Progressive Nation

A Travel Guide

with 400+ Left Turns

and Inspiring Landmarks

★ Jerome Pohlen ★

CHICAGO
REVIEW
PRESS

Library of Congress Cataloging-in-Publication Data
Pohlen, Jerome.
Progressive nation : a travel guide with 400+ left turns and inspiring landmarks / Jerome Pohlen.
— 1st ed.
    p. cm.
Includes index.
ISBN 978-1-55652-717-3
1. Historic sites—United States—Guidebooks. 2. United States—Guidebooks. 3. United
States—History, Local. 4. Progressivism (United States politics)—History—Anecdotes. 5.
Political activists—United States—Biography—Anecdotes. 6. New Left—United States—His-
tory—Anecdotes. 7. Liberalism—United States—History—Anecdotes. 8. United States—Poli-
tics and government—Anecdotes. 9. United States—Social conditions—Anecdotes. I. Title.
E159.P59 2008
917.304'93—dc22   2007044624

Cover design: Trudi Gershenov Design
Interior design: Pamela Juárez

3 1969 01883 9901

Photo credits: **Library of Congress Prints and Photographs Division:** p. 12, 2004672776;
p. 108, ggb2004007435; p. 29, 2004672098; p. 33, 2004664386; p.58, 97519946; p. 63,
89707024; p. 65, 2004671911; p. 69, 2003654393; p. 78, 2003674596; 81; 2005693027; p. 96,
2003688123; p. 98, ggb2005023903; p. 105, 2004672096; p. 120, 2003688131; p. 123, 97500087;
p. 127, 2002725182; p. 146, 2005677239; p. 165, 2004672077; p. 189, 2005696376; p. 209,
brh2003001739/PP; p. 216, ggb2006013628; p. 231, 2003675321; p. 236, 2002725222; p. 243,
2005688160; p. 250, 92519594; p. 258, 97513239; p. 264, 98510365; p. 269, 2004672784; p. 282,
92521943; p. 292, ggb2004005640; p. 293, 2003688132; p. 299, brh2003000502/PP; p. 305,
96512875; p. 324, 2002709330; p. 327, 2004672788; p. 331, 2002712192; p. 360, 94506170; p.
362, 2004672791; p. 371, 92521945; p. 389, 95514641; p. 391, 2005684057
CORBIS: cover (bus), RH003609, © Robert Holmes/CORBIS; cover and p. v (woman with
picket sign), U295238ACME, © Bettman/CORBIS; p. 72, 42-16744280, © Hyungwon/Reuters/
CORBIS; p. 152, BE001108, © Bettmann/CORBIS; p. 206, BE066792, © Jack Moebes/CORBIS;
p. 393, BE045932, © Bettmann/CORBIS
Almay: cover (map), A6282F; p. 107, A2BF9N, © Richard Levine/Almay; p. 133, A4H5CR, ©
Mark Weidman Photography/Almay; p. 255, A1285W, © Photos 12/Almay; p. 267, A2T3F2, ©
Underwood Archives/Almay; p. 386, A2JNC7, Pictorial Press/Almay
John F. Kennedy Presidential Library and Museum: p. 23, ST-C22-1-62
JSC Digital Image Collection: p. 37, S86-25191
Office of Senator Bernie Sanders: p. 45
Democratic National Committee: p.47
Helen Prejean, CSJ: p. 195
Senator John Edwards: p. 203
Gordon Wells: p. 257
Author Photos: cover (Lorraine Motel), p. 48, 61, 101, 112, 159, 161, 168, 184, 186, 221, 234,
276, 334

Published by Chicago Review Press, Incorporated
814 North Franklin Street
Chicago, Illinois 60610
ISBN 978-1-55652-717-3
Printed in the United States of America
5 4 3 2 1

★ For Jim ★

Contents

Introduction

I do not know of any salvation for society except through
eccentrics, misfits, dissenters, people who protest.
—William O. Douglas

Social progress is not automatic. Change does not occur unless somebody of vision, courage, and determination makes it happen. Nearly every progressive movement in American history can be traced back to a person who said "This must change" and then set out to change it. This travel guide celebrates those individuals, their accomplishments, and the movements and communities they inspired.

Most of the people in this book have had a profound impact on the way you live your life today. Be glad they did. Over the past several years it has, at times, been difficult to be hopeful about the direction of this nation. Yet, as the stories in this book demonstrate, progressives have faced far greater challenges and have emerged victorious, despite setbacks. Segregation? Women's suffrage? *Slavery?*

Read and take heart—progressives will win in the end. They always do. Susan B. Anthony understood this, for though she would die 14 years before women were guaranteed the right to vote under the constitution, the final three words she ever uttered in public were "Failure is impossible." Anthony had faith that others would pick up the mantle and move forward, and they did.

When I think about Anthony's proclamation, I believe she was expressing a faith in progressivism itself. The people profiled in this book held and hold a variety of personal and political beliefs, and would likely disagree on a great many issues. But what they would agree on is that injustices need to be resolved. To be liberal is to hold a position, the same way being conservative is. But to be *progressive* means you are actively working at moving society from what it is to what it should be: a just, peaceful society that respects all of its citizens.

> There are many ways of going forward, but only one way of standing still.
> —*Franklin Delano Roosevelt*

A Note on Selection

I have cast a fairly wide net in selecting the histories in this book. I have tried to include as many movements from as many aspects of American society as possible. Yet for every progressive found here, there are dozens more that could not fit on these pages. Explore the museums, books, and online resources discussed in this guide and you will find a progressive history that runs far deeper than any one book can summarize.

> Peculiar travel suggestions are dancing lessons from God.
> —*Kurt Vonnegut*

A KEY FOR READERS

Each site listed in this book is followed by an icon (or two) to aid you on your travels. When planning your progressive road trip, keep the following in mind:

 A museum or historic site—it might take some time to explore.

 A monument or landmark—a good photo opportunity, but a quick stop.

 An extant site of a progressive event, but no historic marker currently exists.

 An organization that continues the work of its founding progressive(s)—not necessarily a tourist destination, but a worthwhile institution to contact. Tours might be arranged by appointment.

 A long-gone site, with nothing to photograph. However, you can still stop by and soak up the lingering progressive aura.

 Private property; view this landmark from the street.

To the extent that phone numbers are available for the sites above, they have been included. If the current occupants or caretakers of a particular site are not associated with the history discussed—several public schools come to mind—their phone numbers have not been included. Please do not bother them.

1
New England

★ Connecticut ★ Maine ★

★ Massachusetts ★

★ New Hampshire ★

★ Rhode Island ★ Vermont ★

One of the most disturbing elements of the Uniting and Strengthening of America by Providing Appropriate Tools Required to Intercept and Obstruct Terrorism Act, better known as the USA PATRIOT Act, is a provision allowing federal authorities to search library and bookstore records of patrons and customers without their knowledge *and without a court order*. What's more, when librarians (or bookstore owners) are served with a National Security Letter (NSL) requesting this information, they are legally restrained from revealing that agents ever set foot in their buildings, to say nothing of what they didn't take when they weren't there.

In August 2005 the Library Connection, a resource-sharing cooperative serving 26 Connecticut libraries, was served with an NSL demanding access to its computer database. It refused. An NSL was not a warrant under the Constitution, it said, and the ACLU concurred. Four librarians—Barbara Bailey, Peter Chase, George Christian, and Jan Nocek—filed suit against the NSL provision of the act. A federal judge agreed with the plaintiffs, and ruled they could go public with their lawsuit. But the Justice Department appealed to the U.S. Supreme Court and the gag order stood.

While the high court sat on the appeal, the Bush administration lobbied for reauthorization of the USA

> The right of the people to be secure in their persons, houses, papers, and effects, against unreasonable searches and seizures, shall not be violated, and no Warrants shall issue, but upon probable cause, supported by Oath or affirmation, and particularly describing the place to be searched, and the persons or things to be seized.
>
> —*Fourth Amendment,
> Bill of Rights*

PATRIOT Act. Alberto Gonzales told Congress that the NSL had *never* been used at any library . . . but wanted to keep the provision anyway. (Remember when perjury was a crime?) Six weeks after the act was renewed, in April 2006, the government dropped its appeal and allowed the plaintiffs to speak about their case. One month later the FBI abandoned its demands for the original information listed on the NSL. The ACLU has vowed to continue its battle to unseal records of NSL abuse by the Justice Department.

LEARN MORE
How Would a Patriot Act? by Glenn Greenwald (Working Assets, 2006)

Canterbury

Prudence Crandall's Forbidden Schoolhouse
Prudence Crandall School and Museum, Routes 14 and 169, PO Box 58, Canterbury, CT 06331 · (860) 546-7800

Prudence Crandall was running the Canterbury Female Boarding School in January 1833 when she admitted a young woman named Sarah Harris. Parents and locals were outraged at Crandall's decision. Why? Sarah Harris was black and the other students were white.

Crandall had a choice to make. Rather than submit to the racist pressure she closed her doors in February, then traveled around New England recruiting "young ladies and little misses of color." Seventeen students arrived through the spring of 1833 when the school—the first of its kind in New England—reopened.

Crandall and her pupils were harassed from the opening day. Windows were smashed, manure was thrown down the school's well, and businesses refused to sell her food and supplies. The Canterbury Congregational Church, just across the street from the school, turned away the students who wanted to attend services, so the girls walked miles to the Packerville Baptist Church. Crandall was charged with contributing to vagrancy under an antiquated law, but the charge was thrown out of court. When the bullying didn't work, locals went to the state legislature. Connecticut passed a bill dubbed the Black Law making it illegal to instruct black nonresidents, and Crandall was arrested and thrown into the nearby Brooklyn jail. Though she could have posted bail she stayed behind bars for a night in protest . . . twelve years *before* Thoreau engaged in a similar action in Massachusetts (see page 20).

> In the midst of this affliction I am as happy as at any point in my life.
> —*Prudence Crandall, in a letter to a friend, 1833*

After three trials a court overturned the Black Law on technical grounds, and Crandall returned to teaching. But a year and a half after she started, arsonists torched the school's cellar. And on September 9, 1834, a masked mob descended on the school, broke in with a battering ram, and trashed the main floor as Crandall and her students hid upstairs. Fearing for her students' safety, Crandall reluctantly closed her doors and fled Canterbury.

Crandall would eventually settle in Elk Falls, Kansas. Well into her 70s, she helped former slaves, known as "Exodusters," settle into new lives on the prairie. In 1886, prodded in part by Mark Twain, the Connecticut legislature tried to make amends by voting Crandall a $400 pension. She died on January 28, 1890, and was buried in the Elk Falls Cemetery. Today her former Connecticut school is a museum.

LEARN MORE

www.chc.state.ct.us/crandall%20museum.htm

The Forbidden Schoolhouse by Suzanne Jurmain (Houghton Mifflin, 2005)

Prudence Crandall by Marvis Olive Welch (Jason Publishers, 1983)

Farmington

The *Amistad*

Farmington Historical Society, 71 Main Street, Farmington, CT 06032

In the early morning of July 2, 1839, off the coast of Cuba, a slave named Sengbeh Pieh and two others broke free of their chains and seized control of the Honduras-bound *Amistad*. All but two of the Spanish crew were killed or escaped in lifeboats, and the remaining 50 captives were then unshackled. Sengbeh Pieh, also known as Joseph Cinque, demanded that the crew set the ship on a course toward the rising sun, back to Africa. Over the next 63 days the *Amistad* sailed eastward by day, but was redirected west at night. It landed off Long Island where it was boarded by a navy patrol. The former captives were arrested and brought to New London, Connecticut.

The Africans were imprisoned in a New Haven brig while awaiting their trial in Hartford for murder, mutiny, and piracy. On January 23, 1840, Judge Andrew Judson ruled that the group were free men, not property, and that they could return to Africa. But the case was appealed to the U.S. Supreme Court. They were defended by former president John Quincy Adams, who secured their release on March 9, 1841. Justice Joseph Story ruled they had been "illegally kidnapped and had the right to self defense from their captors."

But how would they get back home? On March 19, residents of Farmington, many of whom were abolitionists, welcomed the Africans, all Mende, into their community until funds could be raised for passage back to their homeland. The Mende attended morning classes six days a week, and in the afternoon farmed a 10-acre plot given to them by the community. On Sundays they were welcomed at the First Church of Christ, Congregational (75 Main Street).

The Mende lived in Farmington for eight months. When sufficient funds were raised, they departed for Sierra Leone on November 25, 1841, after a tearful farewell at the church. Their experiences with the *Amistad* refugees led many in Farmington to become more active in the abolitionist movement, including work as conductors on the Underground Railroad.

A half-hour reenactment of the *Amistad* trial is performed on Tuesdays and Thursdays in the Old State House in Hartford (800 Main Street) where the first trial took place. In New Haven you can find a monument on the site of the navy brig where the escapees were imprisoned (165 Church Street). A replica of the *Amistad*—the *Freedom Schooner Amistad*—was launched from Mystic, Connecticut, in 2000 and visits ports around the world. Its home port is New Haven's Long Wharf Pier.

LEARN MORE

www.farmingtonhistoricalsociety-ct.org

Amistad America, www.amistadamerica.org, (203) 495-1839

Old State House, www.ctosh.org, (860) 522-6766

Black Mutiny by William A. Owens (Black Classics, 1997)

Mutiny on the Amistad by Howard Jones (Oxford, 1987)

Hartford

Alice Cogswell, Thomas Gallaudet, and the American School for the Deaf
Gallaudet Square, Farmington and Asylum Avenues, Hartford, CT 06105

Around 1810, two-year-old Alice Cogswell was left deaf after a bout with spotted fever. Without the ability to hear she gradually lost her ability to speak. But in 1815 the Cogswells' neighbor, a young preacher named Thomas Hopkins Gallaudet, read about revolutionary methods used to educate the deaf in Europe. He convinced the girl's father, Dr. Mason Cogswell, to send him to l'Institut National de Jeunes Sourds in Paris with the goal of returning to Hartford to teach Alice. Gallaudet did return, along with deaf priest Laurent Clerc, and established America's first school for the hearing impaired on April 15, 1817. Class was held in the Old City Hotel on Main Street (since torn down). Three students, including Alice Cogswell, were the first pupils.

Cogswell went on to be the first deaf student to receive a comprehensive education in the United States. The American School for the Deaf grew quickly, and had 33 students by the end of the first year. Within a few years it had 100 students and a new, permanent building. Gallaudet continued as its principal until he resigned in 1831. He died on September 10, 1851, and was buried in Hartford's Cedar Hill Cemetery (453 Fairfield Avenue).

In 1921 the American School for the Deaf relocated to West Hartford (139 N. Main Street). The original building was eventually torn down, but a monument to Cogswell now stands just east of the site in what is today Gallaudet Square. Another statue, with both Gallaudet and Cogswell signing the letter A, stands in front of the school's current location in West Hartford.

Thomas Gallaudet's influence continued even after his passing. In 1864 his son, Edward Miner Gallaudet, became the first president of Gallaudet College (later Gallaudet University) in Washington, D.C. (see page 64).

LEARN MORE
www.asd-1817.org, (860) 570-2300
A Deaf Child Listened by Anne E. Neimark (William Morrow, 1983)

Horace Bushnell and the Birth of the Municipal Park
Bushnell Park, 166 Capitol Avenue, Hartford, CT 06106

When it was first proposed it was a novel idea. Minister Horace Bushnell offered a solution for the urban eyesore along Hartford's Hog River: a public park. On January 5, 1854, the City of Hartford voted to purchase a stretch of land that was being used by local tanneries and a soap factory as a dumping ground. The land was cleaned up and opened to the general public. Three days before Bushnell's death, on Valentine's Day 1876, the nation's first municipal park was renamed in his honor.

LEARN MORE
www.healthy.hartford.gov/OpenSpace/osParks.htm#Bushnell

New Haven

Griswold v. Connecticut: **The Right to Privacy**
Clinic Site, 79 Trumbull Street, New Haven, CT 06511

In the early 1960s Connecticut still had an 1879 law on its books that made it a crime to use birth control. Hardly a holdover, it was codified by the state legislature as late as 1958: "[A]ny person who uses any drug, medicinal article, or instrument for the purpose of preventing contraception shall be fined not less than fifty dollars or imprisoned not less than sixty days nor more than one year or be both fined and imprisoned." Physicians and counselors who provided birth control information faced the same punishment.

The Planned Parenthood League of Connecticut (PPLC), under executive director Estelle Griswold, actively challenged the state's draconian statute. It established a clinic in New Haven for the sole purpose of getting Griswold arrested, and announced its intentions, "[The PPLC], with the full backing of the national birth control movement, will take steps as rapidly as possible to offer, under medical supervision, all contraceptive techniques." The clinic opened its doors on November 1, 1961, and on November 2 Griswold held a press conference and confirmed that it had provided birth control advice to six women the day before.

A day later, James Morris, a night manager of a local rental car agency, swore out a complaint against the clinic. That afternoon two detectives showed up and Griswold enthusiastically assisted with their investigation. On November 10, arrest warrants were issued for Griswold and Dr. C. Lee Buxton, the clinic's head physician. Both turned themselves in and were released on $100 bonds, and the clinic was closed. The triumphant Morris observed, "I think that a Planned Parenthood Center is like a house of prostitution. It is against the natural law, which says that marital relations are for procreation and not entertainment."

Griswold and Buxton were found guilty at their first trial, and in appeals before the state's appellate and supreme courts. The U.S. Supreme Court overruled those decisions on May 11, 1964. Writing for the 7–2 majority, Justice William O. Douglas wrote, "Would we allow the police to search the sacred precincts of marital bedrooms for telltale signs of the use of contraceptives? The very idea is repulsive to the notions of privacy surrounding the marriage relationship." Douglas went even further, asserting that the Bill of Rights cast a penumbra of "peripheral rights" to privacy that weren't specifically detailed in the Constitution. For example, freedom of the press included not just the right to *publish* information, but to *distribute* that information, *read* that information, and *teach* that information.

The *Griswold* decision only applied to married couples; contraceptive rights for single persons were not affirmed until 1972 with the court's *Eisenstadt v. Baird* decision (see page 18).

LEARN MORE
www.plannedparenthood.org, (212) 541-7800
Griswold v. Connecticut by John W. Johnson (University Press of Kansas, 2005)

Woodbury

Bishop Samuel Seabury and the Separation of Church and State
Glebe House, 49 Hollow Road, Woodbury, CT 06798 · (203) 263-2855

When the American colonies issued the Declaration of Independence, they weren't just breaking away from the British monarchy, but the Church of England as well. Shortly after the American Revolution began, a group of Episcopalians met in the home of priest John Rutgers Marshall—Glebe House—and elected Reverend Samuel Seabury to be the first Episcopal bishop in the new United States. Given their negative experiences with the British, the group also proclaimed that in his new capacity Seabury should *not* mix their religion with the government. Their action set the foundation for separation of church and state in the new republic.

LEARN MORE

www.theglebehouse.org

Samuel Seabury, 1729–1796 by Bruce Steiner (Ohio University, 1972)

MAINE

Each morning the sun shines on Maine before every other state, which explains Maine's motto: "Dirigo," Latin for "I lead." So when Governor John Baldacci launched a bold healthcare initiative in 2003, the first of its kind in the United States, he titled it the Dirigo Health Reform Act. The bill's goal was to provide affordable health insurance to Maine's uninsured working families and poor, while instituting measures to keep a lid on spiraling costs yet improve the overall quality of care. Enrollees would receive subsidized health insurance based upon their ability to pay. By heading off problems before they got worse, participants could avoid expensive medical procedures and emergency room visits.

The legislation passed with broad, bipartisan support, but has since run into criticism from insurance companies. Even though they were receiving state funds (and additional customers), they complained that they were not seeing any financial benefit from the program. Maine's insurance commissioner ran the numbers and found that companies had saved $43.7 million in the two years since Dirigo was launched, but apparently that wasn't enough. The industry, backed by GOP lawmakers and conservative foundations, sued the state to revise or scrap the program. Baldacci's opponents used it to bad-mouth him in the 2006 election. "Leave it to the private sector," they said, presumably because the free market has worked so well in the past . . .

Baldacci won reelection in a four-way race, and Dirigo marches on.

LEARN MORE
www.dirigohealth.maine.gov
Sick by Jonathan Cohn (HarperCollins, 2007)
Sicko (2007)

Augusta

Samantha Reed Smith, "America's Littlest Ambassador"
Samantha Reed Smith Memorial, Maine Archives Building, State and Capitol
Streets, Augusta, ME 04333

Like so many in Ronald Reagan's America, 10-year-old Samantha Reed Smith was worried about a nuclear war between the United States and the Soviet Union. So in November 1982 she penned a letter to Soviet leader Yuri Andropov and asked if his country wanted to conquer the world, and if not, how he planned to avoid a conflict with the west. To Smith's surprise, Andropov responded, and invited her family to come for a visit.

During a two-week sojourn in the summer of 1983, Smith found that the Soviet Union wasn't quite the "Evil Empire" Reagan had described. She visited Moscow, the Crimea (where she attended a youth camp named Artek), and Leningrad. Her visit helped thaw a few cold hearts, and was an early indication of the *glasnost* that would usher in a new era.

Sadly, Smith would not live to see the fall of the Berlin Wall. She and her father Arthur, and six others, perished in a private airplane crash on August 25, 1985, while on approach to the Auburn-Lewiston Municipal Airport. Smith's mother, Jane, established the Samantha Smith Foundation to support youth exchanges between the Cold War superpowers. Ironically, though Smith had been warmly greeted in the Soviet Union, in 1987 the first group of youth from that country to visit the United States was greeted with threats from unidentified Americans.

A statue of "Maine's Young Ambassador of Good Will" has been erected on the grounds of the state capitol. Smith holds a dove of peace in her hands while a black bear cub, symbol of both the state of Maine and the Soviet Union, sits at her feet.

> I have been worrying about Russia and the United States getting into a nuclear war. Are you going to vote to have a war or not? If you aren't please tell me how you are going to help to not have a war.
> —*Samantha Reed Smith, in her letter to Yuri Andropov*

LEARN MORE
Journey to the Soviet Union by Samantha Smith (Little, Brown and
    Company, 1984)

Brunswick

Harriet Beecher Stowe and *Uncle Tom's Cabin*
First Parish Church, Maine Street at Bath Road, Brunswick, ME 04011 · (207) 729-7331

Harriet Beecher Stowe always claimed that God dictated *Uncle Tom's Cabin* to her; she just wrote it down. God first told Stowe to write an antislavery novel on March 2, 1851, while she sat in Pew #23 of the First Parish Church, listening to an abolitionist sermon. She returned home to what is now known as Stowe House (63 Federal Street), near the Bowdoin College campus where her husband Calvin was a professor, and fired off the final chapter first.

God may have dictated the book, but the stories were all Stowe's, collected over the first four decades of her life. She was born in Litchfield, Connecticut, on June 14, 1811, the daughter of Roxanna and Lyman Beecher, a Congregational minister and abolitionist. Her brother, Henry Ward Beecher, would go on to be a prominent abolitionist preacher. Their half-sister, Isabella Beecher Hooker, was one of the founders of the New England Woman Suffrage Association. In 1831 the Beechers moved to Cincinnati, Ohio, where Harriet witnessed Kentucky slavery up close. Harriet married Calvin Stowe in 1836. The Stowes moved to Maine in 1850.

Uncle Tom's Cabin was America's first popular social protest novel, but was first published in weekly serial form in the *National Era*, starting in 1851. A year later the installments were collected as a book, about the time the Stowes left Brunswick. When Southern apologists complained that the fictional story was inaccurate, Stowe penned *A Key to Uncle Tom's Cabin* in 1853, detailing the research she used to shape her story.

Today, Stowe House is a restaurant and hotel. Admirers of Stowe's work should visit her final home in Hartford, Connecticut (77 Forest Street) where they can see the desk

Harriet Beecher Stowe, c. 1880

on which she wrote the book, along with her family's personal effects and Stowe's sketches and watercolors.

LEARN MORE

www.firstparish.net

www.harrietbeecherstowe.org, (860) 522-9258

Uncle Tom's Cabin by Harriet Beecher Stowe (Norton, 1994)

A Key to Uncle Tom's Cabin by Harriet Beecher Stowe (Applewood, 1998)

Harriet Beecher Stowe by Joan D. Hedrick (Oxford, 1994)

Hampden

Dorothea Dix, Mental Health Pioneer

Dorothea Dix Memorial Park, Main Road (Route 1A), Hampden, ME 04444

Dorothea Dix was born south of Hampden on April 4, 1802, and lived here until her family moved to Worcester, Massachusetts, when she was 12 years old. By 14 she was teaching young children, and by 19 had opened her own school. She might have continued as a teacher had she not collapsed from a lung ailment in 1836. Dix traveled to Europe to recuperate, where she met several progressives who educated her about prison reform and new treatments for the mentally ill. When she returned to the United States she had a new mission in life.

After a visit to the basement of a Boston prison in 1841, where "insane" prisoners were shackled, Dix began collecting harrowing information she would later use to force the hands of legislators. Her first major success came in 1845 when she convinced New Jersey lawmakers to fund a new facility in West Trenton. Dix called the New Jersey State Lunatic Asylum, which opened in 1848, her "firstborn child." It was later renamed the Trenton Psychiatric Hospital (Route 29 and Sullivan Way).

Over the next 40 years Dix would be instrumental in establishing 32 hospitals for the mentally ill, includ-

> I come as the advocate of helpless, forgotten, insane men and women; of beings sunk to a condition from which the unconcerned world would start with real horror.
>
> *—Dorothea Dix, to the Massachusetts legislature*

ing St. Elizabeth's Hospital (2700 MLK Avenue SE) in Washington, D.C. During the Civil War Dix served as Superintendent of Nurses for the Union Army, well past her 60th birthday. Before the war, female nurses were looked at with skepticism, but not after.

Dix retired to New Jersey in 1881, and lived in a small apartment at the hospital she founded. She died there on July 17, 1887, and was buried in Mount Auburn Cemetery (580 Mount Auburn Street) in Cambridge, Massachusetts. A memorial park now marks her Hampton birthplace.

LEARN MORE

Voice for the Mad by David L. Gollaher (Free Press, 1995)

Stranger and Traveler by Dorothy Clarke Wilson (Little, Brown and Company, 1975)

Harborside

Helen and Scott Nearing Live the Good Life

The Good Life Center, 372 Harborside Road, Harborside, ME 04642 · (207) 326-8211

Sometime in their late 40s Helen and Scott Nearing decided they'd had enough. To them, New York City had grown dirty and unlivable. They found it difficult to locate the organic produce they needed as vegetarians. And the world around them seemed to glorify militarism rather than the pacifism they practiced. And so they packed up and moved to Vermont. The year? 1968?

Try 1932. The Nearings didn't know they were launching the back-to-the-land movement when they put down $300 for the old Ellonen place at the foot of Stratton Mountain, but they were.

Over the next 20 years they planted gardens and tilled the soil, rebuilt a collapsing farm house in stone, and learned how to harvest and convert maple sugar into syrup, which met their modest cash needs. Was it all toil and backbreaking work? After working out the kinks, the Nearings estimated that they only needed to perform six months of "bread labor"

> We desired to liberate and dissociate ourselves, as much as possible, from the cruder forms of exploitation: the plunder of the planet; the slavery of man and beast; the slaughter of men in war, and of animals for food.
> —*Helen Nearing*

each year, leaving the other six months for traveling, lecturing, reading, writing, and daydreaming.

But the Nearings' success was its undoing, at least in Vermont; they received so much attention and hosted so many uninvited visitors that they decided to move to an even more remote location. In 1952 they sold Forest Farm and moved to the Maine coast and started all over again. Their second homesteading venture, in Harborside, was as successful as the first. Scott lived to be 100 years old, and Helen 91. Their Vermont memoir, *Living the Good Life*, was published in 1954. *Continuing the Good Life*, detailing the Maine years, was published in 1979. Today Harborside is home to the Good Life Center, which offers workshops on everything from caring for fruit trees to making herbal medicine.

LEARN MORE
www.goodlife.org
The Good Life by Helen Nearing (Schocken, 1989)
The Making of a Radical by Scott Nearing (Chelsea Green, 2000)

Newcastle

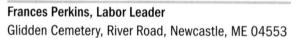

Frances Perkins, Labor Leader
Glidden Cemetery, River Road, Newcastle, ME 04553

Frances Perkins was the first American woman to hold a position in a presidential cabinet, appointed Secretary of Labor by Franklin Delano Roosevelt. FDR knew Perkins; she'd served as New York's Industrial Commissioner when he was governor. In 1911 she'd witnessed the Triangle Shirtwaist factory fire (see page 114) and dedicated herself to the issues of the working class. By 1929 she held the highest labor post in state government.

During her 12 years in federal office, from 1933 to 1945, Perkins oversaw the New Deal's progressive expansion of unemployment relief, union rights, the raising of the minimum wage, the establishment

> Every man and woman in America who works at a living wage, under safe conditions, for reasonable hours, or who is protected by unemployment insurance or Social Security, is in her debt.
> *—Labor Secretary W. Willard Wirtz, at Perkins's death, 1965*

of maximum hours, the abolition of child labor, and the founding of Social Security. Though Roosevelt received much of the credit, most of the ideas were suggested, not to mention implemented, by Perkins. She also successfully lobbied Congress to pass the 1938 Fair Labor Standards Act, the foundation of modern labor law.

Perkins resigned her post after Roosevelt died, but was appointed to the U.S. Civil Service Commission by Harry Truman. She died on May 14, 1965, and was buried in her hometown.

LEARN MORE
The Roosevelt I Knew by Frances Perkins (Harper, 1946)

MASSACHUSETTS

Despite its witch-hunting Puritans and Boston bluebloods, Massachusetts has been far ahead of the curve on many progressive issues. On April 23, 1635, the Boston Latin School opened in the home of Philemon Pormont, becoming the first public school in the colonies. In 1747 the commonwealth mandated "a teacher for every community of 50 families or more." And in 1837 Horace Mann, the state's first commissioner of education, established Massachusetts's public school system, basing it on the German model of grouping children by grade level according to age. Today Mann is generally acknowledged as the "Father of American Public Education."

Massachusetts has also been the birthplace of many American hell-raisers, including Benjamin Franklin, Henry David Thoreau, Susan B. Anthony, William Lloyd Garrison, and 200+ patriots who dumped 342 chests of British tea into Boston Harbor on December 16, 1773, to protest the Townshend Act. It was in Boston that David Walker published his *Appeal* in 1829, in which he used passages from the Bible, the Declaration of Independence, and the U.S. Constitution to denounce slavery and advocate direct action to destroy the institution. Massachusetts is also the birthplace of the New England Anti-Slavery Society, the tactic of civil disobedience, and American environmentalism.

In recent history the Bay State has maintained its progressive tradition. In 1972 it was the only state to not cast its electoral college votes for Richard Nixon; citizens later plastered "Don't Blame Me—I'm from Massachusetts!" bumper stickers on their cars. And in 2003 the Massachusetts Supreme Judicial Court ruled in *Goodridge v. Department of Health* that gay and lesbian couples should be offered the same marriage rights as heterosexual couples. The court ordered

> Be ashamed to die until you have won some victory for humanity.
>
> *—Horace Mann*

17

the legislature to craft a plan, which it did, and just after midnight on May 17, 2004, dozens of same-sex couples marched into city halls and made their unions legal.

That's plenty to be proud of, but read on for more.

Boston

Eisenstadt v. Baird: Birth Control Is for Singles, Too
Boston University, 1 Sherborn Street, Boston, MA 02215

In 1964 the U.S. Supreme Court ruled in *Griswold v. Connecticut* that married couples had the right to purchase and use birth control (see page 7), but it was eight more years before *Eisenstadt v. Baird* established that unmarried adults had the same right.

The case began on April 6, 1967. About 680 Boston University students had signed a petition inviting birth control advocate William Baird to speak on campus. During his lecture he handed out free samples of Emko Vaginal Foam. After the talk he was arrested and charged with exhibiting a birth control device, and distributing that device to an unmarried person.

Baird was eventually found guilty of the distribution charge and was tossed into Boston's Charles Street jail for three months. But that didn't deter him from challenging the law under which he was imprisoned. His case made it to the U.S. Supreme Court, which in 1972 struck down the Massachusetts law (and others like it) in a 6–1 ruling. Unlike *Griswold*, which was decided on privacy grounds, *Eisenstadt* was resolved using the Equal Protection Clause of the Fourteenth Amendment; if married couples were given access to birth control, so should unmarried individuals.

> [T]he marital couple is not an independent entity with a mind and a heart of its own, but an association of two individuals each with a separate intellectual and emotional makeup. If the right of privacy means anything, it is the right of the individual, married or single, to be free of unwanted governmental intrusion into matters so fundamentally affecting a person as the decision whether to bear or beget a child.
>
> —*Justice William Brennan, in*
> **Eisenstadt v. Baird, *1972***

Keith McHenry and Food Not Bombs
Federal Reserve Bank, 600 Atlantic Avenue, Boston, MA 02210

Food Not Bombs (FNB) began more as a "not bombs" organization than a "food" organization. Keith McHenry and others who were active in the 1970s movement against nuclear power wanted to broaden their scope to address the issue of misplaced corporate and governmental priorities. Their first action sought to bring attention to the issues of homelessness and hunger. In March 1981 the First National Bank of Boston was scheduled to hold its annual stockholders' meeting at the Federal Reserve Bank in Boston, and McHenry's group decided to host a breadline on the sidewalk out front. With a load of donated day-old bread, fruit from a local co-op, and a large pot of vegetable soup, they set up a table and served more than 100 people who had been invited from Boston's shelters. With the help of the Clamshell Alliance they were also able to explain to passersby the unholy alliance between the bank, the nuclear utilities, and local governments in the misappropriation of valuable public resources.

As the FNB collective grew it expanded its actions to provide daily vegetarian meals to Cambridge-area homeless and food for antinuclear demonstrations. In late 1981 FNB marched on MIT's Draper Weapons Research Lab in Cambridge (555 Technology Square) and sponsored concerts to raise consciousness about the arms race and money for their group. In time, additional chapters of FNB sprang up around the nation. There are currently hundreds of active (and informal) chapters around the United States and the world.

> **Food Not Bombs's central unifying principles are a commitment to nonviolence, free unrestricted access to vegetarian food, and an honest attempt to make decisions as a group without hierarchy.**
>
> **—Keith McHenry**

LEARN MORE

www.foodnotbombs.net

Food Not Bombs by C. T. Butler, Keith McHenry, and Howard Zinn (See Sharp, 2000)

Concord

Henry David Thoreau and Civil Disobedience

Monument Square (jail torn down), Main Street and Lexington Road, Concord, MA 01742

In July 1846, midway through his stay at Walden Pond, Henry David Thoreau took a walk into Concord to join a huckleberry-picking party. Before he found his friends a constable found him, and he asked Thoreau to pay a nine-shilling state tax. Thoreau knew that part of the fee was being levied to pay for the ongoing Mexican War, an illegal war of aggression that he found repugnant. To protest he refused to pay the tax and was tossed into the Concord jail.

Sitting in his cell, Thoreau reflected on his decision. Sometime during his stay Ralph Waldo Emerson came to visit and asked him what he was doing "in there," to which Thoreau asked what Emerson was doing "out there." The next day Thoreau was released; somebody, either Emerson or Thoreau's aunt, had paid his fine to make the whole incident go away.

But it didn't. Thoreau's experience served as the cornerstone of his influential and famous essay "Resistance to Civil Government," better known today as "Civil Disobedience." It was first delivered as a lecture at the Concord Lyceum (156 Belknap Street) in January 1848, and was published a year later. The essay would later influence Mahatma Gandhi and Martin Luther King Jr. in their struggles against government-sanctioned oppression.

> Unjust laws exist; shall we be content to obey them, or shall we endeavor to amend them, and obey them until we have succeeded, or shall we transgress them at once?
> —Henry David Thoreau, in "Resistance to Civil Government"

LEARN MORE

A Historical Guide to Henry David Thoreau by William E. Cain (Oxford, 2000)

The Higher Law by Henry David Thoreau (Princeton, 2004)

Henry Thoreau by Robert Richardson Jr. (University of Georgia, 1986)

**PROGRESSIVE THOUGHTS OF
HENRY DAVID THOREAU**

- It is never too late to give up your prejudices.
- Any fool can make a rule, and any fool will mind it.
- Aim above morality. Be not simply good; be good for something.
- What's the use of a house if you haven't a tolerable planet to put it on?
- The heads of conservatives have a puny and deficient look, a certain callowness and concavity, as if they were prematurely exposed on one or both sides.
- There will never be a really free and enlightened State until the State comes to recognize the individual as a higher and independent power, from which all its own power and authority are derived.
- The best thing a man can do for his culture when he is rich is to endeavor to carry out those schemes which he entertained when he was poor.

Walden
Walden Pond State Reservation, 915 Walden Street, Concord, MA 01742 · (978) 369-3254

"I went to the woods because I wished to live deliberately, to front only the essential facts of life, and see if I could not learn what it had to teach, and not, when I came to die, discover that I had not lived." So wrote Henry David Thoreau in what became the seminal work of the American environmental movement: *Walden; Or Life in the Woods*.

On Independence Day 1845, needing time and silence to work on *A Week on the Concord and Merrimack Rivers*, Thoreau retreated to a one-room cabin he had built on the northern shore of Walden Pond. He ended up staying two years, two months, and two days. His daily observations of the natural world became the first draft of his best-known work. But although *Walden* is praised for its ecological sensibility, it is as much about finding oneself through a simple, introspective, nonmaterialistic lifestyle, as it is about the environment.

Thoreau's cabin was dismantled in the 1850s, its lumber salvaged for other structures around Concord. Today you'll find a replica near the Walden gift shop, and a marker at the site where the original once stood. In an attempt to preserve the site, only a thousand visitors are allowed on the 400-acre Walden Pond State Reservation at any one time. The Concord Museum (200 Lexington Road) has Thoreau's bed, desk, and chair from the Walden cabin, as well as his flute, original manuscripts, and correspondences with Ralph Waldo Emerson.

> Simplicity, simplicity, simplicity! I say, let your affairs be as two or three, and not a hundred or a thousand; instead of a million count a half-dozen, and keep your accounts on your thumbnail.
> —*Henry David Thoreau*,
> *in* Walden

Thoreau died from tuberculosis on May 6, 1862, at the age of 44. He is buried on Author Ridge in Sleepy Hollow Cemetery (Bedford Street at Court Lane) in Concord, as are Ralph Waldo Emerson, Louisa May Alcott, and Nathaniel Hawthorne.

LEARN MORE
www.mass.gov/dcr/parks/northeast/wldn.htm
www.walden.org, (781) 259-4770
Walden Or Life in the Woods: A Fully Annotated Edition by Henry
   David Thoreau and Jeffrey S. Cramer, ed. (Yale, 2004)
No Man's Garden by Daniel B. Botkin (Island Press, 2001)

Dorchester

John F. Kennedy and the New Generation
John F. Kennedy Presidential Library, University of Massachusetts–Dorchester, Columbia Point, Dorchester, MA 02125 · (866) JFK-1960

You can make a fairly convincing argument that John F. Kennedy, if he was progressive, was only barely so. On the issue of civil rights he rarely made a move that would jeopardize his relationship with Southern Democrats. His Bay of Pigs invasion was reckless and misguided. He oversaw a tremendous increase in the nation's defense budget. But Kennedy, for all his faults, negotiated and signed the Nuclear Test Ban, initiated antipoverty legislation,

The Kennedy family, 1962

launched the Apollo program, and inspired Americans to serve their country and the world's poor through the Peace Corps (see page 256). That's got to count for something.

The John F. Kennedy Presidential Library details the 35th president's life and legacy. It begins with Kennedy's 1960 nomination to head the Democratic ticket and continues through his assassination in 1963. Along the way you'll see exhibits dedicated to the Kennedy–Nixon debates, his inauguration, the Cuban Missile Crisis, Jackie Kennedy, the Space Race, and a replica of the Oval Office as it was during his administration.

Each year since 1990 the Kennedy Library Foundation has selected an individual for the Profile in Courage Award, specifically given for "political courage." Past recipients have included John Lewis, Viktor Yushenko, and John Murtha. A monument to all past winners can be found in the pavilion as you exit the library.

> The problems of the world cannot possibly be solved by skeptics or cynics whose horizons are limited by the obvious realities. We need men who can dream of things that never were.
>
> *—John F. Kennedy*

Kennedy fans might also enjoy visiting his birthplace in nearby Brookline (83 Beals Street). John Fitzgerald Kennedy was born here on May 29, 1917. The family moved to 131 Naples Road (now 51 Abbottsford Road) when John was four years old. Robert was born here on November 20, 1925. JFK's birthplace is open for tours.

LEARN MORE
Library, www.jfklibrary.org
Birthplace, www.nps.gov/jofi, (617) 566-7937
John F. Kennedy by Michael O'Brien (Thomas Dunn, 2005)
An Unfinished Life by Robert Dallek (Little, Brown and Company, 2003)

Great Barrington

Alice's Restaurant's Church
The Church, 4 Van Deusenville Road, Great Barrington, MA 01230 · (413) 528-1955

If there was an anthem to draft resistance in the 1960s it had to be Arlo Guthrie's "Alice's Restaurant Massacree." The 18-minute ballad was a true tale that began on Thanksgiving Day, 1965. Guthrie's friends Alice and Ray Brock (and Fasha the dog) had asked him to haul away a load of garbage left over from the turkey-day gathering at their home, which was a converted church. But when he discovered the local dump was closed for the holiday, Guthrie tossed the junk over a cliff along Glendale Middle Road, west of Stockbridge. There was already a pile at the bottom of the cliff, so rather than make two small piles, Guthrie reasoned, he made one large pile.

Officer William Obanhein—Officer Obie—discovered the mess, traced an envelope back to Guthrie, and arrested him for littering. Guthrie didn't have much of a defense, as Officer Obie had 27 8x10 color glossies with circles and arrows and paragraphs on the back. Guthrie was found guilty and fined $50.

None of this would be remembered today had Guthrie not received notice from the Selective Service in 1967 to report for induction. During the course of his intake he was asked if he had ever been convicted of a crime, which he had, and he was dismissed as unfit for service.

Guthrie turned the incident into a song in which he encouraged young men to tell their local draft boards, "You can get anything you want, at Alice's Restaurant," and walk out. If enough draftees followed his lead, perhaps it might bring a quicker end to the war. At the very least, it provided an option for young men to express their opposition to the Vietnam War.

In 1990 Arlo Guthrie purchased and restored Alice's old home/church to house the Guthrie Foundation, a nonprofit that supports many worthy causes—assistance for families dealing with HIV/AIDS, a computer education center for disadvantaged children, and the Berkshire County Association for Retarded Citizens. (Guthrie's youthful indiscretion might have been one of the best things that ever happened to this community.)

> **You want to know if I'm moral enough to join the army, burn women, kids, houses, and villages after bein' a *litterbug*?**
> —*Arlo Guthrie, in "Alice's Restaurant Massacree"*

Every May the Guthrie Center hosts a 6.3-mile Garbage Trail Walk to raise money for Huntington's disease research (see page 324), where participants visit all the massacree landmarks.

LEARN MORE
www.guthriecenter.org
Arlo, Alice & the Anglicans by Laura Lee (Berkshire House, 2000)

W. E. B. Du Bois and *The Souls of Black Folk*
W. E. B. DuBois Memorial Park, Route 23, Great Barrington, MA 01230

William Edward Burghardt Du Bois was born east of Great Barrington on February 23, 1868. Over the next 95 years he would be involved in almost every civil rights struggle *preceeding* the civil rights movement of the 1950s. He was the leading critic of Booker T. Washington's accommodationism, a founding member of the NAACP (see page 102), and the international president of the Pan-African Congress.

Du Bois was primarily a sociologist, earning his Ph.D. from Harvard in 1895. During a professorship at Atlanta University he wrote *The Souls of Black Folk*, which was published in 1903. The book's 14 essays outlined the status of African Americans at the turn of the century, and argued for their immediate, full integration into all aspects of American society. It was only one of 23 books he wrote during his lifetime, in addition to hundreds of articles, studies, and essays. He was also the founding editor of the NAACP's *Crisis* magazine, serving from 1910 to 1934.

Du Bois's advocacy of socialism would eventually lead to his self-imposed exile. In 1948 he backed Henry Wallace's Progressive Party run for the presidency (see page 253), a stance that got him ousted from the NAACP. Two years later he ran for the senate in New York on a platform advocating world peace and coexistence with the Soviet Union, and received a quarter of a million votes. In 1951 the federal government came after him, charging Du Bois with failing to register as a foreign agent. He was acquitted at trial, but the State Department refused to issue him a passport until 1958. Du Bois spent many of his final days traveling and lecturing abroad, and in 1961 emigrated to Ghana. He died on August 27, 1963 (the day before the March on Washington), and was buried in Accra.

All that remains of Du Bois's birthplace today is a chimney and a stone foundation. The site was made into a memorial park in 1969.

W. E. B. Du Bois, c. 1905

We claim for ourselves every right that belongs to a free-born American; and until we get these rights, we will never cease to protest and assail the ears of America. The battle we wage is not for ourselves, but for all true Americans.

—*W. E. B. Du Bois*

LEARN MORE

www.library.umass.edu/spcoll/duboishome/index.html, (413) 545-2780

The Souls of Black Folk by W. E. B. Du Bois (Norton, 1999)

The Autobiography of W. E. B. Du Bois by W. E. B. Du Bois (International Publishers, 1968)

W. E. B. Du Bois, Black Radical Democrat by Manning Marable (Twayne, 1986)

Lowell

The Bread & Roses Strike

Lowell National Historic Site, 169 Merrimack Street, Lowell, MA 01852 · (978) 970-5000

Several Polish-born workers at Lowell's Everett Cotton Mills were the first to open and count their pay envelopes on January 11, 1912. When the women discovered they'd each been cheated of 32¢ they shut down their looms and marched through the factory shouting, "Short pay!" Before the end of the day 23,000 mill workers walked out of two dozen local mills. What became known as the Bread & Roses Strike began the next day.

Only a week earlier the Massachusetts legislature had enacted a law reducing the 56-hour work week to 54, so the mills responded by speeding up their looms, and though the workers were producing just as much, they were now being paid less. The average mill worker earned $8.76 . . . per *week*.

Organizers from the Industrial Workers of the World (IWW), including 21-year-old Elizabeth Gurley Flynn, rushed to Lawrence to assist the strikers. Each union meeting was translated into 25 languages to include every participant, most of whom were women and children. The strikers made four demands: a true 54-hour work week, a 15 percent pay raise, double-pay for overtime, and no retribution for union members.

The mayor called in the militia to crush the strike, and two strikers were killed. When the police started arresting picketers for loitering, the women invented the moving picket line, the first time it had ever been used. Authorities turned fire hoses on the picketers in the dead of winter. And when the workers began shipping out their children to live with supporters until the dispute was resolved, the city forbade the practice. A melee erupted at the train station on February 24 when police tried to stop more kids from leaving; a pregnant woman was beaten so severely she miscarried.

National and international pressure forced Congress to open investigations, and the mill owners conceded. On March 12 workers

> Our lives shall not be sweated from birth until life closes/ Hearts starve as well as bodies; give us bread but give us roses!
>
> —*James Oppenheimer, in the song "Bread and Roses"*

from the American Woolen Company accepted raises from 10 to 25 percent, time-and-a-quarter overtime, a true 54-hour week, and no punishment for strikers. Other mills quickly followed, and two days later workers called off the strike.

And what of the name "Bread & Roses"? As histories were written of the strike, some reported a placard reading, "We Want Bread, and Roses, Too!" demanding respect in addition to fair pay. Some question if the sign ever existed, though everyone agrees the sentiment certainly did.

LEARN MORE
www.nps.gov/lowe
www.mass.gov/dcr/parks/northeast/llhp.htm, (978) 369-6312
www.breadandroses.net, (978) 794-1655
Bread & Roses by Bruce Watson (Viking, 2005)

Roxbury

William Lloyd Garrison and *The Liberator*
Garrison House National Historic Landmark, 125 Highland Street, Roxbury, MA 02119

Few abolitionists were as outspoken as William Lloyd Garrison; certainly none were as prolific. Between January 1, 1831, and December 29, 1865, Garrison published *The Liberator*, a four-page weekly, and never missed an issue, even during the Civil War. In the paper's first editorial, "To the Public," Garrison threw down the gauntlet:

> I am aware that many object to the severity of my language; but is there no cause for severity? I *will be* as harsh as truth, and as uncompromising as justice. On this subject, I do not wish to think, or speak, or write, with moderation. . . . I am in earnest—I will not equivocate—I will not excuse—I will not retreat a single inch—and I will be heard.

In its more than three decades in print, *The Liberator* never had a large number of subscribers—at its peak only 3,000—and yet its impact was tremendous. Garrison used it as a tool to rally and organize slavery's opponents, and as a springboard for his lecture tours. He was an early advocate of women's suffrage, pacifism, and civil disobedience. And he so angered Southern leaders that mere possession of a copy of the paper in most states was grounds for imprisonment.

Garrison's stridency lost him many friends, even those who agreed with most of his positions. He was not above criticizing a supporter for hypocrisy. He railed against organized religious institutions that he felt enabled slavery (which were most of them), preferring instead to take the gospels at their word—love thy neighbor, help the poor . . . all that stuff—rather than have them interpreted by ministers. He even burned a copy of the Constitution during a rally condemning the Three-Fifths Compromise; "So perish all compromises with tyranny!" he shouted, as the document went up in flames.

William Lloyd Garrison, c. 1875

> The apologist for oppression becomes himself the oppressor. To palliate crime is to be guilty of its perpetuation.
> —*William Lloyd Garrison*

After the Civil War was over, Garrison faded from public discourse, living out his final years at his home in Roxbury. When his health permitted he spoke out on issues of the day. Garrison died on May 24, 1879, and was buried in Forest Hills Cemetery (95 Forest Hills Avenue) in Jamaica Plain.

LEARN MORE
All on Fire by Henry Mayer (St. Martin's, 1998)
William Lloyd Garrison and the Fight Against Slavery by William E. Cain, ed.
   (Bedford Books, 1995)

Somerville

Our Bodies, Ourselves
New England Free Press, 60 Union Square, Somerville, MA 02143

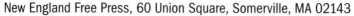

The Boston Women's Health Book Collective started as a discussion group at a feminist conference in 1969. The topic was "Women and Their Bodies." In very short order a common thread emerged from the participants' stories: their doctors were primarily male and were often insensitive, and at times condescending, toward their patients. Worse yet, the doctors assumed a paternalistic tone and failed to provide their patients with the basic information the women truly needed.

Eleven women in the group pledged to do something about it. They started by educating themselves on medical issues, and by fall began presenting their findings to larger groups. The courses became a book, *Our Bodies, Ourselves*, first published in 1970 by the nonprofit New England Free Press. Its stated purpose was to "empower women with knowledge of their bodies, health, and sexuality." At a hefty 600+ pages, it covered not only the medical but the social and psychological aspects of being a woman in the modern world, all without judgment or shame. Many editions and updates later, this revolutionary work is still in print.

> Learning to understand, accept, and be responsible for our physical selves, we are freed of some of these preoccupations and can start to use our untapped energies. Our image of ourselves is on a firmer base, we can be better friends and better lovers, better *people*, more self-confident, more autonomous, stronger and more whole.
>
> —*Boston Women's Health Book Collective, in Our Bodies, Ourselves*

LEARN MORE
Our Bodies, Ourselves: A New Edition for a New Era by the Boston Women's Health Book Collective (Touchstone, 2005)

Springfield

Dr. Seuss National Memorial Sculpture Garden
The Quadrangle, State and Chestnut Streets, Springfield, MA 01103

Few modern writers have influenced the lives of children as richly as Theodor Seuss Geisel—Dr. Seuss. Geisel was born in Springfield (22 Howard Street) on March 2, 1904, but grew up in the city's Forest Park neighborhood (74 Fairfield Street). After studying at Dartmouth and Oxford, Geisel embarked on his artistic career. He worked in the advertising department of Standard Oil for 15 years, and on the side sold adult cartoons to magazines such as *Life, Vanity Fair*, and *The Saturday Evening Post*. The first children's book he both wrote and illustrated, *And to Think That I Saw It on Mulberry Street*, was rejected 27 times before being published by Vanguard Press in 1937.

Geisel injected a healthy dose of progressivism into his works. *Yertle the Turtle* (1958) was a fable on totalitarianism in the wake of the McCarthy era. *The Sneeches* (1961) examined prejudice at the height of the civil rights movement. *The Lorax* (1971) became many kids' introduction to conservationism, just as *The Butter Battle Book* (1984) was a primer on the nuclear arms race.

Geisel won the Pulitzer Prize in 1984 "for his special contribution over nearly half a century to the education and enjoyment of America's children and their parents." He died on September 24, 1991, was cremated, and his ashes scattered. Today his birthplace honors his memory with the Dr. Seuss National Memorial Sculpture Garden. It includes life-sized statues of Horton the Elephant, Sam-I-Am, the Grinch, and more of his most popular characters. Geisel is also rendered in bronze, seated at his drawing table while the Cat in the Hat looks over his shoulder.

LEARN MORE
www.catinthehat.org/memorial.htm
Dr. Seuss & Mr. Geisel by Judith and Neil Morgan (Random House, 1995)

Watertown

Perkins School for the Blind
175 N. Beacon Street, Watertown, MA 02472 · (617) 924-3434

With a property gift from Thomas Perkins, Dr. Samuel Gridley Howe (husband of Julia Ward Howe) founded the Perkins School for the Blind in 1833, the first such school in the United States. Though most of its pupils were sightless, in 1843 the school successfully educated Laura Bridgman, who was deafblind. Charles Dickens visited Perkins in 1842, and wrote favorably about his experience in *American Notes*.

One of the school's most famous graduates was Anne Sullivan, who was born in Feeding Hills, Massachusetts, on April 14, 1886. Sullivan had been blinded by a childhood disease, but her eyesight had been partially restored by an operation at Perkins. After graduation Sullivan went to Tuscumbia, Alabama, where she had been hired to teach Helen Keller (see page 164). The Keller family had learned about the school after reading Dickens's book. Sullivan returned with Keller to live at Perkins in 1888, and the pair stayed five years. Keller went on to finishing school, then Radcliffe, where she graduated cum laude.

Perkins continues to meet the needs of the blind community through onsite education, outreach, parental support, and Braille publications put out through Howe Press.

LEARN MORE

www.perkins.org

Perkins School for the Blind by Kimberly French and the Perkins School for the Blind (Arcadia, 2004)

West Brookfield

Lucy Stone, Feminist Icon
Birthplace (burned down), Coy Hill Road, West Brookfield, MA 01585

Lucy Stone, born in West Brookfield on August 13, 1818, didn't take guff from anyone. Her father didn't believe his daughter should be educated, so Stone taught herself. When he refused to help her with college, she taught school to raise her tuition at Oberlin, and in 1847 became the first woman from Massachusetts to earn a college degree.

After graduation, Stone toured the United States lecturing against slavery and for women's right to vote. Hostile audiences hurled prayer books and worse at her, but during one 1850 speech she inspired abolitionist Susan B. Anthony to join the cause for suffrage.

On May 1, 1855, Stone married Henry Blackwell in her family's home in what turned out to be a groundbreaking ceremony. First, she kept her family name, a practice that was not unheard of at the time, but was unusual enough that women who followed her lead were dubbed "Lucy Stoners." What made the marriage even more revolutionary was that the couple signed a document believed to be the world's first prenuptial agreement. It established Stone and Blackwell as equal partners in their union. Copies were distributed to local clergy, who were encouraged to use it as a model for future ceremonies. Few at the time did.

Lucy Stone, c. 1850

The couple moved to Orange, New Jersey (16 Hurlbut Street), in 1857 where, on September 14, Stone gave birth to their first daughter, Alice Stone Blackwell. A year later a tax collector showed up at their door. Stone turned him away, saying she would happily pay the tax if given the right to vote, but not before. The bureaucrat retaliated by seizing the couple's household goods to sell at auction, including Alice's cradle. One of the family's sympathetic neighbors purchased their property and returned it to them.

> We believe that personal independence and equal human rights can never be forfeited, except for crime; that marriage should be an equal and permanent partnership, and so recognized by law.
> —*Lucy Stone and Henry Blackwell, in their marriage agreement, 1855*

Stone's strong convictions on civil rights led to a rift among suffragists following passage of the Fourteenth and Fifteenth Amendments. Angry that former slaves were being given the vote before women, Susan B. Anthony and Elizabeth Cady Stanton broke away to form the National Woman Suffrage Association. Stone then founded the American Woman Suffrage Association in 1869. (Alice Stone Blackwell would broker the reunification of the two groups in 1890, forming the National American Woman Suffrage Association.)

Lucy Stone died on October 18, 1893. Her last words to her daughter were "Make the world better." Per Stone's wishes, her body was cremated, making her the first person to do so in New England. Her ashes are interred at Forest Hills Cemetery in Jamaica Plain (95 Forest Hills Avenue).

LEARN MORE

www.westbrookfield.org/lucystone.htm

Lucy Stone by Alice Stone Blackwell (University of Virginia, 2001)

Lucy Stone by Andrea Moore Kerr (Rutgers, 1992)

Loving Warriors by Leslie Wheeler, ed. (Dial, 1981)

NEW HAMPSHIRE

The "Live Free or Die" citizens of New Hampshire are a crusty, cantankerous bunch—people like Dorris Haddock of Dublin. In the late 1990s, as Congress began consideration of what would later be known as the McCain–Feingold Campaign Finance Reform Bill, Haddock pledged to walk from coast to coast to raise awareness of government corruption in elections. Haddock, known to most as Granny D., had arthritis and emphysema, and she was pushing 90. "It would be better to die out [there], spending myself in a meaningful pursuit, than at home in my old chair," she wrote.

Granny D. started her trek on January 2, 1999, in Pasadena, California. Heading west through the Mojave Desert, she walked 10 miles each day. She greeted thousands of well-wishers, talked to school assemblies, marched in local parades, spoke in front of the offices of congress members and senators, and got citizens to sign her petition for campaign finance reform.

In Arizona she wanted to meet with GOP Senator Jon Kyl, but he refused to come out of his office to speak to her. She lambasted Senator Mitch McConnell from the steps of his Kentucky offices by answering a rhetorical question he had asked on the senate floor as he filibustered the bill: "How can it be corruption if no

> You are being raised in a society that ever tries to trivialize your life. Your life is not trivial. It is not designer labeled. It is not online or virtual. It is real. You are a free man or woman in a land of free people who have served each other with dignity and sacrifice for many centuries. Do your duty to those who came before you. Do your duty to your own freedom and to the freedom of Americans to come.
> —Dorris "Granny D." Haddock, to Maryland college students, February 2000

one is corrupt?" Granny D. spoke of a senator who had taken $791,945 from insurance companies and blocked a patient rights bill, and who had taken $602,885 from oil and gas companies and scuttled pollution controls, and $597,915 from telecoms to allow digital communication monopolies, and so on. Of course, that senator was Republican Mitch McConnell.

More than a year after she started, on January 24, 2000 (her 90th birthday), Granny D. arrived in Cumberland, Maryland. By then winter was in full force. Unable to continue her walk on the icy highways, she strapped on cross-country skis and finished the last 184 miles along the towpath of the old C&O barge canal. On February 29 she marched from Arlington National Cemetery into Washington with 2,200 supporters, down K Street and Lobbyist Row, and around to the U.S. Capitol where she gave a barnburner of a speech. Due in no small part to Granny D.'s efforts, the McCain–Feingold bill was later passed and signed into law.

In 2004 Granny D. ran for the U.S. Senate and, though she took no corporate contributions, received 34 percent of the vote against incumbent Judd Gregg.

LEARN MORE
www.grannyd.com
Granny D. by Dorris Haddock (Villard, 2001)
Run Granny Run (2006)

Concord

Christa McAuliffe, Pioneering Teacher
Christa McAuliffe Planetarium, 3 Institute Drive, Concord, NH 03301 · (603) 271-STAR

Teachers are inherently progressive. Millions have dedicated their lives to educating future generations, and some have even *given* their lives. Social studies teacher Christa McAuliffe volunteered to become the first private citizen to ride into orbit aboard the Space Shuttle, and was selected from among 11,500 other teachers who wanted the chance. After six months of training she boarded the *Challenger* on January 28, 1986, while her students watched on television. Fifty-one seconds after liftoff the spacecraft exploded, and all seven

Christa McAuliffe, during zero-G training, 1986

crew were killed. The 37-year-old's remains were returned to Concord for burial at Blossom Hill Cemetery (207 N. State Street).

McAuliffe's dream of teaching children about space lives on in her hometown. Concord built and dedicated a state-of-the-art planetarium in her honor.

LEARN MORE

www.starhop.com

I Touch the Future by Robert T. Hohler (Berkley, 1988)

A Journal for Christa by Grace George Corrigan (University of Nebraska, 2000)

She helped people. She laughed. She loved and is loved. She appreciated the world's natural beauty. She was curious and sought to learn who we are and what the universe is about. She relied on her own judgment and moral courage to do right. She cared about the suffering of her fellow man. She tried to protect our spaceship earth. She taught her children to do the same.

—Epitaph on Christa McAuliffe's grave

West Lebanon

Sharon Underwood Takes No Prisoners

Valley News, 24 Interchange Drive, West Lebanon, NH 03784 · (603) 727-3217

It was the gay rights editorial heard round the progressive world, and it was first published by the *Valley News* of West Lebanon, New Hampshire. Penned by computer programmer Sharon Underwood of White River Junction, Vermont, the essay opens fire on readers who had expressed their concerns about "the homosexual agenda" in the pages of local papers following the gay civil unions debate in Vermont (see page 49).

"I am the mother of a gay son," she began, "and I've taken enough from you good people." Underwood went on to describe the injustices suffered by her boy during childhood and adolescence, which led to an attempted suicide at the age of 17. She dismissed every notion that God would approve of the actions of anti-gay zealots, or that homosexuality was a sin. "You use your religion to abdicate your responsibility to be thinking human beings," she concluded, adding, "There are a vast number of religious people who find your attitudes repugnant."

The editorial might have only been noticed by a fraction of the *Valley News* readers, but it was picked up by two other New England newspapers. From there it was spotted by Andrew Tobias, treasurer of the Democratic National Committee, who posted it on his Web site and e-mailed it to friends. If you have been lucky enough to have been on the receiving end of this daisy chain in 2000 or 2001, you probably remember the essay. If you haven't, you can easily find the full text online.

LEARN MORE
www.vnews.com

RHODE ISLAND

Rhode Island has a long history of independence and tolerance. It was founded by Roger Williams, who had fled Massachusetts and the Puritans in search of religious freedom (see page 42). It also proclaimed its independence from Britain a full two months before the Declaration of Independence was signed. And then there was the ill-fated Dorr Rebellion.

It started on May 3, 1842, when Thomas Wilson Dorr was inaugurated as the "People's Governor." This was a shock to Samuel King, who the 5,000 landowning voters of Rhode Island had already elected to the post—land ownership was a requirement to vote under the state's 1663 charter. To get around it, the state's 12,000 working-class citizens had drafted a new constitution in 1841 during a People's Convention, and had held their own statewide election. (Though the election was a big step forward, it was still only open to white males.) When King refused to step down or ratify the new constitution, Dorr and a band of supporters launched a raid on the Providence armory. They were quickly defeated when their only cannon misfired. Dorr fled to Massachusetts, but was arrested a year later, tried for treason, and sentenced to life at hard labor.

But local sentiment was still with Dorr. In 1843 Rhode Island drew up a new constitution extending suffrage to any white male who could afford a $1 poll tax. It was a start. Dorr was pardoned after serving 20 months, and died on December 27, 1854. He is buried at Swan Point Cemetery in Providence (585 Blackstone Boulevard).

LEARN MORE
Right & Might by Joyce M. Botelho (Rhode Island Historical Society, 1992)
The Dorr Rebellion by Marvin Gettleman (Random House, 1973)

Cumberland

Aaron Fricke Goes to Prom
Cumberland High School, 2600 Mendon Road, Cumberland, RI 02864

Some high school students look forward to their senior prom, and others feel it's a ridiculous waste of time and money. But until the 1980s gay and lesbian students didn't even have the option of deciding either way. Were it not for brave students like Aaron Fricke, that might still be the case.

In the spring of 1980 Fricke asked his Cumberland High School principal, Mr. Lynch, if he could bring a male companion to the senior prom. Fricke knew Lynch would deny the request—Fricke's date was to be Paul Guilbert, who had asked Lynch to attend the junior prom a year earlier. Guilbert was 17 years old at the time and had no legal recourse without his parents' support (which he didn't have). But Fricke was 18 and, with the assistance of the National Gay Task Force, sued Lynch for the right to attend.

The case was filed in federal district court and argued before Judge Raymond Pettine on May 21, 1980. Fricke and Lynch were the only witnesses to testify. On May 28 Pettine ruled that Fricke was being denied his first amendment right to political expression. If the school was concerned about "safety," as it had alleged, it should provide proper security. Lynch appealed to the circuit court, but the case was thrown out.

Two days later, on May 30, Fricke and Guilbert put on their blue tuxes and drove to the prom at the Pleasant Valley Country Club (95 Armsby Road) in nearby Sutton, Massachusetts. Bishop Louis Gelineau of the Providence Archdiocese asked Roman Catholics to stay home that night, and pray. Meanwhile, the seniors of Cumberland High danced to the B-52's "Rock Lobster" while having, according to Fricke's memoir, a great time together.

> The First Amendment does not tolerate mob rule by unruly schoolchildren.
> —*Judge Raymond Pettine, in Fricke v. Lynch, 1980*

LEARN MORE
www.cumberlandri.org
Reflections of a Rock Lobster by Aaron Fricke (Alyson, 1981)

Newport

Touro Synagogue National Historic Site
85 Touro Street, Newport, RI 02840 · (401) 847-4794

In 1658, 15 Sephardic Jews emigrated from Barbados to Newport, seeking the opportunity to worship freely in Roger Williams's new colony. Their community had earlier fled Brazil for the Caribbean during the Inquisition, but anti-Semitism had followed them. In Newport they established a new congregation, Jeshuat Israel (Salvation of Israel), and in 1677 purchased and consecrated the first Jewish cemetery in America.

For a century the community worshiped in the homes of its members, but in 1758 its new spiritual leader, Isaac Touro, encouraged them to construct a synagogue. The temple was dedicated during Hanukkah in 1763, and remains the oldest active synagogue in the United States.

Following the American Revolution the congregation was concerned that the religious freedom they had previously enjoyed might be in jeopardy. The congregation's warden, Moses Seixas, wrote a letter to George Washington in 1790—a year before the Bill of Rights was ratified—asking assurance that they, like all other religions, would be allowed to worship in freedom. Washington wrote back that the new government would "give to bigotry no sanction, to persecution no assistance." A copy of his letter is on display in the synagogue today.

LEARN MORE
www.tourosynagogue.org
History of Touro Synagogue by Rabbi Theodore Lewis (Touro Synagogue, 1975)

Providence

Roger Williams, Founder of Religious Liberty

Roger Williams National Memorial, 282 N. Main Street, Providence, RI 02903 · (401) 521-7266

The American colonies were established, for the most part, by those fleeing religious and civil persecution in Europe. However, that didn't prevent the colonists from practicing their own brand of religious intolerance, as Roger Williams discovered in Massachusetts soon after he arrived from England in 1631. Williams advocated the radical notion of the separation of church and state, and for that was tried in 1635 and banished from Boston.

But before Williams could be exiled to Europe he fled into the New England wilderness with his wife, Mary. The pair wandered for three months before setting up a new colony at the headwaters of the Narragansett River: Providence. Unlike other colonizers, Williams negotiated and paid a fair price to the native Narragansett for the land he needed. What's more, he didn't ask the king's permission to do so, and neither did he harbor notions of "Christianizing" the Narragansett. By the 1640s the Providence settlement had become a model of religious tolerance and coexistence with the indigenous population. Cotton Mather, who had orchestrated Williams's banishment from Massachusetts, dismissed the new colony as "the sewer of New England."

Some sewer! Williams established a democratic system of government where each head of the household participated in decisions that affected the colony. The colonists elected Williams the chief officer, and he used his position to request funds to support the colony's widows, orphans, and the mentally ill who had difficulty making ends meet. And he advocated, in a tract titled *The Bloudy Tenent*, that religious liberty be extended not only to Christians but to those who were "paganish, Jewish, Turkish, or anti-christian."

Williams died in 1683. His experiment in the separation between church and state became the model for the new republic after independence. Providence honored Williams with an enormous monument in 1939, built high atop a hill overlooking the town he founded. He is buried two blocks east of the monument.

LEARN MORE

www.nps.gov/rowi

Roger Williams by Edwin S. Gaustad (Oxford, 2005)

Separating Church and State by Timothy L. Hall (University of Illinois, 1998)

Vermont still carries on a New England tradition every progressive should appreciate: Town Meeting Day, a triumph of participatory democracy. Each year on the first Tuesday in March (following the first Monday), banks and schools are closed so that residents can gather in their communities to discuss issues of local and national importance. The meetings' agendas are announced by selectmen for each town in a format called a "warning," and almost anything is open for debate.

In recent years national issues have dominated the meetings, including the impeachment of George W. Bush. Forty assemblies took a vote in 2007 to demand the U.S. House of Representatives begin impeachment proceedings against the president, for knowingly launching a war based on lies, for illegal surveillance of the public by the National Security Agency, and for perjury and obstruction of justice in both matters. Thirty-five communities approved the resolution. Only five declined.

LEARN MORE

Real Democracy by Frank M. Bryan (University of Chicago, 2003)

The Impeachment of George W. Bush by Elizabeth Holtzman and Cynthia L. Cooper (Nation Books, 2006)

Articles for Impeachment Against George W. Bush by the Center for Constitutional Rights (Melville House, 2006)

Burlington

Ben & Jerry's Ice Cream
First Store (torn down), St. Paul and College Streets, Burlington, VT 05401

When Ben Cohen and Jerry Greenfield opened Ben & Jerry's Homemade, an ice cream and crepe eatery, on May 5, 1978, they had no idea how big they would become. They also didn't know how long they would last, which is probably why they handed out several memberships in the Ice Cream for Life Club to folks willing to give them essential freebies, such as copper tubing for their sinks.

Their first store was a converted gas station in downtown Burlington. These New Yorkers had chosen Vermont because it was the only state in the union without a Baskin-Robbins franchise. With a five-dollar correspondence course in ice cream making from Penn State, a player piano, and a knack for wacky marketing, they were ready to roll. Their business grew fast, and within two years they were also selling pints to local stores and restaurants. In 1981 the first franchise opened in Shelburne, and in 1986 the duo opened a state-of-the-art ice cream factory in nearby Waterbury (1401 Waterbury-Stowe Road), which is still open for tours.

So what does all this have to do with progressivism? Showing that business can be a force for good, not profit alone, Ben and Jerry built a corporation based on ecologically sound manufacturing and economic justice for their employees and the communities in which they operated. They donated 7.5 percent of their pretax profits to charity through the Ben & Jerry Foundation, and their flavors often focused on specific issues: Peace Pops, promoting their "1 Percent for Peace" campaign; Rainforest Crunch, aiding conservation efforts; and One Sweet Whirled, fighting global warming. They used their visibility to protest the Seabrook nuclear power plant, support Farm Aid (see page 232), and sponsor the Newport Folk Festival. And though the company was bought by Uni-

We have a progressive, non-partisan social mission that seeks to meet human needs and eliminate injustices in our local, national, and international communities by integrating these concerns into our day-to-day business activities. Our focus is on children and families, the environment, and sustainable agriculture on family farms.
—*From Ben & Jerry's Corporate Mission Statement*

lever in 2000, it maintains an independent board of directors to maintain the business's social mission.

LEARN MORE
www.benjerry.com, (866) BJ-TOURS
Ben & Jerry's by Fred "Chico" Lager (Crown, 1994)

Bernie Sanders, a True Independent
Burlington City Hall, 149 Church Street, Burlington, VT 05401

For those who think third-party candidates are tilting at windmills, consider the political history of Bernie Sanders. In 1971 he joined Vermont's Liberty Union Party, a small group of antiwar progressives who were sick of the entrenched establishment. In 1972 Sanders ran as its senatorial candidate and captured 2 percent of the vote. Before the decade was out he ran once more for senate and twice for governor, and lost each time. Then, in 1981, he took on the six-term Democratic mayor of Burlington, Gordon Paquette. Running as an independent, Sanders cobbled together a coalition of UVM students, working-class citizens, and the city's police union, which had been snubbed by Paquette during labor negotiations. Sanders won at last . . . by 12 votes.

Once he was in office, the Burlington city council worked to undermine Sanders, and would schedule official meetings without informing the mayor. Sanders used its actions as a club to beat the council at the next election, charging members with violating the public trust. Burlingtonians agreed, and voted many of them out of office.

Bernie Sanders, 2007

Sanders served four terms as mayor, establishing a Youth Office, a Women's Council, and an Arts Council, and earned accolades for running a clean, efficient City Hall. Voter participation in elections doubled during his tenure. In 1990 he was elected to the U.S. House of Representatives as an independent. Vermont's only congressman garnered national attention by highlighting skyrocketing prescription costs after leading bus caravans full of seniors across the U.S.–Canadian border. He was also a vocal opponent of the USA PATRIOT Act and the Iraq War before either position was popular. And in 2006 he was elected to the U.S. Senate as an independent, where he serves today.

LEARN MORE
www.sanders.senate.gov, (202) 224-5141
Outsider in the House by Bernie Sanders (Verso, 1997)

Howard Dean Enters Politics
Burlington Bike Path, Lake Champlain Waterfront, Burlington, VT 05401

Howard Dean's entry into politics, and his rise to chairmanship of the Democratic National Committee, demonstrates that citizens can (and should) get involved in government. Originally from New York's Long Island, Dean moved to Vermont in May 1978 to begin his residency in the ambulatory care program at the University of Vermont. He and wife Judy Steinberg eventually established a family practice in Shelbourne, in south suburban Burlington.

Dean believed in supporting his community, and in the late 1970s he, along with Rick Sharp and Tom Hudspeth, founded the Citizens' Waterfront Group. Their goal was to convert an abandoned railroad right-of-way, which ran along Lake Champlain through Burlington, into a public park. After much work with the city, county, and business community, they won; the park and its nine-mile-long bike path are still enjoyed today.

With a growing interest in politics, Dean became the Democratic Party chair of Chittenden County in 1980. In 1983 he was elected a state representative, beating Burlington mayor Bernie Sanders (see page 45). Two years later he secured the post of minority whip, and in 1986 was elected lieutenant governor.

Dean assumed the state's highest office on August 14, 1991, when Governor Richard Snelling died. Though Snelling was a Republican, Dean pledged to continue his economic recovery plan for the balance of his term. A pragmatic politician, fiscally conservative and socially progressive, Dean was reelected in 1992, and four more terms after that. And on June 23, 2003, Dean announced that he would run for president while standing on a stage on Church Street in Burlington, just blocks from the park where he first got his feet wet.

Howard Dean, 2007

LEARN MORE
www.enjoyburlington.com/
  Parks/BikePath1.cfm
Winning Back America by Howard
  Dean (Simon & Schuster,
  2003)
You Have the Power by Howard
  Dean (Simon & Schuster,
  2004)

I'm here to represent the Democratic wing of the Democratic Party.
                              —*Howard Dean*

Glover

The Bread & Puppet Theater
753 Heights Road (Route 122), Glover, VT 05839 · (802) 525-1271

You've no doubt seen the Bread & Puppet Theater's work—oversized, gangling puppets rising above protests against the Vietnam War, and the anti-nuclear marches of the 1970s and '80s. The troupe was founded on Manhattan's Lower East Side by David Schumann during the 1960s. But Schumann longed to work on an even larger scale than was possible in New York, and moved the

Bread & Puppet Theater masks

theater to Goddard College in Plainfield, Vermont, in 1970. Four years later it moved to its current location in Glover.

The Bread & Puppet Theater developed and performed grand pageants—circuses, actually—on the large, hillside field across the road from its Glover farm. Hundreds of puppeteers would collectively explore eight archetypal themes: Death, Fiend, Beast, Human, World, Gift, Bread, and Hope. Though the circuses had foundations in ancient storytelling traditions, their messages were quite modern, including environmental issues and critiques of the G8, IMF, and World Bank.

The circuses were drawing 30,000 visitors by the late 1990s when tragedy struck; a drunken fight in the farm's campground left one man dead from a fall. Schumann decided the theater had strayed from its original mission, so it now hosts several small weekend circuses rather than one large performance. But it still addresses issues of the day, such as a recent circus titled Homeland Security Day in the Life of a Vermont Dairy Cow.

Even if you can't make it for one of the theater's performances, you can always visit its museum, which fills two stories of a 135-year-old barn on the property. Thousands of masks, costumes, and puppets from previous circuses hang from the rafters and walls. You can also purchase works of Cheap Art in the abandoned school bus nearby. Cheap Art is a movement started by the theater's artists in 1984, fostering a noncapitalistic, nonelitist approach to art. Prices range from 10¢ to $10.

> **The tortured world *needs* its solidarity whereas the consumer society manages astonishingly well without it . . .**
> —*Peter Schumann, founder of the Bread & Puppet Theater*

LEARN MORE

www.breadandpuppet.org

Rehearsing with Gods by Ronald T. Simon and Marc Estrin (Chelsea Green, 2002)

Milton

Vermont Establishes Gay Civil Unions

Milton Town Clerk, 43 Bombardier Road, Milton, VT 05468

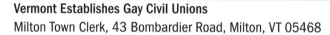

When Lois Farnham and Holly Puterbaugh walked into the Milton Town Clerk's office on April 25, 1997, and asked for a marriage license, they knew they would be denied an application. They had warned the clerk, a friend of theirs, the day before. He handed the couple a letter explaining why he was not able to issue them a license. That letter would be the first step on the road to civil unions in Vermont.

Farnham and Puterbaugh were joined by couples Nina Beck and Stacy Jolles, and Stan Baker and Peter Harrington, in a lawsuit (known as the *Baker* case) challenging Vermont's marriage statutes. The couples had been carefully selected by Susan Murray and Beth Robinson, lawyers who had established the Vermont Freedom to Marry Task Force in 1995. Filed July 22, 1997, the *Baker* case took two and a half years to make it through the courts.

On December 20, 1999, the Vermont Supreme Court handed down a ruling that didn't actually allow same-sex couples to marry, but forced the state legislature to come up with a plan to extend to gay and lesbian couples wanting to marry all the civil rights afforded heterosexual unions. Whether that was through out-and-out marriage or another remedy was up to them, but if lawmakers didn't act the court would impose a plan of its own.

Though Vermont initially divided along traditional political lines, the conservative "values" crowd overplayed its hand. Lawmakers in the middle of the political spectrum had no trouble understanding the vitriol faced by gays and lesbians when they were verbally attacked at town hall forums by gay marriage opponents, just for considering various solutions to the court-ordered mandate.

Meanwhile, brave Vermont citizens came out, spoke out, and educated their neighbors. In the end the legislature settled on a compromise that completely pleased neither side, but was a step forward. Same-sex couples could be united under a "civil union" and many of the legal benefits of a heterosexual marriage, though it wouldn't be called a marriage.

> The extension of the Common Benefits Clause to acknowledge plaintiffs as Vermonters who seek nothing more, nor less, than legal protection and security for their avowed commitment to an intimate and lasting human relationship is simply, when all is said and done, a recognition of our common humanity.
> —Chief Justice Jeffrey Amestoy, in the Baker decision, 1999

The law went into effect July 1, 2000. Just after midnight Carolyn Conrad and Kathleen Peterson became the first same-sex couple to be granted a civil union. After swearing an oath on their license in the Brattleboro town clerk's office (230 Main Street) they walked across the street from the municipal building and had a public ceremony. Puterbaugh and Farnham waited until 9:00 A.M. that day, and signed their civil union license in the office of the South Burlington city clerk (575 Dorset Street), near their new home, followed by a religious ceremony at the First Congregational Church (38 S. Winsooki Avenue) in Burlington.

LEARN MORE
Civil Wars by David Moats (Harcourt, 2004)

2
The Mid-Atlantic

★ Delaware ★

★ District of Columbia ★

★ Maryland ★

★ New Jersey ★ New York ★

★ Pennsylvania ★

★ West Virginia ★

DELAWARE

Delaware might be one of the smallest states in the union, even mocked as "two counties when the tide is up—and only three when the tide is down," but what it lacks in acreage it makes up for in decisiveness: it was the first state in the new republic to ratify the U.S. Constitution. Thirty lawmakers met on the Green in Dover (State Street and Bank Lane) and on December 7, 1787, approved the document on a unanimous vote. By doing so, Delaware became the first state.

Hockessin and Claymont

Bulah v. Gebhart and *Belton v. Gebhart*: Desegregating Delaware Schools
School 107 (now the Hockessin Community Center), 4266 Millcreek Road, Hockessin, DE 19707 · (302) 239-2363

Claymont High School (now the Claymont Community Center), 3301 Green Street, Claymont, DE 19703 · (302) 792-2757

The Delaware State Board of Education was hit with two desegregation lawsuits in 1951, and though it was a long way from Topeka, Kansas, the cases would eventually be linked with the U.S. Supreme Court's *Brown v. Board of Education* decision.

The Delaware lawsuits were filed independently. The Hockessin school district refused to transport Sarah Bulah's daughter Shirley to School 107, the district's one-room schoolhouse for elementary-age black children, though every white child was driven door to door. Bulah wrote a letter to the state's Department of Instruction, but it went unanswered. She then wrote the governor. He lamely responded that his hands were tied—white kids rode the school bus, which meant Shirley could not ride with them. The law was the law.

Meanwhile, Ethel Belton of Claymont was dealing with the state's secondary schools. Her daughter was being forced to spend two hours on a bus each day in order to attend Delaware's only four-year high school for African Americans: Howard High School (401 E. 12th Street), wedged between the factories and warehouses of downtown Wilmington. Worse yet, Claymont had a high school on a beautiful 14-acre campus, but it was restricted to white students.

Both mothers, about the same time, filed suit against the state board of education; Francis Gebhart was a board member. The initial trials were heard together in Chancery Court, Delaware's civil court, by Chancellor (judge) Collins Jacques Seitz. The 36-year-old jurist shocked the establishment when he sided with the parents and ordered the state to admit black students to its white schools. The state supreme court upheld Seitz's ruling, though it left open the possibility of resegregation once black and white school facilities were "substantially equalized."

Neither side was comfortable with the high court's ruling, and appealed to the U.S. Supreme Court. It would roll the Delaware appeal into the Brown case, and answer the question of "separate but equal" facilities two years later (see page 293).

Wilmington

Emily Bissell and Christmas Seals
Emily P. Bissell Hospital, 3000 Newport Gap Pike, Wilmington, DE 19808 · (302) 995-8400

In 1907 Emily Bissell, a social worker with the Delaware Red Cross, received a letter from Dr. Joseph Wales—her cousin—asking that she help him raise $300 to keep Wales's tuberculosis sanitarium solvent. Bissell had recently read an article about a Danish postal clerk who had collected funds through the sale of a stamp-like seal. Bissell decided to launch a similar fundraiser. With $40 collected from friends (and a credit from her printer) she was able to get 50,000 Christmas-themed seals printed.

Bissell began selling them from a table in the lobby of the Wilmington post office on December 7, 1907. One penny for 25 seals. Sales were modest, and Bissell began to worry that she wouldn't clear $300. So she hopped a train to Philadelphia where she met with Leigh Mitchell Hodges, a columnist with the *North American* newspaper. Hodges publicized the seals through his paper, and soon Bissell was printing 50,000 more. By the end of the campaign she had raised $3,000. And the next year? $120,000!

Today Christmas Seals are a major part of the American Lung Association's annual appeal. Bissell's contribution has not been forgotten; when the hospital where she worked was torn down, the 200-bed structure erected in its place was named after her. Today the facility houses a nursing home.

LEARN MORE
www.christmasseals.org
www.lungusa.org, (800) LUNG-USA

Thomas Garrett and the Underground Railroad
Garrett Home Site (torn down), 227 Shipley Street, Wilmington, DE 19801

Over 38 years, starting in 1822 when he moved to Wilmington, Thomas Garrett helped more than 2,700 slaves escape north. And he wasn't shy about his activities, either. When Garrett learned that a slaveholding neighbor had threatened to shoot him on sight, he showed up at the man's door and said, "Here I am. Thee can shoot me if thee likes." The man backed down. In another confrontation, Garrett was tossed from a moving train by slavecatchers while trying to rescue a runaway.

Then, in 1848, Garrett challenged a Delaware sheriff who was holding a family of six. He was able to confuse the officer by pointing out inconsistencies in the group's papers. Once freed, he shuttled the family to Philadelphia, where they disappeared into the Underground's clandestine network. When the sheriff discovered he'd been duped, Garrett was arrested and tried for harboring and transporting slaves. He was found guilty and fined $5,000.

> Thou has left me a dollar, but I wish to say to thee, and all in this courtroom, that if anyone knows of a fugitive who wants a shelter and a friend, send him to Thomas Garrett.
>
> *—Thomas Garrett, to the judge, after being convicted of harboring escaped slaves*

Though the verdict left him penniless, Garrett was undeterred. Abolitionists collected donations to help him reestablish his operations, and his new home became a popular stopover for Harriet Tubman (see page 78). Garrett continued his work up until the Civil War. He died on January 25, 1871, and was buried in the Wilmington Friends Meeting House Cemetery (401 N. West Street). Though his home is long gone, a statue of Garrett and Tubman has been erected in Wilmington's Peter Spence Plaza (French and Ninth Streets).

LEARN MORE

www.wilmingtondefriendsmeeting.org, (302) 652-4491

Station Master on the Underground Railroad by James A. McGowen and William
   C. Kashatus (McFarland & Company, 2004)

DISTRICT OF COLUMBIA

For progressives, the District of Columbia is a treasure chest of democracy in action . . . so long as they avoid K Street, the *Washington Times*, and the backrooms of Congress. Of course, no Washington shrine is more sacred than the National Archives (700 Pennsylvania Avenue NW, www.archives.gov), repository of the Declaration of Independence, the U.S. Constitution, and the Bill of Rights. Outside the building's rotunda the exhibits rotate, and depending on when you visit you might see the Emancipation Proclamation, the 1965 Voting Rights Act, or Richard Nixon's letter of resignation.

Several blocks west of the Archives on the Mall is the National Museum of American History (14th Street and Constitution Avenue NW, www.americanhistory.si.edu), the Smithsonian's crown jewel of progressive artifacts. Here you can find Susan B. Anthony's red shawl, FDR's Fireside Chat microphone, César Chávez's union jacket, Helen Keller's Braille watch, Mister Rogers's sweater, Einstein's pipe, Ben Franklin's walking stick, Jonas Salk's polio vaccine syringe and empty vials, Abe Lincoln's stovepipe hat, Alice Paul's desk, Archie and Edith's chairs, Muhammad Ali's gloves, Thomas Jefferson's annotated Bible, Kermit the Frog, and the Woolworth's lunch counter and stools from Greensboro, North Carolina.

But those two museums only scratch the surface of what can be found in Washington—museums and monuments too numerous to list. But there are a few historic sites that demand special attention . . .

Alice Paul, the National Women's Party, and the Equal Rights Amendment
NWP Headquarters, Sewall-Belmont House, 144 Constitution Avenue NE,
Washington, DC 20002 · (202) 546-1210

Though Susan B. Anthony gets much of the credit, the person most responsible for securing the vote for American women is Alice Paul. Born in Mount Laurel, New Jersey (128 Hooten Road), on January 11, 1885, Paul received her political education while attending the London School of Economics. Women in Great Britain were demanding the vote, and she joined them; Paul was arrested seven times during demonstrations, was jailed three times, and was force fed during a hunger strike. On returning to the states in 1909, she vowed to fight for the franchise in her home country.

Working on behalf of the National American Woman Suffrage Association (NAWSA), Paul organized a march—the Suffrage Procession and Pageant—in Washington, D.C., on the eve of Woodrow Wilson's inauguration. On May 3, 1913, more than 5,000 women paraded along the inauguration route behind a banner that read, "We Demand an Amendment to the Constitution of the United States Enfranchising the Women of This Country." Along the way they were heckled and harassed, and the police did little to stop (and in some cases encouraged) the attackers. But the abuse they suffered, when reported, drew national attention and supporters to their cause.

Paul demanded that the NAWSA continue its activist posture, and when they refused she founded the Congressional Union, which became the National Women's Party (NWP) in 1916. "It is better, as far as getting the vote is concerned I believe, to have a small united group than an immense debating society," Paul confided to a friend. When she advocated more drastic measures, Paul was banned from the NAWSA.

The NWP's first action took place on January 10, 1917; four women hoisted banners outside the White House. The silent vigil continued through June 22, when 27 women were arrested. Six were eventually convicted for "causing a crowd to gather and thus obstructing traffic," and when they refused to pay their $25 fines they were tossed into jail for three days.

The protests continued, and by August mobs had destroyed more than 200 of the NWP's banners. Thirty-three women, including Paul, were ordered to the Occoquan Workhouse for disorderly conduct, with sentences ranging from six days to six months. Even more were sent to the District jail. Paul launched a hunger strike—the first person to do so in U.S. history—and was joined by other inmates. Public outrage eventually forced Wilson to pardon the suffragists.

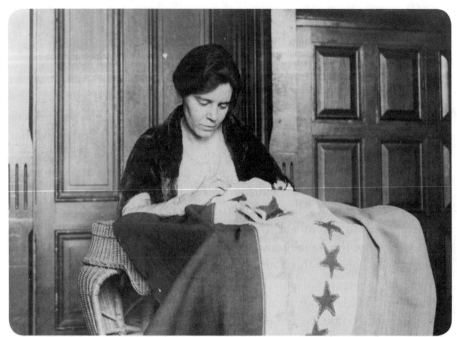

Alice Paul, sewing another star onto her ratification banner, c. 1919

When Congress reconvened in January 1918, the president endorsed ratification of the "Susan B. Anthony Amendment." It passed the House by one vote, but when it stalled in the Senate the NWP resumed its protests. The bill failed when the Senate fell two votes short, primarily because of Southern opposition. Paul established a perpetual "watch fire" in front of the White House where the NWP would burn Wilson's democracy speeches "as fast as he made them in Europe." Though Congress had adjourned, Wilson ordered it back into special session, where the amendment passed in June and was sent to the states. The Nineteenth Amendment was finally adopted in August 1920 (see page 214). Alice Paul was just 35 years old at the time.

But Paul didn't stop there. She drafted the Equal Rights Amendment in 1923, when it was introduced to Congress: "Equality of rights under the law shall not be denied or abridged by the United States or by any state on account of sex." The amendment was brought forward every session, but didn't make it to the floor until 1972, and was sent to the states in March. Hawaii was the first to approve it, followed by Nebraska.

> I always thought once you put your hand on the plough you don't remove it until you get to the end of the row.
>
> —Alice Paul

Unfortunately, the ratification process expired on June 30, 1982, three states short of adoption.

LEARN MORE
www.sewallbelmont.org
www.alicepaul.org, (856) 231-1885
From Equal Suffrage to Equal Rights by Christine Lunardini (NYU, 1986)
The Equal Rights Amendment by Sarah Slavin, ed. (Haworth, 1982)
Iron-Jawed Angels by Linda G. Ford (University Press of America, 1991)

THE BIRTH OF NOW

In July 1966 Betty Friedan and 27 other women met to form a national organization to address the concerns of American women. Three months later they held the First National Conference of the National Organization for Women—NOW—in Washington. On October 19 the delegates adopted a "Statement of Purpose" that outlined their beliefs and goals on gender equality: "The purpose of NOW is to take action to bring women into full participation in the mainstream of American society now, exercising all the privileges and responsibilities thereof in truly equal partnership with men."

Though the organization suffered from internal conflicts in the early years, including an unsuccessful and unfortunate attempt by Friedan (who served as president until 1970) to ban lesbian members from leadership positions, the group eventually coalesced around a single issue: passage of the Equal Rights Amendment. Their campaign peaked in the late 1970s, but the amendment died in 1982 before being ratified by enough state legislatures. NOW, however, was not defeated, and continues to fight for women, reproductive freedom, constitutional equality, and diversity, and against domestic violence through more than 550 active chapters across the United States. (www.now.org)

We strive to ensure that no party, candidate, president, senator, governor, congressman, or any public official who betrays or ignores the principle of full equality between the sexes is elected or appointed to office.

—*NOW, in its "Statement of Purpose," 1966*

Bolling v. Sharpe: Desegregating the District
John Philip Sousa Junior High, 3650 Ely Place SE, Washington, DC 20019

The third of five cases to be rolled into the *Brown v. Board of Education* decision (see page 293) originated in the nation's capital. Gardner Bishop had long been trying to integrate the district's schools; in 1947 he'd attempted to enroll his daughter Judine at all-white Eliot Junior High instead of the school she'd been assigned, the all-black Browne Junior High. Though Eliot had the capacity for 918 students, and only 765 enrollees, Judine was sent back to Browne. That building was made to hold 783 students and had 1,638—students were taught in double shifts. So Bishop showed up at a school board meeting with 40 Browne students and announced that they, and all the other students, would not return to classes until conditions improved. After seeing picketing students in the newspaper, the board promised to end the double shifts, and the strike ended.

Not surprisingly, the board had made an empty promise. The next school built in the district, John Philip Sousa Junior High, opened in 1950 with an all-white student body. Bishop arrived on September 11, 1950, with 11 African American students ready to enroll, and was turned away. One of the students that day, 12-year-old Spottswood Bolling Jr., was named in a lawsuit against the president of the district's school board, Melvin Sharpe.

Bolling v. Sharpe was argued on Fifth Amendment due-process grounds. While it was making its way through the federal courts, the lawyer on the case learned from the clerk of the U.S. Supreme Court that it would be added to its docket under *Brown*.

CODEPINK: Women for Peace and the Iraq War Vigil
The White House, 1600 Pennsylvania Avenue NW, Washington, DC 20500

One of the most assertive (and entertaining!) responses to the Bush administration's militaristic "foreign policy" has been CODEPINK: Women for Peace. The organization was formed in 2002 by several women with a lifelong commitment to progressive causes, including Medea Benjamin and Jodie Evans. The White House had just issued its preposterous color-coded Homeland Security Advisory System and the women decided to add a color . . . one that expressed women's role in safety and security, one that didn't come with politically timed terror alerts or at the point of a bayonet.

CODEPINK, preparing to be arrested at the White House, 2005

In one of its first actions, CODEPINK launched a nonstop vigil outside the White House during the four months leading up to the Iraq War. On March 8, 2003, International Women's Day, more than 10,000 pink-clad demonstrators marched to Lafayette Park to protest the looming war, and many were arrested. The group also sent peace delegations to Iraq and other Middle Eastern countries to demonstrate that there were Americans who were opposed to the president's deadly scheme.

CODEPINK members have a knack for popping up where war hawks least expect them, disrupting congressional hearings, unfurling enormous "pink slip" banners outside Bush's speaking engagements, and sitting in at the offices of elected officials. Several CODEPINKers even materialized on the floor of the 2004 Republican National Convention, interrupting Bush's acceptance speech with demands to end the bloodshed; delegates chanted "Four more years!" to drown out the protesters, who somehow managed to pull on bright pink slips before being dragged out by security. Not only did it disrupt Bush's swaggering delivery, it was great theater!

CODEPINK has chapters in more than 200 cities around the nation. The chapters are exceedingly democratic and open to anyone, including men, who wants to do more than just talk about peace and justice, but take action.

LEARN MORE

www.codepinkalert.org

Stop the Next War Now by Medea Benjamin and Jodie Evans (Inner Ocean, 2005)

Mothers Say NO to War (2006)

Coxey's Army

U.S. Capitol Building, First Street and Pennsylvania Avenue, Washington, DC 20002

Though the Bill of Rights clearly states that citizens have the right to "peaceably assemble," it wasn't until 1894 that somebody actually thought of the idea of marching on Washington for a "redress of grievances." And when he did, it wasn't entirely clear that he would be allowed to do so.

Jacob Coxey believed that the federal government needed to aggressively address the economic crisis of the 1890s by launching a public works program. In 1891 he proposed a Good Roads Bill to put unemployed laborers to work. After months of unsuccessfully lobbying, Coxey joined forces with Carl Browne to announce a "petition in boots"—hundreds of out-of-work men and boys would march 700 miles from Massillon, Ohio, to the nation's capital to demand relief. Browne was a populist with a knack for showmanship; he usually sported a full-length leather coat and a sombrero. Browne encouraged Coxey to wrap the march in religious symbolism. Hence, the "Commonweal of Christ" marchers—better known as Coxey's Army—departed Massillon on March 25, 1894: Easter Sunday.

The press first mocked the marchers as tramps and urchins "not belonging to the bone and sinew of the country." As they got closer to Washington the newspapers started to echo the concerns of the political establishment: Coxey's Army was a mob bent on trouble. "The very purpose and the method of this organized movement are hostile to the spirit of our Government, and at war with the fundamental principle upon which free institutions rest," wrote the *New York Tribune*.

Grover Cleveland urged police to announce that they'd arrest the marchers for vagrancy if they ever reached town. Despite Cleveland's efforts, public opinion rested with the "mob." Police cited the 1882 Act to Regulate the Grounds of the Capitol when they announced that Coxey's Army would not be allowed to set foot on any federal property. Coxey replied, "I will test the constitutionality of the law," and said he'd give a speech from the steps of the Capitol. On May 1, more than 30,000 spectators turned out to watch the 900

Jacob Coxey, addressing his "army," 1914

Commonwealers arrive. They marched in via Georgia, New Hampshire, and Pennsylvania Avenues, and were met at the U.S. Capitol Building by hundreds of police. Coxey walked up five steps and was arrested; Browne was clubbed and taken away.

Rather than return to Ohio, the marchers established camps in Maryland and Virginia and awaited the fate of their leaders. Coxey and Browne were released on June 11. Coxey then left for Ohio to run for the House on the Populist ticket, while Browne tried to keep the Commonwealers together. Virginia and Maryland authorities harassed the marchers until they disbanded in late summer.

It wasn't entirely clear until later that Coxey had indeed established a precedent through his demonstration. However, when the Capitol police conceded (under public pressure) the Commonwealers' right to march through the district, a new form of protest was born.

Fifty years to the day later, Coxey returned to Washington and delivered his original speech . . . from the steps of the Capitol.

LEARN MORE

Coxey's Army by Carlos Schwantes (University of Nebraska, 1985)

Deaf President Now!

Gallaudet University, 800 Florida Avenue NE, Washington, DC 20002 · (202) 651-5050

Though it was founded in 1857, Gallaudet University (originally the Columbia Institution for the Instruction of the Deaf and Dumb and Blind) had never had a deaf president for its first 130 years. That all changed in 1988 in a movement known as Deaf President Now! (DPN). On March 6 the school's board of trustees announced its selection of a new president, Elisabeth Zinser. Though she had an impressive administrative resume, Zinser was not deaf, in contrast to several of the finalists under consideration.

The decision brought out long-festering resentment about the board's insensitivity to the school's deaf culture. Students revolted, with faculty support, and secured the campus; they blocked the campus entrances with school buses and let the air out of their tires, and sealed the gates with tangled bike locks. DPN then made four demands: a deaf president to replace Zinser, the resignation of the board chair, a majority deaf representation on the board, and promises of no reprisals for DPN participants. They brought their demands to Congress as well, and seized the national spotlight. One week into the protests, Dr. I. King Jordan was named to replace Zinser, and the board accepted the rest of DPN's demands.

DPN had a greater impact than just who had the corner office at Gallaudet. Later that year the U.S. Congress passed the Telecommunications Accessibility Enhancement Act, mandating TDD circuits on phones, followed in 1990 by the Television Decoder Circuitry Act, which established closed-caption circuits in all new TVs. Legislators credited both laws to DPN's education campaign. And also in 1990, Congress enacted the Americans with Disabilities Act, the most sweeping civil rights legislation since the 1960s.

LEARN MORE

www.gallaudet.edu

Deaf President Now! by John B. Christiansen and Sharon N. Barnartt
  (Gallaudet, 1995)

Frederick Douglass, Abolitionist Leader
Frederick Douglass House, Cedar Hill, 1411 W Street SE, Washington, DC 20020 ·
(202) 426-5961

"What, to the American slave, is your Fourth of July? . . . To him, your celebration is a sham; your boasted liberty, an unholy license; your national greatness, swelling vanity; your sounds of rejoicing are empty and heartless; your denunciation of tyrants, brass-fronted impudence; your shouts of liberty and equality, hollow mockery; your prayers and hymns, your sermons and thanksgivings, with all your religious parade, and solemnity, are, to him, mere bombast, fraud, deception, impiety, and hypocrisy—a thin veil to cover up crimes which would disgrace a nation of savages." Frederick Douglass was never one to mince words, and true to form, delivered this assessment during a speech at the 1852 Independence Day celebration in Rochester, New York.

Douglass knew firsthand what he was talking about. He was born into slavery on the Holme Hill farm near Tuckahoe, Maryland (Kingston Landing Road) on February 14, 1818. In 1826 he was sent to Baltimore to be the house servant to the family of Hugh Auld. Sophia Auld, Hugh's wife, broke the law by teaching Douglass to read. "I looked forward to a time at which it would be safe for me to escape," he later wrote. "I wished to learn to write, as I might have occasion to write my own pass."

When it came time, he would use the identification papers of a free black seaman. On September 3, 1838, he boarded a train to Delaware, and then a steamer to Philadelphia. He eventually ended up in Massachusetts, where he met William Lloyd Garrison (see page 28). The abolitionist firebrand convinced Douglass to lecture before the Massachusetts Anti-Slavery Society in 1841. He became a popular orator, and in 1845 published his autobiography. Supporters worried

Frederick Douglass, c. 1870

that because of his notoriety he could be kidnapped back into slavery, so he left for the British Isles. Europeans eventually purchased his freedom, and he returned in 1843.

Douglass moved to Rochester in 1847, and began publishing the *North Star* the same year. Its motto was "Right is of no Sex—Truth is of no Color—God is the Father of us all, and we are all brethren." He was a friend and ally of Susan B. Anthony, John Brown, and William Seward, and an advisor to Abraham Lincoln. When his Alexander Street home burned down under mysterious circumstances in 1872, he moved to Washington, D.C.

In 1877, he purchased Cedar Hill in the capital's Anacostia neighborhood. In addition to running the Freedman's Savings and Trust Company, Douglass advised presidents Hayes and Harrison and was appointed to several government posts. He served as U.S. marshal for the District, recorder of deeds, minister-resident and consul general to Haiti, and chargé d'affaires for the Dominican Republic.

Douglass died of a stroke at Cedar Hill on February 20, 1895. His funeral was held at the Metropolitan A.M.E. Church (1518 M Street NW) in Washington before his body was returned to Rochester's Mount Hope Cemetery (791 Mount Hope Avenue). Today, there is also a monument to him in Rochester's Highland Park (Central Avenue and St. Paul Street). It was dedicated in 1899 by then-governor Teddy Roosevelt. It was the first public monument to an African American in the United States.

> If there is no struggle there is no progress. Those who profess to favor freedom, and yet deprecate agitation, are men who want crops without plowing up the ground. They want rain without thunder and lightning.
> —*Frederick Douglass*

LEARN MORE

www.nps.gov/frdo

http://memory.loc.gov/ammem/doughtml/doughome.html

Frederick Douglass by William S. McFeely (Norton, 1991)

Narrative of the Life of Frederick Douglass, an American Slave Written by Himself by Frederick Douglass (Norton Critical Edition, 1997)

Frederick Douglass by Philip S. Foner, ed. (Lawrence Hill, 1999)

Jim and Sarah Brady's Campaign to Prevent Gun Violence
Washington Hilton, 19th Street Entrance, 1919 Connecticut Avenue NW,
Washington, DC 20009

The modern drive to establish sane gun policies in the United States began in 1974 with Dr. Mark Borinsky's founding of the National Council to Control Handguns (NCCH). But the movement did not gain wide popular support until John Hinkley opened fire outside the Washington Hilton on March 30, 1981. Hinkley squeezed off six shots, hitting Ronald Reagan, press secretary James Brady, Secret Service agent Timothy McCarthy, and D.C. policeman Thomas Delehanty. Brady was struck in the forehead, but survived. The shooting moved his wife Sarah to become the National Rifle Association's most relentless (and effective) adversary.

Sarah Brady joined Handgun Control, the new name for the NCCH, in 1985, and a year later persuaded Congress to ban armor-piercing "cop-killer" bullets, a move the NRA opposed. In 1988 the NRA also lost its insane fight to keep plastic handguns, which cannot be detected by airport x-ray machines, legal. And on November 30, 1993, Bill Clinton signed the Brady Bill into law. It required a five-day waiting period and owner background check on all handgun purchases. A year later Clinton signed the Assault Weapons Ban.

Though the background check was struck down by the U.S. Supreme Court, the waiting period remains, albeit with the "gun show loophole." Handgun Control was renamed the Brady Campaign to Prevent Gun Violence in 2001, and continues to battle the NRA through state and national legislation, keeping faith with the *full* text of the Second Amendment: "A *well regulated* Militia, being necessary to the security of a free State, the right of the people to keep and bear Arms, shall not be infringed." (The NRA typically ignores the opening clause.)

> The gun lobby finds waiting periods inconvenient. You have only to ask my husband how inconvenient he finds his wheelchair from time to time.
> —*Sarah Brady*

LEARN MORE
www.bradycampaign.org, (202) 898-0792
A Good Fight by Sarah Brady (PublicAffairs, 2002)
Bowling for Columbine (2002)

Leonard Matlovich, Gay Military Pioneer
Congressional Cemetery, 1801 E Street SE, Washington, DC 20003 · (202) 543-0539

Long before the "Don't Ask, Don't Tell" policy was dreamed up by a bunch of straight guys in the 1990s, a gay serviceman fought the Pentagon's anti-gay policy . . . and won.

Technical sergeant Leonard Matlovich volunteered for three tours in Vietnam. He earned the Bronze Star, and a Purple Heart when he stepped on a land mine in Da Nang. His U.S. Air Force career eventually led him to an assignment in Langley, Virginia, in 1975. And that same year, citing the *Brown v. Board of Education* decision as inspiration, he gave a letter to his commanding officers announcing that he was gay. After review by a military panel, Matlovich was discharged as "unfit for duty," though his service record was spotless.

Matlovich sued the air force for reinstatement, and the Pentagon eventually offered him his commission back, as long as he promised to never "practice homosexuality" again. He declined, and the suit continued. In 1978 a federal court ordered him reinstated with back pay, but the government appealed. Two years later, in an out-of-court settlement, the air force upgraded his dismissal to an "honorable discharge" and gave him $160,000 in back pay.

In 1986 Matlovich learned he had contracted HIV, and would become one of the first patients to volunteer for AZT trials. He died from AIDS complications on June 22, 1988, and was buried in Washington, D.C. His tombstone, with its blunt epitaph, has become a rallying location for many who oppose the Pentagon's continued devotion to its outdated, homophobic policy.

> **Never Again, Never Forget**
> —*A Gay Vietnam Veteran*
>
> *When I was in the military they gave me a medal for killing two men and a discharge for loving one.*
>
> —*Epitaph on Leonard Matlovich's tombstone*

LEARN MORE
Matlovich by Mike Hippler (Alyson, 1989)
Conduct Unbecoming by Randy Shilts (St. Martin's, 1993)

The March on Washington for Jobs and Freedom

Lincoln Memorial, West Potomac Park, Constitution Avenue and 23rd Street, Washington, DC 20037 · (202) 426-6841

Most commonly associated with Martin Luther King Jr.'s "I Have a Dream" speech, the March on Washington for Jobs and Freedom did not originate with King, but with labor leader A. Philip Randolph and civil rights activist Bayard Rustin. Back in 1941, Randolph announced a 100,000-person march that would descend on the nation's capital on July 1. His goal was to force the federal government to end segregation in the armed forces and the defense contracting industry. When it became clear that Randolph meant business, FDR issued Executive Order 8802 on June 25, which established the Fair Employment Practices Committee and outlawed racial discrimination by defense contractors. Having achieved most of his objectives, Randolph called off the march.

The March on Washington, 1963

MARCHING ON THE LINCOLN MEMORIAL

From the very day it opened to the public, the Lincoln Memorial (www.nps.gov/linc) has been the backdrop to many marches and demonstrations. Here are just a few.

- **The Dedication (May 31, 1922):** As shocking as it sounds, the Lincoln Memorial's dedication ceremony was a *segregated* event. African Americans were invited, but they had to sit in a section across the road from where the white attendees sat. Twenty-one invitees walked out in protest.

- **Marian Anderson's Easter Concert (April 9, 1939):** Opera contralto Marian Anderson had been invited to perform for an Easter Sunday concert in Washington, but when promoters applied for the performance to be held at Constitution Hall (1776 D Street NW), the request was denied. The hall was controlled by the Daughters of the American Revolution, which cited "local custom" for its refusal; Anderson was African American, and Constitution Hall was a segregated venue. Outraged, Eleanor Roosevelt resigned her DAR membership in her syndicated newspaper column, then persuaded Interior Secretary Harold Ickes to open the Lincoln Memorial for the event. Ickes welcomed Anderson and 75,000 onlookers with a speech observing, "When God gave us this wonderful outdoors and the sun, the moon, and the stars, he made no distinction of race, creed, or color." Anderson began her performance by singing "America."

(continued)

But in 1963, as the modern civil rights movement approached its second decade, there was still plenty to be done. Bayard Rustin was planning a two-day effort in Washington that would include citizen lobbying, sit-ins, and a rally at the Lincoln Memorial. Randolph and Rustin joined forces, and invited other organizations to participate. Randolph, King of the SCLC, Whitney Young of the National Urban League, Roy Wilkins of the NAACP, James Farmer of CORE, and John Lewis of SNCC formed the "Big Six" who first endorsed the march. Rustin, who organized it all, was purposely downplayed because he was gay and had once been a member of the Communist Party.

- **Harry Truman Addresses the NAACP (June 29, 1947):** Harry Truman was the first president to address the NAACP, and he did so from the steps of the Lincoln Memorial on the last day of the group's 1947 conference. During his speech he proclaimed, "[W]e can no longer afford the luxury of a leisurely attack upon prejudice and discrimination. . . . [W]e cannot, any longer, await a growth of a will to action in the slowest state or the most backward community. Our national government must show the way." As he descended the podium Truman turned to NAACP Executive Secretary Walter White and promised, "I meant every word of it—and I'm going to prove that I do mean it." On July 26, 1948, Truman signed Executive Order 9981, desegregating the U.S. military, which many claim opened the governmental floodgates of the modern civil rights era.

- **The Poor People's Encampment (May 12, 1968):** Organized by Martin Luther King Jr. and others, the Poor People's Encampment was designed to focus attention on endemic poverty in America. Contingents of all races were to descend on the capital from across the nation, the first group starting from Marks, Mississippi. Once in D.C. they would set up a Resurrection City on the Mall, and not leave until Congress drafted a Poor People's Bill of Rights. But before they arrived, King was assassinated in Memphis (see page 220). The campaign went forward, arriving in Washington on May 12. The 7,000 protesters lobbied for more than a month, but on June 24 helmeted police moved in with tear gas and clubs and drove them off the Mall. Jesse Jackson Jr., standing on a flatbed truck at the corner of 14th and U Streets, addressed the retreating crowd, and was later credited with quelling a potential riot.

(The Big Six were later joined by Walter Reuther of the United Auto Workers, Rabbi Joachim Prinz of the American Jewish Congress, Rev. Eugene Blake of the National Council of Churches, and Mathew Ahmann of the National Catholic Conference, to form the Big Ten.)

Though a CORE contingent walked 230 miles from Brooklyn, most of the 250,000 marchers were bussed in and walked from the Washington Monument to the Lincoln Memorial. The August 28 event was broadcast on national TV, the first time an event like it received live coverage. King's speech came near the end of the rally, and most of it was not from his prepared text. Rustin closed the day by delivering the march's 10 Demands, followed by a pledge led by Randolph, which was repeated by the crowd: "I will march and I will write letters. . . . I will demonstrate and I will vote."

The National Park Service is currently building a memorial to King along the Tidal Basin, midway between the Lincoln and Jefferson Memorials.

LEARN MORE

Like a Mighty Stream by Patrik Henry Bass (Running Press, 2002)
The Dream by Drew D. Hansen (Ecco, 2003)

Stephen Colbert Bombs
Washington Hilton, 1919 Connecticut Avenue NW, Washington, DC 20009

The verdict from inside the beltway was almost unanimous: comedian Stephen Colbert bombed at the 2006 White House Correspondents' Association Dinner. Any objective viewer would have to agree. He bombed the presi-

Stephen Colbert, bombed Bush in background, 2006

dent. He bombed the press. He bombed the Joint Chiefs of Staff. He bombed the entire Washington establishment that had been propping up George W. Bush's failed presidency for five years.

If you ever needed evidence of how far in bed the press corps is with the White House it covers—covers *for*, actually—the media silence the next day was all you needed to (not) hear. If reporters or anchors mentioned the dinner at all, it was to gush about Bush's routine earlier in the evening—an act inspired by the Doublemint twins. Stephen Colbert? Stephen . . . Stephen *who?*

But Colbert's performance, with a Helen Thomas assist, vaulted over the arbiters of Washington taste (the same folks who find Mark Russell and the Capitol Steps hilarious) via the blogosphere and YouTube. Viewers outside the beltway cheered Colbert's brass-balls attack on Bush and his enablers. When they challenged the silent pundits the press dismissed Colbert as either unfunny or "not the right fit for the audience."

And what audience was that? Just two years earlier George Bush gave a slide presentation at the same annual dinner. He showed photos of himself looking behind the curtains and under the furniture in the Oval Office. "Those weapons of mass destruction gotta be around here somewhere," he chuckled. And the correspondents roared with laughter. They *roared.*

That's your "liberal media," all right.

> I stand by [George W. Bush] because he stands *for* things, and not only for things, he stands *on* things, things like aircraft carriers, and rubble, and recently flooded city squares. And that sends a strong message: that no matter what happens to America she will always rebound with the most powerfully staged photo ops in the world!
>
> —*Stephen Colbert, at the White House Correspondents' Association Dinner, 2006*

LEARN MORE

www.colbertnation.com

I Am America (and so Can You!) by Stephen Colbert (Grand Central, 2007)

Watchdogs of Democracy? by Helen Thomas (Scribner, 2006)

The Trail of Broken Treaties and the Native American Embassy
Bureau of Indian Affairs Building, 1951 Constitution Avenue NW, Washington, DC 20006

The idea came from Robert Burnette, a former tribal chairman on the Rosebud Reservation in South Dakota: a Native American march on Washington, D.C., to coincide with the 1972 presidential election. The Trail of Broken Treaties, as it became known, was to start from three different locations, Los Angeles, San Francisco, and Seattle, with caravans to converge on the nation's capital on November 1. Along the way the protesters would educate communities about the unfulfilled promises made to American Indians over the years. And when they arrived, they'd present the White House with their demands: the Twenty Points.

Unfortunately, the Trail organizers made a major tactical mistake: few politicians would even be in D.C. in the days leading up to the election—they were back in their districts campaigning. The caravans arrived the Wednesday before the election to a half-empty city. Then, during an unplanned visit to the Bureau of Indian Affairs (BIA) office to secure additional lodging for the group, police from the General Services Administration arrived in full riot gear. A fight broke out, and the protesters ended up barricading themselves inside the BIA building.

Within hours, a banner reading "Native American Embassy" was unfurled from the roof, and the standoff was on. Realizing they were sitting atop the repository of the U.S. government's treaty and land records, the group began digging through the BIA's files. On Monday, November 6, a judge ordered the protesters to vacate by 6:00 P.M. The ruling had the opposite effect of what was intended; the protesters trashed the offices that had been responsible for so much hardship on their home communities over the years, through

> When history recalls our efforts here, our descendants will stand with pride knowing their people were the ones responsible for the stand taken against tyranny, injustice, and the gross inefficiency of this branch of a corrupt and decadent government.
> —Sign left in the Native American Embassy, 1972

inaction, insensitivity, and corruption. If the message wasn't clear, somebody spray painted a quote from Red Cloud on a hallway wall: "They made us many promises, more than I can remember, but they never kept but one; they promised to take our land, and they took it." The last of the protesters left on November 8.

LEARN MORE

www.doi.gov/bureau-indian-affairs.html

Behind the Trail of Broken Treaties by Vine Deloria Jr. (University of Texas, 1985)

MARYLAND

If anyone in the modern era picked up the torch of social criticism once carried by Mark Twain and Robert Ingersoll, it was H. L. Mencken, the "Sage of Baltimore." He was a passionate defender of free speech who lambasted fundamentalists of all stripes through biting satire.

Henry Louis Mencken was born in Baltimore (380 W. Lexington Street, torn down) on September 12, 1880. When he was three his family moved to a new home (1524 Hollins Street) where Mencken would live for the rest of his life, with the exception of a five-year marriage to Sara Haardt. (She died of tuberculosis in 1935.) In 1899 the *Baltimore Morning Herald* hired Mencken as a reporter, and seven years later he moved to the *Baltimore Sun*, where he first wrote his popular editorials. In 1924 he teamed up with George Nathan and Alfred Knopf to publish *The American Mercury*, a literary magazine that would give first voice to many well-known writers.

Mencken was an outspoken critic of the rabid patriotism of World War I, and the Wilson administration's assault on civil liberties under the Espionage and Sedition Acts. He denounced the KKK, the common American "booboisie," and virtually all religious doctrine, particularly at the Scopes Monkey Trial (see page 216). His satire was often caustic, and his criticism at times ventured into elitist bigotry. He died on January 29, 1956. In 1989, per instructions in his will, his personal diary was released. It revealed several shocking racist and anti-Semitic passages. At heart, he was a libertarian, and didn't believe in sugar-coating anything, not even his often contradictory legacy.

Mencken House is open for tours, by appointment. The largest Mencken archive can be found at the Enoch Pratt Free Library (400 Cathedral Street) in Baltimore, which has rotating exhibits in its Mencken Room.

LEARN MORE
www.mencken.org
www.menckenhouse.org
Mencken by Marion Elizabeth Rodgers (Oxford, 2005)
The Skeptic by Terry Teachout (HarperCollins, 2002)

CRUSTY OBSERVATIONS FROM H. L. MENCKEN

- It doesn't take a majority to make a rebellion; it takes only a few determined leaders and a sound cause.

- In this world of sin and sorrow there is always something to be thankful for; as for me, I rejoice that I am not a Republican.

- Democracy is the art and science of running the circus from the monkey cage.

- The whole aim of practical politics is to keep the populace alarmed by menacing it with an endless series of hobgoblins, all of them imaginary.

- It is even harder for the average ape to believe that he has descended from man.

- The trouble with Communism is the Communists, just as the trouble with Christianity is the Christians.

- A Sunday school is a prison in which children do penance for the evil conscience of their parents.

- Most people want security in this world, not liberty.

LEARN MORE
The Days of H. L. Mencken by H. L. Mencken (Dorset, 1943)

Cambridge

Harriet Tubman, "Moses of Her People"
Harriet Tubman Museum, 424 Race Street, Cambridge, MD 21613

Harriet Tubman was born into slavery near Bucktown, Maryland, in 1821, and was given the name Araminta, or "Minty." At the age of 17 she threw herself between an overseer and the slave he was trying to kill, and was hit in the head by a large lead weight. The brain damage caused her to suffer from seizures and narcolepsy for the remainder of her life. But after the injury Tubman claimed to have visions and hear voices, one of which said, "Arise, flee for your life." She did, in September 1849, leaving her husband and children behind at the Brodess Plantation.

"I looked at my hands to see if I was the same person," she later wrote, about crossing the border into Pennsylvania. "There was such glory over everything. The sun came up like gold through the trees and I felt I was in heaven." Though she ended up in Philadelphia, Tubman vowed to return to the South.

And she did. During 19 trips back, Harriet Tubman rescued more than 300 slaves, many of whom were family members, including her parents, children, sister, brothers, and their children. Her husband John Tubman, a free black, had remarried after she fled; he chose *not* to leave his new family. Slaveowners placed a $40,000 bounty on Tubman's head, but she eluded capture for 15 years and never lost a passenger. Even more amazing, Tubman served as a scout for the Union forces during the Civil War, and led a raiding party into South Carolina.

Though she spent a lot of time in the United States, Tubman officially lived in St. Catherines, Ontario, until after the war. William Seward

Harriet Tubman, c. 1866

> I would have been able to free a thousand more slaves if I could only have convinced them that they were slaves.
>
> —*Harriet Tubman*

(see page 88) convinced her to return to the States to a home on his street in Auburn, New York (180–182 South Street), where she lived with her parents. Tubman died there on March 10, 1913, and was buried with full military honors in Fort Hill Cemetery (19 Fort Street) beneath a headstone that reads "Servant of God, Well Done." Her will stated that her home was to be used as a home for poor and elderly African Americans, to be run by the A.M.E. Zion Church.

LEARN MORE

www.harriettubman.com

Harriet Tubman by Catherine Clinton (Back Bay, 2004)

Bound for the Promised Land by Kate Clifford Larson (Ballantine, 2003)

Catonsville

The Catonsville Nine

Knights of Columbus Hall (Draft Board 33 site), 1010 Frederick Road, Catonsville, MD 21228

As the Vietnam War began to ratchet up in the late 1960s, radical priests (and brothers) Daniel and Philip Berrigan felt more desperate measures were called for if the killing was to be stopped. On October 26, 1967, they and three others entered the U.S. Customs House in Baltimore (40 S. Gay Street) and poured blood into the file cabinets that contained draft records for the Selective Service. To ensure that their message was clear, they waited for police to arrive, and were arrested.

The trial was swift, and the defendants were found guilty; they never denied the charges. In fact, they vowed to do it again. Sure enough, while awaiting sentencing, the Berrigans and seven others broke into Catonsville's Local Draft Board 33 on May 17, 1968, and seized two wire baskets filled with documents.

> We have been accused of arrogance, but what of the fantastic arrogance of our leaders? What of their crimes against the people, the poor, and the powerless?
>
> —*Philip Berrigan, at trial*

> Our apologies, good friends, for the fracture of good order, the burning of paper instead of children.
>
> —*Daniel Berrigan, at trial*

Outside, in the parking lot, they torched 378 draft files using homemade napalm. And where did they get the recipe? From a U.S. Army manual.

The "Catonsville Nine" appealed to the judge and jury's consciences to render verdicts based upon their own feelings about the war, and not just on the group's actions. How should citizens respond to an unjust and immoral war? Is the destruction of property to prevent the killing of innocents justified?

Though the Nine made their case, the jury had been stacked with government bureaucrats and skeptical veterans. All of the defendants were found guilty and received sentences ranging from two to three and a half years behind bars. An appeals court upheld their convictions and the group was ordered to prison. Daniel Berrigan, who was facing three years in prison, jumped bail and went underground. The FBI placed him on its Ten Most Wanted List, and he was eventually apprehended. He was not released until 1972.

LEARN MORE
http://c9.mdch.org
Uncommon Martyrs by Fred A. Wilcox (Addison-Wesley, 1991)
The Trial of the Catonsville Nine by Daniel Berrigan (Bantam, 1970)

Glen Echo

Clara Barton and the American Red Cross
Clara Barton National Historic Site, 5801 Oxford Road, Glen Echo, MD 20812 ·
(301) 320-1410

In 1833, David Barton fell from the rafters of his parents' unfinished barn in North Oxford, Massachusetts (68 Clara Barton Road), and severely injured himself. It took him two years to recover, and all the while he was cared for by his sister Clara. She was only 11 years old when he fell, but by 13 she had learned to be a nurse.

Barton's life path changed, however, when she became a schoolteacher at the age of 16. She taught in North Oxford until she moved away in 1840 to take a teaching assignment in Bordentown, New Jersey. Barton's six-student school (142 Crosswicks Street) grew until there were 600 pupils. After she convinced the locals to build a new facility, they hired a male principal to take over, and Barton resigned in protest.

When the Civil War broke out, Barton organized a group to bring medical supplies to the wounded, and bring soldiers back from the front lines. She initially met resistance, but by 1864 she was in charge of the Army of the James hospital. Near the end of the war, Abraham Lincoln gave Barton the responsibility of finding 30,000 missing Union soldiers, most of whom were buried in unmarked graves. Through newspaper articles, personal letters, and visits to places such as the Andersonville Prison, she was able to bring closure to many families.

The work left her exhausted, and in 1869 a group of U.S. doctors sent Barton to Europe to recuperate. Of course, she was not the type to relax, and volunteered with the International Committee of the

Clara Barton, c. 1904

Red Cross during the 1870 Franco-Prussian War. She returned to the States in 1873 and began lobbying to establish the American Red Cross (ARC). Originally dismissed—"We'll never have another Civil War"—she was able to convince leaders that the ARC could be used for disaster relief as well. The ARC was founded on May 21, 1881, with Barton as its president. The first local ARC chapter was established at St. Paul's Lutheran Church (21 Clara Barton Street) in Dansville, New York, on August 22, 1881. It is today called the Clara Barton Chapter No. 1.

The ARC's unique disaster relief mission was first tested during the 1884 Ohio River Flood. Barton went to Evansville, Indiana, to set up a base of operations (at Iowa and Mary Streets, site of a memorial today). She and her volunteers traveled up and down the river on the steamer *Josh V. Throop*, bringing help to victims. What Barton learned was put to use in later disasters, including the 1889 Johnstown Flood.

For many of its early years, the Red Cross was headquartered in Barton's Glen Echo home. It was built in 1897 using the same floor plan as the Johnstown hotel/hospital where she organized flood relief, and even included wood salvaged from that building. She died there April 12, 1912. Her home is now a museum, as is her Massachusetts birthplace.

LEARN MORE
www.nps.gov/clba
www.clarabartonbirthplace.org, (508) 987-5375
www.redcross.org, (800) RED-CROSS
Clara Barton by Elizabeth Brown Pryor (University of Pennsylvania, 1987)
Champions of Charity by John F. Hutchinson (Westview, 1996)

Hagerstown

Mary Titcomb and the Birth of the Bookmobile

Hagerstown Library, 100 S. Potomac Street, Hagerstown, MD 21740 · (301) 739-3250

The world's first bookmobile was actually a Hagerstown book wagon set up by librarian Mary Titcomb in 1904. Titcomb had founded the Washington County Free Library in 1901, the second free public library in the United States. Three years later she put boxes of books on a horse-drawn wagon driven by Joshua Thomas and sent them out into the community. Titcomb established 66 deposit stations around the county, and each received 30 new volumes on a rotating basis.

All went well until August 1910 when the wagon met a freight train at a crossing in St. James, and lost. Two years later the library purchased a motorized vehicle, and the modern bookmobile was born.

> No better method has ever been devised for reaching the dweller in the country. The book goes to the man, not waiting for the man to come to the book.
> —*Mary Titcomb, in* The Story of the Washington County Free Library

LEARN MORE
www.whilbr.org/bookmobile/index.aspx

NEW JERSEY

James Dale loved the Boy Scouts. He joined as a Cub Scout when he was eight years old, and eventually earned his Eagle Scout badge. In college he volunteered as an assistant scoutmaster, but in 1990 was expelled. Why? Not for any impropriety; the Boy Scouts discovered that Dale was also the head of the Lesbian/Gay Alliance at Rutgers. The organization tried to justify its decision by claiming Dale had violated the organization's Scout Oath and Law to be "morally straight" and "clean." He disagreed, and took the Scouts to court.

In 1999 the New Jersey Supreme Court unanimously ruled that the Boy Scouts of New Jersey had discriminated against Dale, but it was overruled by the U.S. Supreme Court a year later. In a 5–4 decision the high court claimed that as an "expressive association"—one that promotes a certain viewpoint—the Boy Scouts could skirt the antidiscrimination laws of the state. The conservative justices who sided with the Boy Scouts made no effort to determine whether Dale had violated the Scout Oath, which made no mention of homosexuality. Indeed, he had not. Just being gay was reason enough to be labeled "morally crooked" and "unclean."

The decision was criticized by congressional scholars from both left and right. It essentially opened a Pandora's box whereby any organization could refuse to comply with antidiscrimination statutes simply by citing its bylaws. For example, could

> The only apparent explanation, then for the majority's holding . . . is that homosexuals are simply so different from the rest of society that their presence alone—unlike other individual's—should be singled out for special 1st Amendment treatment.
>
> —Justice John Paul Stevens, in his dissent on Boy Scouts of America v. Dale, 2000

the American Legion, whose constitution states that its goal is "to foster and perpetuate a 100 percent Americanism," assert that a particular group, such as gays or women or Muslims, was antithetical to this goal, however preposterous the assertion might be? The court's ruling suggested so.

The U.S. Supreme Court will hopefully overturn its flawed decision someday, but in the meantime, the Boy Scouts' policy remains officially *pro*-discrimination.

Atlantic City

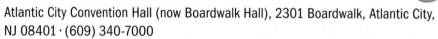

Miss America Meets the Women's Liberation Front
Atlantic City Convention Hall (now Boardwalk Hall), 2301 Boardwalk, Atlantic City, NJ 08401 · (609) 340-7000

There were two Miss Americas crowned in 1968: Debra Barnes (Miss Kansas), and a bleating sheep. Robin Morgan of the New York Radical Women reasoned that if Barnes was going to be paraded around like livestock at a county fair, why not go all the way? So on September 7, 1968, in a protest outside the Atlantic City Convention Hall, Morgan and the newly formed Women's Liberation Front brought a real barnyard animal for the pageant's judges.

And that's not all. About 200 women picketed on the Boardwalk, then threw "instruments of torture to women"—bras, high-heeled shoes, makeup, curlers, and *Playboy*—into a Freedom Trash Can. (This is believed to be the origin of the "bra-burning" myth, even though the items were never torched.) Later, during the live television broadcast, several women were able to disrupt the show by unfurling a banner and shouting at participants.

Of course, sexism has been only part of the problem with the pageant; racism has long been a problem at Miss America as well. Not until 1984 did an African American, Vanessa Williams, win the crown, and she soon resigned after nude photographs surfaced. Apparently objectifying yourself for a scholarship was acceptable, but objectify-

> The Pageant contestants epitomize the roles we are all forced to play as women. The parade down the runway blares the metaphor of the 4-H Club county fair, where the nervous animals are judged for teeth, fleece, etc., and where the best "specimen" gets the blue ribbon.
> —Robin Morgan, in "No More Miss America!"

ing yourself to pay the rent was not. As it turns out, Williams didn't need the pageant; she bounced back with musical and dramatic careers, has been nominated for a Grammy 15 times, won an NAACP Image Award in 1987, and now stars on *Ugly Betty*.

LEARN MORE
"There She Is, Miss America" by Elwood Watson and Darcy Martin, eds. (Palgrave, 2004)

Morristown

Dorothy Eustis, Morris Frank, and the Seeing Eye
Washington Valley Road, Morristown, NJ 07693 · (973) 539-4425

The idea of using dogs to assist the blind grew out of a tragic necessity; thousands of soldiers had been blinded on the battlefields of World War I, and needed help. Throughout their domesticated history, dogs had been used to assist the handicapped, but nobody had ever formalized a method for doing so. A school was established in Potsdam, Germany, to train German shepherds, which caught the attention of Dorothy Eustis, an American living in Switzerland. Eustis wrote an article about the program for a 1927 edition of the *Saturday Evening Post*. Morris Frank, a blind man in Nashville, Tennessee, heard about the article and wrote to Eustis, asking her if she would train a dog for him. In return, he would use his experience to establish a school for dog guides in the United States. Eustis agreed, and Frank went to Europe, where he was paired up with Buddy, his first dog guide.

With a $10,000 gift from Eustis, Frank returned to Nashville and in 1929 started the Seeing Eye, the first dog guide school in the United States. Before the end of the year, 17 students had completed the course. Two years later the Seeing Eye relocated to Whippany, New Jersey, and in 1965 moved to its current home in Morristown. More than 10,000 dogs have been trained by the school since its inception.

The Seeing Eye has never raised its fees in 70+ years; students pay

> The mission of the Seeing Eye is to enhance the independence, dignity, and self-confidence of blind people through the use of Seeing Eye dogs.
>
> —*The Seeing Eye's mission statement*

$150 for the four-week course, and leave with a fully trained companion. See-ing Eye dogs work from 7 to 10 years before they need to retire, and if they are not taken in as pets by their owners, the Seeing Eye finds them adoptive homes. If you live in the tri-state area, the organization is always looking for volunteers to raise and socialize puppies, and to adopt retired dogs.

LEARN MORE
www.seeingeye.org
The Seeing Eye by Steve Swanbek (Arcadia, 2002)

Perth Amboy

Thomas Peterson and the Fifteenth Amendment
St. Peter's Church Cemetery, 183 Rector Street, Perth Amboy, NJ 08861

In the wake of the Civil War, the United States added three new amendments to the U.S. Constitution, the last of which, the Fifteenth Amendment, granted voting rights to African Americans. (Though the amendment didn't exclude women specifically, women were not allowed to vote at the time.) It would take years to overcome obstacles designed to block black enfranchisement—poll taxes, literacy tests, and outright intimidation—but as far as the Constitution was concerned, African American men could officially vote starting March 30, 1870, the date the amendment was ratified.

One day later, on March 31, Thomas Peterson voted in a local election to revise the Perth Amboy city charter, becoming the first African American to exercise his franchise. Peterson was a school custodian and would go on to become active in local politics. Perth Amboy awarded him a gold medal in 1884 to honor his service to the community. He died on February 4, 1904, and was buried in the St. Peter's Church Cemetery.

> The right of citizens of the United States to vote shall not be denied or abridged by the United States or by any State on account of race, color, or previous condition of servitude.
> —*Fifteenth Amendment,*
> *U.S. Constitution*

NEW YORK

Of all the progressive movements that started in New York, and there are a lot, few are as underappreciated today as the Chautauqua Institution. It was founded in 1874 by Methodist Bishop John Heyl Vincent and businessman Lewis Miller as a training camp for Sunday school teachers. The pair quickly realized its potential as a much broader educational institution, and were soon offering adult coursework on topics as varied as Greek philosophy, evolution, and Mozart.

In 1878, Vincent launched the Chautauqua Literary and Scientific Circle, America's first book club/correspondence course. Then, in 1887, the institution was granted a university charter, the first time a college of part-time students was given degree-granting authority. Because women had fewer opportunities to attend traditional colleges, the Chautauqua Institution was more popular with women than men. Each August, students who had completed their coursework were invited to collect their diplomas at the Recognition Day ceremony in the Hall of Philosophy, a tradition that continues to this day.

The Chautauqua Institution also inspired a much larger, unaffiliated movement that spread west in the early 1990s. Roving "tent Chautauquas" would move from one small town to another, offering lectures on many topics over the course of their stays. They were also instrumental in developing public support for many progressive ideas, including school lunch programs, physical fitness, juvenile courts, food safety laws, and the graduated income tax.

The tent Chautauquas were eventually eclipsed by more powerful media—radio and movies—in the 1920s. However, the original Chautauqua Institution soldiers on, a living reminder that there really were good old parts of the Good Ol' Days.

LEARN MORE
www.ciweb.org, (800) 836-ARTS
The Chautauqua Moment by Andrew Chamberlin Rieser (Columbia, 2003)
The Romance of Small-Town Chautauquas by James R. Schultz (University of Missouri, 2002)

Auburn

William and Frances Seward, Abolitionist Heroes

Seward House, 33 South Street, Auburn, NY 13021 · (315) 252-1283

Though William Henry Seward is best known today as the man who negotiated the purchase of Alaska from Russia—"Seward's Folly"—in his day he was better known as an ardent abolitionist. As governor of New York, and later senator, he denounced slavery, an institution he had witnessed as a young man while teaching in Georgia. He bailed out fellow abolitionists from jail over the years, and in 1850 he was instrumental in seeing that California was admitted to the Union as a free state.

Before the Civil War, Seward and his wife, Frances, harbored runaways in a secret room above their woodshed in Auburn. Because William was often in Washington, Frances organized most of the Underground Railroad work herself. William Seward served as Lincoln's secretary of state, having lost to him for the Republican Party's presidential nomination. Seward was gravely wounded by Booth conspirator Lewis Powell on the same night the president was assassinated.

After recovering from his stab wounds, Seward lived out his last years in Auburn. He convinced Harriet Tubman (see page 78) to return to the United States from Canada, sold her a home in Auburn, and convinced the federal government to award her a pension for her work as a Union scout during the war. He died on October 10, 1872, and was buried in Auburn's Fort Hill Cemetery (19 Fort Street) beside Frances, who had died seven years earlier.

LEARN MORE
www.sewardhouse.org
William Henry Seward by John M. Taylor (HarperCollins, 1991)

Canandaigua

Susan B. Anthony Votes
Trial Site, Ontario County Courthouse, 27 N. Main Street, Canandaigua, NY 14424

On November 5, 1872, armed with the newly ratified Fourteenth Amendment and a legal brief written by Judge Henry Selden, Susan B. Anthony and 14 other women marched into a Rochester polling location and voted. The registrars made no attempt to stop them, as Selden's interpretation of Section I of the Fourteenth Amendment made sense; the women were indeed citizens under the amendment, and don't citizens have the right to vote? The amendment begins:

> All persons born or naturalized in the United States and subject to the jurisdiction thereof, are citizens of the United States and of the State wherein they reside. No State shall make or enforce any law which shall abridge the privileges or immunities of citizens of the United States; nor shall any State deprive any person of life, liberty, or property, without due process of law; nor deny any person within its jurisdiction the equal protection of the laws.

On November 28 a U.S. marshal showed up at Anthony's Rochester home (17 Madison Street) and arrested her. (The other women and the registrars were arrested as well.) Anthony was taken by streetcar to the courthouse, but when asked for her fare she told the conductor, "I'm traveling at the expense of the government. This gentleman is escorting me to jail. Ask him for my fare." Anthony was the only person charged who did not post bail, though her lawyer did, claiming, "[I] could not see a lady I respect put in jail."

The trial took place on June 17, 1873, in Canandaigua. The venue had to be moved because Anthony, in the months leading up the trial, had taken her case directly to the citizens of Monroe County through a series of speeches. Learning of the change of venue, she toured Canandaigua's Ontario County as well. She explained herself in one lecture: "We no longer petition legislature or Congress to give us the right to vote, but appeal to women everywhere to exercise their too long neglected 'citizen's right.' . . . [W]e throw to the wind the old dogma that governments can give rights."

Anthony was refused the right to testify at trial, and Judge Ward Hunt *ordered* the jury to find her guilty, and to do so without even voting. They complied. Anthony was fined $100, and upon learning the verdict told the judge she would never pay it. And neither has anyone else; it is still uncollected.

Anthony lived in Rochester until her death on March 13, 1906. Her last public words were "Failure is impossible," which she delivered on

> May it please your honor, I will never pay a dollar of your unjust penalty . . . "Resistance to tyranny is obedience to God."
>
> —*Susan B. Anthony, on receiving her sentence, 1873*

her 86th birthday. Women would not get the vote for another 14 years. A bust of Anthony can be found in the Ontario County Courthouse today.

LEARN MORE

www.susanbanthonyhouse.org, (585) 235-6124

Failure Is Impossible by Lynn Sherr (Crown, 1995)

Susan B. Anthony by Kathleen Barry (Authorhouse, 2000)

Dresden

Robert Ingersoll, the Great Agnostic

Ingersoll Birthplace and Museum, 61 Main Street, Dresden, NY 14441 · (315) 536-1074

Would you find it hard to believe that the most popular public speaker of the late 19th century was a relentless and blistering critic of the religious right, as well as an advocate for African Americans' civil rights and suffrage for women? Or that this person was heard by more Americans than any other before the era of radio, television, and movies? Who was this popular radical? Robert Green Ingersoll, the Great Agnostic.

Ingersoll was born the son of a Presbyterian minister in Dresden on August 11, 1833. He struck out on his own in his late teens, and landed in Mount Vernon, Illinois, where he studied for the bar. Once passed, he set up a law practice in Peoria with his brother Ebon. Ingersoll ran for Congress in 1860, but lost because he denounced the Fugitive Slave Act. At the outbreak of the Civil War he organized the 11th Illinois Cavalry Regiment, served as a colonel, and fought at the battle of Shiloh.

After the war Ingersoll was appointed the first attorney general of Illinois, the only public office he ever held, primarily because of his outspokenness.

After leaving office he accepted unpopular clients, gave lectures explaining his agnosticism, and worked to educate the public about Darwin's theory of evolution. A brilliant orator, people crammed theaters to hear him speak, gladly paying a dollar each (a large sum at the time) to have their beliefs challenged and their worldviews expanded. Not surprisingly, Ingersoll was denounced by clergy wherever he spoke.

During the last 10 years of his life Ingersoll lived in New York City (52 Gramercy Park). He died on July 21, 1899, while visiting family in Dobbs Ferry, New York, and was buried in Arlington National Cemetery. His final home was torn down to make way for the Gramercy Park Hotel (2 Lexington Avenue), which honors him with a plaque at its entrance. His birthplace, the only extant home from his long life, is now a museum run by the Council for Secular Humanism.

LEARN MORE

www.secularhumanism.org

What's God Got to Do with It? by Tim Page, ed. (Steerforth, 2005)

Freethinkers by Susan Jacoby (Metropolitan, 2004)

PROGRESSIVE THOUGHTS OF ROBERT INGERSOLL

· Intellectual liberty is the air of the soul, the sunshine of the mind, and without it, the world is a prison; the universe is a dungeon.

· There is something wrong in a government where they who do the most have the least. There is something wrong when honesty wears a rag, and rascality a robe; when the loving, the tender, eat the crust, while the infamous sit at banquets.

· The man who invented the telescope found out more about heaven than the closed eyes of prayer ever discovered.

· Capital punishment degrades and hardens a community and it is the work of savagery.

· Let us do away forever with the idea that to care for the sick, for the helpless, is charity. It is a duty. . . . It is no more a charity than it is to pave or light the streets.

Hyde Park

Franklin and Eleanor Roosevelt

Franklin Delano Roosevelt National Historic Site (Springwood), 4079 Albany Post Road, Hyde Park, NY 12538 · (800) 337-8474

Eleanor Roosevelt National Historic Site (Val-Kill), 519 Albany–Post Road, Hyde Park, NY 12538 · (800) 337-8474

If America were to give an award for the greatest progressive couple in history, the Roosevelts would win it going away. They ushered the nation through two of its greatest crises, the Great Depression and World War II, and set the standard for honest, responsive public service on behalf of all Americans, not just their wealthy friends (and they had plenty of those).

Franklin Roosevelt was born in Hyde Park, New York, on January 30, 1882. He worked his way up through the political ranks, first as state senator, then as assistant secretary of the navy, and finally as governor of New York. Three years into the Great Depression, he was elected president. Immediately after taking office, he instituted a "banking holiday" to prevent further collapse of the financial industry. He then called Congress into special session; four days later it passed the Emergency Banking Act. To keep depositors calm, he went to the radio for weekly Fireside Chats, reminding Americans that "The only thing we have to fear is fear itself." (Contrast that to "The only thing we have is fear" message spouted today.)

Consider for a moment the bold initiatives enacted during the Roosevelt administration: Social Security, the Civilian Conservation Corps, the Works Progress Administration, the Fair Labor Standards Act, the Agricultural Adjustment Act, the Farm Credit Administration, the Tennessee Valley Authority, the Federal Emergency Relief Administration, the Indian Reorganization Act, the National Labor Relations Board, the Rural Electrification Administration, and the Home Owners' Loan Act. Roosevelt desegregated the defense contracting industry, appointed the first woman to a cabinet post (see page 15), and established a federal minimum wage. Not only did he put the nation on a strong progressive footing, many of his New Deal programs and ideals survive to this day.

And Eleanor Roosevelt was no slouch, either. "It isn't enough to talk about peace," she said, "One must believe in it. And it isn't enough to believe in it. One must work at it." She campaigned on behalf of civil rights (see page 70), workers' rights, and veterans. In 1945, after FDR's death, she was appointed a delegate to the United Nations by Harry Truman, where she chaired the Commission on Human Rights. In 1948 it drafted and adopted the Universal Declaration of Human Rights, one of the greatest documents of the 20th century.

> **All human beings are born free and equal in dignity and rights. They are endowed with reason and conscience and should act towards one another in a spirit of brotherhood.**
> —*Article I, International Bill of Human Rights*

LEARN MORE

www.nps.gov/hofr

www.nps.gov/elro

FDR by Jean Edward Smith (Random House, 2007)

Eleanor Roosevelt, Volume 1 by Blanche Wiesen Cook (Viking, 1992)

Eleanor Roosevelt, Volume 2 by Blanche Wiesen Cook (Viking, 1999)

Freedom from Fear by David M. Kennedy (Oxford, 1999)

The International Bill of Human Rights by Paul Williams, ed. (Entwhistle, 1981)

Ithaca

Keith Olbermann's Moral Force

Cornell University, Barton Hall, Campus Road and Garden Avenue, Ithaca, NY 14853

Nobody expected the convocation speech at the 1998 Cornell graduation to be memorable. But anchorman Keith Olbermann (Class of '79) gave an address that delighted the audience, infuriated his bosses, and lambasted the press corps and the Washington establishment.

The speech was delivered in the midst of the Clinton-Lewinsky investigation, which Olbermann characterized as a politically vindictive freak show foisted on the American public by a sensation- and ratings-obsessed media. And he, as host of MSNBC's *The Big Show with Keith Olbermann*, was part of the problem. As his cable network began covering the scandal "28 hours out of every 24" Olbermann was seduced enough by his growing ratings to agree to expand his broadcast from one hour to two.

"I'd love to tell you the punch line to this story. But, I can't because it ain't over yet," he said of the march toward impeachment. "All I know is that if even the slightest part of any religion known to man is factually correct, all of these people are going to meet again some day—in Hell." The crowd roared. And then he revealed what only a few MSNBC brass knew at that time: three weeks earlier Olbermann had decided to listen to his Moral Force, as he described it, and had told his bosses that he wanted to leave the show, to step away from the circus, "to choose what I felt in my heart was right over what I felt in my wallet was smart." He had given them no specific timetable, but by reveal-ing his plan in the Cornell speech, he forced their hands. Rather than keep him on the air, they had him ride out the remainder of his con-tract in silence. (The complete text of Olbermann's Cornell address can still be found online.)

Olbermann eventually returned to MSNBC with a new format and a new commitment. *Countdown with Keith Olbermann* pulls no punches during its weeknight broadcasts, on the right or the left, and has become a must-watch for progressives.

> [I]f you keep your Moral Force intact just sufficiently so that you can stand up once or twice in the rest of your life and say, "You know what? This is wrong for me and for people I know and for people I don't know and I'm not going to do it," you will have improved the world.
>
> —*Keith Olbermann, 1998*

LEARN MORE
http://thenewshole.msnbc.msn.com
Truth and Consequences by Keith Olbermann (Random House, 2007)
The Worst Person in the World by Keith Olbermann (Wiley, 2006)

New Hyde Park

Engel v. Vitale: No Prayer in Public Schools
New Hyde Park School District, 1950 Hillside Avenue, New Hyde Park, NY 11040

In 1951 the New York State Board of Regents adopted a prayer that was to be recited daily in the state's public schools, following the Pledge of Allegiance: "Almighty God, we acknowledge our dependence upon Thee, and we beg Thy blessings upon us, our parents, our teachers, and our Country." Its purpose, so the board said, was to instill character and good citizenship. But it was the regents who ended up with the civics lesson. Five parents whose children attended classes in the New Hyde Park School District objected to the board's intrusion into the religious instruction of their children, as well as its violation of the First Amendment; they took William Vitale Jr., the chairman of the Union Free School District No. 9, to court. Parent Stephen Engel's name was listed first on the lawsuit.

The parents lost at the first trial, though the school board was ordered to devise a plan for students who did not want to participate in the prayer. On appeal to the U.S. Supreme Court, the school board asserted that prayer was a *significant* element of the nation's heritage, but that the Regents' Prayer was so *insignificant* a part of the school day that it wasn't worth the justices' consideration. With logic like that, is it any wonder it lost the case by a 6–1 vote? Writing on behalf of the majority, Hugo Black pointed out that when a prayer is written by government officials, and citizens are compelled to recite it, that is a de facto violation of the Establishment Clause.

Justice William O. Douglas went even further, writing in his concurring opinion that "In God We Trust" should be removed from U.S. currency, that government officials should not swear on the Bible when taking office, and that churches should be denied tax-exempt status. (None of these suggestions was implemented as part of the case's narrow ruling.)

In the wake of the decision, some in Congress proposed a constitutional amendment establishing prayer in public schools. More than 220 constitutional law professors testified against having legislators mess around with the Bill of Rights. The bill eventually died, but is revived from time to time, usually in an election season.

> The constitutional prohibition against laws respecting an establishment of religion must at least mean that in this country it is in no part the business of government to compose official prayers for any group of the American people to recite as part of a religious program carried on by government.
> —*Justice Hugo Black, in* Engel v. Vitale, *1962*

New York/Brooklyn/Bedford-Stuyvesant

Shirley Chisholm, Unbought and Unbossed

12th Congressional District Offices (closed), 587 Eastern Parkway, Brooklyn, NY 11216

Politicians underestimated Shirley Chisholm at their peril. Her motto—Unbought and Unbossed—was not an empty slogan.

The maverick congresswoman was born in Brooklyn's Brownsville neighborhood on November 30, 1924. She attended elementary school in Barbados, but returned in 1934 and later graduated from Brooklyn's Girls' High School (Nostrand Avenue and Halsey Street). She then enrolled in Brooklyn College, where she got an elementary education degree in 1946.

From there, Chisholm worked in education and got involved in Brooklyn politics. Effectively barred from the Democratic political machine, she joined the Bedford-Stuyvesant Political League and in 1960 formed the Unity Democratic Club, which was designed to promote black candidates. In 1964, at the age of 40, she was elected to the New York State Assembly, where she was the only woman, and one of only a handful of blacks. During the first three years of her tenure the boundaries of her district were redrawn three times, but she won all three redistricting elections.

In 1968 Chisholm campaigned for the U.S. House from New York's newly created 12th Congressional District against the well-known founder of CORE, James Farmer. She had decided to run when a group of poor mothers presented her with a collection they'd taken to get her started: $9.62. She beat two other candidates in the primary, and during the general campaign was hospitalized to remove a benign abdominal tumor. Against her doctor's orders, she went back to the streets to campaign. Chisholm won by a 2-to-1 margin, becoming the first African American woman elected to the U.S. House.

Shirley Chisholm, 1972

In her first speech before the body, in March 1969, she announced, "I intend to vote against any money bill that comes to the floor of Congress that provides any funds for the Department of Defense. Any bill whatsoever, until the time comes when our values and sense of duty to the citizens is turned right side up again, until our country starts to use its wealth for people and for peace, not profits and war." When assigned to the Agricultural Subcommittee on Forestry and Rural Villages (neither of which was prevalent in Brooklyn), she attached an amendment to the committee assignments until she was reassigned to Veterans Affairs.

"I did not come to Congress to behave myself and stay away from explosive issues so I can keep coming back," she told reporters. But her constituents loved her, and returned her 13 more times, where she focused on inner city jobs development, education, and securing minimum wage protection for domestic workers. In 1972 Chisholm ran for president and, though she was not successful in gaining the nomination, pushed the debate to include issues of concern to women, minorities, and working-class Americans. She died on January 1, 2005.

> I'm trying to show young people, black people, poor people, by my every action and word, not to give up. The government belongs to them. They should know it and take responsibility for running it. Politics has a negative sound to it, but we have to take it out of the local clubhouses and give it to the people.
>
> —Shirley Chisholm

LEARN MORE
The Good Fight by Shirley Chisholm (Harper & Row, 1973)
Unbought and Unbossed by Shirley Chisholm (Avon, 1970)
Chisholm '72 (2005)

New York/Brooklyn/Brownsville

Margaret Sanger's First Birth Control Clinic
46 Amboy Street, Brooklyn, NY 11212

It's hard to believe that a column titled "What Every Girl Should Know" could get its author in deep trouble, but when Margaret Sanger started discussing health issues in the *New York Call* in 1912, she ran afoul of the 1873 Comstock Law outlawing "obscenity" sent through the mail. Sanger often wrote about birth control, and distributed a flyer titled *Family Limitation*. Facing arrest and prison, she fled to Europe in 1914 under an assumed name. But she returned a year later on a mission: she was going to establish a birth control clinic for poor women.

It opened on October 16, 1916. Patients could get family planning advice for 10¢, and about 500 women did so in its first nine days before an undercover operation shut it down. Sanger, her sister Ethel Byrne, and Fania Mindell were arrested. They spent 30 days in prison, but emerged resolute. Sanger expanded her advocacy beyond New York, touring the United States and abroad to lecture before audiences large and small, friendly and hostile. By 1918, New York law was changed to allow doctors to prescribe contraceptives.

Margaret Sanger, c. 1916

Sanger eventually reopened the clinic in Manhattan, at 104 Fifth Avenue, and later moved to a building at 46 W. 15th Street. In 1921 she founded the American Birth Control League (ABCL), which would evolve into Planned Parenthood. Two years later the ABCL launched a Clinical Research Bureau at 17 W. 16th Street—Sanger's home— to study and improve birth control methods and STD prevention.

Sanger was not without her faults. Like many in her era, she was a supporter of eugenics. But on witnessing the horror of the Nazis' European genocide, she condemned them. She died in Tucson, Arizona, on September 6, 1966.

> By knowing ourselves, by expressing ourselves, by realizing ourselves more completely than has ever before been possible, not only shall we attain the kingdom ourselves but we shall hand on the torch of life undimmed to our children and the children of our children.
>
> —Margaret Sanger, 1920

LEARN MORE
Woman of Valor by Ellen Chesler (Simon & Schuster, 1992)
The Autobiography of Margaret Sanger by Margaret Sanger (Dover, 1971)

New York/Manhattan/Central Park

Strawberry Fields and *Angels in America*
72nd Street and Central Park West, New York, NY 10023 · (212) 310-6600

If you're a progressive visiting New York and are looking for a little green space, head on up to Central Park and Strawberry Fields, the memorial to John Lennon. The teardrop-shaped garden contains at least one plant from every country in the world; "Imagine" is inscribed in tile along its pathway. The garden was built in part with a $1 million gift from Yoko Ono and Sean Lennon. John Lennon was murdered outside the Dakota, to the west of the garden, on December 8, 1980.

If you walk east from Strawberry Fields you'll come to the Bethesda Terrace. The "Angel of the Waters" statue atop its fountain was carved in 1873 by sculptor Emma Stebbins. The figure later became the inspiration for Tony Kushner's powerful two-part AIDS drama, *Angels in America*.

LEARN MORE
www.centralparknyc.org

New York/Manhattan/Chelsea

Air America to the Rescue!
641 Avenue of the Americas, New York, NY 10011

To progressives everywhere, the debut of Air America on March 31, 2004, seemed as if the cavalry had arrived. Al Franken's *The O'Franken Factor* led the charge, with guests like Al Gore and Michael Moore between news items, political sketches, and anti-Bush rants. It was followed by Randi Rhodes, who served up guest Ralph Nader's Democrats-and-Republicans-are-all-the-same head on a radio platter. Talk radio had a new voice, and it wasn't just another conservative crank who hated taxes, "furriners," and unscreened calls.

And then, two weeks later, Air America went silent in two of its five markets. Its primary financier didn't have the money he'd promised, and the fledging network looked like it might fold before using up the toner in its fax machines. Much of the talent and staff rallied, and they persevered while new investors stepped up to the plate. What emerged and flourished in the months to come was fertile ground for progressives vying for a national spotlight. Though Franken and Rhodes already had national exposure, others emerged. Standup comic Marc Maron cohosted *Morning Sedition* (with Mark Riley), a morning zoo with substance that included call-ins from Planet Bush Bureau Chief Lawton Smalls, Pendejo the Revolutionary, Cardinal Mort Milfington, and Sammy the Stemcell. In the evening, Sam Seder was a goofy, fact-filled compliment to Janeane Garafalo's Red Bull–inspired (but entertaining!) diatribes on *The Majority Report*. David Bender, Rachel Maddow, Mike Papantonio, and Laura Flanders were also introduced to a national audience, not to mention dozens of underexposed progressive pundits who made regular appearances.

Unfortunately, Air America has since suffered from a series of bad programming decisions. Maron's show was canceled, Franken left to run for the senate in Minnesota, and Seder was shuffled to a weekend slot. But the network marches on, and can be found in large and small markets across the United States, as well as satellite radio. Its lineup is often supplemented by other syndicated progressives, such as Ed Schultz (see page 303), and while it has yet to reach the enormous assprint of Rush Limbaugh, it has made considerable headway.

LEARN MORE

www.airamerica.com

Road to Air America by Sheldon Drobney (SelectBooks, 2004)

Air America, the Playbook by David Bender, et al. (Rodale, 2006)

Left of the Dial (2005)

New York/Manhattan/Chinatown

Amy Goodman and *Democracy Now!*

87 Lafayette Street, New York, NY 10013 · (212) 431-9090

For everyone who is appalled by the current state of mainstream American media, there is an alternative: *Democracy Now!* Launched on Pacifica Radio to cover the 1996 elections, it continued production after listeners begged for it to stay on the air. The format was expanded to include a wide spectrum of domestic and foreign news, uncovering stories typically (or deliberately) ignored by corporate media. Journalist and cohost Amy Goodman has reported on the Indonesian military's massacre of 200,000 East Timorese, pollution and murder by international oil conglomerates in Nigeria, and the Battle in Seattle (see page 407), and *always from the scene.* Nothing is filtered through a government spokesperson or prechewed by a pundit—she goes directly to those affected, then returns to authorities to demand answers. In 2000 she and reporter Gonzalo Aburto grilled Bill Clinton for a half hour about his presidential legacy, and he charged them with being "confrontational" and "disrespectful." Boo. Hoo.

Amy Goodman, 2007

> The greatest threat to corporate power, interestingly enough, is globalization—grassroots globalization. It's what those powers fear the most. We can turn their own actions and mechanisms, their own empowerment, against them.
>
> *—Amy Goodman*

In 2001, *Democracy Now!* began simulcasting its radio show on cable TV and the Internet, and can now be found on 450+ public radio, satellite TV, PBS, and cable access stations across the nation. So fear not—the spirit of Thomas Paine isn't dead, it's broadcasting from a converted firehouse in New York's Chinatown. Independent media lives!

LEARN MORE

www.democracynow.org

The Exception to the Rulers by Amy Goodman and David Goodwin (Hyperion, 2004)

Static by Amy Goodman and David Goodman (Hyperion, 2006)

Lizzie Jennings, 19th-Century Rosa Parks
Arrest Site, Chatham Square (Bowery and Division Street), New York, NY 10038

More than a hundred years before Rosa Parks did the same in Montgomery, Alabama (see page 157), schoolteacher Lizzie Jennings boarded a horse-drawn carriage at the corner of Pearl and Chatham Streets in Manhattan, site of present-day Chatham Square. It was July 16, 1854, and she was on her way to play the organ at the Sunday services of the First Colored Congregational Church (Sixth Street and Second Avenue). The driver refused her fare, claiming the carriage was reserved for whites only (and it was), but she got on anyway. When she refused to leave, the driver physically assaulted Jennings and tried to eject her, but she held firm until police backups were called.

The 24-year-old schoolteacher sued the Third Avenue Railway Company, and was represented by future president Chester Alan Arthur. Judge William Rockwell ruled in her favor: "Colored persons if sober, well behaved, and free from disease, had the same rights as others and could neither be excluded by any rules of the Company, nor by force or violence." She received $22.50 in court costs and $225 in damages . . . and by 1860 New York's public transportation was integrated.

New York/Manhattan/East Village

Birthplace of the NAACP
Cooper Union, Cooper Square (Astor Place and Fourth Avenue), New York, NY 10003 · (212) 353-4100

On February 12, 1909, the 100th anniversary of Abraham Lincoln's birth, the National Association for the Advancement of Colored People (NAACP) was founded in New York City. Just six months earlier a two-day race riot in Springfield, Illinois, had left eight African Americans dead (two of them lynched) and more than 50 injured. Thousands more fled Lincoln's hometown fearing for their lives. Accounts of the tragedy shocked a group of progressive intellectuals into action; they met in a New York apartment in early January 1909 and drafted "The Call." The February 12 document was signed by 60 individuals, including Jane Addams, John Dewey, W. E. B. Du Bois, Ida B. Wells-Barnett, and Mary Ovington White. It outlined their goals, and announced a May 30 organizing conference to be held at the Cooper Union.

In the beginning, the NAACP was a mostly white organization whose goal was to work within the American legal system to effect change. It adopted many of the goals of Du Bois's Niagara Movement, primarily the full implementation and enforcement of the Thirteenth, Fourteenth, and Fifteenth Amendments. Within a decade the NAACP had 90,000 members and had achieved modest successes. However, not until it hired the dean of the Howard University Law School, Charles Houston, in 1935 did its legal strategy kick into high gear. Houston created the NAACP Legal Defense and Education Fund in 1940, and named his protégé, Thurgood Marshall, as its first director.

Marshall racked up an impressive record of legal victories, including the landmark *Brown v. Board of Education* decision (see page 293). But as the civil rights movement grew, so did criticism of the NAACP. The organization officially opposed "extralegal" actions such as civil disobedience, though many of its members were active in the movement. Perhaps that is why the NAACP survived to be one of the nation's preeminent African American organizations today.

> [W]e call upon all the believers in democracy to join in a national conference for the discussion of present evils, the voicing of protests, and the renewal of the struggle for civil and political liberty.
> —*From "The Call" to organize the NAACP, 1909*

LEARN MORE
www.naacp.org, (877) NAACP-98
Freedom's Sword by Gilbert Jonas (Routledge, 2005)
Inheritors of the Spirit by Carolyn Wedin (Wiley, 1997)
Groundwork by Genna Rae McNeil (University of Pennsylvania, 1983)

Dorothy Day, Peter Maurin, and the Catholic Worker
Catholic Worker Soup Kitchen, 36 E. First Street, New York, NY 10003

Dorothy Day first met Peter Maurin in December 1932. Day was a crusading journalist covering the nation's descent into the Great Depression, and Maurin was a wandering, French Catholic scholar who had been following her writings. Maurin proposed that they found a newspaper, *The Catholic Radical*, with the goal of building a society "in which it [was] easier for people to do good." The first issue was sold for one cent at a Communist rally in New York's Union Square on May 1, 1933, under a new name: *The Catholic Worker*.

From its inception the Catholic Worker, both the paper and the movement, was not just interested in providing spiritual direction to its followers, but to live out its message. Day and Maurin wanted every parish across the nation to establish a shelter for the homeless and to feed the poor, so they founded the first "house of hospitality" on the Lower East Side. They also advocated "voluntary poverty," giving whatever excess they had to those who had none.

The Catholic Worker has always been militantly pacifist, and criticized the Church's "just war" doctrine. During the depth of the 1950s Cold War, Day organized protests against New York's annual civil defense drill. Residents were told to run for cover when air raid sirens blew, but Day defied the orders by picketing in City Hall Park, and was repeatedly arrested. Protests grew year after year until the city abandoned the drill as unworkable.

In the 1960s and '70s Day spoke out against the Vietnam War and on behalf of the United Farm Workers (see page 383). For much of the latter part of her life she lived at Maryhouse (55 E. Third Street) with New York's poor. She died there on November 29, 1980. Today, there are many Catholic Worker communities across the nation.

> Young people say, 'What good can one person do? What is the sense of our small effort?' They cannot see that we must lay one brick at a time, take one step at a time; we can be responsible only for the one action of the present moment.
>
> —*Dorothy Day*

LEARN MORE
www.catholicworker.org
Resources, www.catholicworker.com
The Catholic Worker Movement by Mark and Louise Zwick (Paulist, 2005)
A Harsh and Dreadful Love by William D. Miller (Image, 1974)
By Little and By Little by Robert Ellsberg, ed. (Knopf, 1983)
The Long Loneliness by Dorothy Day (HarperSanFrancisco, 1952)

Emma Goldman, American Anarchist
Goldman's *Mother Earth* Home, 210 E. 13th Street, New York, NY 10003

The motto of Emma Goldman's *Mother Earth* newspaper was "No Gods, No Masters." Goldman lived it every day. Born in Kaunas, Lithuania, on June 27, 1869, she immigrated to the United States in 1886. She worked in Rochester, New York, as a sweatshop seamstress, but not for long. Goldman vowed to change the squalid labor and living conditions of those around her, and moved to New York to join the anarchist movement. The anarchists advocated an end to hierarchical government and exploitive capitalism, and the expansion of personal freedom.

In New York Goldman met Alexander Berkman, who in 1892 was arrested and jailed for attempting to kill Henry Clay Frick, a factory manager in Homestead, Pennsylvania, who had hired Pinkerton "detectives" to murder striking steelworkers. Berkman's actions were denounced by many anarchists, and Goldman by association. Back in New York, she turned her oratory skills to much greater effect . . . with a price. In 1893 Goldman was arrested in Union Square for telling the unemployed to take bread if they could not afford it, and spent a year in jail at Roosevelt Island (then known as Blackwell's Island).

After she was released, Goldman returned to her activism for women's and workers' rights. In 1903 she rented two sixth-floor tenements, from which she began publishing *Mother Earth* in 1906. In 1916, shocked by the growing number of back-alley abortions in poor communities, Goldman began distributing information about contraception, and was arrested. She spent 14 months behind bars.

In the run-up to World War I, Goldman helped organize No Conscription Leagues and denounced the European conflict. "Conceit, arrogance, and egotism are essentials of patriotism," she wrote. "Patriotism assumes that our globe is divided into little spots, each one surrounded by an iron gate. Those

Emma Goldman, c. 1911

who had the fortune of being born on some particular spot, consider themselves better, nobler, grander, more intelligent, than the living beings inhabiting any other spot." For her antiwar work, Goldman was arrested in 1917 under the Espionage Act and spent two years in federal prison. Not long after her release, she was deported to the Soviet Union, along with 248 other political "undesirables," by a young J. Edgar Hoover. (Her citizenship had been revoked in 1908, but she was living in the United States as a resident alien.)

Goldman was no less critical of the USSR's oppressive regime than she had been of America's. In 1921 she moved to Great Britain, and later, at the age of 67, joined those fighting fascism in the Spanish Civil War. Three years later, while visiting Toronto, Canada, she died of a stroke on May 14, 1940. Her body was returned to the United States, where it was buried beside the Haymarket Martyrs (see page 234).

> [G]overnments ordain, judge, condemn, and punish the most insignificant offenses, while maintaining themselves by the greatest of all offenses, the annihilation of individual liberty.
>
> —*Emma Goldman*

LEARN MORE

Red Emma Speaks by Emma Goldman (Humanity Books, 1996)

The World's Most Dangerous Woman by Theresa Moritz (Subway, 2001)

Anarchy! An Anthology of Emma Goldman's Mother Earth by Peter Glassgold, ed. (Counterpoint, 2001)

Reverend Billy and the Church of Stop Shopping
St. Mark's Church in-the-Bowery, 131 E. 10th Street, New York, NY 10003 · (212) 674-6317

Bill Talen had had enough. From his apartment in Hell's Kitchen he'd been witnessing the Disneyfication of Times Square—the transforming of a unique, gritty neighborhood into an obscene shrine to consumerism run amok. Something had to be done. *Immediately.* So he grabbed a white tux coat left over from his catering days, strapped on a clerical collar, and pomaded his hair up high, "like Conway Twitty." On the march over to Broadway he picked up a pulpit from a Christian supply store on 43rd Street, which he erected on the sidewalk facing the Disney Store.

Reverend Billy, 2006

"Mickey Mouse is the Antichrist!" he testified to the shocked crowd, their arms weighed down with the day's purchases. "Remember, when that *product* smiles at you, you are actually at that point walking into the Lake of Fire!!" Reverend Billy and the Church of Stop Shopping were born.

Though Talen was an actor, this was no act. Reverend Billy has been sent to save America from the Shopocalypse. Today he enters Starbucks, lays his hands on the cash register, and exorcises the demons within. His followers stroll the aisles of high-end stores, loudly yakking on their cell phones, "Oh, I don't think we should buy them that, honey. They use *sweatshops* to make this stuff!" And at Wal-Marts they Whirl—dozens of nonshoppers perform ballets with empty carts in a brazen display of "corporate disobedience." No big box store is safe.

Reverend Billy now has a Stop Shopping Choir, and holds old-time revivals at St. Mark's Church in-the-Bowery and on the road. So cut up those credit cards! Buying stuff will not fill that emptiness in your heart—that hole has been *manu-*

> Anyone who isn't here to buy something will be arrested!
> —*Disney Store manager, on the arrival of Reverend Billy*

factured by the same demons who pay Indonesian children pennies to stitch Pocahontas dolls! Save your soul—step away from the merchandise!!!!

LEARN MORE

www.revbilly.com

www.stmarkschurch-in-the-bowery.com

What Should I Do If Reverend Billy Is in My Store? by Bill Talen (New Press, 2003)

What Would Jesus Buy? by Reverend Billy (PublicAffairs, 2006)

New York/Manhattan/Financial District

Seeger v. United States: CO Status Is Extended to the Nonreligious

Whitehall Induction Center, 39 State Street, New York, NY 10004

For many years the only way a young draftee could claim conscientious objector (CO) status was to profess belief in a Supreme Being, and be a member of an accepted pacifist religion. That posed a problem for Daniel Seeger: he didn't believe in God. So in 1957 Seeger wrote a letter to his Queens draft board. "I have concluded that war, from the practical standpoint, is futile and self-defeating, and from the more important moral standpoint, it is unethical." The board sent him Form 150, the application for CO status. As directed by a 1940 law, Form 150 asked whether Seeger believed in God, and rather than answer yes or no, he drew in a third box and attached an explanation. "Skepticism or disbelief in the existence of God does not necessarily mean lack of faith in anything whatsoever," he wrote.

The army, never big on nuance, rejected Seeger's application. In October 1958 he was ordered to report to the Army Induction Center for a preinduction physical. He appealed the order, and his case made it to the federal courts as *Seeger v. United States*. Originally found guilty of refusing the draft, his conviction was overturned in a unanimous decision by the U.S. Supreme Court in 1965. Though the justices only ruled on Seeger's

> What is necessary for . . . conscientious objection to all war is that this opposition to war stem from . . . moral, ethical, or religious beliefs about what is right or wrong and that those beliefs be held with the strength of traditional religious convictions.
>
> —*Justice Hugo Black, in* Welsh v. United States, *1970*

particular case, it was the foot in the door to change CO guidelines forever. In 1970, the high court expanded on its ruling in *Welsh v. United States*, and the military was ordered to rewrite its procedures to eliminate the religious requirement altogether.

New York/Manhattan/Greenwich Village

Henry Bergh and the American Society for the Prevention of Cruelty to Animals

Clinton Hall (now the District 65 Building), Astor Place and Lafayette Street, New York, NY 10003

In late April 1866 Henry Bergh came upon a carriage driver who was beating his lame horse on Manhattan's Fifth Avenue, at 22nd Street. Bergh demanded the driver stop the cruelty or he would have him arrested. The driver thought Bergh was joking, and laughed before resuming whipping the animal. Bergh left, but his campaign against animal exploitation and abuse had just begun.

Bergh was actually within his power to arrest the man; as the founding leader of the American Society for the Prevention of Cruelty to Animals (ASPCA) he had lobbied the New York legislature to pass a law outlawing the mistreatment of horses and other animals. Passed on April 19, 1866, the groundbreaking statute also deputized members of the ASPCA (and similar groups) as "humane officers" who could bring violators before a judge for prosecution. The ASPCA had only been in existence for two months at the time. Bergh launched the organization with a public lecture on animal cruelty before a packed crowd at New York's Clinton Hall. In his February 8 talk he unveiled the "Declaration of the Rights of Animals," the founding document of the ASPCA. The organization was granted a state charter on April 10.

The day after his run-in with the carriage driver, Bergh confronted another man who was brutally transporting livestock . . . and this time Bergh arrested him. When the offender was brought into court, the judge claimed no knowledge of the new statute and let the man go. Bergh continued his efforts and a few weeks later secured the first conviction under the law; a butcher was fined $10 for mishandling livestock. And by the end of the year the ASPCA had successfully prosecuted 66 cases. By the late 1880s it had 12,000 convictions under its belt in New York City alone.

Bergh and his band of activists brought even more attention to the plight of work horses by strategically ordering drivers to unhitch overburdened teams, or by forcing riders to step off crammed omnibuses. The ensuing traffic fiascos raised the ASPCA's visibility, and its membership. The group also advocated the installation of water troughs and fountains along busy thoroughfares, and got them.

Though the ASPCA was the first American anticruelty society, it quickly spawned similar organizations in more than 20 U.S. cities.

LEARN MORE
www.aspca.org, (212) 876-7700
Crusade for Kindness by John Loeper (Macmillan, 1991)

Jeanne Manford Starts PFLAG

United Methodist Church of the Village (formerly Metropolitan Duane UMC), 201 W. 13th Street, New York, 10011

When Jeanne Manford saw her son Morty on television being punched and pushed down an escalator at the New York Hilton while police stood idly by, she did what any caring mother would: she got mad. Manford called the *New York Times* and demanded that they investigate the assaults at the gay rights protest. They hung up on her. So Manford wrote a letter to the *New York Post*, published April 29, 1972, in which she proclaimed, "I have a homosexual son and I love him."

The response was overwhelmingly positive from the gay community, but less so from the school where she worked as a teacher. Some staff and parents complained, but Manford told the principal it was none of their business. That June, Morty asked his mom to march with him in the Christopher Street Liberation Day Parade, so she hand-printed a sign that asked other parents to support their children. The crowd went wild, and she got hugs and cheers all along the parade route. Even she was surprised at the reaction.

Manford got so many requests to speak to individuals' parents that on March 11, 1973, she hosted a support group titled Parents of Gays at the Metropolitan Duane United Methodist Church. About 20 people attended. Her movement grew to include family members and friends, and took on the name Parents and Friends of Lesbians and Gays—PFLAG. The

> **Parents of Gays: Unite in Support of Our Children**
> *—Jeanne Manford's sign at the Christopher Street Liberation Parade, 1972*

group flourished after a 1980 column by "Dear Abby," and today includes more than 500 chapters nationwide. And to this day, PFLAG contingents always get the loudest applause at every Pride parade.

LEARN MORE
www.pflag.org, (202) 467-8194
www.thevillagechurchumc.org, (212) 243-5470
Beyond Acceptance by Carolyn W. Griffin and Marian J. Worth (St. Martin's
   Griffin, 1997)

The Stonewall Riot
51–53 Christopher Street, New York, NY 10014

It started at 1:20 A.M. on June 28, 1969. For the second time in a week, Deputy Inspector Seymour Pine of the NYPD First Division of the Public Morals led a raid on the Stonewall Inn, a mafia-run gay bar in Greenwich Village. But unlike the earlier bust, the patrons actually resisted the police harassment. Perhaps it was the full moon. After the bartenders and managers were loaded into the paddy wagon, the cops began arresting customers, including several men in drag. By this time, a crowd had gathered and began tossing coins at the police. If the officers missed the not-too-subtle allusion to the department's notorious corruption, the crowd made it clear, shouting, "Here's your payoffs!" Three drag queens under arrest shoved the cops, and the crowd grew angrier. Then, when a handcuffed lesbian fought back while being manhandled into a squad car, the coins turned to bottles and rocks. The police retreated into the bar, and the Stonewall Riot was on.

The 10 police inside were no match for the hundreds gathered outside. A phalanx of street hustlers and drag queens led the charge, and used a parking meter as a battering ram to bust down the front door. Others tossed paving stones through the shattered front window. The police found a firehose and sprayed water out of the building at the rioters. Backups arrived, but could not control the chaos. A group of men in heels formed a kick line and taunted the cops, while others circled around through alleys and attacked the police from behind. The cat-and-mouse game went on until sunrise.

Word of the riot drew thousands to the Village the next night, and the gutted Stonewall served free soft drinks to happy, liberated patrons standing in

The Stonewall Inn today

the rubble. Police showed up later, and another battle erupted. They weren't any more successful in quelling the uprising than they had been the night before. Only 13 people were arrested that weekend.

The Stonewall Riot is commemorated each year at the end of June through Pride parades across the nation. The first march, dubbed Christopher Street Liberation Day, took place on June 28, 1970. About two thousand people walked from Sheridan Square (across from the Stonewall) up Seventh Avenue to Central Park, where they held a rally at the Sheep Meadow.

> We are the Village girls!
> We wear our hair in curls!
> We wear our dungarees,
> Above our nelly knees!
> —*Kick-line protesters at the Stonewall Riot, 1969*

LEARN MORE
www.stonewallvets.org
Stonewall by David Carter (St. Martin's, 2004)
Stonewall by Martin Duberman (Dutton, 1993)

LGBT ACTIVISM IN NEW YORK

- **Oscar Wilde Memorial Bookshop (15 Christopher Street, www. oscarwildebooks.com, (212) 255-8097):** Craig Rodwell opened America's first LGBT bookstore at 291 Mercer Street two years *before* the Stonewall Riot. The store was a meeting place for the city's gay community before there was a community center. It has since moved to a new location, just a block from the Stonewall Inn.

- **Gay Activist Alliance Firehouse (99 Wooster Street, gone):** The Gay Liberation Front was founded in response to the Stonewall Riot, but its political goals were too broad for many in the new movement. Later in 1969, activist Jim Owles founded the Gay Activist Alliance to address specific issues in the community. The GAA purchased a former firehouse in 1970, to be used as a community center for meetings and Saturday night "Liberation Dances." The highly visible building was often threatened by arsonists, and burned to the ground on October 15, 1974.

- **Lesbian, Gay, Bisexual & Transgender Community Services Center (208 W. 13th Street, www.gaycenter.org, (212) 620-7310):** The LGBT community found a new home in 1984 in a former elementary school, P.S. 6. The center has seen the first public meetings of ACT UP (see page 115), GLAAD (www.glaad.org), and Queer Nation. It continues to offer cultural programs, community outreach, counseling, government relations, and youth services.

LEARN MORE

Gay New York by George Chauncey (Basic Books, 1995)

About Time by Martin Duberman (Dutton, 1991)

Gay American History by Jonathan Katz (Plume, 1992)

Triangle Shirtwaist Factory Fire
Brown Building, 29 Washington Place, New York, NY 10003

In a 1909 strike organized by the International Ladies Garment Workers Union (ILGWU) against the Triangle Shirtwaist Factory, 20,000 employees walked off the job for 14 weeks. But despite the ILGWU's efforts, the Greenwich Village sweatshop never unionized. One hundred forty-six workers, mostly immigrant women, paid the price on March 25, 1911.

It was a Saturday, so only half the usual workforce was on the clock when a fire broke out in a scrap bin. The blaze quickly spread from the 8th to the 10th floor as the management escaped via the roof. Most of the women were trapped behind locked doors; the owners had been locking the exits to prevent union organizers from entering. The building's only fire escape collapsed, and without a way to escape, many jumped to their deaths to avoid being burned alive. The building's hoses couldn't reach the upper floors, nor could the fire department's ladders.

The labor movement was able to force some reforms in the aftermath. For the first time New York created a Bureau of Fire Prevention. The state's Joint Board of Sanitary Control set new standards for workplace conditions. But Triangle management received only paltry fines for stacking sewing machines against the doors, and opened for business five days later at a new location. They also paid the victims' families $75 each for their losses. No, that's not a typo.

The original building still stands and is today an NYU office building. You can see a memorial plaque on the northwest corner of Washington Place and Greene Street.

LEARN MORE
www.ilr.cornell.edu/trianglefire
Triangle by David Von Drehle (Atlantic Monthly, 2003)

New York/Manhattan/Midtown

ACT UP at St. Patrick's Cathedral
460 Madison Avenue, New York, NY 10022

The AIDS Coalition to Unleash Power—ACT UP—was created in March 1987 after playwright Larry Kramer warned an audience at New York's LGBT Community Center (see page 113) that they had better start fighting back or two-thirds of them would be dead within five years. Two days later, 300 people met at the center and vowed to force the FDA to release new experimental drugs and to radically overhaul its approval process.

ACT UP's first demonstration took place on March 24 in the shadow of Wall Street. About 250 protesters hung President Reagan's FDA head, Dr. Frank Young, in effigy in front of Trinity Church (Broadway and Wall Street), then tied up traffic for several hours. More demonstrations took place at drug corporations and public hearings. ACT UP protesters later chained themselves to the balcony at the New York Stock Exchange. Yet no action drew as much attention as their demonstration at St. Patrick's Cathedral.

John Cardinal O'Connor was a member of the Presidential AIDS Policy Panel, which ACT UP had targeted for its criminally negligent foot dragging. O'Connor had never been a friend of the gay community, and it showed on the panel. So on December 10, 1989, over 5,000 ACT UPers descended on the church to disrupt services while O'Connor was saying mass. As the cardinal sat on the altar, they made a point of reminding him of Jesus' command to help the sick, while police arrested 111 shouting protesters.

Did it work? In many ways, yes. The FDA made changes to its drug approval process, extending the lives of countless victims, and ACT UP deserved much of the credit.

> As long as the epidemic rages and the Church fights in direct opposition to the policies recommended by responsible doctors, scientists, and public health officials, ACT UP will never be silent—not in the streets, not in the capital, and not even in the Church itself.
>
> —from ACT UP's Post-Action Position Statement, 1989

LEARN MORE
www.actupny.org
Reports from the Holocaust by Larry Kramer (St. Martin's, 1994)
And the Band Played On by Randy Shilts (Penguin, 1987)

Flora Kibbe and the No-Kill Animal Shelter
Bide-a-Wee, 410 E. 38th Street, New York, NY 10016 · (212) 532-6395

Most of the nation's first humane associations were primarily interested in "ending the suffering" of strays—euthanasia was commonplace. Animal shelters held animals before they could be put to sleep, but adoption was not a priority. But in 1903, Flora D'Auby Jenkins Kibbe designed and built America's first no-kill animal shelter. Her Bide-a-Wee Home Association was based upon the Barrone d'Herpents Dog Refuge, which Kibbe had visited while traveling in France.

Kibbe's shelter opened in a small building near her Manhattan home. Bide-a-Wee would adopt stray or neglected animals, mostly dogs, and feed and house them until a suitable home could be found. Kibbe also worked to place watering troughs around the city when draft animals were still common.

Bide-a-Wee was housing 200 dogs by 1909, and some of its neighbors began to complain about the barking. Faced with eviction from the neighborhood, Kibbe had a new facility constructed, which the association still operates to this day. In its first century of operation, Bide-a-Wee has placed more than a million pets with loving families.

 **LEARN MORE**
www.bideawee.org

Jon Stewart Slays *Crossfire*
CNN Studios, 10 Columbus Circle (1 Time Warner Center), New York, NY 10019

It says a lot about today's media landscape that many people (correctly) trust "fake news" shows on Comedy Central more than "real news" broadcasts on CNN and Fox. But seldom have viewers seen a cage match between the forces of good and evil before the *Daily Show*'s Jon Stewart took on CNN's *Crossfire* on its own turf. On October 15, 2004, Stewart appeared on the show and blindsided cohosts Tucker Carlson and Paul Begala. Stewart explained, "Right now, you're helping the politicians and the corporations. . . . You're part of their strategies. You are partisan . . . what do you call it? . . . *hacks.*"

Carlson took exception. "You had John Kerry on your show and you sniff his throne and you're accusing *us* of partisan hackery?"

Stewart clarified, "You're on CNN. The show that leads into me is puppets making crank phone calls. *What is wrong with you?*" Carlson then accused Stewart of being Kerry's "butt boy" and the show went gloriously downhill from there.

"I do think you're more fun on your show—just my opinion," Carlson offered.

"You're as big a dick on your show as you are on *any* show," Stewart concluded, and the studio audience—the CNN audience—cheered in agreement. CNN must have agreed with Stewart's brutal evaluation of *Crossfire*; the show was cancelled shortly thereafter.

LEARN MORE

www.comedycentral.com/shows/the_daily_show/index.jhtml

New York/Manhattan/Morningside Heights

Maggie Kuhn and the Gray Panthers
International House, Columbia University, 500 Riverside Drive, New York, NY 10027

Maggie Kuhn had spent her entire adult life in social work, from her first job with the YWCA in Philadelphia, to the USO during World War II, to the Social Education and Action Department of the Presbyterian Church, which she directed. But in 1970, seven months before her 65th birthday, she was told by church officials she would have to retire, regardless of whether she could still perform her duties.

Legally there was nothing Kuhn could do. She organized a lunch date with five others in the same predicament, and they decided to call a general meeting of men and women interested in social action but who were being pushed into retirement against their wishes. It took place at the International House at Columbia University in May 1970. About 100 people attended.

They originally called themselves the Consultation of Older Persons, and their first issue of concern was opposition to the Vietnam War. They attended antiwar rallies and built alliances with student groups, developing their slogan "Age and Youth in Action." They invited speakers for teach-ins on housing, age discrimination, and health care.

The organization remained the Consultation of Older Persons until Kuhn shared a cab with Reuben Gums, a producer with WPIX-TV in New York.

"You know, that name doesn't sound like what you have in mind. I think you should call yourselves the Gray Panthers," Gums suggested. Kuhn couldn't stop laughing. And at the next meeting the group's members endorsed the new name.

In the early days the Gray Panthers operated out of Kuhn's Philadelphia row house. As the organization grew she was offered a space in the basement of the Tabernacle United Church (3700 Chestnut Street) in West Philadelphia—the broom closet. Here, in 1971, Kuhn set up a desk, a phone, two chairs, a mimeograph machine, and a filing cabinet.

One of Kuhn's first local projects was to pressure the First Pennsylvania Banking and Trust Co. to address a problem faced by local seniors: Social Security recipients were often mugged on the way home from cashing their monthly checks. The bank wouldn't allow the elderly poor to open checking accounts . . . until Kuhn arrived at its boardroom with three dozen seniors. First Pennsylvania established an interest-bearing checking account for depositors over 65, and got a wealth of positive publicity to boot.

By 1973 the Gray Panthers absorbed the members of Ralph Nader's Retired Professional Action Group and established 11 chapters from Syracuse to San Francisco. By 1976 Kuhn was traveling more than 100,000 miles annually on behalf of the organization. By 1981 it had 90 chapters with 9,000 members.

> Older persons in our society constitute a great national resource which has largely been unrecognized, undervalued, and unused. The purpose of our meeting is to consider how retirees can be involved in new and really significant ways.
>
> *—Maggie Kuhn, in her invitational flyer to the first meeting of what would become the Gray Panthers, 1970*

LEARN MORE

www.graypanthers.org, (800) 280-5362

No Stone Unturned by Maggie Kuhn with Christina Long and Laura Quinn (Ballantine, 1991)

Get Out There and Do Something About Injustice by Margaret E. Kuhn (Friendship Press, 1972)

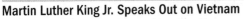

Martin Luther King Jr. Speaks Out on Vietnam
Riverside Church, 490 Riverside Drive, New York, NY 10027 · (212) 870-6700

Though Martin Luther King Jr.'s "I Have a Dream" speech is better known, no less moving was his denunciation of the Vietnam War at New York's Riverside Church on April 4, 1967. Sponsored by Clergy and Laymen Concerned About Vietnam, it was the first time King spoke out against the war in a big way. "Somehow this madness must cease. We must stop now," he said. "I speak for the poor of America who are paying the double price of smashed hopes at home and death and corruption in Vietnam. I speak as a citizen of the world, for the world as it stands aghast at the path we have taken. . . . The great initiative in this war is ours. The initiative to stop it must be ours."

King was denounced by some for speaking out on a subject other than civil rights, but he brushed aside the critics. "I have been fighting against segregation all my life," he told a reporter, "I refuse to segregate my conscience." Following the speech, King began planning a campaign to convince youth of all races to register as conscientious objectors. The plan never came to fruition; one year to the day after the Riverside speech King was assassinated.

> A nation that continues year after year to spend more money on military defense than on programs of social uplift is approaching spiritual death.
> —*Martin Luther King Jr., 1967*

LEARN MORE
www.theriversidechurchny.org

New York/Manhattan/Washington Heights

Malcolm X, Gone Too Soon
Audubon Ballroom, 3940 Broadway, New York, NY 10032

On February 21, 1965, while standing on the stage of New York's Audubon Ballroom, Malcolm X was gunned down in front of his wife and children. He was just shy of his 40th birthday. Three members of the Nation of Islam (NOI) were eventually convicted of the crime. There's some debate whether they were the only parties involved, or whether they were railroaded, but the tremendous loss of a great leader is not debatable.

Malcolm X was born Malcolm Little in Omaha, Nebraska (3448 Pinkney Street, torn down), on May 19, 1925. His family moved a number of times during his childhood, but they eventually ended up in Lansing, Michigan. In 1929 their home (4705 S. Logan Street) burned to the ground under mysterious circumstances. Two years later, while living in East Lansing, his father was run over by a streetcar. Again, foul play was suspected. Little's mother had a nervous breakdown and her eight children were shipped off to foster homes.

In 1944 Little was arrested in Boston for carrying a weapon and fencing stolen goods. He served a short sentence, but was imprisoned again in 1946, for burglary. He bounced between three Massachusetts prisons—Charlestown, Concord, and Norfolk—where he spent his time studying the writings of Elijah Muhammad and copying words and definitions out of an abridged dictionary to improve his vocabulary. When he was released on parole August 7, 1952, he took a new name: Malcolm X.

Within two years Malcolm X was the head of the NOI's Mosque #7 in Harlem. His charismatic speaking style brought many followers to the NOI, and national attention for their message. He criticized civil rights leaders for being too passive, denounced the racist white establishment, and advocated confrontation over integration. He passionately defended the NOI's teachings, yet became disillusioned after learning that Elijah Muhammad had fathered children by several NOI secretaries. He officially severed ties with the organization in early 1964 and made a pilgrimage to Mecca. There, side-by-side with Muslims of many races and nationalities, he had a new awakening. Returning to the states, he renounced some of his earlier rhetoric, founded the Organization of Afro-American Unity, and changed his name to El-Hajj Malik El-Shabazz. Still advocating on behalf of black self-determination, he expanded his message to include

Malcolm X, 1964

a "true brotherhood" of man. But in less than a year, he was murdered.

The façade on the old Audubon Ballroom remains the same as when he died, but its interior has been renovated to be part of a hospital complex. Plans are in the works to make part of it into the Malcolm X Museum.

> You're not to be so blind with patriotism that you can't face reality. Wrong is wrong no matter who does it or says it.
> —*Malcolm X*

LEARN MORE

www.cmgworldwide.com/historic/malcolm/

www.themalcolmxmuseum.org

The Autobiography of Malcolm X by Malcolm X and Alex Haley (Grove, 1964)

Malcolm X Speaks by George Breitman, ed. (Grove, 1994)

X (1992)

Niagara Falls

Lois Gibbs and Love Canal

93rd to 100th Streets, between Frontier Avenue and Colvin Boulevard, Niagara Falls, NY 14304

Lois Gibbs was not an activist in the mid-1970s, but a mother with two children in Niagara Falls' Love Canal neighborhood. When her son kept getting the same medical problems, and nobody could determine exactly what was causing them, she began to worry that the reports of chemical contamination in the area might be true. Armed with a clipboard, she visited her neighbors and logged how many had also suffered unexpected illnesses. She then took her findings to the New York Department of Health and started asking questions.

The answers shocked her. First, the subdivision had been built atop the Hooker Chemical Company's old dump. Worse still, the elementary school had been located over the largest concentration of leaky drums, barely concealed by a thin layer of soil. The state immediately closed the school and ordered 239 families to vacate the area. Gibbs formed the Love Canal Homeowners Association to give residents a voice, to monitor health concerns, and to demand relocation funds. State and federal money was slow in coming until members detained two EPA officials on May 10, 1980. The media rushed to the scene, and within a week Jimmy Carter declared a state of emergency and $15 million was approved for 810 families.

In 1980 Gibbs moved to Washington, D.C., where she established the Citizen's Clearinghouse for Hazardous Waste. Today it is known as the Center for Health, Environment, and Justice.

LEARN MORE
www.chej.org, (703) 237-2249
Love Canal by Lois Marie Gibbs (New Society, 1998)

Seneca Falls

Elizabeth Cady Stanton and the Seneca Falls Convention
Women's Rights National Historic Park, 136 Fall Street, Seneca Falls, NY 13148 · (315) 568-2141

On July 13, 1848, Elizabeth Cady Stanton and four friends, including Lucretia Mott, had gathered for a social visit when the discussion turned to women's rights. Angered at being relegated to second-class status, the women resolved to do something about it . . . and quickly. They called for a Women's Rights Convention, to be held in Seneca Falls a week later. Announcements went out and Stanton began working on a draft of a "Declaration of Rights and Sentiments."

About 300 people, Frederick Douglass among them, attended the gathering at Wesleyan Chapel (Fall and Water Streets) on July 19 and 20. After much discussion and debate the attendees adopted the declaration, which Stanton based upon the Declaration of Independence. It clarified that "all men *and women* are created equal" and made a dozen demands, including the right to vote and access to all areas of employment and public life comparable to men. At the end of the convention, 68 women and 32 men signed the document. The women's rights movement was born.

In its early days the fight for suffrage was strongly tied to the issue of abolition. Susan B. Anthony was working with the American Anti-Slavery Society, as well as temperance and teachers' issues, before she joined the struggle for women's rights in 1851. But as the nation careened toward the Civil War, women's suffrage received less attention. After the war, when African American men were given the franchise by the Fourteenth Amendment, a deep rift developed in the women's movement. Angry that former slaves received the vote before them, Anthony and Stanton formed the mostly white, all female National Woman Suffrage Association (NWSA) in May 1869. Lucy Stone and husband Henry Blackwell (see page 32) formed the American Woman Suffrage Association (AWSA) in November of the same year, but it was open to women and men of all races.

Elizabeth Cady Stanton and Susan B. Anthony, c. 1895

The NWSA looked to the federal government to address the issue of suffrage, which didn't happen until 1920 (see page 214). The ASWA had more success at the state and local level, though not much more. The groups eventually reconciled and merged to become the National American Woman Suffrage Association (NAWSA) in February 1890, with Anthony as its president. She retired in 1900.

Today Seneca Falls is home to the Women's Rights National Historic Park, as well as the National Women's Hall of Fame (76 Fall Street). The latter museum honors outstanding American women from Harriet Tubman and Dolley Madison to Sally Ride and Oprah Winfrey. The nearby Seneca Falls Historical Society (55 Cayuga Street) has Stanton's rocking chair, manuscripts of Anthony's speeches, and some of Amelia Bloomer's personal effects, among other artifacts.

LEARN MORE

www.nps.gov/wori

www.greatwomen.org, (315) 568-8060

The Birth of American Feminism—The Seneca Falls Convention of 1848 by Virginia Bernhard and Elizabeth Fox-Genovese, eds. (Brandywine, 1995)

The Elizabeth Cady Stanton-Susan B. Anthony Reader by Ellen Carol DuBois, ed. (Northeastern University, 1991)

Not for Ourselves Alone by Geoffrey C. Ward and Ken Burns (Knopf, 1999)

PENNSYLVANIA

Many of this nation's most important progressive documents were penned in Pennsylvania—Philadelphia specifically. Thomas Jefferson wrote and rewrote the Declaration of Independence in a home now known as Declaration House (701 Market Street), which was then signed at Independence Hall (500 Chestnut Street). Eleven years later, on September 17, 1787, the U.S. Constitution was adopted in the same building, and sent to the states for ratification. You can learn the whole story at the new National Constitution Center (525 Arch Street).

Yet Philadelphia's progressive tradition doesn't stop there. The American Anti-Slavery Society was founded in the City of Brotherly Love during a convention in 1833. At it, William Lloyd Garrison's Declaration of Sentiments was approved: "[N]o man has a right to enslave or imbrute his brother—to hold or acknowledge him, for one moment, as a piece of merchandise—to keep back his hire by fraud—or to brutalize his mind by denying him the means of intellectual, social, and moral improvement," it stated. Six years later another abolitionist group, the Friends of Liberty, saw the inscription on the State House Bell, which was first rung on the

> We hold these Truths to be self-evident, that all Men are created equal; that they are endowed by their Creator with certain unalienable Rights; that among these are Life, Liberty, and the Pursuit of Happiness—That to secure these Rights, Governments are instituted among Men, deriving their just Powers from the Consent of the Governed, that whenever any Form of Government becomes destructive to these Ends, it is the Right of the People to alter or to abolish it, and to institute new Government . . .
>
> —*From the Declaration of Independence, 1776*

reading of the Declaration of Independence: "Proclaim liberty throughout all the land, unto the inhabitants thereof." They renamed it the Liberty Bell and used it as a symbol for their cause.

And Philadelphia's progressive tradition has continued well into the 20th century. In 1977 Reverend Leon Sullivan, the pastor of the Zion Baptist Church (2600 N. Broad Street), drafted the Sullivan Principles. These guidelines for corporate behavior concerning the apartheid regime in South Africa became the framework around which the 1980s American divestiture movement was based.

LEARN MORE

Independence Hall, www.nps.gov/inde, (215) 965-2305

National Constitution Center, www.constitutioncenter.org, (215) 409-6600

Sacred Scripture by Pauline Maier (Knopf, 1997)

Moving Mountains by Leon H. Sullivan (Judson, 1998)

Abingdon

Abingdon School District v. Schempp: No Prayer in Public Schools

Abingdon Senior High School, 900 Highland Avenue, Abingdon, PA 19001

In the 1950s the state of Pennsylvania required that its schools begin the day by reading 10 New Testament verses and the Lord's Prayer. Students could be excused with a note from a parent or guardian. But Edward and Sidney Schempp didn't believe in state-sponsored religious indoctrination, nor that their three children should have to request what was their constitutional right, so in 1956 they filed suit against the school district. The Schempps were not atheists, they were Unitarians who felt *they* were responsible for their children's religious education, not Pennsylvania lawmakers. They also objected to the burden the policy was putting on non-Christian students.

The Schempps won their first court case, and when the district's appeal reached the U.S. Supreme Court it was combined with another suit from Baltimore, Maryland. Madalyn Murray (later O'Hair), who was an atheist, didn't want her son Bill to be required to say a mandatory prayer at Woodbourne Junior High School (1526 Winford Road) each day. To protest, Bill Murray refused to go to class for three weeks until the school allowed him to opt out. Meanwhile, Madalyn Murray proceeded with her lawsuit, *Murray v. Curlett*, to have the prayer, voluntary or not, declared unconstitutional.

The court ruled 8–1 on June 17, 1963, that prayer had no place in public school. The justices ruled the constitution intended "to create a complete and permanent separation of the spheres of religious activity and civil authority." The opinion is still vilified today by religious leaders who claim it was the moment the country began sliding downhill.

LEARN MORE

An Atheist Epic by Madalyn O'Hair (American Atheist Press, 1989)

> While the Free Exercise Clause clearly prohibits the use of state action to deny the rights of free exercise to anyone, it has never meant that a majority could use the machinery of the State to practice its beliefs. . . . In the relationship between man and religion, the State is firmly committed to a position of neutrality.
>
> —Justice Tom Clark, in Abingdon School District v. Schempp, *1963*

Dover

Intelligent Design and the Dover Area School Board

Dover Area High School, 46 W. Canal Street, Dover, PA 17315

In the spring of 2003 Alan Bonsell, the newest board member of the Dover Area School District, brought up creationism with the principal and several biology teachers at Dover High School. He wanted it taught alongside evolution, and when the principal refused to entertain the idea she was forced to resign. And while they didn't begin teaching creationism, several science teachers began treading lightly around the subject of evolution.

When Bonsell was elected board president in January 2004, he was then advocating Intelligent Design (ID). As would later come out at trial, ID was creationism by another name, popularized through a book titled *Of Pandas and People* (Davis and Kenyon) and material from the Discovery Institute, a conservative anti-evolution organization. The teaching of creationism in public schools had already been declared unconstitutional by the U.S. Supreme Court, so ID specifically avoided any biblical references . . . yet used most of the same arguments to make its points.

During the summer of 2004 the board clashed over the purchase of new biology textbooks, with several members vowing they would only approve a new core text if *Pandas* was purchased as well. When public funds were not approved, two board members accepted donations to buy 60 copies of *Pandas* for classroom use. In protest, the remaining moderate board members resigned, and Bonsell replaced them with fundamentalists. The new board then mandated the teaching of ID during all biology classes.

Dover High School teachers revolted. They refused to read aloud a statement, in class, drafted by the board that was critical of evolution. Eleven parents filed suit against the board, claiming its new ID policy "was added to the curriculum precisely because of its religious contents and nature," thus violating the constitution's Establishment Clause.

A federal district judge (a Republican appointed by George W. Bush) would later rule in *Kitzmiller v. Dover Area School District* that the board had overstepped its authority. What's more, he confirmed what everyone knew: because ID invoked the idea of "supernatural causation," it was indeed a faith-based theory, and therefore unconstitutional in public schools.

The ruling followed an even more stinging defeat for the school board; on November 8, 2005, voters replaced eight of the nine board members who had adopted the ID policy. On the *700 Club* the next day Pat Robertson warned, "I'd like to say to the good citizens of Dover, if there is a disaster in your area, don't turn to God. You just rejected Him from your city." When criticized, he clarified, "I recommend they call on Charles Darwin. Maybe he can help them."

Well, Darwin's dead. But in Dover schools, thanks to active citizens, science is still being taught. It could probably be of some use in a disaster.

Charles Darwin, welcome again in Dover, c. 1875

> The students, parents, and teachers of the Dover Area School District deserve better than to be dragged into this legal maelstrom, with its utter waste of monetary and personal resources.
>
> —Judge John Jones, in Kitzmiller v. Dover Area School District, *2006*

LEARN MORE

40 Days and 40 Nights by Matthew Chapman (Collins, 2007)

Creationism's Trojan Horse by Barbara Forest (Oxford, 2004)

Dublin

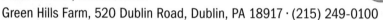

Pearl S. Buck, Humanitarian

Green Hills Farm, 520 Dublin Road, Dublin, PA 18917 · (215) 249-0100

Though she was born in Hillsboro, West Virginia (Route 219), on June 26, 1892, Pearl S. Buck (née Sydenstricker) spent the first 40 years of her life with her missionary parents in China. From the moment she started writing, her goal was to promote understanding between East and West. Buck's portrayal of peasant life in China, *The Good Earth*, won her the Pulitzer Prize in 1923. And, for that novel and others, Buck was awarded the 1938 Nobel Prize for Literature, the first American woman to receive the honor.

Buck purchased the Green Hills Farm estate in Dublin in 1935, where she and her husband raised eight children, some of whom the couple had adopted in Asia. Incensed that many agencies considered mixed-race children "unadoptable," she founded Welcome House in 1949. The plight of Amerasian children, particularly in the wake of the Korean War and the growing American involvement in Vietnam, led her to expand Welcome House into the Pearl S. Buck Foundation in 1964. In its four decades of operation it has placed more than 25,000 children.

Buck was also active in civil rights causes, advocated passage of the Nuclear Test Ban, and spoke out for women's rights and humanitarian relief, particularly for China. She died in Danby, Vermont, on March 6, 1973, and was buried beneath a large ash tree at Green Hills Farm. The estate is now a museum, and the headquarters of the Pearl S. Buck Foundation.

LEARN MORE

www.psbi.org

Pearl S. Buck by Peter Conn (Cambridge, 2002)

The Good Earth by Pearl S. Buck (Pocket, 2005)

Franklin

Johnny Appleseed's First Nursery
13th Street and Franklin Avenue, Franklin, PA 16323

The real life story of John Chapman—Johnny Appleseed—has been so tainted by folklore that it's often difficult to separate fact from fiction. But Franklin's claim that Chapman planted his first apple nursery here is as good as any town's. Local historians believe that he established the nursery along French Creek sometime between 1797 and 1804.

Chapman was born in Leominster, Massachusetts, on September 26, 1774. As a young man he trained as a nurseryman near Wilkes-Barre, Pennsylvania, where he converted to the Swedenborgian faith. Imbued with the spirit and a new trade, Chapman headed west in 1797, just ahead of a wave of new settlers. He established hundreds of nurseries over 100,000 square miles from New England to Indiana, and as far south as Kentucky. As settlers arrived, Chapmen greeted them with fruit trees, day lily bulbs, and herb seeds. Deeply religious, he also passed out as many religious tracts and Bibles as he did saplings.

Chapman has been called America's first hippie. He was a pacifist and vegetarian, made peace with Native Americans, and preferred to go barefoot, even in the winter. The latter habit turned out to be his undoing; on a trip to Fort Wayne, Indiana, in March 1845, he contracted pneumonia after trudging through the snow to visit one of his orchards. He was 72 years old at the time, but never made it to 73. He died on March 18 and was buried north of town. Though the exact location of his grave is unknown, it is believed to be somewhere in what is today Johnny Appleseed Memorial Park (4000 Parnell Avenue).

LEARN MORE

Johnny Appleseed by William Ellery Jones, ed. (Chrysalis, 2000)

Johnny Appleseed by Robert Price (Indiana University, 1954)

King of Prussia

The Plowshares Eight

General Electric Nuclear Missile Re-Entry Division, 230 Mall Boulevard, King of
Prussia, PA 19406

On September 9, 1980, eight activists, including Daniel and Philip Berrigan,
entered the General Electric Nuclear Missile Re-Entry Division plant in King
of Prussia on a biblical mission. Following the words of Isaiah 2:4, "And they
shall beat their swords into plowshares, and their spears into pruning hooks;
nation shall not lift up sword against nation, neither shall they learn war any-
more," the group took sledgehammers to the nosecones of two Mark 12A
nuclear warheads, poured blood onto nearby documents, and offered prayers
for peace. When police arrived, the group surrendered without incident.

The following February the Plowshares Eight went on trial on a variety of
charges. The judge denied them the right to present a "justification defense,"
which would have allowed testimony on the destructive potential of the weapons they were attempting to disable. All were found guilty and received sentences of 1½ to 10 years in prison. Eventually, through a decade of appeals,
they were able to present more of their defense, which they saw as their moral
duty.

Though the original eight were behind bars for months, the Plowshares
movement was anything but slowed. Every month or so a new group of protesters would walk into a facility, row out to a nuclear submarine, or sneak onto
a military base and start pounding on the instruments of war. Each action
was given its own name—the Per-
shing Plowshares, the Silo Pruning
Hooks, the Doves of Peace Disarmament Action—and was designed to
draw maximum media attention to
the threat posed by militarism and
the manufacture of weapons of mass
destruction. More than 75 Plowshares protests were carried out over
the next two decades, in the United
States and abroad. And they're still
going on.

> The only message I have to the
> world is: We are not allowed
> to kill innocent people. We are
> not allowed to be complicit in
> murder. We are not allowed
> to be silent while prepara-
> tions for mass murder proceed
> in our name, with our money,
> secretly.
> —*Philip Berrigan, at trial*

LEARN MORE

Swords into Plowshares by Arthur J. Laffin, ed. (Rose Hill, 2003)

To Construct Peace by Michael True (Twenty-Third Publications, 1992)

In the King of Prussia (1982)

Langhorne

Sesame Street

Sesame Place, 100 Sesame Road, PO Box L579, Langhorne, PA 19047 · (215) 752-7070

On November 10, 1969, *Sesame Street* debuted on public television. Some educators were concerned because its format was developed using Madison Avenue sales techniques—fast-paced segments designed to look like commercials, but instead of pushing cereal they taught young children letters, shapes, and numbers, as well as life skills, simple words, and basic addition, subtraction, and Spanish. The segments mixed puppets and live actors, which some felt could confuse or even disturb young children.

Well, experts aren't always right; *Sesame Street* was a gargantuan hit. Even Mississippi's Commission for Public Television, which originally refused to air the show because of its multicultural cast, relented to public pressure. To date, the Children's Television Workshop (now the Sesame Workshop) has produced more than 4,100 episodes, and has spun off more than 30 international versions, each sensitive to its home country's particular cultural needs. In the Middle East, *Sesame Stories* is a joint venture between Israelis, Palestinians, and Jordanians aimed at cross-cultural understanding. And in 2002 South Africa's *Takalani Sesame* introduced Kani, an HIV-positive Muppet, to address the region's AIDS crisis.

You're probably wondering if I can tell you how to get, how to get to Sesame Street. The show is set on a fictitious street in Brooklyn Heights, New York, where some of the original writers lived. However, there is a facsimile located in suburban Philadelphia: Sesame Place. The theme park not only has a re-creation of the show's set, but has kiddie rides, parades, and a water park run by Ernie and his rubber ducky.

LEARN MORE
www.sesameworkshop.org
www.sesameplace.com
Sesame Street and the Reform of Children's Television by Robert W. Morrow (Johns Hopkins, 2006)
Sesame Street Unpaved by David Borgenicht (Hyperion, 1998)
It's Not Easy Being Green by Jim Henson (Hyperion, 2005)

Latrobe

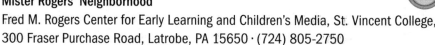

Mister Rogers' Neighborhood

Fred M. Rogers Center for Early Learning and Children's Media, St. Vincent College, 300 Fraser Purchase Road, Latrobe, PA 15650 · (724) 805-2750

In spring 1951, a month from college graduation and preparing to enter the Pittsburgh Theological Seminary, Fred McFeely Rogers returned home for Easter vacation. His parents had just purchased a TV, and it was the first time he'd seen one. "I just hated it," he reflected. "I looked at those people on television throwing pies into each other's faces. And I thought: I'm just going to go into television!" So began the most charmingly subversive and militantly decent career in broadcasting.

Rogers headed for New York where he landed a job on the NBC *Television Opera Theatre*. That led to work as an assistant producer on *The Kate Smith Hour, The Voice of Firestone,* and *Your Lucky Strike Hit Parade,* and eventually a position as the NBC floor director. And then, two years after he began, he quit. The nation's first public television station, WQED, was being launched in Pittsburgh, and Rogers felt a calling.

At WQED, he and Josie Carey coproduced *The Children's Corner*; Carey was the host, and Rogers was the puppeteer and musician. He also re-entered the seminary and studied child psychology at the Arsenal Family and Children's Center. Rogers was ordained a Presbyterian minister in 1963, but instead of taking on a congregation, was given the ministry of reaching children through mass media. The Canadian Broadcasting Corporation hired him to create *Misterogers,* the predecessor to *Mister Rogers' Neighborhood.* That show debuted on WQED when he returned in 1967. A grant from the Sears Roebuck Foundation allowed the show to be broadcast nationwide.

And then in 1969 Richard Nixon announced that he wanted to cut in half a $20 million grant to the Corporation for Public Broadcasting (CPB), money that would be used for children's educational programming. He messed with the wrong guy. Rogers went before Congress to plead CPB's case, and in eight short minutes turned Rhode Island Senator John Pastore, the gruff committee chairman overseeing the CPB budget, into an enthusiastic champion for the cause. Rogers' brilliant and heartfelt talk (available on the DVD below) ranks as one of the most outstanding pieces of testimony in congressional history.

Rogers went on to found Family Communications, Inc. (FCI), in 1971. Throughout his adult life, he was a strict vegetarian and a committed pacifist, and rarely watched

Mister Fred Rogers, 1975

TV. Fred and Joanne Rogers were married for 51 years, and had two sons. Rogers received an Emmy for Lifetime Achievement in 1997, was inducted into the Television Hall of Fame in 1999, and was awarded the Presidential Medal of Freedom in 2002. Rogers died on February 27, 2003, and was buried in Unity Cemetery (McCullough and Unity Cemetery Roads) in his hometown of Latrobe. FCI continues his work today, as does the Fred M. Rogers Center for Early Learning and Children's Media at St. Vincent College.

For true Fredophiles, there are two Rogers attractions not far from Latrobe. The Children's Museum of Pittsburgh (10 Children's Way, www.pittsburghkids. org) invites children to explore a re-creation of Mister Rogers's television home, to watch how things are made on Picture Picture, to sit on the front porch in a sweater and sneakers, and to play with puppets in X the Owl's tree. And if you're an adult looking for something a bit more your size, visit Mister Rogers' Neighborhood of Make-Believe at Idlewild Park (Route 30, www.idlewild. com) in Ligonier. There you'll ride a trolley past King Friday XIII and Queen Sarah's castle, Lady Elaine Fairchilde's Museum-Go-Round, Daniel Striped Tiger's clock, and more.

LEARN MORE

www.fredrogerscenter.org

www.fci.org

Mister Rogers' Neighborhood by Mark Collins and Margaret Mary Kimmel, eds.
(University of Pittsburgh, 1996)

Fred Rogers, America's Favorite Neighbor (2003)

PROGRESSIVE THOUGHTS OF MISTER ROGERS

- Try your best to make goodness attractive.

- There are millions and millions of people doing wonderful things all over the world, and they're generally not the ones being touted in the news.

- Our world hangs like a magnificent jewel in the vastness of space. Every one of us is a part of this jewel; and, in the perspective of infinity, our differences are infinitesimal. We are intimately related. May we never pretend that we are not.

- You are a very special person. There is only one like you in the whole world. There's never been anyone exactly like you before, and there never will be again. Only you. And people can like you exactly as you are.

- I'm proud of you for standing up for something you believed in—something that wasn't particularly popular, but that assured the rights of someone less fortunate than you.

- The opposite of love is not hate, it's indifference.

- A person can grow to his or her fullest capacity only in mutually caring relationships with others.

- All we're ever asked to do in this life is to treat our neighbors—especially our neighbor who is in need—exactly as we would hope to be treated ourselves. That's our ultimate responsibility.

LEARN MORE

The World According to Mister Rogers by Fred Rogers (Hyperion, 2003)

Life's Journeys According to Mister Rogers by Fred Rogers (Hyperion, 2005)

Many Ways to Say I Love You by Fred Rogers (Hyperion, 2006)

Minersville

Minersville School Board v. Gobitis: A Setback for the First Amendment
Minersville Area Elementary School Center, Fifth Street, Minersville, PA 17954

Anyone who argues that patriotic ceremonies in schools, such as the Pledge of Allegiance, should be compulsory ought to hear the story of Lillian and William Gobitas. As brother and sister, they listened with their family to a radio speech given by Joseph Rutherford in October 1935. In it Rutherford, leader of the American [Jehovah's] Witnesses, commended Carleton Nicholls for refusing to salute the American flag in his Massachusetts third-grade classroom, as a matter of religious freedom, and was *arrested*. (Two years earlier Adolf Hitler had banned the Witnesses in Germany for refusing to salute the Nazi flag. More than 10,000 Witnesses were sent to concentration camps, and half perished.) The Gobitas children decided they would stop saluting the flag in class as well. And did.

When school superintendent Charles Roudabush learned that Lillian and William Gobitas had sat down during the morning flag pledge, he contacted their parents. They supported their children's decisions, so Roudabush went to the school board. It enacted a policy whereby children were required to salute the flag or face punishment for insubordination. When the Gobitases refused to comply, they were expelled. Walter Gobitas, their father, filed suit against the school board in federal court. In the meantime, the children attended a nonpublic "Kingdom School" on a farm in New Ringgold.

The first court's ruling went in favor of the children. "The refusal of these two earnest Christian children cannot even remotely prejudice or imperil the safety, health, morals, property, or personal rights of their fellows," wrote Judge Albert Maris. On appeal, the Gobitases won again. When the case reached the U.S. Supreme Court the clerk misspelled the family's name as Gobitis. It was an omen. In an 8–1 ruling on June 3, 1940, the high court supported the board's expulsion policy. Justice Harlan Fiske Stone was the lone dissenter, writing that the policy was "the surrender of the constitutional protection of the liberty of small minorities to the popular will."

In the immediate aftermath of the decision, hundreds of vigilantes attacked Jehovah's Witnesses across the country, burning Kingdom Halls, beating canvassers, and even castrating one Nebraska Witness. Court observers believed that several jurists on the high bench likely realized they had made a grave error, and that they might be open to overturning their decision. It came three years later in the case of *West Virginia Board of Education v. Barnette*.

LEARN MORE
To the Flag by Richard J. Ellis (University Press of Kansas, 2005)

WEST VIRGINIA BOARD OF EDUCATION V. BARNETTE

The U.S. Supreme Court was rightfully criticized for its weak reasoning in the *Minersville* decision. The fact that the traditional arm-upraised salute looked disturbingly Nazi-esque didn't help matters, particularly while Germany was marching across Europe.

Still, many school boards adopted compulsory flag-salute rules for their districts, including West Virginia. Dozens of children, mostly Jehovah's Witnesses, were expelled from the state's public schools when they declined to participate, including Walter Barnette's two daughters of the Slip Hill grade school. The case was first filed in August 1942, but quickly made its way to the U.S. Supreme Court. It reversed its 8–1 ruling in *Minersville* by a 6–3 margin. The decision was handed down on Flag Day (June 14) 1943.

Those who begin coercive elimination of dissent soon find themselves exterminating dissenters. . . . If there is any fixed star in our constitutional constellation, it is that no official, high or petty, can prescribe what shall be orthodox in politics, nationalism, religion, or other matters of opinion or force citizens to confess by word or act their faith therein.
—*Justice Robert Jackson, in* West Virginia Board of Education v. Barnette, *1943*

Philadelphia

Benjamin Franklin, Founding Progressive
Franklin Court Underground Museum, 314–322 Market Street, Philadelphia, PA 19106 · (215) 597-2760

Though never a president, Benjamin Franklin had as profound an influence on the birth of the United States as any chief executive. What's more, he was a diehard progressive. He founded America's first anti-slavery society, its first lending library, its first volunteer fire department, and its postal service. He was also a scientist and inventor, and came up with the lightning rod, swim fins, bifocals, the odometer, and the potbelly stove. Yet not every idea was brilliant; he devised a new alphabet (doing away with c, j, q, w, x, and y) and suggested the turkey as the national bird.

Franklin was born in Boston (17 Milk Street, torn down) on January 17, 1706. He attended the Boston Latin School, but dropped out at age 10. Two years later he was apprenticed to his brother James, a printer, but at 17 he ran away to Philadelphia, worked a few jobs, and left for London. He returned in 1726, and in 1730 founded his first newspaper, *The Pennsylvania Gazette*. Three years later he published the first edition of *Poor Richard's Almanack*.

In the War of Independence, Franklin became the revolutionaries' elder sage, and famously summed up their dilemma: "We must all hang together, or assuredly we shall all hang separately." As a commissioner to France on behalf of the new republic, he was able to secure France's support in the war, and in doing so likely saved the union.

Like many of the Founding Fathers, Franklin was a Deist. In the true spirit of the Enlightenment, he separated morality from organized religion. "I have found Christian dogma unintelligible," he wrote. "Early in life I absented myself from Christian assemblies." He did, however, believe in a higher power . . . he just didn't go overboard.

> Those who would give up essential liberty to purchase a little temporary safety, deserve neither liberty nor safety.
> —Benjamin Franklin

Franklin died in Philadelphia on April 17, 1790, and was buried in the Christ Church Burial Ground (Fifth and Arch Streets). His home no longer exists, but a museum now sits on the site.

LEARN MORE

www.nps.gov/inde/franklin-court.html

www2.fi.edu, (215) 448-1200

Benjamin Franklin by Walter Isaacson (Simon & Schuster, 2003)

The Autobiography of Benjamin Franklin by Benjamin Franklin (Touchstone, 2003)

The Wit and Wisdom of Benjamin Franklin by Benjamin Franklin (Barnes & Noble Books, 1995)

Caroline Earle White, the Morris Animal Refuge, and the American Anti-Vivisection Society

Morris Animal Refuge, 1242 Lombard Street, Philadelphia, PA 19147 · (215) 735-3256

Before the late 1800s, stray animals were routinely killed in most American cities. But in 1870 Caroline Earle White convinced the mayor of Philadelphia to let her spearhead an effort to gather strays and lost pets, help find their owners or put them up for adoption, and euthanize those for which she could not find homes. (It would be another three decades before the nation's first no-kill shelter opened—see page 116.) The city gave her $2,500 to get started.

White enlisted the support of Elizabeth Morris and Annie Wahn to create the first shelter. Since 1858 Morris and Wahn had been independently rescuing strays in the Philadelphia area, and paying for it out of their own pockets. In 1874 the Morris Refuge Organization for Homeless and Suffering Animals (later renamed the Morris Animal Refuge) opened its doors.

This was not White's first or last triumph. She had long advanced the revolutionary idea that "animals have certain rights, as inalienable as those of man to life, liberty, and the pursuit of happiness." On June 21, 1868, after two years of organizing, she had founded the Pennsylvania Society for the Prevention of Cruelty to Animals (PSPCA). Under its state charter White, as a woman, could not serve as its president, but her husband sat on the board of managers and spoke on her behalf. White led the Women's Branch of the PSCPA.

But White didn't stop there. In 1883 she also founded the American Anti-Vivisection Society (AAVS) to combat the abuse of animals in medical research. Newspapers had been printing horror stories of puppies sewn together, and dogs (often stolen pets) with their spines shattered or their paws slowly crushed "in the name of science." The AAVS forced the medical establishment to draw up guidelines for ethical research behavior, and got public schools to end the practice of vivisection (the "cutting up of life"— dissecting *live* animals) as part of science instruction.

> *Non facias malum ut inde fiat bonum* (You cannot do evil that good may result)
> —*Motto of the American Anti-Vivisection Society*

LEARN MORE
www.morrisanimalrefuge.org
www.aavs.org, (215) 887-0816

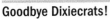

Goodbye Dixiecrats!
Convention Hall (torn down), 3400 Civic Center Boulevard, Philadelphia, PA 19104

In his early political career, Hubert Humphrey was more idealistic than pragmatic. As the 37-year-old mayor of Minneapolis, he worked to repair the city's reputation for anti-Semitism, and on behalf of civil rights. And at the 1948 Democratic National Convention he showed up at the Platform Committee with four planks he wanted inserted: to abolish poll taxes, to enact a federal antilynching law, to integrate the armed services, and to establish a permanent presidential fair employment commission.

Humphrey's proposals were opposed and eventually rejected in committee . . . so he brought them before the full convention on the night Harry Truman was to be renominated. Humphrey's passionate speech moved the delegates to approve the planks, 651½ to 582½. The Alabama and Mississippi delegations were moved as well; the 35 Southern delegates walked out, and eventually into the welcoming arms of the Republican Party. South Carolina's Democratic governor Strom Thurmond ran for president on the Dixiecrat ticket in 1948. The Dixiecrats won 38 electroral college votes, enough to keep the *Republicans* from a majority, and Harry Truman in the White House.

Sadly, while Hubert Humphrey was instrumental in the advancement of civil rights in 1948, he played just the opposite role at the 1964 convention in Atlantic City. Lyndon Johnson made Humphrey's nomination as vice president contingent on suppressing the Mississippi Freedom Democratic Party's petition to be seated (see page 200). "Do you mean to tell me that your position is more important to you than 400,000 black people's lives?" Fannie Lou Hamer asked Humphrey. He did not answer.

> To those who say that we are rushing this issue of civil rights, I say to them we are 172 years too late! . . . The time has arrived in America for the Democratic Party to get out of the shadow of state's rights and walk forthrightly into the bright sunshine of human rights!
>
> —*Hubert Humphrey, at the 1948 Democratic National Convention*

Richard Allen and the Mother Bethel AME Church
419 S. Sixth Street, Philadelphia, PA 19147 · (215) 925-0616

In 1769 Richard Allen was assigned to Philadelphia's St. George's Methodist Church (235 N. Fourth Street) by the American Methodist Church. As the denomination's first black preacher, it was a big step forward. But Allen and his associate Absalom Jones set their sights even higher: they insisted that St. George's end its practice of segregating black congregants in the balcony. The church hierarchy refused the pair's request, and it led to a split in 1787.

Allen purchased a plot of land in 1793, and on it built the Mother Bethel Church a year later. Though the church structure has been rebuilt three times, the land beneath it remains the oldest property continuously owned by African Americans in the United States. To signal its independence from the Methodist Church, Mother Bethel formed the African Methodist Episcopal (AME) Church in 1816, the first black religious denomination in the United States. When Allen died in 1831, he was interred in a crypt in the church's basement.

In addition to Allen's religious accomplishments, he and Jones founded the Free African Society on April 12, 1787, the first black organization in the United States. The Free African Society was a mutual aid society, but its members were instrumental in forming the AME Church.

LEARN MORE
www.motherbethel.org

Schenck v. United States: A Blow to Free Speech
Socialist Party Offices, 1326 Arch Street, Philadelphia, PA 19107

On May 18, 1917, the U.S. Congress passed the Conscription Act, which established the Selective Service at the outset of World War I. The Socialist Party was opposed to the draft, and printed 15,000 flyers stating why. The pamphlet quoted the Thirteenth Amendment: "Neither slavery nor involuntary servitude, except as a punishment for crime whereof the party shall have been duly convicted, shall exist within the United States or any place subject to their jurisdiction." It went on to urge young men to challenge their orders, and advocated the repeal of the Conscription Act.

But Congress had also passed the 1917 Espionage Act, which authorities used to charge the Socialist Party's general secretary Charles Schenck with sedition. The government could not prove that anyone had been *prevented* from enrolling using the flyers, nor did it even try. Instead, Schenck was prosecuted for expressing his opinion on a public issue. He was found guilty at his first trial, and on appeal.

The U.S. Supreme Court reviewed the case and on March 3, 1919, issued a chilling unanimous decision that read, in part, "When the nation is at war many things that might be said in time of peace are such a hindrance to its effort that their utterance will not be endured so long as men fight and that no court could regard them as protected by any constitutional right." Justice Oliver Wendell Holmes then cited a previously unknown "clear and present danger" exception to the First Amendment, a ruling that is never mentioned by the right wing when it rails against the abuses of "activist judges."

Schenck's three 10-year sentences were affirmed, and he was sent off to federal prison to serve them concurrently. He was released six months later.

> **LONG LIVE THE CONSTITUTION OF THE UNITED STATES**
> —*Headline on the pamphlet that earned Charles Schenck a conviction for sedition, 1917*

Springdale

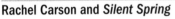

Rachel Carson and *Silent Spring*
Rachel Carson Homestead, 613 Marion Avenue, Springdale, PA 15144 · (724) 274-5459

The 1962 publication of *Silent Spring* is often cited as the moment when the modern environmental movement was born. In it, author Rachel Carson detailed the growing threat posed by the overuse of pesticides, particularly DDT. Carson was dismissed by the chemical industry, first as a "hysterical" woman, and later in print through a $250,000 organized smear campaign.

But Carson's scientific credentials were impressive. She was the first woman ever employed by the U.S. Fish and Wildlife Service, and rose to be the editor in chief for all its publications. She also wrote nature articles for the *Baltimore Sun*.

Carson's love of the environment started early. She was born on her family's rural homestead on May 27, 1907, and lived with her parents until she was 22 years old. She earned a bachelor's in marine biology, and a master's in zoology from Johns Hopkins. From there she was hired to write radio scripts for the U.S. Fish and Wildlife Service, and stayed with the agency for most of her career.

> Can anyone believe it is possible to lay down such a barrage of poisons on the surface of the earth without making it unfit for all life? They should not be called "insecticides" but "biocides."
>
> —*Rachel Carson, in* Silent Spring

Carson was diagnosed with breast cancer shortly after *Silent Spring* was published. The disease took her life on April 14, 1964, at the age of 56. She was buried in Parklawn Memorial Park (12800 Veirs Mill Road) in Rockville, Maryland. Today her family's homestead is a pilgrimage site for those who care about the earth.

LEARN MORE

www.rachelcarson.org

www.rachelcarsonhomestead.org

Silent Spring by Rachel Carson (Houghton Mifflin, 1962)

Rachel Carson by Linda J. Lear (Henry Holt, 1997)

Lost Woods by Rachel Carson (Beacon, 1997)

WEST VIRGINIA

Since independence, the region that became West Virginia never quite liked the rest of the state, in part because of the Three-Fifths Compromise. The residents were underrepresented, in their opinion, because so few in the Appalachians owned slaves. Also, under the state's constitution, only landowners were allowed to vote, and were only considered landowners if they had 25 acres of "improved" land or 50 acres of fallow land. That excluded many in the mountainous west. Western Virginians tried to push through reforms, and some changes were eventually made to the state constitution, but the region continued to get the short end of the electoral stick.

Shortly after the battle at Fort Sumter, South Carolina, state lawmakers met to draft articles of secession. A group of western Virginians, led by John S. Carlile, walked out on April 17, 1861, vowing to remain loyal to the Union. The new group met in Wheeling on May 13–15, and announced their opposition to the upcoming Ordinance of Secession referendum. The measure passed statewide on May 23, and Virginia joined the Confederacy.

But all was not lost. The Union Army soon took control of northwestern Virginia, allowing another convention to take place in Wheeling, from June 11 to 25, 1861. Delegates approved the Restored Government charter, which regional voters approved on October 24. Once its constitution was written, President Lincoln and the U.S. Congress approved West Virginia's reentry to the Union, even though it was unconstitutional for one state to be formed from another without its full permission. The new legislature considered several new names, including Kanawha, Augusta, and Western Virginia, but settled on West Virginia.

Fairmont

Grace Clayton and Father's Day

Central United Methodist Church, 301 Fairmont Avenue, Fairmont, WV 26554 ·
(304) 366-3351

Despite what you might think, Father's Day was not dreamed up by Hallmark
to sell cards. The spring holiday actually marks a dark day in American labor
history.

On December 6, 1907, an explosion rocked the West Virginia mining town
of Monongah. Two mines owned by the Consolidated Coal Company of Boston, Mine #6 and Mine #8, were demolished when a combination of methane
gas and coal dust ignited. Only four miners escaped the blast; 361 miners
perished, 210 of whom were fathers. It remains the worst coal mining disaster
in American history.

To honor the dead, and to support the fatherless children left behind, Grace
Clayton of nearby Fairmont suggested a special service be held in their honor.
On July 5, 1908, the first Father's Day was celebrated at the Central United
Methodist Church, presided over by Reverend Robert Webb. Others adopted
the holiday over time, and in 1968 President Lyndon Johnson officially recog-
nized the special day, though his signing didn't go into effect until 1972.

LEARN MORE
www.cumcwv.org

Grafton

Anna Jarvis, Julia Ward Howe, and Mother's Day

International Mother's Day Shrine, Andrews Methodist Episcopal Church, 11 E. Main
Street, PO Box 513, Grafton, WV 26354 · (304) 265-1589

As with Father's Day, Mother's Day had its origins in a progressive cause.
Anna M. Jarvis was concerned about the bad blood lingering between North
and South in the wake of the Civil War, so in 1868 she established a Mothers Friendship Day in her community. Her goal was to build relationships
between women who'd lost sons on both sides of the conflict, not to honor
motherhood.

Two years later, poet Julia Ward Howe, author of "The Battle Hymn of the
Republic," issued a declaration calling for a Mother's Day for Peace. She had

learned of Jarvis's efforts, and believed mothers were in a unique position to effect change. Though her call for an international summit of women was never acted upon, the idea for a Mother's Day was kept alive.

When Jarvis died in 1905 her daughter, also named Anna, decided to honor her mother's efforts at building a lasting peace. Three years later, more than 400 people filed into Andrews Methodist Episcopal Church, each carrying a white carnation in honor of his or her mother. It was such a success that Anna emptied her life savings to lobby Congress to make Mother's Day an official holiday. In 1914 Woodrow Wilson signed a federal bill designating the second Sunday in May as Mother's Day. But in a sickening, dishonest turn, Wilson used the holiday to rally American sentiment for America's entry into World War I . . . "to defend American mothers."

The folks in Grafton have converted the church where Anna's mother taught, and where the first ceremony took place, into the Mother's Day Shrine. It has two stained glass windows: one of Anna, and one of her mother.

> Our sons shall not be taken from us to unlearn all that we have been able to teach them of charity, mercy, and patience.
> —Julia Ward Howe, in her "Mother's Day Proclamation," 1870

LEARN MORE
www.mothersdayshrine.com
Mother's Day by Susan Tracy Rice (Kessinger, 2005)

Harpers Ferry

John Brown's Raid
Harpers Ferry National Historic Park, PO Box 65, Harpers Ferry, WV 25425 · (304) 535-6029

On October 16, 1859, abolitionist John Brown and 19 others launched a raid against the federal armory at Harpers Ferry. His goal was to seize enough guns and ammunition to launch an armed insurrection that would drag the nation into a civil war and end slavery. Brown's plan was not very well thought out, and was soon thwarted by the local militia. One of Brown's sons died in the initial assault on the arsenal (and another two days later, from wounds), as did eight other followers. In retreat, Brown barricaded himself in the armory's firehouse. He was captured two days later by a squad of marines commanded by Robert E. Lee.

Three raiders escaped, but Brown and four allies were captured and sent to Charles Town. His trial commenced October 27, when he was well enough to be brought into the courtroom on a cot. On the first day at the Jefferson County Court-house (100 E. Washington Street), Brown's appointed lawyers moved that he be declared insane, but Brown would have none of that. "I look upon this as a miserable pre-text of those who ought to take a different course in regard to me," Brown shouted. The men were dis-missed and replaced by two others who were no better at slowing the runaway train toward conviction.

John Brown, 1859

After a week-long trial, the jury took less than an hour to find Brown guilty of insurrection and murder. (The others were later tried and found guilty as well.) On November 2, Brown was sentenced to death,

> I am not terrified by the gallows, which I see staring at me in the face, and upon which I am soon to stand and suffer death for doing what George Washington was made a hero for doing.
> —*John Copeland, one of Brown's followers*

and was given a chance to address the courtroom. "Had I so interfered in behalf of the rich, the powerful . . . every man in this court would have deemed it an act worthy of reward rather than punishment," he said. "I believe that to have interfered as I have done . . . in behalf of [God's] despised poor, was not wrong, but right."

Approximately 1,500 troops and bystanders witnessed Brown's execution in Charles Town on December 2. The Civil War he predicted started 16 months later. The armory in Harpers Ferry was burned by retreating Union troops dur-ing the conflict. Later, the firehouse ruins were shipped to the 1893 Colum-bian Exposition in Chicago, and a historic marker was placed on its original site. Eventually the building's bricks made it back to town, where the firehouse was reconstructed.

Stones from Brown's Charles Town jail cell were pulled from the postwar rubble and arranged in a pyramid at the site where Brown was put to death (515 S. Samuel Street), and remain to this day. The Jefferson County Courthouse has a display on Brown's trial; the Jefferson County Museum (200 E. Washington Street) has the wagon Brown rode to the scaffold, sitting atop his coffin.

LEARN MORE

www.nps.gov/hafe

John Brown by David S. Reynolds (Vintage, 2005)

John Brown Raid Handbook by the National Park Service (National Park Service, Undated)

John Brown's Holy War (2000)

The Secret Six by Edward J. Renehen (University of South Carolina, 1997)

Matewan

The Matewan Uprising

Matewan Shootout Site, Main and Mate Streets, Matewan, WV 25678

The right to unionize in the United States has been marked by many battles, and one of the biggest was the Matewan Uprising. In 1919 the United Mine Workers, under John L. Lewis, were trying to organize West Virginia's southern coal mines. They were being harassed by company goons and local law enforcement who were in the pockets of the mine owners, so Lewis called for a strike on November 1.

For the most part the owners crushed the union's efforts, with the exception of the mines in Mingo County, particularly around the town of Matewan. Mayor Cabell Testerman, police chief Sid Hatfield, and Mingo County sheriff George Blankenship backed the miners, and faithfully administered the laws that protected them. Then, in May 1920, the Stone Mountain Coal Company announced that employees who joined the union would be fired and evicted from their company-owned homes. On May 19, thirteen agents from the Baldwin-Felts detective agency showed up in Matewan and asked the mayor for permission to mount machine guns atop buildings around town . . . "to keep the peace" as they evicted miners . . . and offered Testerman a

$1,000 bribe. The mayor ignored the offer and told the group that if they tried to evict the miners they would be arrested themselves. After a tension-filled day, the mayor and Albert Felts met up in front of Chambers Hardware, across from the train station. Felts shot Testerman in cold blood, and in the ensuing shootout two miners and seven agents were killed. Testerman died on the way to the hospital.

Public sympathy was with the union, and membership surged. More mines came under strikes, and picketers blocked rail lines and vandalized property. Governor John Cornwell called for federal troops to keep the situation from further deteriorating, and for the most part they were successful. In July Sid Hatfield and 22 miners were charged with conspiracy to murder the Baldwin-Felts agents. Seven months later, a jury acquitted them all.

By spring West Virginia had a new governor, Ephraim Morgan, who was determined to quell the uprising; state police were ordered into Matewan and surrounding communities in May 1921, and pitched gunfights erupted everywhere. Morgan proclaimed martial law on the anniversary of the Matewan shootout, and replaced all local police sympathetic to the strikers. Several union-friendly newspapers were shut down. Hatfield was charged with criminal conspiracy, but when he showed up at the McDowell County Courthouse (90 Wyoming Street) in Welch on July 29, he was shot four times by Baldwin-Felts agents seeking revenge.

Hatfield's death spurred an armed protest march on the Capitol by 10,000 union members. The governor called in state police and local militias, and deputized mine supporters, who met the advancing union column at Blair Mountain, east of Logan. A gun battle raged for 10 days before the U.S. Army stepped in, and threatened to *bomb* the marchers from the air. Many of the strikers had fought in World War I, and were not interested in fighting it over again at home, and a cease-fire was negotiated. Retreating marchers were attacked, however, and violence flared up again. Tear gas and pipe bombs were eventually dropped on miners from three biplanes. A second cease-fire, starting September 4, held. The death toll from the uprising has been estimated between 20 and 50. Though the strikers' grievances were with mine owners, the uprising was spun as an attack on the government, and the unions suffered from the misplaced public outrage.

LEARN MORE

The Battle of Blair Mountain by Robert Shogan (Westview, 2004)

Thunder in the Mountains by Lon Savage (University of Pittsburgh, 1990)

Matewan (1987)

3
The South

★ Alabama ★ Arkansas ★

★ Florida ★ Georgia ★

★ Kentucky ★ Louisiana ★

★ Mississippi ★

★ North Carolina ★

★ South Carolina ★

★ Tennessee ★ Virginia ★

ALABAMA

Alabama was center stage for the three best-known battles of the civil rights movement: the Montgomery Bus Boycott, the Birmingham demonstrations, and the Selma to Montgomery March. Each saw thousands of nonviolent protesters facing seemingly insurmountable odds, and winning. But the odds were never as great as those faced by the Freedom Riders.

In 1960 the U.S. Supreme Court ruled that interstate bus facilities could not be segregated (see page 226). Southerners defied the decision, so a small group of CORE organizers came up with a plan to confront their intransigence: the Freedom Rides. Thirteen volunteers, trained in pacifism by James Farmer, would travel by bus through the South and enter segregated waiting areas at each stop.

The first group, six men including John Lewis of SNCC, left Washington, D.C., on May 4, 1961, for Fredericksburg, Virginia. By the time they arrived, the station's "White" and "Colored" signs had been removed. Other Virginia stations refused them service. When they reached Rock Hill, South Carolina, a mob assaulted Lewis and Al Bigelow as they tried to enter a waiting room.

On May 14, Klan members attacked the Freedom Riders at the Anniston, Alabama, Greyhound station. The riders retreated to the bus, which raced west out of town, chased by 50 cars. Six miles later the bus stopped as its slashed tires went flat. The driver fled and the mob threw a firebomb inside. As riders spilled out of the burning vehicle they were beaten again, before the Alabama state troopers arrived.

Meanwhile, a Trailways bus passed through Anniston carrying seven more Freedom Riders. Thugs boarded and clubbed the riders with baseball bats. The bus left town with the attackers still aboard. When it arrived in Birmingham, the police were absent as whites descended on the bus. Journalists trying to record the melee had their cameras stolen and smashed. Following the riot, the drivers refused to take the riders any farther. Stranded in a hostile town, the riders flew to New Orleans, their final destination.

If the thugs felt they'd won, it was short-lived. A second wave of Freedom Riders arrived on May 17, from the sit-in movement in Nashville. Though not part of the original group, they bought tickets when they heard about the Anniston firebombing. They were arrested when they arrived in Birmingham, and the next day a police convoy took seven back across the Tennessee border and abandoned them on a country road after dark. "We'll be back in Birmingham by the end of the day," rider Catherine Burks told Eugene "Bull" Connor before he drove off.

She was right. Friends rescued the seven . . . and drove them right back to Birmingham. Others joined them there. Now 21 strong, the riders boarded a Greyhound for Montgomery on May 20. Justice Department officials flanked the bus with 32 squad cars, but when the bus arrived at the Montgomery city limits, the promised police escort was nowhere to be found. The bus proceeded downtown where more than 1,000 locals appeared with bats, pipes, and chains, and attacked the riders, reporters, and federal authorities.

More volunteers appeared in Montgomery after seeing events unfold, and when two buses left Montgomery on May 24 there were 27 Freedom Riders aboard. The Alabama National Guard escorted the bus to the Mississippi border. When they reached Jackson they were arrested and charged with disturbing the peace. Refusing to pay the fines, they were jailed, some for as long as six weeks. Outside, hundreds of new Freedom Riders appeared on interstate buses and were also arrested, jamming the state's prisons.

Was it all worth it? You bet! Under public pressure the Interstate Commerce Commission issued regulations on September 22, 1961, desegregating interstate terminals, and forced bus companies and municipalities to comply.

> We felt we could count on the racists of the South to create a crisis so that the federal government would be compelled to enforce the law.
>
> —*James Farmer*

LEARN MORE
www.preserveala.org/greyhoundstation.aspx?sm=g_i
Freedom Riders by Raymond Arsenault (Oxford, 2006)
Walking with the Wind by John Lewis (Harcourt, 1998)

Birmingham

Dogs and Firehoses
Birmingham Civil Rights Institute, 520 16th Street North, Birmingham, AL 35203 · (205) 328-9696

By early 1963 little had changed in Birmingham regarding institutional segregation, and it was unlikely to unless the issue was addressed head-on. Civil rights leaders called for a citywide boycott of white-owned businesses to coincide with the Easter buying season. The boycott was supported by a series of marches, and on Palm Sunday, Public Safety Commissioner Eugene "Bull" Connor turned police dogs against protesters, to the horror of television viewers across the United States.

The marches continued, and on Good Friday, April 12, Martin Luther King Jr. and Ralph Abernathy were arrested and thrown in jail (501 Sixth Avenue South). Criticized by some religious leaders for "provoking" Connor, King wrote an open letter to those idle on the sidelines (see below).

With King and Abernathy behind bars, local youth responded to SCLC's Jim Bevel and Fred Shuttlesworth's call for action. On May 2 a thousand

Birmingham demonstrators, 1963

children and teens met at the Sixteenth Street Baptist Church, then marched downtown where they were arrested. The following day 1,500 kids repeated the march, but this time were met in Kelly Ingram Park (Fifth to Sixth Avenues, 15th to 16th Streets) by Connor's German shepherds and firehoses. News crews filmed the marchers being blown off their feet and mauled, galvanizing opinion against the segregationists. Seven days later Birmingham agreed to integrate its stores, hire black clerks, and establish a civil rights commission.

Today Kelly Ingram Park is a shrine to the movement, and contains statues of its leaders and children facing down Connor's forces. Adjacent to the park

"LETTER FROM BIRMINGHAM JAIL"

When Birmingham police jailed Martin Luther King Jr. and Ralph Abernathy on April 12, 1963, they probably thought they'd decapitated the movement. Yet four days later an essay from King appeared that rallied his followers. King had secretly penned "Letter from Birmingham Jail" in the margins of newspaper scraps that were then smuggled out of his cell by visitors; the pieces were reassembled by his aide, Wyatt Walker.

King's letter was a blistering indictment of those who claimed to support integration, yet stood on the sidelines during the struggle. "[T]he Negro's great stumbling block in the stride toward freedom is . . . the white moderate who is more devoted to 'order' than to justice; who prefers a negative peace which is the absence of tension to a positive peace which is the presence of justice," King wrote. His honest assessment shamed some into action, and inspired others.

King and Abernathy were eventually bailed out by Harry Belafonte. Today, "Letter from Birmingham Jail" is considered one of the key documents of the era.

LEARN MORE

Blessed Are the Peacemakers by J. Southern Bass (LSU, 2001)
Why We Can't Wait by Martin Luther King Jr. (Signet Classics, 2000)

you'll find the Sixteenth Street Baptist Church and the Birmingham Civil Rights Institute, which preserves the jail cell in which King and Abernathy were held.

LEARN MORE
www.bcri.org
Carry Me Home by Diane McWhorter (Touchstone, 2002)
But for Birmingham by Glenn T. Eskew (University of North Carolina, 1997)

Sixteenth Street Baptist Church
1530 Sixth Avenue North, Birmingham, AL 35203 · (205) 251-9402

On Sunday, September 15, 1963, four cowards tossed a bundle of 15 sticks of dynamite from a passing car at the Sixteenth Street Baptist Church. It landed under the church's front stairway. Inside, in the basement, choir members were preparing for services. The explosion killed four girls in the women's lounge: Cynthia Wesley, Carole Robertson, Addie Mae Collins, and Denise McNair. Wesley, Robertson, and Collins were 14 years old; McNair only 11. Twenty-four others were injured.

As with the year's earlier events in Kelly Ingram Park, the nation was horrified. Birmingham erupted in riots that left two more dead. But the bombing pushed even some local holdouts in the white community—albeit grudgingly—toward integration.

Four KKK suspects were immediately identified, but not until 1977 was anyone convicted for the murders. Robert Chambliss, a city employee known around town as "Dynamite Bob," was sentenced to life in prison. He died there in 1985. Two others, Thomas Blanton Jr. and Bobby Frank Cherry, received life sentences after trials in 2001 and 2002. Herman Cash, the final suspect, died in 1994 before ever being charged.

> **May men learn to replace bitterness and violence with love and understanding.**
> *—Memorial plaque at the Sixteenth Street Baptist Church*

LEARN MORE

Until Justice Rolls Down by Frank Sikora (Fire Ant, 2005)

Long Time Coming by Elizabeth H. Cobbs and Petric J. Smith (Crane Hill, 1994)

4 Little Girls (1997)

Hale County

Samuel Mockbee and the Rural Studio
Rural Studio, PO Box 278, Newbern, AL 36765 · (334) 624-4483

Samuel Mockbee never believed architecture was meant only for rich clients. The Auburn professor felt that, done right, architecture could address the economic, social, and civic needs of America's poorest communities, and he launched Rural Studio to make his vision a reality. In 1992 he and 12 students went to Hale County, Alabama, to see how they could put their skills to the best use, and to develop a professional social ethic in the process. He called the experiment "context based learning."

Rural Studio's first client was the Bryant family of Mason's Bend. Students developed fresh methods and styles while getting hands-on construction experience with recycled and nontraditional materials. The Bryant's home was built using stucco-encased hay bales, industrial Fiberglas roofing panels, salvaged wooden beams, and recycled highway signs.

The Bryant House became the prototype for future projects. Rural Studio would work through the county's Department of Human Resources to identify clients, not just families in need of housing but communities in need of public facilities. Each semester 15 second-year students would get hands-on training in Mockbee's "classroom of the community" building a home. Design teams would present plans to the client who had the last call as to what would be built. Meanwhile, 15 fifth-year students would be similarly engaged on a civic project, from community centers to sports facilities to boys and girls clubs.

In 2000 Mockbee received a MacArthur "genius grant" for his work. Though he died a year later from leukemia, his vision lives on and the work continues. The studio's

> Everybody wants the same thing, rich or poor . . . not only a warm, dry room, but a shelter for the soul.
>
> —*Samuel Mockbee*

finished works can be found throughout Hale County. While the homes are private property, visitors can easily find the public works, such as the Farmer's Market in Thomaston, the HERO Playground and Children's Center in Greensboro, the Mason's Bend Community Center, the Akron Pavilion, the Yancey Chapel in Sawyerville, and the Newbern Baseball Field.

LEARN MORE
www.cadc.auburn.edu/soa/rural-studio
Rural Studio by Andrea Oppenheimer Dean and Timothy Hursley (Princeton, 2002)

Marion

Coretta Scott King, Civil Rights Leader
Scott Home Site, County Road 29 North, Marion, AL 36756

Coretta Scott was born on a farm in rural Perry County, 12 miles north of Marion, on April 27, 1927, the second of three children of Obadiah and Bernice Scott. During Coretta's youth, the Scotts were attacked twice by arsonists, first burning her father's lumber mill, and then the family's home on Thanksgiving Day, 1942.

Scott graduated valedictorian from Marion's Lincoln High School, the country's only high school for African Americans. From there she attended Antioch College in Yellow Springs, Ohio, and then the New England Conservatory of Music in Boston, where she studied voice and violin. It was here that she met Martin Luther King Jr., who was working on his doctorate at Boston University. On June 18, 1953, they were married in Scott's hometown, and a year later King accepted his first position, as pastor of the Dexter Avenue Baptist Church in Montgomery (see page 159).

Coretta Scott King was her husband's closest confidant, and often put her own life in jeopardy. Three days after her husband's assassination, the day before his funeral, King marched in his place in Memphis to support striking garbage workers. Ten days later the strikers were offered a new contract.

Widowed with four children, King continued her civil rights activism. She was the driving force behind the creation of the Martin Luther King Jr. Center for Nonviolent Social Change in 1969, where she served as president until retiring in 1994. She was instrumental in getting King's birthday made a national holiday in 1986. And since 1970 her name has honored works of children's literature that promote tolerance; the Coretta Scott King Book Award is given annually by the American Library Association.

King died January 31, 2006, and was buried beside her husband in Atlanta (see page 183).

> Hate is too great a burden to bear. It injures the hater more than it injures the hated.
> —*Coretta Scott King*

LEARN MORE
www.ala.org/csk
www.mlkday.gov
Coretta by Octavia Vivian (Augsburg Fortress, 2006)
My Life with Martin Luther King Jr. by Coretta Scott King (Henry Holt, 1994)

Montgomery

Claudette Colvin, Mary Louise Smith, Jo Ann Gibson Robinson, and Rosa Parks
Rosa Parks Library and Museum, Troy State University Montgomery, 252 Montgomery Street, Montgomery, AL 36104 · (334) 241-8661

The story of the Montgomery bus boycott does not begin on December 1, 1955, the day Rosa Parks refused to give up her seat. It started on March 2, 1955, when 15-year-old Claudette Colvin boarded a bus in front of the Dexter Avenue Baptist Church (see page 159). When a white rider demanded she give up her seat she informed the driver that she was "just as good as any white person" and stayed put. Two policemen arrived, dragged Colvin off the bus, and arrested her. When she was found guilty of breaking the local segregation ordinance and sentenced to indefinite probation, many in the black community refused to ride the buses. The seeds of the boycott were planted.

On October 21 it happened again. Eighteen-year-old Mary Louise Smith was ordered to surrender her seat for a white woman. "I am not going to move out of my seat," Smith told the driver, "I am not going to move anywhere." She was arrested, jailed, and fined $9 for failure to obey a police officer. Jo Ann Gibson Robinson, president of the Women's Political Council (WPC), which had been advocating a boycott, ultimately decided Smith's case wasn't the best opportunity to launch the plan. That would come a month later.

Rosa Parks, a respected member of the community who had trained in nonviolence at the Highlander Folk School (see page 221), was arrested on December 1, and the WPC sprang into action. Parks had boarded the Cleveland Avenue bus across from the fountain in Court Square, and sat near the front. Two blocks north along Montgomery Street a white male passenger demanded her seat, and Parks refused. Driver James Blake called police and Parks was taken into custody. "People always say that I didn't give up my seat because I was tired, but that isn't true," Parks later reflected. "No, the only tired I was, was tired of giving in."

The next day Robinson and the WPC mimeographed thousands of flyers calling for a one-day boycott of city buses on Monday, December 5. Labor leader E. D. Nixon went to Martin Luther King Jr. and asked him to secure the support of other clergy. Initially reluctant, King agreed. Three days later the boycott was a success, and its organizers called a meeting that evening at the Holt Street Baptist Church (903 S. Holt Street). Those attending voted to continue the boycott until the city relented, and formed the Montgomery Improvement Association (MIA) to coordinate their efforts. (The story of the boycott continues below.)

The Rosa Parks Library and Museum recently opened on Montgomery Street at the bus stop where Parks was arrested.

> As we stand and sit here this evening and as we prepare ourselves for what lies ahead, let us go out with a grim and bold determination that we are going to stick together. We are going to work together.
> —Martin Luther King Jr., at the founding of the MIA, 1955

LEARN MORE

http://montgomery.troy.edu/rosaparks/museum

The Montgomery Bus Boycott and the Women Who Started It by Jo Ann Gibson Robinson (University of Tennessee, 1987)

Rosa Parks by Rosa Parks (Dial, 1992)

Rosa Parks by Douglas Brinkley (Viking, 2000)

Martin Luther King Jr. and the Montgomery Bus Boycott
Dexter Avenue King Memorial Baptist Church, 454 Dexter Avenue, Montgomery, AL 36104 · (334) 263-3970

In 1954 the Dexter Avenue Baptist Church hired a 25-year-old, fresh-out-of-divinity-school pastor from Georgia: Martin Luther King Jr. He arrived just weeks after the U.S. Supreme Court's *Brown* decision (see page 293). Following Rosa Parks's 1955 arrest, King was thrust into the leadership of the Montgomery Improvement Association (MIA), and its boycott of city buses.

King and others met stiff, violent opposition. Two months into the boycott, on January 30, 1956, the Kings' parsonage home (309 S. Jackson Street) was bombed. Standing in the rubble of the front porch he addressed a group of supporters who wanted to retaliate. "I did not start this boycott," he said. "If I am stopped it will not stop. . . . We must meet hate with love." Two day later E. D. Nixon's home was bombed.

Meanwhile, the city threw every legal obstacle it could at King and the MIA. Black cab drivers were threatened with fines if they charged any less than 45¢ a ride, so the MIA set up a "private taxi" service of sympathetic car owners to shuttle boycotters. In February King and 88 others were arrested for violating an old statute making it illegal to harm a business through a boycott. A month later King was found guilty of conspiracy and was sentenced to a $500 fine or a year in jail; he appealed, but lost a year later (after the boycott was over) and paid the fine.

The U.S. Supreme Court eventually ruled on the MIA's federal lawsuit, *Browder v. Gayle*, on November 13, 1955. In a 9–0 decision it declared segregated local public transportation illegal. The decision went into effect on December 21, the day the MIA called off its 13-month boycott.

Dexter Avenue King Memorial Baptist Church today

King continued on as Dexter Street's pastor until 1960, when he returned to Atlanta (see page 183). His former church still has an active congregation. Both the church and the parsonage are open for tours, by appointment.

LEARN MORE

www.dexterkingmemorial.org

Stride Toward Freedom by Martin Luther King Jr. (Harper & Row, 1958)

The Thunder of Angels by Donnie Williams and Wayne Greenshaw (Lawrence Hill, 2006)

Daybreak of Freedom by Stewart Burns, ed. (University of North Carolina, 1997)

National Civil Rights Memorial
Southern Poverty Law Center, 400 Washington Avenue, Montgomery, AL 36104 · (334) 956-8200

Forty individuals who lost their lives during the civil rights struggles of the 1950s and '60s have been memorialized outside the Southern Poverty Law Center (SPLC) in Montgomery. Designed by Maya Lin (creator of the Vietnam Memorial), the National Civil Rights Memorial invokes a paraphrase from the Book of Amos often used by Martin Luther King Jr.: ". . . until justice rolls down like waters and righteousness like a mighty stream." Water rises from the center of a circular, black granite table and flows outward over names and events etched into the surface as a time line. While the memorial only marks events occurring between the 1954 *Brown v. Board of Education* decision and King's 1968 assassination, it is intended to encourage continued dedication to combating prejudice, racism, and violence. For the last four decades, the SPLC has been at the forefront of that struggle.

The SPLC was founded in 1971 by Morris Dees and Joseph Levin, and from the beginning has relentlessly pursued the KKK, the Aryan Nations, and other hate groups in court. By winning legal settlements against these terrorist organizations, the SPLC has forced many to liquidate their assets, effectively shutting down their operations (see page 358). It also launched the Klanwatch Project in 1979 to monitor the activities of the KKK and other right-wing hate groups. (It has since been renamed the Intelligence Project, and publishes a quarterly report for law enforcement and SPLC supporters.) It also provides free material to educators on diversity through its popular quarterly journal *Teaching Tolerance.*

National Civil Rights Memorial

LEARN MORE

www.splcenter.org

Free at Last by Sara Bullard (Oxford, 1993)

A Time for Justice by Morris Dees and Steve Fiffer (Charles Scribner's Sons, 1991)

Selma

SNCC's Voter Education Project

National Voting Rights Museum & Institute, 1012 Water Avenue, Selma, AL 36702 ·
(334) 418-0800

Even measured against other Southern communities, Selma and surrounding
Dallas County stood out as a segregationist stronghold. In early 1963 only 335
African Americans were registered to vote in Dallas County, about one percent
of its eligible black population. So the Student Nonviolent Coordinating Committee (SNCC) planned a campaign—the Voter Education Project—aimed
at registering disenfranchised citizens and challenging segregated facilities,

starting in February 1963. The group met with harassment and violence from the white Selma establishment, and Sheriff James Clark led the assault.

After months of grassroots organizing, SNCC called for the first Freedom Day on October 7, 1963. About 350 citizens lined up outside the Dallas County Courthouse (105 Lauderdale Street) to register. As clerks dragged

THE SELMA TO MONTGOMERY MARCH

The Selma to Montgomery March took five days and covered roughly 54 miles. About 3,000 marchers stepped off from the Brown Chapel A.M.E. Church (410 Martin Luther King Jr. Street) on Sunday, March 21. Leading the group was Martin Luther and Coretta Scott King, UN diplomat Ralph Bunche, John Lewis, Andrew Young, Ralph Abernathy, A. Philip Randolph, and Cager Lee, among others. They walked south on Sylvan Street, turned right on Selma Avenue, and then left onto Broad Street, which led out of Selma over the Edmund Pettus Bridge.

The marchers covered seven miles on U.S. Route 80 before stopping for the night at the farm of David and Rosa Belle Hall, near Casey. On the second day they walked 17 miles through Lowndes County, a KKK stronghold where not a single African American was on the voter roles, and camped on the property of Rose Steele, a 70-year-old Whitehall store owner. On the third day they made it 11 more miles and rested at the Gardner family farm near Mt. Sinai.

The final night's campsite was in suburban Montgomery at the City of St. Jude (2048 W. Fairview Avenue), an integrated Catholic church, school, and hospital complex. That night marchers enjoyed a rally and concert, which included Harry Belafonte, Joan Baez, Sammy Davis Jr., Anthony Perkins, Dick Gregory, Leonard Bernstein, and Peter, Paul, and Mary.

The next morning 25,000 walked the last four miles to the Alabama statehouse (600 Dexter Avenue), stopping at the same point where Jefferson Davis's inaugural parade came to an end. There, in front of the first capitol of the Confederacy, King observed, "They said we would not get here, but we are here, and we are not going to let anyone turn us around."

Today the 1965 march route has been designated the Selma to Montgomery National Historic Trail (www.nps.gov/semo).

their feet indoors, forcing applicants to take ridiculously complex qualification tests, Clark's officers beat and arrested SNCC volunteers who tried to provide food and water to those waiting for hours outside.

SNCC's campaign slogged on for another year before the Southern Christian Leadership Conference (SCLC) joined the fight in January 1965. As the campaign grew, so did the backlash. In nearby Marion, on February 18, Jimmie Lee Jackson was shot while protecting his 82-year-old grandfather, Cager Lee, from a police beating. The 26-year-old died a week later. Four thousand mourners showed up for Jackson's funeral, and demanded action.

SNCC would go directly to Governor George Wallace. The original plan was to bring Jackson's casket to the steps of the state capitol. Instead, SNCC announced a march from Selma to Montgomery. On Sunday, March 7, a group of 600, led by SNCC's John Lewis and SCLC's Hosea Williams, left Brown Chapel A.M.E. Church heading for U.S. Route 80. But after they crossed the Edmund Pettus Bridge at the south end of town, they met Sheriff Clark, his deputies, and 50 Alabama state troopers. The police attacked the marchers with clubs, horses, whips, and tear gas, and drove them back across the bridge. John Lewis suffered a fractured skull. The event became known as "Bloody Sunday."

The marchers refused to give up. Hundreds came from around the country to participate in a new march. Two days later 2,000 marchers, led by Martin Luther King Jr., crossed the bridge and came up against Clark's forces. They stopped, knelt, and prayed . . . then turned around and returned to Brown Chapel. That evening a gang of four white men beat Reverend James Reeb and two other ministers from the march; Reeb died two days later.

At the time some questioned King's tactics, but behind the scenes King was working to force the hand of the president. On March 15 Lyndon Johnson addressed a joint session of Congress and urged passage of the 1965 Voting Rights Act. To the shock of the South (and most of the North, too), Johnson ended his speech by proclaiming "we shall overcome."

Organizers had not given up on their plans. On March 21, the fifth anniversary of South Africa's Sharpeville Massacre, more than 3,000 protesters left for Selma (see page 162). A federal judge had ruled a week

> The law is clear that the right to petition one's government for the redress of grievances may be exercised in large groups . . . and these rights may be exercised by marching, even along public highways.
>
> —Judge Frank Johnson Jr.,
> allowing the Selma
> to Montgomery March
> to proceed, 1965

earlier that they had the right to march on a public highway, and that the state could not stop them. By the time they arrived their numbers had swelled to 25,000. And on August 6, Lyndon Johnson signed the 1965 Voting Rights Act into law. By 1975, 60 percent of the eligible African Americans in Dallas County were registered to vote.

Artifacts from the SNCC campaign and march have been collected in the new National Voting Rights Museum & Institute, located near Selma's Edmund Pettus Bridge in a storefront once occupied by the racist White Citizens Council. You'll see logbooks from the emergency room at Good Samaritan Hospital, where many of the injured were treated, the clothes worn by King during the march, and photos of the events.

LEARN MORE
http://selmavotingrightsmuseum.org
Selma 1965 by Charles E. Fager (Beacon, 1985)
Selma, Lord, Selma by Sheyann Webb and Rachel West Nelson (University of
   Alabama, 1980)

Tuscumbia

Helen Keller, Committed Socialist
Ivy Green, 300 W. North Commons, Tuscumbia, AL 35674 · (256) 383-4066

The story of Helen Keller's life is usually told in one of two ways. The first narrative focuses on her struggle to overcome her physical disabilities, and the second underscores her passionate advocacy for socialism, women's suffrage, civil rights, universal education, nuclear disarmament, and birth control. Guess which story is told more often?

Keller was born in Tuscumbia on June 27, 1880. At the age of 19 months she was left blind and deaf by typhoid fever. As Keller grew older she began lashing out at everyone around her, so her parents hired Anne Sullivan, who had been trained in deaf education (see page 31), to try to communicate with her . . . or at the very least teach her some manners. Less than a month after arriving, Keller and Sullivan were at the well, Sullivan tapping out the word W-A-T-E-R on Keller's palm, when Helen suddenly made the mental connection between the word and the object. Within an hour, Keller had a vocabulary of 30 words. Keller would call that March 1887 day her "soul's birthday."

That day is also when most Keller histories abruptly end; the final curtain in William Gibson's *The Miracle Worker* drops at the well. Yet in 1909 she joined the Socialist Party, and supported labor strikes called by the IWW. In 1913 she declared herself a "militant suffragette" and endorsed the birth control efforts of Margaret Sanger (see page 97). Keller protested the militarism of World War I, and in 1916 burned personal bridges to her Alabama family and friends by publicly donating to the NAACP. And when a labor dispute arose between the crew and studio on a film about her life, *Deliverance*, Keller threatened to boycott the premiere. The studio then offered an acceptable contract.

Helen Keller and Anne Sullivan, 1897

Keller was a founding member of the ACLU, though you'll not likely hear about that on the tour at Ivy Green, her birthplace—so be sure to ask. She also kept a red flag beside her writing desk, but that too is suspiciously absent today. In 1964 Keller was awarded the Presidential Medal of Freedom. She died on June 1, 1968, and was buried beside Anne Sullivan in Washington, D.C. (Washington National Cathedral Cemetery, 3101 Wisconsin Avenue NW).

> So long as I confine my activities to social service and the blind, [the newspapers] compliment me extravagantly, calling me an "arch-priest of the sightless," "wonder woman," and "a modern miracle." But when it comes to a discussion of poverty and the industrial system under which we live, that is a different matter.
>
> —*Helen Keller*

LEARN MORE

www.helenkellerbirthplace.org

The Story of My Life by Helen Keller (The Modern Library, 2003)

The Radical Lives of Helen Keller by Kim E. Nielsen (NYU, 2004)

Helen Keller by John Davis, ed. (Ocean Press, 2003)

ARKANSAS

Though Arkansas can claim a number of progressive sons and daughters, any fair assessment of its most famous citizen, Bill Clinton, would have to conclude he was many things—a more than capable administrator and a skilled, perhaps brilliant, politician—but he was only mildly progressive. Never forget that he signed NAFTA, the 1996 Telecommunications Act, and the 1996 Defense of Marriage Act. And on most issues during his administration, he came down on the side of neither the left nor the right, but on the side of corporate America.

You want Arkansas progressives? Try Daisy and L. C. Bates, or the Little Rock Nine. Or Adolphine Fletcher Terry. Or Susan Epperson. They didn't practice Clintonian "triangulation," just determined courage under unimaginable pressure.

Jonesboro

Hattie Caraway, America's First Elected Woman Senator
Caraway House (torn down), 208 Warner Avenue, Jonesboro, AR 72401

When Senator Thaddeus Caraway died in office in 1931, his wife, Hattie, was appointed to fill out his term, as was the political tradition. However, near the end of her short tenure Carraway announced that she would run for reelection in 1932, and won, making her the first woman elected to the U.S. Senate for a full term. Caraway championed rural Arkansas farmers, and was a close ally of Huey Long. She was also a champion of the New Deal, and it was she who seconded Franklin Roosevelt's nomination at the 1936 Democratic National Convention.

The voters returned Caraway to office in 1938, where in 1943 she co-sponsored the Equal Rights Amendment. Unfortunately, Caraway did not support growing calls for racial integration. She was defeated for a third term in 1944 by J. William Fulbright.

> I have observed the Farm Board members testifying before the Senate Agriculture Committee, and they did not know how many elevators and warehouses the Farm Board was operating, but they always had perfectly manicured fingernails.
> —*Hattie Caraway*

LEARN MORE
Silent Hattie Speaks by H. C. and Diane D. Kincaid, ed. (Greenwood, 1979)

Little Rock

Daisy Bates and the Little Rock Nine
Central High School National Historic Site, 2125 W. Daisy L. Gatson Bates Drive (14th Street), Little Rock, AR 72202 · (501) 374-1957

When Minnijean Brown, Elizabeth Eckford, Ernest Green, Thelma Mothershed, Melba Pattillo, Gloria Ray, Terrance Roberts, Jefferson Thomas, and Carlotta Walls—the Little Rock Nine—entered Central High on September 25, 1957, it was the first "saddle shoes on the ground" battle to end official segregation in the United States. In 1954 the U.S. Supreme Court ruled in *Brown v. Board of Education* (see page 293) that all public schools should be integrated "with all deliberate speed," but by 1957 very few districts in the South had done so.

Originally 75 black students had applied for enrollment to Central High, but by the fall only nine remained on the list. The effort was spearheaded by Daisy Bates, president of the Arkansas NAACP and wife of L. C. Bates, publisher of the Arkansas *State Press*. Both the mayor of Little Rock and the city's school board *supported* the plan to integrate Central High. Their mistake was implementing its schedule too slowly; it allowed opposition forces to rally their troops, and soon Governor Orval Faubus warned that "blood would run in the streets" if African American students were allowed entry.

Central High today

Faubus called out the Arkansas National Guard to block the Little Rock Nine from entering on opening day, September 3. A cadre of white bigots calling themselves the Mothers' League sang "Dixie" on the school steps while the Nine waited at the Bates's home (1207 W. 28th Street). Then, due to a miscommunication, Elizabeth Eckford attempted to walk to school the following morning. White protesters spat at her, and a photographer caught a shot of Eckford bravely passing a young woman who was screaming racial epithets. The mob and the National Guard kept the Nine away until a judge ruled on September 20 that they were to be allowed entry. On September 23 they tried, and a riot broke out in the school hallways. The Nine fled to avoid being lynched.

That was it. The national outcry over the chaos in Little Rock forced the hand of a reluctant president. Dwight Eisenhower issued Executive Order 10730, commanding the 101st Airborne and the federalized Arkansas National Guard to secure the area around Central High. Two days later, on September 25, the Little Rock Nine entered for good.

Minnijean Brown would leave Central High before the end of the year, suspended after being provoked into a fight in the cafeteria. But later that spring, Ernest Green walked across the stage at Central High and accepted his

THE WOMEN'S EMERGENCY COMMITTEE TO OPEN OUR SCHOOLS

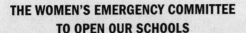

When Orval Faubus closed the Little Rock schools in 1958, local philanthropist Adolphine Fletcher Terry sprang into action. Terry opposed segregation, but had not gotten deeply involved in the issue until the crisis erupted. "I see that the men have failed again," she announced "I'll have to send for the ladies." And she did, with two friends, organizing the Women's Emergency Committee to Open Our Schools. In its five years of operation, WECOOS was instrumental in the recall and defeat of segregationist school board members and other politicians who the women felt were standing in the way of progress on civil rights. Terry was also an advocate for new low-income housing and tuberculosis eradication campaigns in Arkansas.

 LEARN MORE

Breaking the Silence by Sara Alderman Murphy (University of Arkansas, 1997)

diploma in front of a silent audience, to become the first African American to graduate from Central High.

Faubus shut down the Little Rock schools in 1958 as a last-ditch gambit. The superintendent and 44 white teachers protested, and were fired for insubordination. And then, in an ironic turn, local parents organized a recall election and ousted three segregationist school board members. Central High reopened in the fall of 1958.

The Little Rock Nine won the Battle of Little Rock, but the war was far from over. Little Rock's elementary schools did not integrate until much later: 1968. The Little Rock Nine were each awarded the Congressional Gold Medal of Honor in 1999.

 LEARN MORE

www.nps.gov/chsc

www.centralhigh57.org

The Long Shadow of Little Rock by Daisy Bates (University of Arkansas, 1986)

Daisy Bates by Grif Stockley (University Press of Mississippi, 2005)

Warriors Don't Cry by Melba Pattillo Beals (Pocket, 1994)

Epperson v. Arkansas: Schools May Teach Evolution
Central High School, 2125 W. Daisy L. Gatson Bates Drive, Little Rock, AR 72202

In the aftermath of the Scopes Monkey Trial (see page 216), the Arkansas legislature passed an antievolution statute in 1928. It forbade educators from discussing evolution or adopting textbooks that did the same. But since the constitutionality of Tennessee's Butler Act was never determined, Arkansas's law stood on questionable footing. Then, in 1965, biology teacher Susan Epperson, backed by the Arkansas Education Association, deliberately violated the statute by using a copy of *Modern Biology* in her Central High classroom. She simultaneously filed suit in Pulaski County Chancery Court to overturn the law on First Amendment grounds.

Epperson won her original case, but it was overturned by the Arkansas Supreme Court two years later. The U.S. Supreme Court, however, unanimously struck down the Arkansas law on November 12, 1968, citing the Establishment Clause.

That might have been the end of it, had not Ronald Reagan been elected president in 1980 with strong evangelical support. Emboldened, the religious right pushed an "equal time" law through the Arkansas legislature. It forced teachers to teach creationism alongside evolution. The ACLU filed suit, and was able to get several local ministers to act as *plaintiffs*. The Arkansas attorney general tried to recruit credible scientists to testify for the defense, but failed. A federal judge declared the law unconstitutional in 1982.

> Government in our democracy, state and national, must be neutral in matters of religious theory, doctrine, and practice. It may not be hostile to any religion or the advocacy of no-religion; and it may not aid, foster, or promote one religion or religious theory against another.
> *—Justice Abe Fortas, in* **Epperson v. Arkansas,** *1968*

FLORIDA

If progressives had grown complacent during the 1990s, they got a rude awakening during the 36-day fiasco surrounding the 2000 presidential vote count in Florida. Few realized until it was too late that the Bush campaign had developed a plan to ensure that the state was delivered to his column. It certainly helped that Jeb Bush was governor and Katherine Harris, co-chairperson of Florida's Bush for President campaign, was secretary of state. In 1999 she hired ChoicePoint Database Technologies (out of Texas) to "scrub" names of potential felons from voter lists, and told them they only needed to exceed an "80 percent match" on its names lists in order to remove them from the roles. More than 57,000 residents, disproportionately black and Latino, lost their right to vote for no other reason than their names were 80-something percent similar to a known felon . . . in another state.

But that was just the tip of the conspiracy. Read any of the books below and ask yourself why people weren't thrown in jail. Vote tampering, funneling state funds to GOP campaign events, misusing elected offices for partisan purposes, "re-creating" ballots, physical intimidation of poll judges, and more. Virtually every documented "irregularity" worked in the favor of George W. Bush. Funny, that. When journalist Greg Palast later questioned the Florida Department of Elections director Clayton Roberts about improprieties in the 2000 election, Robert tore off his mike and mumbled, "Ya know, if y'all want to hang this on me that's fine," and ran off.

> Although we may never know with complete certainty the identity of the winner of this year's presidential election, the identity of the loser is perfectly clear. It is the nation's confidence in the judge as an impartial guardian of the rule of law.
> —Justice John Paul Stevens, in his Bush v. Gore dissent, 2000

Still, the greatest injustice was perpetrated by the U.S. Supreme Court when five Republican-appointed justices ordered the Florida recount stopped with Bush 537 votes ahead of Gore. Constitutional scholars have generally agreed that the decision was one of the most egregious abuses of judicial power in American history.

So while it is difficult for modern progressives to think of Florida without gritting their teeth, there are several bright stories to come from the Sunshine State. Read on.

LEARN MORE

Jews for Buchanan by John Nichols and David Deschamps (New Press, 2001)
The Best Democracy Money Can Buy by Greg Palast (Plume, 2002)
Down & Dirty by Jake Tapper (Little, Brown and Company, 2001)
The Betrayal of America by Vincent Bugliosi (Nation Books, 2001)

Belle Glade

Harvest of Shame
Migrant Parking Lot, Fifth Street and SW Avenue D, Belle Glade, FL 33430

On Thanksgiving Day 1960 the American public, already stuffed with turkey, sat down in front of their televisions for a final course: a heaping helping of guilt. That night CBS broadcast Edward R. Murrow's *Harvest of Shame*, a blistering exposé on the lives and working conditions suffered by the nation's migrant workforce. The documentary started and ended in a Belle Glade parking lot, where picking crews gathered to begin their six-month trek northward, following the harvest.

At the time migrants earned, on average, $900 per year, and without permanent addresses they were ineligible for unemployment, welfare, health, or education benefits for their children. "We used to own our slaves," a farmer told Murrow, "Now we just rent them."

Harvest of Shame led to new federal protections for migrant workers, including the extension of child

> Is it possible to have love without justice? Is it possible that we think too much in terms of charity, in terms of Thanksgiving Day baskets, in terms of Christmas baskets, and not in terms enough of eliminating poverty?
>
> —*Rev. Julian Griggs*, in
> Harvest of Shame, *1960*

labor laws to the agricultural sector, workman's compensation, and some regulation of crew leaders and workplace conditions. The first minimum wage for migrant workers was established in 1966.

 **LEARN MORE**
Harvest of Shame (1960)

Daytona Beach
Mary McLeod Bethune, Educator
Mary McLeod Bethune Home, Bethune-Cookman College, 640 Mary McLeod Bethune Boulevard, Daytona Beach, FL 32114 · (386) 481-2000

Mary McLeod was born on July 10, 1875, five miles north of Mayesville, South Carolina. She attended the Mayesville Mission School near her home, a rare opportunity for the daughter of former slaves. She excelled in her studies, and eventually went on to Barber–Scotia Seminary in North Carolina and Moody Bible Institute in Chicago. Following college, she taught in several southern schools for African Americans, and met and married Albertus Bethune in Sumter, South Carolina, in 1898. They later had one son, Albert, but she had to raise him alone; Albertus died in 1904.

Following her husband's death, Bethune moved to Florida and opened the Daytona Normal and Industrial Training School for Negro Girls. At the time she had $1.50 to her name. Her first class on October 3, 1904, consisted of five girls and her son in a ramshackle cabin, but through Bethune's boundless energy and talent for fundraising, the school grew. Students sold ice cream and sweet potato pies to railroad crews and raised enough money to buy the adjacent city dump, on which the school expanded. In 1923 Bethune merged her school with Jacksonville's Cookman Institute for Boys, which in 1931 became a junior college with a new name: Bethune–Cookman College. Ten years later it became a fully accredited four-year college.

Bethune became a sought-after advisor for several U.S. presidents. Herbert Hoover appointed her to the White House Council on Child Health in 1930. She was a close friend of Eleanor Roosevelt, and advised FDR's administration on the abolition of the poll tax, expanding voting rights, and enacting federal antilynching legislation. In 1936 FDR named her the director of the Division of Negro Affairs at the National Youth Administration, a year after she founded the National Council of Negro Women (NCNW). She also counseled Harry Truman on civil rights and education matters, and acted as his personal representative at inauguration ceremonies in Liberia.

Bethune lived in Washington, D.C., at Council House (1318 Vermont Avenue NW) from 1943 to 1955, the year she died. (Bethune is buried on the Bethune–Cookman campus.) Today the house is a museum dedicated to her memory and the contributions of African American women to this nation. A statue of Bethune stands in Lincoln Park (13th and East Capitol Street NE). When it was erected in 1974, it was the first monument to a black woman erected in a public park in the nation's capital.

> I leave you love. I leave you hope. I leave you the challenge in developing confidence in one another. I leave you a thirst for education. I leave you respect for the use of power. I leave you faith. I leave you racial dignity.
> —*Mary McLeod Bethune, in her will, 1955*

LEARN MORE
www.bethune.cookman.edu
DC Home, www.nps.gov/mamc, (202) 673-2402
NCNW, www.ncnw.org, (202) 737-0120
Mary McLeod Bethune by Earl Devine Martin (Xlibris, 2004)

Immokalee

The Coalition of Immokalee Workers
PO Box 603, Immokalee, FL 34143 · (239) 657-8311

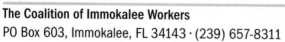

The history of the Coalition of Immokalee Workers (CIW) is not one of David and Goliath, but David and a half-dozen Goliaths . . . and counting. Few expected the migrant farmworkers of southwest Florida to become such a powerful labor force when they organized in 1993. Yet in little more than a decade these 2,500 Mexican, Guatemalan, and Haitian immigrants have racked up an impressive list of victories.

The struggle hasn't been easy. It took three general strikes, a 230-mile march, and a month-long hunger strike for the CIW to earn wage concessions from tomato growers in 1998. The group also rescued more than 1,200 pickers from "debt bondage" through its late-1990s Anti-Slavery Campaign. (Yes, there still is slavery in America.) Three local crewleaders eventually served time in federal prison for immigrant smuggling.

Then, in 2001, the CIW took on one of the nation's largest fast food companies: Taco Bell. The "Boot the Bell" campaign consisted of a 50-state boycott, hunger strikes, and nonviolent actions in Kentucky and California. Taco Bell eventually acquiesced in March 2005 and pledged to use its considerable corporate muscle to improve wages and working conditions among its suppliers.

Did the CIW stop there? Nope—they turned their sights on the golden arches. This time it took McDonald's just two years to see the light, agreeing in April 2007 to raise the price it paid for tomatoes by 1¢ a pound and monitor its suppliers for abuses.

And Burger King's next.

LEARN MORE
www.ciw-online.org

Panama City

Gideon v. Wainwright: **The Right to Counsel**
Bay Harbor Poolroom (torn down), 109 N. Everitt Avenue, Panama City, FL 32401

One of the fundamental rights afforded you under America's modern judicial system is your right, under the Sixth Amendment, to be represented by a lawyer in a court of law. But you can thank a 51-year-old drifter, railroaded four decades ago in Panama City, for making this right more than a vague promise.

Clarence Earl Gideon was accused of burglarizing the Bay Harbor Poolroom on June 3, 1961, stealing money from the cigarette machine and jukebox. Because Gideon was not charged in a capital case, and because he was poor, he was forced to defend himself in court.

The state's case hinged on the "eyewitness" testimony of Henry Cook. Gideon did not explore contradictory statements made by his accuser on the stand, and failed to uncover evidence pointing to Cook's questionable motives. As a result, Gideon was found guilty and sentenced to five years in prison.

But Gideon didn't accept his verdict. He applied for a writ of habeas corpus to the Florida Supreme Court, saying he had been illegally imprisoned. The court rejected it. He went over the court's head and filed a writ of certiorari with the U.S. Supreme Court. Amazingly, the justices decided to hear his case. This time *Gideon v. Wainwright* was argued by Abe Fortas (who would later be named to the high court). On March 18, 1963, the justices ruled 9–0 that Gideon was entitled to a new trial, but this time with a lawyer.

> Lawyers in criminal courts are necessities, not luxuries.
> —Justice Hugo Black, in
> Gideon v. Wainwright, *1963*

The second time Gideon was tried in Panama City, Cook's testimony fell apart under cross-examination. Gideon wasn't the only victor when the jury declared him not guilty on August 5, 1963; the judicial system was a winner as well.

LEARN MORE
Gideon's Trumpet by Anthony Lewis (Vintage, 1989)

Vero Beach

Pelican Island, the First National Wildlife Refuge
Pelican Island NWR, 1339 20th Street, Vero Beach, FL 32960 · (772) 562-3909, extension 275

Back in the Victorian Era, the greatest threat to wild birds wasn't pesticides or development, but fashion. Haberdashers were using exotic plume feathers to adorn women's hats, and pushing many species to the brink of extinction. Ornithologist Frank Chapman believed that if the government didn't set aside land for bird sanctuaries, many species could disappear altogether.

While conducting a survey of habitats, Chapman learned that a five-acre mangrove island near Sebastian was the last brown pelican rookery on the east coast of Florida, and thought it a perfect candidate to suggest for protection. He and conservationist William Dutcher approached Theodore Roosevelt who, on March 14, 1903, signed an executive order making Pelican Island a federal bird reservation. It would be the first of 55 such sanctuaries (later known as National Wildlife Refuges) set aside by the president.

German immigrant Paul Kroegel was named the refuge's first manager and was paid $1 a month by the Florida Audubon Society. He had been trying to protect the birds of Pelican Island for years on his own, chasing off poachers at the point of a gun. Kroegel continued in the post until his retirement in 1923.

In 1968 the refuge was expanded to include 4,760 acres of surrounding islands and submerged land along the Indian River Lagoon north of Vero Beach. Pelican Island has also been named a National Historic Landmark for its place in conservation history.

LEARN MORE
www.fws.gov/pelicanisland/

GEORGIA

In the waning days of the Civil War, Georgia was the site of a truly progressive idea: reparations for the victims of slavery. On January 12, 1865, General William Sherman met with 20 freed African American leaders at his field headquarters in the Green–Meldrim House (14 W. Macon Street) in Savannah. The men asked that all former slave families be given a plot of land on which to start their new lives. That meeting led to Special Field Order 15, issued four days later.

The field order was first announced at a meeting at the Second African Baptist Church (127 Houston Street). The federal government had seized 400,000 acres of land along the coast stretching from Charleston, South Carolina, to Florida's St. John's River—rice plantations, mostly. Former slaves and white Southern Unionists could apply with the newly formed Bureau of Refugees, Freedmen, and Abandoned Lands—the Freedmen's Bureau—for title to 40-acre plots. They could also borrow a mule from the army to help establish their farms. Though 40,000 refugees settled on land set aside by the order, the federal government, on Andrew Johnson's orders, reneged on the plan and turned the land back over to the original plantation owners.

It's impossible to say whether African Americans in the South could have avoided endemic rural poverty had the plan been allowed to continue. But the sharecropping system that arose instead—de facto slavery—certainly perpetuated a social, racial, and economic caste system that haunts America today.

LEARN MORE
Reparations by Boris I. Bittker (Beacon, 2003)
The Debt by Randall Robinson (Dutton, 2000)

Americus

Koinonia Farm and Habitat for Humanity
121 Habitat Street, Americus, GA 31709 · (800) HABITAT

Koinonia Farm was founded near Americus in 1942 by Clarence Jordan. A recent graduate of Southern Baptist Seminary, Jordan and several others were looking to live out what they felt were the true messages of the gospels: social justice, pacifism, and community, regardless of race. For this, the Koinonians were verbally and physically threatened, and shot at after dark, yet they persevered.

In 1965 Millard Fuller, a self-made millionaire who had recently divested himself of his worldly belongings, found Koinonia. Three years later he moved his family to Georgia to work with the poor. Here, in 1969, Fuller and Jordan developed the idea of "partnership housing" where families needing homes would work side-by-side with volunteers (building "sweat equity") constructing their new homes. The homes would then be sold to the families at cost, interest free, and the mortgage payments would be funneled back to a revolving fund to be used for new projects. Bo and Emma Johnson of Americus became the first homeowners in 1969, and paid off the last of the loan in 1990.

Millard and Linda Fuller wanted to see if partnership housing would work in developing nations, so in 1973 they moved their family to Zaire. The project was so successful they returned to the states three years later and founded Habitat for Humanity. The organization gained a powerful spokesperson, and worker, in Jimmy Carter in 1984. To date, Habitat for Humanity has built more than 100,000 homes worldwide, and counting. Millard Fuller was presented the Presidential Medal of Freedom in 1996.

> What the poor need is not charity but capital, not caseworkers but co-workers. And what the rich need is a wise, honorable, just way of divesting themselves of their overabundance.
> —*Clarence Jordan*

LEARN MORE
www.habitat.org
www.koinoniapartners.org, (229) 924-0391
Cotton Patch for the Kingdom by Ann Louise Coble (Herald, 2001)
Interracialism and Christian Community in the Postwar South by Tracy Elaine K'Meyer (University of Virginia, 1997)
One Family at a Time by Habitat for Humanity (Habitat for Humanity, 2001)
Briars in the Cotton Patch (2003)

Athens

Birthplace of the American Garden Club
Lumpkin House, 973 Prince Avenue, Athens, GA 30606

In January 1891 a dozen women gathered at the home of Mary Lumpkin to form what would become the first garden club in the United States. The Ladies' Garden Club of Athens started by inviting horticulturalists to speak to the group, and a year later held its first flower and vegetable show. Though started by local socialites, the group was soon open to "every lady in Athens who might be interested in growing anything, from a cabbage to a chrysanthemum."

The spirit of the original club never died, and neither has its original garden. The Founders' Memorial Gardens (325 S. Lumpkin Street) is maintained by the Garden Club of Georgia, the descendant of the original Athens club, whose office stands adjacent to the gardens.

LEARN MORE
www.uga.edu/gardenclub/

Integration of the University of Georgia
University of Georgia, Holmes Hunter Academic Building, Broad Street at College Avenue, Athens, GA 30602

Though the integration of the universities of Alabama and Mississippi are better known, the *first* major victory in the battle for open higher education in the deep South was won at the University of Georgia. After two years of legal wrangling, Charlayne Hunter and Hamilton Holmes registered for classes on January 9, 1961, becoming the first African American students in the school's 176-year history. They were escorted by their lawyer, Vernon Jordan, who would go on to lead the Urban League.

The Athens campus erupted in two days of riots that included cross burnings, death threats, and a 2,000-person mob descending on Hunter's dormitory. Both Hunter and Holmes were suspended "for their own good," but returned once order was established. Hunter graduated in 1963 and went on to a distinguished career in journalism, including several years on PBS's *The News Hour,* and later as South Africa Bureau Chief for CNN. Holmes graduated the same year as Hunter and went on to medical school; the Atlanta orthopedic surgeon died in 1995. On the 40th anniversary of the school's integration, the university renamed the building in which the pair registered the Holmes Hunter Academic Building.

LEARN MORE

In My Place by Charlayne Hunter Gault (Farrar, Straus and Giroux, 1992)

UNIVERSITY INTEGRATION BATTLES

In the eyes of most white Southerners, the integration of the University of Georgia was hardly a precedent for college doors to swing open to everyone, regardless of race. Most universities witnessed their own versions of the struggle in Athens during the early 1960s.

It took 30,000 federalized troops and U.S. marshals to get air force veteran James Meredith into the University of Mississippi in Oxford in the fall of 1962. During the violence surrounding his entry, fanned by Governor Ross Barnett, snipers murdered a newsman and a bystander. The final standoff between state and federal officials took place in front of Lyceum Hall, where Meredith was allowed to enter and register on October 1. Soldiers had to guard Meredith for the remainder of the year.

The following summer another showdown took place at the University of Alabama in Tuscaloosa. On June 11, 1963, Governor George Wallace stood in the doorway of Foster Auditorium to block the entry of James Hood and Vivian Malone. Wallace had claimed he would rather have a "barbed-wire enema" than see African Americans admitted to the university. When federal agents led by Nicholas Katzenbach, number two at Kennedy's Department of Justice, explained that they could accommodate the governor's request, the governor stepped aside.

LEARN MORE

Mississippi, An American Insurrection by William Doyle (Doubleday, 2001)

Three Years in Mississippi by James Meredith (Indiana University, 1996)

Alabama, The Schoolhouse Door by E. Culpepper Clark (Oxford, 1993)

Atlanta

Bowers v. Hardwick: Challenging Sodomy Statutes
The Cove (closed), Atlanta, GA 30309

Sometime after midnight on August 3, 1982, police officer Keith Torick showed up at the home of Michael Bowers in Atlanta. A friend who was sleeping on Bowers's couch let Torick in. The officer went to Hardwick's bedroom where he found him engaging in oral sex with another man. Both were arrested for sodomy and thrown in jail until posting bail 12 hours later.

But *why* was Torick in Hardwick's bedroom in the first place? The officer had ticketed Hardwick for public drinking several weeks earlier outside the Cove, a gay bar where Hardwick worked. Though Hardwick had already paid his $50 fine, Torick got an arrest warrant without checking the case file. Torick was notorious for harassing gay men with misdemeanor violations.

Hardwick was contacted by the ACLU, which hoped to use his case to challenge the constitutionality of the Georgia sodomy law. Though he faced up to 20 years in prison if found guilty, Hardwick agreed. But because Torick had improperly obtained the warrant, Georgia's attorney general, Michael Bowers, dropped the charges. The ploy didn't stop the ALCU or Hardwick, who filed suit in federal court against the statute on Fourteenth Amendment due process grounds, established in *Griswold v. Connecticut* (see page 7).

The case made it to the U.S. Supreme Court in 1986. At its core it was about the right to privacy, but the Georgia lawyer played on several justices' homophobia. The strategy worked. In a stunning 5–4 ruling, the court used moral and Biblical arguments (as opposed to constitutional ones) to render its majority opinion. Chief Justice Burger claimed the sodomy law was "firmly rooted in Judeo-Christian moral and ethical standards" and that to overturn it would "cast aside millennia of moral teaching."

Justice Harry Blackmun wrote a scathing dissent in which he said, "depriving individuals the right to choose for themselves how to conduct their intimate relationships poses a far greater threat to the values most deeply rooted in our Nation's history than tolerance and nonconformity could ever do." He also wrote that he hoped the court would one day reverse itself. In 2003, ruling in *Lawrence v. Texas* (see page 342), it did just that.

LEARN MORE
Courting Justice by Joyce Murdoch and Deb Price (Basic Books, 2001)

Heart of Atlanta Motel v. United States: The 1964 Civil Rights Act Stands
Heart of Atlanta Motel (torn down), 255 Courtland Street NE, Atlanta, GA 30303

The 1964 Civil Rights Act specifically prohibited discrimination in public accommodations, particularly in restaurants and hotels. Under the statute no customer could be refused service because of race, color, religion, or national origin. But the owner of Georgia's Heart of Atlanta Motel wanted to continue to discriminate against African Americans, and challenged the act in court (along with Ollie's Barbecue in Birmingham, Alabama).

The suits were fast-tracked to the U.S. Supreme Court, which ruled unanimously in late 1964 that based on its interpretation of the Commerce Clause, the Congress indeed had the power to regulate such matters. No longer could states hide behind the shield of "states' rights" when it came to issues that affected the entire nation.

Martin Luther King Jr. Center for Nonviolent Change
Martin Luther King Jr. National Historic Site, 450 Auburn Avenue NE, Atlanta, GA 30312 · (404) 730-3112

"I have a dream that one day this nation will rise up and live out the true meaning of its creed: 'We hold these truths to be self-evident; that all men are created equal.'" Martin Luther King Jr. announced his vision from the steps of the Lincoln Memorial on August 28, 1963, and, as few Americans before or since, forced America to start living up to that creed.

Though King was born in Atlanta, it was not here that he made his greatest contributions to civil rights. From the Montgomery Bus Boycott to the March on Washington, from the Selma to Montgomery March to his denunciation of the Vietnam War to his ultimate martyrdom while supporting poor garbage workers in Memphis, King confronted injustice wherever he could.

Still, King's Georgia connections run deep. He was born in Atlanta (501 Auburn Avenue) on January 15, 1929. At the time, his father was the pastor of the nearby Ebenezer Baptist Church (407 Auburn Avenue). The King family moved to a new home (193 Boulevard Street) in 1941; Martin Jr. lived here while attending Morehouse College, where he enrolled at the age of 15.

After graduating from Morehouse in 1948, King went on to Crozer Theological Seminary in Pennsylvania, and then on to Boston University where he was awarded his doctorate in theology in 1955. King, newly married to Coretta

Martin Luther King Jr.'s tomb

Scott, then accepted a job as pastor of Dexter Avenue Baptist Church in Montgomery, Alabama (see page 159).

The Kings and their children returned to Atlanta (234 Sunset Avenue NW) in 1960 where Martin would head up the SCLC. He also shared the pastorship of Ebenezer Baptist with his father until his death.

King's funeral was held at Ebenezer Baptist Church. His body was then interred in South View Cemetery until 1977, when it was relocated to an above-ground tomb just east of the church, at the center of a reflecting pool outside the Martin Luther King Jr. Center for Nonviolent Change. Coretta Scott King had established the center shortly after her husband's assassination and was its first president. Today the Martin Luther King Historic District—"Sweet Auburn" to Atlantans—includes his birthplace, Ebenezer Baptist Church, and the Freedom Hall Complex, where you can see King's 1964 Nobel Peace Prize.

PROGRESSIVE THOUGHTS OF
MARTIN LUTHER KING JR.

- The ultimate measure of a man is not where he stands in moments of comfort and convenience, but where he stands at times of challenge and controversy.

- A time comes when silence is betrayal.

- Freedom is never voluntarily given by the oppressor; it must be demanded by the oppressed.

- The purpose of direct action is to create a situation so crisis-packed that it will inevitably open the door to negotiation.

- The hope of a secure and livable world lies with disciplined nonconformists who are dedicated to justice, peace, and brotherhood.

- A man can't ride your back unless it's bent.

- Nonviolence is a powerful and just weapon, which cuts without wounding and ennobles those who wield it. It's a sword that heals.

LEARN MORE
The Words of Martin Luther King Jr. by Coretta Scott King, ed.
    (Newmarket, 1987)

LEARN MORE
www.nps.gov/malu
www.thekingcenter.org, (404) 526-8900
Parting the Waters by Taylor Branch (Simon & Schuster, 1988)
Pillar of Fire by Taylor Branch (Simon & Schuster, 1999)
At Canaan's Edge by Taylor Branch (Simon & Schuster, 2006)

The NAMES Project Foundation AIDS Memorial Quilt
The NAMES Project Foundation, 637 Hoke Street NW, Atlanta, GA 30318 · (404) 688-5500

It started in a San Francisco storefront, and within years grew to become the largest community artwork in the world: the NAMES Project Foundation AIDS Memorial Quilt. The idea came from Cleve Jones, a gay rights activist who had been organizing the city's annual candlelight march to remember Harvey Milk and George Moscone (see page 392). For the 1985 march he'd asked participants to write the names of friends who'd died of AIDS on placards, which were later taped to the walls of the city's federal building to protest government inaction during the crisis.

The event inspired Jones and his friends to plan a permanent memorial to those lost to the disease. The first three-by-six-foot panel—by design, roughly the size of a grave—was created in memory of Marvin Feldman in 1987. The NAMES Project Foundation (NAMES being an acronym for National AIDS Memorial Education and Support) was established that June.

AIDS groups across the nation began contributing panels of their loved ones, and when it was first unfurled in Washington on October 11, 1987, it already had 1,920 panels and was larger than a football field. From there it went on a 20-city tour, raising awareness and money for AIDS service organizations. By the end of the tour it was 6,000+ panels large.

The quilt returned to the nation's capital in October 1988 with 8,288 panels, spread out on the Eclipse in front of the White House to Ronald Reagan's shame. It would be displayed in Washington several more times, but the last time it was seen in its entirety was in 1996, when it blanketed the Mall from the Washington Monument to the U.S. Capitol Building.

Of course the goal was never to make the largest AIDS memorial in

The NAMES Project Foundation AIDS Memorial Quilt, 1992

the world—hopefully some day there will be no additional panels because there will be no more victims. Until then, the foundation continues to raise donations and accept panels. You can see some of them on display at its offices in Atlanta.

LEARN MORE
www.aidsquilt.org
Stitching a Revolution by Cleve Jones (HarperSanFrancisco, 2001)
Lest We Forget (1996)
Common Threads: Stories from the Quilt (1989)

Columbus

Fr. Roy Bourgeois and the School of the Americas Watch
SOA Watch, PO Box 3330, Columbus, GA 31903 · (202) 234-3440

If a terrorist training camp was operating on American soil, wouldn't you think the U.S. government would be concerned?

It's a trick question: the answer is yes, *unless they're the ones running it.* Every year the Western Hemisphere Institute for Security Cooperation—the School of the Americas (SOA)—trains hundreds of military officers from Central and South America at Fort Benning. The school was founded in Panama by the U.S. government in 1946. However, following the Panama Canal Treaty, the Panamanian president kicked it out, calling it "the biggest base for destabilization in Latin America." The U.S government then reestablished it in Georgia.

The SOA's 60,000 alumni are a rogue's gallery of thugs, assassins, and death squad leaders. They've been responsible for massacres of entire villages, the murder of nuns and priests, the rape and torture of civilians, and the assassination of Salvadoran Archbishop Oscar Romero . . . using "skills" taught them using your tax dollars.

Well not forever, not if Fr. Roy Bourgeois has anything to say about it. In 1983 he and two friends snuck onto the base at Fort Benning and scaled a tree outside the Salvadoran trainee barracks. From there, Bourgeois blasted a tape recording of the homily delivered by Archbishop Romero on the day he was murdered. For this, Bourgeois was sentenced to 18 months in federal prison.

After his release, Bourgeois returned to Georgia where, in 1990, he founded the School of the Americas Watch, a clearinghouse for information on SOA's graduates and their atrocities. SOA Watch has obtained copies of SOA train-ing manuals (which you can view online) that include instructions on inter-rogation techniques, psychological warfare, and commando operations.

SOA's reputation will likely be its undoing; in 2004 Venezuela's Hugo Chávez stopped sending troops to the school, and was followed by Argentina and Uruguay in 2006, and Costa Rica in 2007. Every November SOA Watch organizes a vigil outside Fort Benning, which includes a mock funeral proces-sion, the reading of the names of SOA victims, and civil disobedience. In 2006 more than 22,000 attended, and the number grows each year.

LEARN MORE

www.soaw.org

Disturbing the Peace by James Hodge and Linda Cooper (Orbis, 2004)

School of Assassins by Jack Nelson-Pallmeyer (Orbis, 2001)

Plains

Jimmy Carter, Farmer, President, Nobel Prize Laureate

Jimmy Carter National Historic Site, 300 N. Bond Street, Plains, GA 31780 · (229) 824-4104

Ever since he was crushed in his bid for reelection, Jimmy Carter has been the butt of conservative, right-wing jokes. They invoke his name, roll their eyes, and give that "'nuff said" look. Human rights, alternative energy, nuclear disarmament, the Camp David Accords . . . yeah, what a *loser*. One of the first things Ronald Reagan did after his inauguration was have Carter's solar panels torn off the White House roof. If that's what passes for "leadership," give me malaise any day.

James Earl Carter Jr. was born on October 1, 1924, in Plains. He grew up in a home southwest of town on Old Plains Road, and graduated from Plains High School in 1941. Carter attended the U.S. Naval Academy and served as a nuclear engineer on one of the first atomic submarines in the U.S. fleet.

Rosalynn Smith also grew up in Plains, graduating from Plains High in 1944. She married Carter on July 7, 1946, at the Plains United Methodist Church (301 W. Church Street). Jimmy Carter mustered out of the navy in 1953 when his father died, and returned to Plains to take over the peanut operation. For three years the Carters lived in public housing (Paschall and Thomas Streets, Unit 9A) before moving to a home on Archery Road.

Jimmy Carter at the Democratic National Convention, 1976

Carter entered public life as a state senator and served two terms. He lost his first bid at the governorship, but won in 1970. After four years in office, he launched his presidential campaign from the old train depot in downtown Plains. In the wake of Watergate, the American public was looking for change, and Carter fit the bill: a decent, honest, humble peanut farmer. And a Democrat.

Though his presidency was not without its mistakes, could it at least be acknowledged that the American public made one crucial error at that time, too? On July 15, 1979, Jimmy Carter addressed the nation, and urged citizens to conserve energy, to look to alternative sources, to stop driving gas-guzzlers, and to support his plan to wean the United States from its dependency on foreign oil. "Too many of us now tend to worship self-indulgence and consumption," he warned. And, by and large, people dismissed him.

> My concept of human rights has grown to include not only the rights to live in peace, but also to adequate health care, shelter, food, and economic opportunity.
>
> —*Jimmy Carter*

After being defeated in 1980, the Carters returned to Plains and the home they still own on Woodland Drive. They would later open the Carter Center in Atlanta (One Copenhill, 453 Freedom Parkway). Much more than a presidential library, the center has spearheaded efforts at international conflict resolution, election monitoring, disease eradication, and more. For this, Jimmy Carter was awarded the 2002 Nobel Peace Prize. The next time you get the Jimmy Carter eye roll, ask your GOP friend how long before George W. Bush wins one of those.

LEARN MORE

www.nps.gov/jica

www.cartercenter.org, (404) 420-5100

An Hour Before Daylight by Jimmy Carter (Simon & Schuster, 2001)

Keeping Faith by Jimmy Carter (Bantam, 1982)

Our Endangered Values by Jimmy Carter (Simon & Schuster, 2005)

Savannah

Juliette Gordon Low and the Girl Scouts

Girl Scout National Center, 142 Bull Street, Savannah, GA 31401 · (912) 233-4501

Juliette "Daisy" Gordon was born to a wealthy family in Savannah (10 E. Oglethorpe Avenue) on October 31, 1860, and lived with them until marrying Andrew Low, a cotton broker, in 1886. Low was a philanderer, and when he died in 1898 Juliette found herself in court, arguing with his mistress over his sizable estate.

Low won, but felt embarrassed to show herself around Savannah. So she took off for England where, in 1911, she met Sir Robert Baden-Powell, founder of the Boy Scouts. Low had always been more interested in exploring nature and working with her hands than she was in tea parties and cotillion balls. She soon became obsessed with the idea of starting her own scouting organization, but for girls.

Low returned to Savannah, a woman on a mission. With the advice and blessing of Baden-Powell, and $500,000 from the estate settlement, Low founded the Girl Guides of America. She started small; the first meeting of 18 girls and 8 adult leaders was held in Low's front parlor (329 Abercorn Street) on March 12, 1912. As the organization grew, Low established an office in the carriage house behind her home. By 1915 it had gone national and counted more than 5,000 members. Low moved her operation to Washington, D.C., where it was renamed the Girl Scouts of the USA.

Low died in Savannah on January 17, 1927, and was buried, in full uniform, in her family's plot at Laurel Grove North Cemetery (802 W. Anderson Street). A museum dedicated to the Girl Scouts and Juliette Gordon Low is housed in the Victorian home where the founder was born.

LEARN MORE

www.girlscouts.org/who_we_are/birthplace/

Outdoor Education in Girl Scouting by Carolyn L. Kennedy (Girl Scouts of the USA, 1996)

KENTUCKY

In 1999 public officials from Kentucky's neighboring McCreary and Pulaski counties voted to install displays of the Ten Commandments in their courthouses. They intended to recognize the nation's Christian heritage, they asserted, separation of church and state be damned.

But the framed Old Testament rules caught the attention of several local residents who, in turn, called the ACLU of Kentucky. Faced with a First Amendment lawsuit, the counties added copies of the Declaration of Independence, the Mayflower Compact, and a letter from Abraham Lincoln to their displays, all of which referenced a divine being.

The plan didn't work; a federal judge ordered them all removed. Defying the order while on appeal, Jerry Falwell's Liberty Counsel lawyers advised that the counties add even *more* to their walls—the Magna Carta, the Bill of Rights, and the lyrics to the "Star Spangled Banner"—to make them "Foundations of American Law" exhibits. (The national anthem, adopted in 1931, is a "foundation of American law"?)

Combined as *McCreary County v. ACLU of Kentucky*, the U.S. Supreme Court called the two displays "unmistakably religious statement[s]" and ordered them taken down. The 5–4 decision was criticized by Antonin Scalia who asserted in his dissent that "the Establishment Clause permits this disregard of polytheists and believers in unconcerned monotheists, just as it permits the disregard of devout atheists." Yikes . . .

> It is true that many Americans find the Commandments in accord with their personal beliefs. But we do not count heads before enforcing the First Amendment.
> —Justice Sandra Day O'Connor, in her concurring opinion in McCreary County v. ACLU of Kentucky, 2005

Berea

Berea College and the Birth of Integrated College Education
Berea College, Main and Chestnut Streets, Berea, KY 40404 · (859) 985-3000

In 1855 Reverend John Fee and J. A. R. Rogers, funded by abolitionist Cassius M. Clay, opened an elementary school in their Kentucky church. That school would eventually become Berea College, the first integrated college in the United States. Even back then, several institutions of higher learning were open to African Americans, but Berea was the first in which white and black students were taught in the same classrooms. What made it even more remarkable was that Kentucky was a slave state at the time.

None of this sat very well with local slaveholders. Shortly after John Brown's failed raid at Harpers Ferry (see page 145), vigilantes threatened the lives of Fee and Rogers, and when the governor refused to protect the men they fled the state. In 1866, after the Civil War, Fee and Rogers reopened Berea with 187 students, half of whom were black and the other half white. In 1904 the Kentucky legislature passed the Day Law, which forced private educational institutions to segregate . . . a statute that applied only to Berea. The college fought the law all the way to the U.S. Supreme Court, which ruled in *Berea College v. Commonwealth of Kentucky* (1908) that the state could enforce its racist statute.

Berea used its development funds to establish the Lincoln Institute in Simpsonville (Route 60 West). African American students were taught at Lincoln until 1950, when the Day Law was amended to allow integration in higher education. Berea immediately reintegrated.

> **God has made of one blood all peoples of the earth.**
> —*Berea College Motto*

LEARN MORE
www.berea.edu
www.lincolnfdn.org, (502) 585-4733
Berea College by Shannon H. Wilson (University Press of Kentucky, 2006)

LOUISIANA

If you believe Hurricane Katrina destroyed New Orleans, you're misinformed. The U.S. government flooded the city, which is why it has an obligation to fully compensate residents for the damage. The Bush administration, the state government, and the city all bear responsibility for their flat-footed, incompetent *response* to the disaster, but they didn't *cause* the flood any more than they caused the hurricane. The U.S. Army Corps of Engineers did.

For decades, the corps improperly built and failed to maintain the Mississippi River's flood walls. The levees weren't in much better shape, but the levees didn't fail in 2005. The flood walls collapsed because they were never built to the corps' own standards. They've even admitted to their error in two formal assessments of the disaster, and have been backed up by other independent investigations.

So the question hangs out there: why hasn't the federal government stepped up to pay New Orleans residents for the damage it caused? The 2005–2008 answer is simple: the Bush administration never takes responsibility for *anything*, and the current Congress never forces it to. There's nothing stopping future chief executives and legislators from doing so. Progressives should demand that their representatives approve full reparations for the victims of the U.S. government's negligence, just as they would a corporation that placed a defective product on the market.

 LEARN MORE
Breach of Faith by Jed Horne (Random House, 2006)
Path of Destruction by John McQuaid and Mark Schleifstein (Little, Brown and Company, 2006)

Angola

Sister Helen Prejean and Louisiana's Death Row
Louisiana State Penitentiary, Route 66, Angola, LA 70712

Sister Helen Prejean was not plan-ning on become a national spokes-person against the death penalty when she began her correspon-dence with Elmo Patrick Sonnier in 1981. Sonnier was locked up in the Louisiana State Penitentiary await-ing execution for a brutal double murder, and was looking for a spiri-tual advisor in his final days. But Prejean's experience with Sonnier led her to speak out against capi-tal punishment, which she felt was part of a consistent pro-life position (which included opposition to abor-tion, euthanasia, and suicide). Sen-sitive to criticism that she focused too much on the perpetrators of crimes, Prejean founded Survive in 1988 to help crime victims and their families.

Sister Helen Prejean, 2007

> I used to think that America had the best court system in the world. But now I know differently.
>
> —*Sister Helen Prejean*

Prejean would go on to write *Dead Man Walking*, an account of Sonni-er's final months, as well as those of Robert Lee Willie, whom she also counseled. She was then tapped to head up the National Coalition to Abolish the Death Penalty from 1993 to 1995.

"Rightful" executions aside, Prejean has expanded her criticism of capital punishment to include the issue of "wrongful" executions, writing about the cases of two men she met on Louisiana's death row who she believes were innocent of the crimes for which they were put to death. Her unique ministry continues through the Death Penalty Discourse Center in New Orleans.

LEARN MORE
www.prejean.org, (504) 948-6557
www.deathpenaltydiscourse.org
www.ncadp.org, (202) 331-4090
Dead Man Walking by Sister Helen Prejean (Random House, 1993)
The Death of Innocents by Sister Helen Prejean (Random House, 2005)
Dead Man Walking (1995)

New Orleans

Plessy v. Ferguson: A Big Step Backward
Penn Street Station (torn down), Penn Street, New Orleans, LA 70112

On June 7, 1892, Homer Plessy purchased a first-class ticket to Covington on the East Louisiana Railway. He boarded the train in New Orleans and took a seat in the first-class coach. The conductor asked him to vacate the car because he was Creole, an "octoroon" (one-eighth black), and when Plessy refused he was hauled off to jail.

Plessy had anticipated the arrest. He and the American Citizens' Equal Rights Association were directly challenging the state's 1890 law mandating separate railroad cars for white and nonwhite passengers. Plessy was particularly angry that the state was allowing railroad conductors to be the "autocrat[s] of Caste" by giving them the authority to determine who was black and who was not.

Plessy's case would end up having much wider implications for the institutionalization of Jim Crow laws in the South. After losing in district and state court, Plessy's appeal reached the U.S. Supreme Court in 1896. Eight of the nine justices agreed that the Fourteenth Amendment "could not have been intended to abolish distinctions based on color, or to enforce social, as opposed to political, equality, or a commingling of the two races upon terms unsatisfactory to either." Of course, that "logic" ignored the very wording of the amendment. It says, in part, ". . . nor shall any State deprive any person of life, liberty, or property, without due process of law; *nor deny any person within its jurisdiction the equal protection of the laws.*"

> In respect of civil rights, all citizens are equal before the law.
> —*Justice John Marshall Harlan,* in his Plessy v. Ferguson *dissent, 1896*

Only one justice, John Marshall Harlan, saw the case clearly. Writing in his dissent he asserted, "Our Constitution is color-blind, and neither knows nor tolerates classes among citizens." Unfortunately, the majority ruling established just the opposite: institutionalized "separate but equal" public accommodations until the *Brown v. Board of Education* case of 1954 (see page 293).

LEARN MORE

Plessy v. Ferguson by Brook Thomas (Bedford, 1996)

The Color-Blind Constitution by Andrew Kull (Harvard, 1992)

Ruby Bridges and *The Problem We All Face*
William J. Frantz School, 3811 N. Galvez Street, New Orleans, LA 70117
McDonogh No. 19 School (now Louis Armstrong Elementary), 5909 St. Claude Avenue, New Orleans, LA 70117

On November 14, 1960, federal marshals escorted Ruby Bridges to her first day of class at Franz elementary school. She needed protection because a group of adults calling themselves the Cheerleaders were awaiting her arrival with taunts and threats to poison her sack lunch. Bridges was six years old, and one of four African American girls who would integrate the New Orleans public schools that year. The other three—Gail Etienne, Tessie Prevost, and Leona Tate—were taken to McDonogh No. 19 School the same day and met a similar reception.

Bridges attended a class of one in Room 202 with her teacher Barbara Henry. Most of the white parents had withdrawn their children rather than integrate. Several parents who kept their kids in class lost jobs when their coworkers found out, and one family fled New Orleans fearing for its safety. The Louisiana legislature then cut off all teacher salaries at the two schools.

> Four big marshals got out of each car and from somewhere in the automobiles they extracted the littlest Negro girl you ever saw. . . . The big marshals stood her on the curb and a jangle of jeering shrieks went up from behind the barricades. The little girl did not look at the howling crowd but from the side the whites of her eyes showed like those of a frightened fawn.
>
> —*John Steinbeck, in*
> **Travels with Charley**

The ugly events were captured for posterity by Norman Rockwell and John Steinbeck. One of Rockwell's best-known paintings, *The Problem We All Face,* shows a confident Bridges walking to school past tossed tomatoes and racist graffiti, framed by the legs of U.S. marshals. The title, of course, refers neither to Bridges nor the marshals, but the girl's faceless attackers. For a chilling portrayal of those hoodlums, check out the final chapters of Steinbeck's *Travels with Charley.* The author had read about the ongoing unrest in the Crescent City and decided to detour through Louisiana on the final leg of his cross-country journey. The result was an unflinching and unflattering conclusion to a mostly upbeat travelogue.

LEARN MORE
www.rubybridges.com
Through My Eyes by Ruby Bridges (Scholastic, 1999)
Travels with Charley by John Steinbeck (Viking, 1962)

MISSISSIPPI

Mississippi has the dubious distinction of being one of the bloodiest states during the civil rights movement. Eighteen of the 40 names listed on the National Civil Rights Memorial in Montgomery, Alabama (see page 160), were murdered in Mississippi. The most famous was Medgar Evers, shot in the back as he got out of his car in front of his Jackson home (2332 Margaret W. Alexander Drive) on June 12, 1963.

A year later, on June 21, James Chaney, Andrew Goodman, and Michael Schwerner, volunteers on the 1964 Freedom Summer campaign, were murdered outside Philadelphia in a plot coordinated by the KKK and Neshoba County deputy sheriff Cecil Price. Years later it was revealed that Price had identified Schwerner's station wagon using information from the Mississippi Sovereignty Commission (MSC).

What was the MSC? Established in 1956 as a propaganda organ for state government, it quickly mutated into Mississippi's own spy agency, with each successive governor's full knowledge. Over the next 21 years it illegally gathered information on 87,000 Americans. Disbanded in 1977, the state legislature ordered that all its records be destroyed. Many of its most damaging files were shredded, but plenty survived; they were released to the public in 1998. The documents revealed that the state had illegally assisted the defenses in both the Evers and Freedom Summer murder trials.

Because of the state's collusion, it took 30 years for a prosecutor to bring Evers's murderer to justice. Relentlessly prodded by Evers's widow, Myrlie Evers, local prosecutors used newly uncovered evidence to put Byron De La Beckwith on trial in 1994. It was the third time he faced a jury, and this time he was found guilty of first-degree murder. Sentenced to life, he died in prison in 2001. Like the

> If I die, it'll be in a good cause.
> —*Medgar Evers*

hands on a clock, the wheels of justice do turn in Mississippi, it's just hard to see them move. And yet, they do move.

LEARN MORE

Evers, *Ghosts of Mississippi* by Maryanne Vollers (Little, Brown and Company, 1995)

Freedom Summer, *Murder in Mississippi* by Howard Ball (University Press of Kansas, 2004)

Ruleville

Fannie Lou Hamer and the Mississippi Freedom Democratic Party
Hamer Home, 626 E. Lafayette Street, Ruleville, MS 38711

When it came to grassroots organizing in the 1960s South, nobody was more grassroots than Fannie Lou Hamer. Born in Montgomery County on October 6, 1917, the youngest of 20 children in a sharecropper family, she was working in the cotton fields by the age of six, full-time by twelve.

On August 27, 1962, Hamer attended a voter registration meeting held by the Council of Federated Organizations (which included CORE, SNCC, the NAACP, and the National Urban League) at the Williams Chapel Missionary Baptist Church in Ruleville (915 Bryan Street). Before it was over, Hamer and 17 others pledged to register in Indianola, the Sunflower County seat. On August 31 the group marched past gun-brandishing whites to the courthouse, where they were given a "literacy" test. The test included obscure questions on Mississippi's constitution, and none of the applicants passed. On their way out of town the SNCC-chartered bus was pulled over . . . for being the wrong color . . . and the driver was fined $100. And when Hamer got back to the Marlow plantation, where she had worked and lived for 18 years, she learned she'd been fired, and was kicked off the property.

Harassed and shot at, Hamer left Ruleville but returned two months later, determined to register. On December 4 she told the courthouse clerk, "Now, you can't have me fired because I'm not living in no white man's house. I'll be here every 30 days until I become a registered voter." On her third visit, Hamer passed the test. As a new field officer for SNCC, she would help thousands of disenfranchised poor achieve the same thing.

Hamer faced violent opposition. She and several civil rights workers were dragged from a bus in Winona on June 9, 1963, and beaten while in custody at the Montgomery County jail, an assault that left Hamer with permanent kidney damage and blindness in one eye. The U.S. Justice Department later charged the officers involved, but an all-white jury acquitted them.

The Winona acquittals convinced Hamer to take on the Mississippi political establishment at the ballot box. In 1964 she helped found the Mississippi Freedom Democratic Party (MFDP), and ran for the state's second congressional district. Challenged in court by the local Democratic machine, Hamer came right back at them . . . at the 1964 Democratic National Convention. On August 22 she testified before the Credentials Committee, demanding that the MFDP's slate of delegates be seated, rather than the all-white delegation. The MFDP lost, but succeeded in exposing the party's racist substructure, particularly in the South.

That November the MFDP held its own election—the Freedom Vote—open to all Mississippians. The results demonstrated just how corrupt the state's elections had become. The MFDP challenged the "official" vote and even got a hearing in the U.S. Congress, though the challenge ultimately failed.

The Freedom Farm Corporation (FFC) was Hamer's final big project. It started in 1969 as a "pig bank." Poor farmers could borrow a sow, and once it had given birth to 20 piglets it would be returned to the FFC. Then, when two of its offspring eventually got pregnant, those sows would be given to another family. The FFC also purchased land for a vegetable-growing co-op. Needy families could help in the harvest and would receive food in return, and the surplus would be sent to poor people around the country. The corporation also helped families secure FHA loans for homes, and gave college and vocational scholarships to graduating seniors.

Fannie Lou Hamer died of heart failure on March 14, 1977. She was buried on former co-op land on Bryan Street in Ruleville, now part of the town's Industrial Park. Today there is a Fannie Lou Hamer Memorial Garden on the site.

> With God's help, without violence, I'll keep on fighting until the constitution means more than a piece of paper.
> —*Fannie Lou Hamer*

LEARN MORE

For Freedom's Sake by Chana Kai Lee (University of Illinois, 1999)

Fannie Lou Hamer and the Right to Vote by Penny Colman (Millbrook, 1993)

This Little Light of Mine by Kay Mills (Dutton, 1993)

NORTH CAROLINA

Though he was born in Seneca, South Carolina, on June 10, 1953, John Edwards grew up in Robbins, North Carolina, where his father worked in a textile mill and his mother was a postal carrier. He became the first member of his family to attend college, and graduated from the University of North Carolina law school. It was here that he met and married Elizabeth Anania.

Edwards began practicing law in 1978 and became a successful personal-injury trial attorney. Then, on April 4, 1996, the Edwards' 16-year-old son Wade was killed when his Jeep was blown off a North Carolina highway. Edwards reevaluated what he wanted to do with the rest of his life, so to honor the memory of his son he chose a path of public service. Quitting the law firm he founded, he ran for the U.S. Senate against GOP incumbent Lauch Faircloth in 1998, and won. During his one term in the senate he established himself as a moderate progressive with a strong but imperfect record; he voted for the USA PATRIOT Act and the Iraq War Resolution, both of which he later admitted were mistakes, and apologized.

In 2003 Edwards announced on *The Daily Show with Jon Stewart* that he would run for the 2004 Democratic Party nomination for president. His populist theme of the "Two Americas"—the have-a-lots and the struggling-to-make-ends-meets—gained wide support, but not enough to win the nomination. He was later tapped as the Democrats' vice-presidential candidate.

The day after conceding the election, Elizabeth Edwards announced that she had been recently diagnosed with breast cancer. She would later write about the experience, and of the loss of her son, in *Saving Graces*. Following Elizabeth's chemotherapy, John Edwards began laying the

> You can be disappointed, but you cannot walk away. This fight has just begun.
>
> —*John Edwards, in his 2004 concession speech*

groundwork for another presidential bid. As part of his 2008 effort, he launched One Corps, an online effort to enlist volunteers to not just stuff envelopes, but to engage in active service in their communities, reflecting the goals and values of his campaign.

In late March 2007, Elizabeth Edwards learned that her cancer had returned, and had spread. Though incurable, doctors believed it to be manageable, and not immediately life-threatening. Determined not to let the diagnosis squelch their dreams and aspirations, the Edwardses committed themselves to continue the campaign, and were lauded by cancer survivors everywhere.

John Edwards, 2007

LEARN MORE
www.wade.org, (919) 836-9355
Four Trials by John Edwards (Simon & Schuster, 2004)
Saving Graces by Elizabeth Edwards (Broadway, 2006)

Afton

Environmental Racism in Warren County
North of Town, Afton, NC 27589

In 1978 the Ward Transformer Company came up with a plan to dispose of 31,000 gallons of PCB-laced oil generated by its North Carolina facility. It hired a trucking company to dump the carcinogenic material along 200 miles of rural ditches in the dark of night. But that wasn't the worst of it. Ronald Reagan's EPA later drafted a controversial cleanup proposal: the contaminated soil would be collected and dumped in a landfill near Afton, in one of the poorest counties in the state. Warren County also had one of North Carolina's highest concentrations of African Americans. Coincidence?

Please. After two NAACP-backed lawsuits were thrown out of court, residents in Warren County turned to civil disobedience in the fall of 1982. More than 500 people were arrested while trying to block dump trucks from getting to the Afton site. Others marched 60 miles to the state capital and presented their demands to the governor. Ultimately, the plan went ahead when the governor made empty promises to "detoxify" the site.

In response to the controversy, Congressman Walter Fauntroy and the Congressional Black Caucus requested a GAO survey of toxic waste landfills in the South, which revealed that three of every four sites were located in poor, black communities. The United Church of Christ's Commission for Racial Justice issued a report in 1987 that showed anecdotal evidence that indeed, this pattern was no coincidence. The term "environmental racism" became a powerful issue in the eco community. Today, the Environmental Justice Resource Center at Clark Atlanta University monitors and documents instances of environmental racism.

LEARN MORE
www.ejrc.cau.edu, (404) 880-6911
Dumping in Dixie by Robert D. Bullard (Westview, 2000)
From the Ground Up by Luke W. Cole and Sheila R. Foster (NYU, 2001)

Edenton

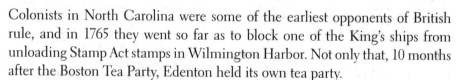

The Edenton Tea Party
Cupola House, 408 S. Broad Street, Edenton, NC 27932 · (252) 482-2637

Colonists in North Carolina were some of the earliest opponents of British rule, and in 1765 they went so far as to block one of the King's ships from unloading Stamp Act stamps in Wilmington Harbor. Not only that, 10 months after the Boston Tea Party, Edenton held its own tea party.

What made the Edenton Tea Party unique was that it was organized and carried out entirely by women. Led by Penelope Barker, 51 women met at the Cupola House to sign a declaration on October 25, 1774, stating they would boycott British tea so long as it was taxed. News of the women's civil disobedience made it back to London, where they were mocked in political cartoons. Fellow colonists felt differently, as the British soon found out.

A display on the Edenton Tea Party can be found in the Cupola House today, and an empty teapot stands as a memorial on Edenton's Courthouse Green.

 **LEARN MORE**
www.cupolahouse.org

The Provincial Deputies of North Carolina have resolved not to drink any more tea, nor wear any more British cloth, &c. many ladies of this Province have determined to give a memorable proof of their patriotism, and have entered into the following honourable and spirited association.

—Edenton Tea Party Resolution

Greensboro

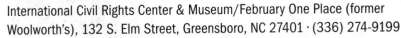

The Woolworth's Sit-In
International Civil Rights Center & Museum/February One Place (former Woolworth's), 132 S. Elm Street, Greensboro, NC 27401 · (336) 274-9199

On Monday, February 1, 1960, four freshmen from North Carolina A&T State College (later University)—Franklin McCain, David Richmond, Joseph McNeil, and Ezell Blair Jr.—walked into the Woolworth's in Greensboro and ordered coffee and doughnuts. The waitress thought the men, who were African American, had made a mistake, and informed them that they could not be served. The students took out their books and started to study, willing to wait as long as was necessary. They stayed at the counter until the store closed.

On Tuesday the four returned, with 25 others. Again, nobody was waited on, and again, they remained in their seats until the end of the day. On Wednesday 85 protesters showed up and filled the counter's 65 seats, plus some. By Saturday numbers topped 900 and the protest spilled over to Kress's Dime Store.

Within a month, lunch counter sit-ins were taking place across North Carolina and the South, and eventually the North. Picketers could be found outside many Woolworth's stores, including former Miss America (and Miss Alabama) Yolande Fox. "I'm a Southern girl, but I'm a thinking girl," she told reporters.

The sit-ins breathed new life into the stalled struggle for civil rights in the United States. Greensboro officials finally yielded to the pressure, and on July 25 opened the city's dining establishments to African Americans.

The original Woolworth's closed in the early 1990s, and the lunch counter and chairs were moved to the Smithsonian (see page 56). Most of the rest of the original facility, however, remained intact, and is being developed into a civil rights shrine.

Woolworth's sit-in, day two, 1960

LEARN MORE
www.sitinmovement.org
Civilities and Civil Rights by William F. Chafe (Oxford, 1980)

Raleigh

Ella Baker and the Student Nonviolent Coordinating Committee
Shaw University, BTI Performing Arts Center (former Memorial Auditorium), 188 E.
South Street, Raleigh, NC 27601

As the sit-in movement that started in Greensboro (see page 205) spread across
the South, civil rights leaders knew they had to capitalize on the enthusiasm
of college-age activists. Ella Baker of the SCLC called for a meeting of civil
rights organizations at her alma mater, Shaw University. The meeting started
in Memorial Auditorium on April 15, 1960. Though Dr. King (of SCLC), the
NAACP, and the Urban League all urged students to join their groups, the
200 attendees wanted to strike out on their own.

On April 17 the group founded the Student Nonviolent Coordinating Committee (SNCC). It was designed to be active and flexible, drawing its energy from the idealism of a new generation of young leaders. Marion Berry was its first chairman.

SNCC walked the walk, and led some of the most dangerous civil rights campaigns of the era. It popularized the "jail-in" (see page 211), joined the Freedom Rides (see page 150), coordinated Alabama's Voter Education Project (see page 161), and proposed the 1964 Freedom Summer. Its many leaders included John Lewis, Diane Nash, Bob Moses, and Stokely Carmichael.

SNCC began falling apart (as an organization) in 1966. Its leadership had grown more militant, and many advocated racial separatism. In a December meeting Carmichael urged members to expel the organization's white members. As a result the group lost several African American leaders in protest, including Fannie Lou Hamer (see page 200). Carmichael left a year later to help lead the new Black Power Party, and SNCC eventually collapsed.

> **Strong people don't need strong leaders.**
>
> —*Ella Baker*

LEARN MORE
www.shawuniversity.edu
SNCC by Howard Zinn (Beacon, 1964)
In Struggle by Clayborne Carson (Harvard, 1981)

SOUTH CAROLINA

South Carolina has a history of intransigence on the issues of race and civil rights. On December 20, 1860, it was the first state to secede from the union, and saw the first battle of the Civil War at Fort Sumter. Four years later, on February 16, 1865, General William Sherman arrived at Columbia and, seeing the Confederate battle flag flying from atop the state capitol dome (Gervais and Assembly Streets), ordered his men to fire on the building. As Confederate forces fled the city they set fire to many structures . . . and later blamed Sherman. His soldiers did, however, break into the capitol to hold a mock general assembly—they voted unanimously to repeal the Ordinance of Secession.

Some today still believe Sherman torched Columbia. But historians have determined that most of the blazes during the Union's occupation can be attributed to drunken or careless soldiers and residents, as well as Southern saboteurs; many fires started in the very buildings where troops were quartered, then spread. During the largest conflagration downtown, more than 2,000 Union soldiers were engaged to fight the blaze *and keep it from spreading*. And far less of the capital city burned—about 30 percent—than is often stated.

South Carolina's historical revisionism has extended to its recent battle over the Confederate battle flag being flown over the state capitol. "It's a celebration of our heritage," folks claimed, "It's always been flown there!" In fact, the first time it flew over the capitol after the Civil War was 1962, as a statement against *integration*. Pressed by an NAACP-led boycott, the state removed the flag in 2000 and placed it north of the building, on the capitol grounds. A monument to local African Americans was erected at the same time. As the progressive stories that follow demonstrate, their contributions to the state and nation cannot be under-memorialized.

LEARN MORE

"Who Burned Columbia?" in *Lies Across America* by James W. Loewen
(The New Press, 1999)

Sherman and the Burning of Columbia by Marion B. Lucas (Texas A&M, 1976)

Georgetown

Joseph H. Rainey, Hero of Reconstruction
Rainey Birthplace, 909 Prince Street, Georgetown, SC 29440

Though born in Georgetown in 1832, Joseph Hayne Rainey (who was African American) was not born into slavery; his parents had been able to purchase their freedom before his birth. The family moved to Charleston in 1846, where Rainey was later drafted as a steward in the Confederate navy. He eventually escaped to Bermuda where he waited out the Civil War.

Shortly after returning to Georgetown in 1866, Rainey became active in local politics. He was elected as a Republican to the state senate in 1870, but resigned later that year to take an appointment to a vacated seat in the U.S. House of Representatives. He became the first African American to serve in the House, starting in December 1870. (Hiram R. Revels of Mississippi was the first African American to serve in the Senate, starting in February 1870.)

Joseph Rainey, c. 1875

Rainey worked to pass legislation enforcing the Fourteenth Amendment, to curtail the KKK's terrorist activities, and to outlaw discrimination in public accommodations—restaurants, hotels, transportation, and theaters—through the Civil Rights Act of 1875. Rainey also worked for more just policies toward Native Americans and Chinese immigrants.

But Rainey's distinguished political career came to an end in 1878. Federal troops withdrew from the South in 1877 and Reconstruction collapsed. Rainey lost his bid for reelection, and in 1883 the U.S. Supreme Court nullified many provisions of the Civil Rights Act. Though he worked for some time for the U.S. Treasury Department in Washington, D.C., Rainey returned to his home state in 1886 and died a year later. He is buried in Georgetown's Baptist Cemetery (Church and Screven Streets).

 **LEARN MORE**
Reconstruction by Eric Foner (Peter Smith, 2001)

Murrells Inlet

Birthplace of the Public Sculpture Garden
Brookgreen Gardens, 1931 Brookgreen Drive, Murrells Inlet, SC 29576 · (843) 235-6000

When it opened in 1931, Brookgreen Gardens was a revolutionary idea in the art world: sculpture placed in a natural setting for the public to enjoy. It was originally intended as a showcase for the works of sculptor Anna Hyatt Huntington (and was financed by Huntington and her husband Archer), but was soon expanded to include works of other artists. During the Depression, the Huntingtons' acquisitions helped feed more than a few starving artists.

Today the gardens include more than 900 works on 300+ acres, including those of Daniel Chester French, Augustus Saint-Gaudens, and Frederic Remington. Brookgreen focuses on figurative art of animals and humans from the Beaux Art and Art Deco periods.

 **LEARN MORE**
www.brookgreen.org

Rock Hill

The Rock Hill Jail-In
McCrory's Lunch Counter (closed down), 135 E. Main Street, Rock Hill, SC 29730

For almost a year students from Friendship Junior College, led by Leroy Johnson, had been trying to integrate the lunch counter at McCrory's department store in Rock Hill. But their sit-ins had not persuaded McCrory's or the city to change their policies. So in a bold move on February 1, 1961, Johnson called the city's bluff: rather than post the $100 bail after their arrests, nine students—the Friendship Nine—opted to stay in jail and serve out their 30-day hard labor sentences at the York County prison farm. Within days four national SNCC organizers—Diane Nash, Ruby Doris Smith, Charles Sherrod, and Charles Jones—had been arrested at McCrory's and joined the others. The "jail-in" was born.

The tactic not only demonstrated a commitment to the civil rights cause, it turned the financial tables on local governments. Rather than surrender money for bail, the protesters forced municipalities to spend money and time to keep them locked up. Two weeks after the original Nine were sentenced, 70 more joined them behind bars. Guards and prisoners claimed the Rock Hill 70 wouldn't stop singing and speaking out on civil rights matters. Soon, protesters were copying the "jail, no bail" strategy throughout the South.

Saint Helena Island

Penn School and the Port Royal Experiment
Penn School Historic Landmark District, PO Box 126, Saint Helena Island, SC 29920 · (843) 838-2432

During the Civil War, as Union forces seized Confederate territory, they had to come up with a plan for meeting the needs of newly liberated slaves. South Carolina's barrier islands at Port Royal Sound were among the first parcels of freed land, on which 10,000 African Americans lived. Abolitionist missionaries presented Treasury Secretary Salmon Chase with a plan: the Port Royal Experiment. The navy expelled the islands' few plantation owners who hadn't already fled, and assisted the abolitionists in setting up trade schools and health services for the population.

Laura Towne and Ellen Murray of the Pennsylvania Freedmen's Relief Association led the operation known as the Penn School. It opened in June 1862 only weeks after St. Helena Island was captured. Charlotte Forten (later Grimké) taught here from 1862 to 1864. The Penn School provided islanders with training in agriculture, carpentry, and other skills. It also established the state's first farm co-op. The Port Royal Experiment also served as a laboratory for many Reconstruction-era programs. Unfortunately, though it provided useful education for the islands' black poor, it was insensitive to the region's Gullah culture in an effort to "Americanize" the people it served.

Towne and Murray, partners in life as well as work, set up a home at the former Frogmore Plantation (Lands End Road). They would live here for another four decades as the Penn School developed into the Penn Normal, Industrial, and Agricultural School. Towne died here in 1901, and Murray passed away in 1907. The school changed its focus and its name in 1948. Penn Community Services, Inc. focused on local needs and preserving the unique culture of the barrier islands. (Today it is known as the Penn Center.) And during the civil rights era it was used to train organizers, register voters, and work toward overcoming segregation.

LEARN MORE
www.penncenter.com
Rehearsal for Reconstruction by Willie Lee Nichols Rose (University of Georgia, 1998)

Summerton

Briggs v. Elliot: Part of *Brown v. Board of Education*
Scott's Branch School (torn down, replace by Scotts Branch Middle School), 1154 Fourth Street, Summerton, SC 29148

The *Brown v. Board of Education* decision of 1954 (see page 293) was a combination of five different school desegregation challenges. The first case was filed in Clarendon County, South Carolina, in November 1949: *Briggs v. Elliot*. Black students there had only one school open to them, the Scott's Branch School in Summerton. Because the school board refused to transport black children, even though it had 30 busses, attending classes was out of the question for many rural families. Even if they were able to attend, the dilapidated building and instructional materials were far inferior to the county's white schools. Indeed, the school board spent $43 a year on each black student, while white students were funded at $179 per child.

So, led by Reverend Joseph DeLaine, Harry Briggs and 19 other parents filed suit against the county's school board, chaired by Roderick Elliot. Briggs was a navy veteran who worked at Summerton's Sinclair gas station, which was owned by the town's 12-term mayor, H. C. Carrington. For filing, the mayor fired Briggs the day before Christmas, and wife Eliza Briggs was dismissed from her job as a maid at a Summerton motel. Other plaintiffs suffered reprisals; they were fired, denied credit at local businesses, firebombed, and shot at. And DeLaine's Liberty Hill A.M.E. Church (23110 Liberty Hill Church Road) was burned to the ground.

But the parents' bravery paid off, for it was at the Scott's Branch School that Dr. Kenneth Clark would conduct the "doll test" that was integral to the *Brown* decision. On May 24, 1951, Clark interviewed 16 young students about their feelings toward four dolls: a black boy, a white boy, a black girl, and a white girl. Ten of the African American children chose to play with a white doll, saying the black dolls looked "bad." The evidence confirmed Clark's earlier studies showing the long-term impact of segregation on the self-image of black children.

A three-judge District Court panel in Charleston ruled 2–1 on June 23, 1951, to uphold the segregated schools, but Judge Julius Waties Waring penned a stinging dissent that ended with five words that would echo in the *Brown* decision: "Segregation is *per se* inequality." *Briggs v. Elliot* was appealed to the U.S. Supreme Court a month after the ruling.

> There is absolutely no reasonable explanation for racial prejudice. It is all caused by unreasoning emotional reactions and these are gained in early childhood.
> —Judge Waring, in his Briggs v. Elliot *dissent, 1951*

LEARN MORE
Simple Justice by Richard Kluger (Vintage, 1977)
A Passion for Justice by Tinsley E. Yarbrough (Oxford, 2001)

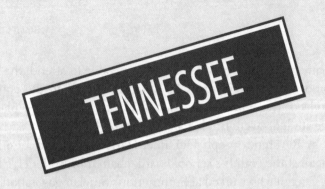

TENNESSEE

The long struggle for women's suffrage came to fruition on August 18, 1920, when the Tennessee legislature ratified the Nineteenth Amendment to the U.S. Constitution. It was the 36th state to approve the measure, putting it over the three-fourths required for adoption. The amendment took effect on August 26.

The Volunteer State's efforts were led by Anne Dallas Dudley, president of the local chapter of the Equal Suffrage League. She had been lobbying for four years, beginning with a march in May 1916 from downtown Nashville to a rally in Centennial Park (26th and West End Avenues). Yet not until the U.S. Congress sent the measure to the states in 1918 did Tennessee lawmakers take up the issue in earnest.

Prodded by Dudley and others, including the NAWSA's Carrie Chapman Catt, the governor called the legislature into special session on August 9 to consider the amendment. During late-night debates, antisuffrage lobbyists plied senators with liquor on the eighth floor of the capitol building, but apparently not enough; the senate successfully passed the bill to the house. Vote-counting suffragists knew the tally in the lower body would be very close. Harry Burn, at 24 the youngest member of the house, cast the deciding vote. Though he was initially opposed to the measure, on the final day of debate he received a note: "Hurrah! And vote for suffrage. . . ." his mother wrote. "Don't forget to be a good boy and help Mrs. Catt. . . ."

Harry was a good boy that day.

> The right of the citizens of the United States to vote shall not be denied or abridged by the United States or by any State on account of sex.
>
> —*Nineteenth Amendment*

LEARN MORE
Century of Struggle by Eleanor Flexner and Ellen Fitzpatrick (Belknap, 1975)

Byrdstown

Cordell Hull and the Birth of the United Nations
Cordell Hull Birthplace and Museum State Park, 1300 Cordell Hull Memorial Drive, Byrdstown, TN 38549 · (931) 864-3247

Few Americans were as instrumental in the founding of the United Nations as Tennessee's Cordell Hull. Though not a household name today, Hull served as secretary of state from 1932 to 1944, longer than any other person before or since.

Hull was born in a log cabin west of Byrdstown on October 2, 1871. His family moved away when he was four years old, but Hull received most of his education in Tennessee and neighboring Kentucky. In 1907 he was elected to the Tennessee legislature, and went on to represent the state in Washington as a congressman and senator. He resigned as senator in 1932 after FDR nominated him to serve as secretary of state.

In August 1943 Hull's State Department drafted the "Charter of the United Nations," which later formed the basis of the international organization. Hull resigned his post in 1944 due to health concerns, but witnessed the founding of the United Nations a year later. That same year he received the Nobel Peace Prize.

Hull died on July 23, 1955, and was buried in Washington National Cathedral. His humble birthplace has been restored, and includes a small museum of his professional and family artifacts, including his 1945 Nobel Prize.

> Peace has become as essential to civilized existence as the air we breathe is to life itself. There is no greater responsibility resting upon peoples and governments everywhere than to make sure that enduring peace will this time, at long last, be established and maintained.
> —*Cordell Hull, on receiving the Nobel Peace Prize, 1945*

LEARN MORE
www.cordellhullmuseum.com
Act of Creation by Stephen C. Schlesinger (Westview, 2003)

Dayton

The Scopes Monkey Trial

Rhea County Courthouse, 1475 Market Street, Dayton, TN 37321 · (423) 775-7801

John Scopes knew it was illegal to teach evolution to Tennessee schoolchildren; so did the Dayton town boosters who encouraged him to do so. State legislators had passed the Butler Act on March 21, 1925, which forbid teaching "any theory that denies the story of the Divine Creation of man as taught in the Bible, and to teach instead that man has descended from a lower form of animals." But many felt the act gave the state an intellectual black eye, and wanted to challenge it in court. In early May, Dayton police were told that a 24-year-old Rhea County High School science teacher had used a state-approved textbook, *A Civic Biology*, to teach Darwin's theory to his classes. On May 7 Scopes was arrested.

The Scopes Monkey Trial, as it became known, pitted defense attorney Clarence Darrow and the ACLU against former Democratic presidential candidate William Jennings Bryan. As the boosters had hoped, the trial injected cash into Dayton's stagnant economy. The town was overrun with reporters, traveling preachers, chimpanzees with their trainers, and con artists of all sorts.

The eight-day trial commenced on July 10 and was broadcast on nationwide radio. Denied the right to present scientific testimony, Darrow hammered away at fundamentalists' interpretation of the Bible. On the last day he called Bryan, a self-proclaimed expert on the holy

John Scopes, 1925

If today you can take a thing like evolution and make it a crime to teach it in the public schools, tomorrow you can make it a crime to teach it in the private schools. . . . And the next session you may ban books and newspapers. . . . Ignorance and fanaticism is ever busy and needs feeding.

—*Clarence Darrow*

book, to the stand. He asked Bryan whether Jonah had really survived in a whale's stomach for three days, and whether Joshua made the sun stand still, and whether the earth was created in six days. When Bryan accused Darrow of ridiculing Christians, Darrow shot back, "We have the purpose of preventing bigots and ignoramuses from controlling the education of the United States, and you know it." And at trial's end, Darrow declined to make a final summation, denying Bryan the right to present a closing argument, where the orator might have shined.

But it didn't matter. The judge instructed the jury to rule only on whether Scopes had violated the Bulter Act, not on the law's constitutionality. Scopes was found guilty and fined $100. Allowed to make a statement, Scopes said, "Your Honor, I feel that I have been convicted of violating an unjust statute. I will continue in the future, as I have in the past, to oppose this law in any way I can. Any other action would be a violation of my ideal of academic freedom— that is, to teach the truth—as guaranteed in our constitution, of personal and religious freedom. I think the fine is unjust." That night, to thank Dayton citizens for their hospitality, the pool reporters hired out a Chattanooga band and invited the town to the village hall. Darrow danced away the evening with high school girls and visited with admirers.

On appeal, the Tennessee Supreme Court ruled that the judge should not have imposed the fine, but that the jury should have, which kept it from having to rule on the law's constitutionality as well. The Butler Act stayed on the books until 1967.

LEARN MORE

Six Days or Forever? by Ray Ginger (Oxford, 1958)

Summer for the Gods by Edward J. Larson (Harvard, 1997)

Memphis

Frances Wright's Nashoba Experiment
Nashoba Plantation (torn down), Riverdale Road, Memphis TN 38138

In 1818 Frances "Fanny" Wright toured the United States and wrote dispatches to her Scottish countrymen. Wright loved America, and because she wasn't afraid to say so, Americans loved her back. Still, she was troubled by slavery and vowed to do something about it. Six years after her original visit she returned to launch a bold experiment in utopian living, certainly for the antebellum South.

Wright purchased the Nashoba Plantation on the south banks of the Wolf River just east of Memphis, and established a colony based on the New Harmony (Indiana) model. She purchased slaves who were to be educated, "upraised," and freed, and hired a former New Harmony resident to oversee it all. It might have worked had not Wright also been a proponent of "free love." Wright saw marriage as an institution that enslaved women, and she didn't intend to advocate it at Nashoba. She also freely admitted that religion "has no place in this institution."

Her financial backers, and the 500 or so residents of Memphis, were alarmed at what appeared to be a godless, race-mixing community in their midst. The ensuing scandal forced Wright to flee Nashoba for New Harmony in 1827. The African American residents she had hoped to help were spirited away to Haiti for their own safety, and freed. The plantation was sold a year later.

> No woman can forfeit her individual rights or independent existence, and no man assert over her any rights or power whatsoever beyond what he may exercise over her free and voluntary affection.
>
> —*Frances Wright*

LEARN MORE
Visions of Utopia by John Egerton (University of Tennessee, 1977)

Ida B. Wells-Barnett, Crusading Journalist
Memphis *Free Speech* Offices (burned down), 379 Beale Street, Memphis, TN 38103

In May 1884, 22-year-old Ida B. Wells purchased a first-class railway ticket from Memphis to Woodstock, where she worked as a teacher. After taking her seat, a conductor told her she had to move back to the "colored" car. Wells refused, and when the conductor (and a baggage handler) tried to drag her out, she bit him. The incident would become a metaphor for her life.

Wells was born into slavery in Holly Springs, Mississippi, on July 16, 1862. In 1878 a yellow fever epidemic orphaned her and five siblings, so at age 16 Wells trained as a teacher to support the family. She and two sisters moved to Memphis in 1880 where she attended Fisk University and commuted to Woodstock.

Wells sued the Chesapeake, Ohio and Southwestern Railroad Company for discrimination, and won a $500 settlement in civil court. However, the judgment was overturned by the Tennessee Supreme Court in 1887. Wells wrote several essays on her case for *Living Way*, a religious weekly, expressing her anger at the ruling and at Southern racism. The essays were widely reproduced and circulated, and launched her journalism career.

Though Wells wrote on a wide range of topics, investigating lynchings occupied much of her energy. In 1891 she founded the Memphis *Free Speech and Headlight* to catalogue the crimes. Then, on March 9, 1892, three black businessmen, owners of the People's Grocery (Walker Avenue and Mississippi Boulevard), were murdered by a white mob. The men had opened their store across the street from a white-owned grocery, and were cutting into its business. Wells outlined the facts of the case and demanded that local officials bring murder charges against the perpetrators.

Angry Memphis residents descended on the *Free Speech*'s offices on May 27, 1892, and ransacked it. Wells, who was in Philadelphia at the time, fled to New York City, where she joined the staff of the New York *Age*. She traveled across the country and to Europe, lecturing on lynching and lobbying for federal action. In 1895 she married Ferdinand Lee Barnett, the founder and owner of the Chicago *Conservator*, Chicago's first black-owned newspaper, and moved to the Windy City. That same year she published *A Red Record*, a groundbreaking statistical analysis of American lynchings.

Wells-Barnett helped found the National Association of Colored Women in 1896, and the NAACP (see page 102) in 1909. She also worked on behalf of women's suffrage. In 1930 Wells ran for the Illinois state senate, and lost. A year later, on March 25, 1931, Wells-Barnett died and was buried in Chicago's Oak Woods Cemetery (1035 E. 67th Street).

> The people must know before they can act, and there is no educator to compare with the press.
>
> —*Ida B. Wells-Barnett*

LEARN MORE

To Keep the Waters Troubled by Linda O. McMurry (Oxford, 1999)

Ida B. Wells-Barnett and American Reform, 1880–1930 by Patricia A. Schechter (University of North Carolina, 2000)

At the Hands of Persons Unknown by Philip Dray (Random House, 2002)

Martin Luther King Jr. Makes It to the Mountaintop

National Civil Rights Museum/Lorraine Motel, 450 Mulberry Street, Memphis, TN
38103 · (901) 521-9699

In early 1968, African American garbage workers in Memphis were locked in
a labor struggle that was, at its heart, a civil rights struggle. The strike began
in response to the unequal treatment of white and black employees. Not only
were blacks paid less than their counterparts, they were prevented from moving up within the department. They also suffered numerous injustices at the
hands of managers; for example, when snow prevented workers from making
their rounds, white employees were typically given the day off with pay, but
black employees were docked a day's salary.

The strike began on February 12. When it became clear that picketing
wasn't working, the union scheduled a demonstration downtown. The march
was scheduled for March 22, but had to be delayed a week because of a snow-
storm. The March 28 demonstration erupted in violence; 280 people were
arrested and one person was shot and killed by police. The city got an injunction preventing further marches, so the union asked Reverend James Lawson
for help. Lawson was minister of Clayborn Temple (280 Hernando Street) and
a longtime civil rights leader. He called Martin Luther King Jr. to help negoti-
ate lifting the injunction.

While in Memphis, King was asked to give a speech at the Mason Temple
(930 Mason Street) on April 3. It was as inspiring as it was eerie. Reassuring
the crowd, he said,

> "We've got some difficult days ahead, but it doesn't matter with me
> now, because I've been to the mountaintop. . . . Like anybody, I would
> like to live a long life. Longevity has its place. But I'm not concerned
> about that now. I just want to do God's will. And he's allowed me
> to go up to the mountain, and I've looked over, and I've seen the
> Promised Land. I may not get there with you, but I want you to know
> tonight that we, as a people, will get to the Promised Land!"

The following evening, standing on the balcony of the Lorraine Motel,
King was struck down by an assassin's bullet. He was 39 years old.

Four days after King's murder, Coretta Scott King led a peaceful march
through downtown Memphis. The following day she buried her husband in
Atlanta (see page 183). On April 18, the sanitation workers were offered and
accepted a new contract, with a 15¢ per hour raise.

The Lorraine Motel balcony today

LEARN MORE
www.civilrightsmuseum.org
Going Down Jericho Road by Michael K. Honey (Norton, 2007)

Monteagle and New Market

Myles Horton, Septima Clark, and the Highlander Research and
Education Center

Original Location, Route 41, Monteagle, TN 37356

Current Location, 1959 Highlander Way, New Market, TN 37820 · (865) 933-3443

The Highlander Folk School was founded by Myles Horton in 1932. Though its adult education classes covered a wide variety of topics, its primary goal was to teach American history and government in order to empower the powerless, and to help students effect change in their home communities. During the Depression the school focused on labor issues, but at the dawn of the civil rights movement it taught Southerners how to organize to fight segregation.

Septima Clark, a teacher from Charleston, South Carolina, joined Highlander in 1956 as its director of education. She would be instrumental in training many of the movement's leaders, including Martin Luther King Jr., Fannie Lou Hamer, Rosa Parks, and Andrew Young. She also developed the idea of Citizenship Schools, which opened throughout the South. They not only taught reading and vocational skills but also became centers for civil rights organizing in many communities.

Tennessee officials were never happy about having a school for rabble-rousers in their midst. The state attorney general raided the Monteagle facility in 1959 and closed it down after uncovering liquor and integrated classrooms, both of which were illegal in Tennessee. Horton reopened the school in Knoxville and renamed it the Highlander Research and Education Center. Following constant harassment by a powerful right-wing businessman, Horton moved the school to New Market in 1970.

Highlander remained under the direction of Horton until 1973. When he died in 1990 he was buried on the grounds of the original school. You can still take courses at Highlander today, including environmental justice, human rights, youth leadership, criminal justice reform, and more.

LEARN MORE

www.highlandercenter.org

Highlander by John M. Glen (University of Kentucky, 1988)

The Long Haul by Myles Horton (Teachers College, 1998)

The Myles Horton Reader by Myles Horton and Dale Jacobs, ed. (University of Tennessee, 2003)

VIRGINIA

If you have a chance to visit Thomas Jefferson's grave at Monticello (931 Thomas Jefferson Parkway, Charlottesville), you may notice something absent from his obelisk: any mention that he ever served as president of the United States. His epitaph does, however, note that he founded the University of Virginia, authored the Declaration of Independence, and wrote Virginia's 1786 Bill for Establishing Religious Freedom. Many people are familiar with his first two accomplishments, but the third?

Jefferson introduced the Bill for Establishing Religious Freedom in 1777 as the Commonwealth rewrote its laws to reflect its new independence. The bill stated, in part, "No man shall be compelled to frequent or support any religious worship, place, or ministry whatsoever, nor shall be enforced, restrained, molested, or burdened in his body or goods, nor shall otherwise suffer, on account of his religious opinions or belief." Jefferson's goal was to avoid the entanglement of church and state that had characterized British rule.

Virginia and the new republic should be founded on the ideals of the Enlightenment, Jefferson believed, writing, "Our civil rights have no more dependence on our religious opinions, any more than our opinions in physics or geometry. . . ." That suggestion didn't go down easy with lawmakers, which is probably why it took nine years, and the political skills of Jefferson's friend James Madison, to pass the bill into law. The Virginia statute was used as the model for the Establishment Clause in the Bill of Rights' First Amendment.

Jefferson made good use of his own religious freedom by creating a book he titled *The Life and Morals of Jesus of Nazareth, Extracted Texturally from the Gospels*, better known as *The Jefferson Bible* today. So blasphemous was the notion that

> All a tyranny needs to gain a foothold is for people of good conscience to remain silent.
> —*Thomas Jefferson*

one could pick and choose elements from the Bible, it was suppressed until first published in 1902.

LEARN MORE
www.monticello.org, (434) 984-9822
Thomas Jefferson by R. B. Bernstein (Oxford, 2005)
American Sphinx by Joseph J. Ellis (Vintage 1998)
The Jefferson Bible by Thomas Jefferson (Beacon, 2001)

Central Point

Loving v. Virginia: An End to Miscegenation Laws
Passing Road, Central Point, VA 22552

Mildred Jeter and Richard Loving were married in Washington, D.C., on June 2, 1958, but they made their first home together in Central Point, Virginia, the town where they both grew up. Their home was raided at 2:00 A.M. by sheriff Garnett Brooks on July 13, 1958, while the couple slept. Brooks asked Richard who the woman in the bed with him was. When Richard told him Mildred was his wife, both were arrested under a 1924 Virginia statute outlawing miscegenation—interracial marriage.

The couple was held for five days before their parents posted bail. Both were charged under the law's evasion clause; residents could not marry in a state where interracial unions were legal, then return to Virginia. Facing one to five years in prison, they pleaded guilty and accepted a plea bargain: they received suspended sentences if they agreed to leave Virginia immediately and not return for 25 years.

The Lovings moved to Washington, D.C., and had three children. But in 1963 they returned to Virginia to be closer to their family. Not wanting to live in secret, Mildred wrote to Attorney General Robert Kennedy to ask whether the miscegenation law was still legal. It was. If the Lovings wanted it overturned they would have to challenge it in court.

Represented by the ACLU, the couple filed suit in November 1963 to vacate the original judgment as "repugnant to the Fourteenth Amendment." The motion was denied by a state court. The Virginia Supreme Court of Appeals, however, overturned the Lovings' 25-year exile as excessive and ordered a new trial. In 1966, before the Lovings returned to county court, the U.S. Supreme Court agreed to rule on the constitutionality of the statute.

Arguing before the high court, the state of Virginia asked that the justices look only at the evasion provision of the law, under which the couple had been convicted. That pig didn't fly. On June 12, 1967, the court ruled 9–0 that the Virginia's Racial Integrity Act of 1924 was unconstitutional under the Fourteenth Amendment's Equal Protection Clause. Richard Loving told reporters of his relief, "Now I can put my arm around my wife in Virginia."

Today June 12 is known nationally as Loving Day.

LEARN MORE
www.lovingday.org
Virginia Hasn't Always Been for Lovers by Phyl Newbeck (Southern Illinois
   University, 2004)

Farmville

Davis v. County School Board of Prince Edward County: **Part of**
Brown v. Board of Education
Robert R. Moton High School, 900 Griffin Boulevard, Farmville, VA 23901

The second of five desegregation lawsuits to be rolled together in the *Brown v. Board of Education* decision (see page 293) concerned the schools of Virginia's Prince Edward County. Unlike the other cases, this lawsuit grew out of the actions of one of the schools' students.

On April 23, 1951, the principal of Moton High School received an anonymous phone call telling him to rush to the local Greyhound station where police were holding two students. The call was bogus; as soon as the principal left the school, 16-year-old Barbara Rose Johns sent her friends around to announce an emergency assembly. Johns took the stage and requested that all 20+ teachers leave the auditorium. She then told the 450 students that they had suffered with their dilapidated building long enough, and that they should not return until the school board fixed the problems *and* integrated the district. The student body agreed.

Johns and her friends had secretly painted and stored picket signs in the school's carpentry shop, which the teens immediately picked up for a march to the courthouse downtown. The school superintendent turned them away, so they marched to the business owned by the school board chairman. He, too, rebuffed them. But the students soon found allies among African American residents. Reverend L. Francis Griffin got them in touch with the NAACP, who filed a discrimination case on behalf of five students. Fifteen-year-old Dorothy Davis was the lead plaintiff.

Despite overwhelming evidence to the contrary, a three-judge panel at the federal trial in Richmond "found no hurt or harm to either race" due to segregation, and voted unanimously to uphold the status quo. The case was then appealed to the U.S. Supreme Court.

Prince Edwards officials thought they'd won, and were outraged to learn otherwise when the *Brown* decision was handed down. Rather then integrate, white officials shut down their schools in 1959 . . . until 1964. A court had to force them to reopen. Students who were denied an education during those five years did not receive their diplomas until a reconciliation ceremony was held in 2003. They also received a long overdue apology from the Virginia legislature.

> **WE ARE TIRED OF TAR-PAPER SHACKS—WE WANT A NEW SCHOOL**
> —*Picket sign at the Moton High School walk-out*

LEARN MORE

http://motonmuseum.com, (434) 315-8775

They Closed Their Schools by R. C. Smith (University of North Carolina, 1965)

Richmond

Boynton v. Virginia: An End to Segregated Interstate Bus Facilities
Trailways Bus Station (gone), Downtown, Richmond, VA 23173

Bruce Boynton was heading home to Alabama from Howard University Law School in 1958 when his Trailways bus stopped in Richmond for a 40-minute layover. Boyton went inside the station for a sandwich. When told he would have to move to the "colored" lunch counter if he wanted to be served, he refused, and was arrested and fined $10.

Boynton soon got a firsthand supplement to his law education when the NAACP's Thurgood Marshall accepted his case and appealed it all the way to the U.S. Supreme Court. As with the case of Irene Morgan (see below), the justices declined to address the issue of equal protection, but ruled instead on the commercial provisions of the Interstate Commerce Act. In a 7–2 decision on December 5, 1960, the court held that facilities associated with interstate travel could not be segregated.

Some Southern waiting rooms and restaurants integrated following the ruling, but most refused. Their intransigence set the stage for the Freedom Riders (see page 150).

MORGAN V. VIRGINIA: AN END TO SEGREGATED SEATING ON INTERSTATE BUSES AND TRAINS

Bruce Boynton's legal challenge to interstate bus facilities followed, by a dozen years, another landmark civil rights decision that came out of this state: *Morgan v. Virginia.* In October 1944 Irene Morgan was traveling from Virginia to Maryland on a Greyhound bus when the driver asked her to give up her seat for a white passenger. When she refused, she was arrested, charged with disorderly conduct, and fined $10 in the circuit court in Middlesex County. Morgan's case was appealed to the U.S. Supreme Court, which ruled on July 3, 1946, that segregating interstate buses and trains—the vehicles themselves—posed an "undue burden" on commerce. Local buses and trains (see page 159) were not affected by the decision.

Patrick Henry: Give Him Liberty or Give Him Death
St. John's Episcopal Church, 2401 E. Broad Street, Richmond, VA 23223 · (804) 649-7938

Few American revolutionaries were as articulate as Patrick Henry, which makes it all the more ironic that he may not have uttered his most famous quote. As a delegate to the 1775 Virginia Assembly, Henry passionately advocated for the colonies to break their ties with Britain. On March 23 he addressed a meeting at St. John's Episcopal Church where he allegedly closed with an ultimatum to King George III: "Give me liberty or give me death!"

Some historians today question whether Henry delivered the speech exactly as attributed. It was not written down until years later, reconstructed by sympathetic biographer William Wirt. Still, the sentiment no doubt reflected his beliefs, and whatever he said tipped the Virginia Assembly toward colonial independence; both George Washington and Thomas Jefferson were in the pews at St. John's that day.

Patrick Henry did not temper his passion for individual liberty after the revolution. His denunciation of the new Constitution, believing that it encroached on individual liberties and states' rights, led to the adoption of the Bill of Rights in 1791. He died on June 6, 1799, and his body was returned to Red Hill, Henry's final Virginia home, in Brookneal (1250 Red Hill Road).

> Is life so dear, or peace so sweet, as to be purchased at the price of chains and slavery? . . . I know not what course others may take, but as for me, give me liberty or give me death!
> —*Patrick Henry (maybe), 1775*

LEARN MORE
www.historicstjohnschurch.org
www.redhill.org, (800) 514-PHMF
A Son of Thunder by Henry Mayer (Grove, 2001)

4
The Midwest

★ Illinois ★ Indiana ★ Iowa ★
★ Michigan ★ Minnesota ★
★ Missouri ★ Ohio ★
★ Wisconsin ★

ILLINOIS

Though he was born in Kentucky and spent some of his childhood in Indiana, Abraham Lincoln lived most of his adult life in Illinois. It was here, at New Salem, that he studied law, ran a store (that failed), and in 1834 was elected to the state legislature as a Whig. Three years later he moved to Springfield to practice law. In 1846 he was elected to the U.S. House of Representatives, and later became a Republican to protest the 1854 Kansas–Nebraska Act.

In 1858 Lincoln campaigned for the U.S. Senate against the author of the bill, Stephen Douglas. On June 16, at the [Old] State Capitol (Fifth and Adams Streets), Lincoln outlined the nation's dilemma before the Illinois Republican State Convention: "'A house divided against itself cannot stand.' I believe this government cannot endure, permanently half slave and half free." It was a message he returned to often during the race, particularly during seven well-attended debates, one in each of the state's congressional districts. Though Lincoln lost the election, two years later he was nominated for president by the Republicans, faced Stephen Douglas again, and won.

On February 11, 1861, from the balcony at Springfield's Great Western Depot (Monroe and Ninth Streets), Lincoln bid farewell to his hometown friends. "To this place, and the kindness of these people, I owe everything," he said. "I now leave, not knowing when, or whether ever, I may return, with a task before me greater than that which rested upon Washington." Indeed, the country erupted in Civil War five weeks after his inauguration.

Lincoln was assassinated on April 14, 1865, and his body was returned to Springfield for burial at Oak Ridge Cemetery (1500 N. Monument Avenue). Today in Springfield you can visit Lincoln's home (413 S. Eighth Street), law offices (209 S. Sixth Street), and the recently completed

> It is a sin to be silent when it is your duty to protest.
> —*Abraham Lincoln*

Abraham Lincoln Presidential Library and Museum (112 N. Sixth Street).

LEARN MORE

Lincoln Home, www.nps.gov/
liho, (217) 492-4241

Lincoln Library, www.alplm.org,
(217) 558-8844

New Salem, www.
lincolnsnewsalem.com,
(217) 632-4000

Lincoln by David Herbert Donald
(Random House, 1995)

Following in Lincoln's Footsteps
by Ralph Gary (Carroll & Graf,
2001)

Abraham Lincoln, c. 1860

Alton

Elijah Lovejoy, Martyr for Abolition

Lovejoy Monument (and Grave), Alton City Cemetery, 1205 E. Fifth Street, Alton, IL 62002 · (618) 465-7774

Reverend Elijah Lovejoy was a persistent, vocal advocate for abolition. In the early 1830s he published the St. Louis *Observer,* an antislavery newspaper. But Missouri was not a free state, and proslavery forces threatened him with prosecution and physical harm if he continued. Lovejoy felt his best strategy was to move his press across the Mississippi River to Alton, Illinois. There, in July 1836, he launched the Alton *Observer* and continued to write and speak out against the nation's "peculiar institution." Not only that, he assisted runaways heading north, and cofounded the Illinois Antislavery Society during a meeting in his home (Clawson and College Streets).

Three times over the next year and a half, Missouri mobs came across the river and destroyed Lovejoy's printing press. Each time his supporters replaced it. Then, on November 7, 1837, Lovejoy was shot while guarding his fourth press. He became a martyr for the abolitionist cause and, in a broader sense, freedom of the press. His murder moved abolitionists across the nation, particularly John Brown, to a new militancy.

A 90-foot monument to Lovejoy now stands in Alton Cemetery, the state's tallest monument to an Illinois resident. The frame from the last destroyed press can be seen at the *Alton Telegraph*'s offices (111 E. Broadway) today.

> As long as I am an American citizen, and as long as American blood runs in these veins, I shall hold myself at liberty to speak, to write, and to publish whatever I please on any subject amenable to the laws of my country for the same.
>
> —*Reverend Elijah Lovejoy*

LEARN MORE
Freedom's Champion by Paul Simon (Southern Illinois University, 1994)

Champaign

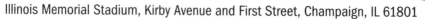

Farm Aid

Illinois Memorial Stadium, Kirby Avenue and First Street, Champaign, IL 61801

The idea came to Willie Nelson in August 1985 while playing the Illinois State Fair: a benefit concert to assist America's struggling farmers. Plummeting crop prices in the early 1980s were bankrupting thousands of family farms, and the Reagan administration was doing little to stop it. So Nelson stepped up, asked the governor to find him a stadium, and started calling his musical friends. Five weeks later, on September 22, the first Farm Aid concert was held at the University of Illinois.

Nelson, John Mellencamp, and Neil Young led the effort; Johnny and June Carter Cash, Bob Dylan, Tom Petty, Bonnie Raitt, Loretta Lynn, Emmylou Harris, Jon Bon Jovi, Joni Mitchell, Merle Haggard, John Denver, Carole King, Billy Joel, Glen Campbell, and others—the largest confluence of country and rock stars ever assembled for a benefit—joined them. Tickets were $17.50. The show raised not only emergency funds for struggling farms but also awareness about the dangerous trend in American agriculture toward corporate, factory-style operations.

> I've always believed that the most important people on the planet are the ones who plant the seeds and care for the soil where they grow.
>
> —*Willie Nelson*

Unfortunately, that trend continues. Farm Aid plows on, and has expanded its mission to address issues surrounding organic farming, biofuels, community agriculture, world hunger, and "growing local" campaigns. The American consumer seems to be coming to the realization that without the family farm, the economic soul of the nation is at risk. The question remains, will enough people realize this before it's too late?

LEARN MORE
www.farmaid.org, (800) FARM-AID
Farm Aid by Holly George-Warren (Rodale, 2005)

Chicago

Carrie Chapman Catt and the League of Woman Voters
Congress Hotel, 520 S. Michigan Avenue, Chicago, IL 60605

Following the ratification of the Nineteenth Amendment, the National American Woman Suffrage Association (NAWSA) found itself without a mission. What would it do next?

How about throw a party! Hundreds of NAWSA members gathered in Chicago to celebrate their victory on February 13, 1920. The party was held in the Congress Hotel's Gold Room. Delegates blew party horns for a half hour, marched up and down the aisles, stood on chairs waving flags, and joined together in singing "America" and "The Star-Spangled Banner." The ceremonies ended with the official disbanding of the NAWSA and the formation of a new organization: the League of Women Voters (LWV). Carrie Chapman Catt, who served as head of the NAWSA from 1900 to 1904, and 1915 to 1920, proposed the nonpartisan league to promote full participation in the nation's electoral process.

> I venture to propose [a memorial] whose benefits will bless our entire nation and bring happiness to the humblest of our citizens—the most natural, the most appropriate, and the most patriotic memorial that could be constructed—a League of Women Voters to "finish the fight" and to aid in the reconstruction of the nation.
>
> —*Carrie Chapman Catt, in "National Call for a League of Women Voters," 1920*

Today the LWV has more than 900 chapters in all 50 states, which regularly host candidate debates, voter drives, and public policy forums. It is one of the original grassroots organizations, where local chapters are encouraged to set their own agendas "to make democracy work for all citizens."

LEARN MORE
www.lwv.org, (202) 429-0854
Carrie Chapman Catt by Jacqueline Van Voris (Feminist Press at CUNY, 2007)

The Haymarket Riot
600 W. Randolph Street, Chicago, IL 60661

On May 4, 1886, a group of workers gathered in Haymarket Square to protest working conditions at the McCormick Farm Machinery Works (Blue Island and Western Avenues) where two protesters had been shot and killed the day before. Central to their demands was the call for an eight-hour work day. By all accounts, the gathering was peaceful; even Chicago Mayor Carter Harrison stopped by for a look.

Then the police arrived. A 176-man battalion confronted the crowd near the corner of Randolph and Des Plaines Streets. Without warning, a bomb was thrown at the police. One officer was killed immediately, and pandemonium erupted. Before it was over, six other cops and four civilians (but probably more) were dead or mortally wounded. An investigation later revealed that most of the police casualties were shot in the back by other trigger-happy cops.

It was never determined who threw the bomb. However, eight men, all anarchists and/or labor organizers, were tried and convicted for the police deaths. Four were eventually hanged on Novem-

Haymarket monument today

ber 11, 1887: August Spies, Albert Parsons, Adolph Fischer, and George Engel. A fifth, Louis Lingg, committed suicide in his cell a day earlier. Before the trap door opened, August Spies shouted, "The day will come when our silence will be more powerful than the voices you are throttling today."

Three men who received prison sentences, Michael Schwab, Samuel Fielden, and Oscar Neebe, were pardoned in 1893 by Illinois Governor John Peter Altgeld. Though scorned and soundly defeated in the next election, Altgeld proclaimed, "No man's ambition has the right to stand in the way of performing a simple act of justice."

LEARN MORE

http://dwardmac.pitzer.edu:16080/Anarchist_Archives/index.html

Death in the Haymarket by James Green (Pantheon, 2006)

Haymarket Revisited by William J. Adelman (Illinois Labor History Society, 1986)

Henry Gerber and the Society for Human Rights
Gerber Home, 1710 N. Crilly Court, Chicago, IL 60614

America's first gay rights organization wasn't founded on either coast, but in the heart of the Midwest. On December 24, 1924, the state of Illinois issued a charter for the Society for Human Rights (SHR), the brainchild of Henry Gerber, who served as its first and only president. While serving in the U.S. Army of Occupation following World War I, Gerber became familiar with Germany's gay civil-rights movement and decided to bring the idea back to the states. The SHR's incorporation documents were written in such a way that those not "in the know" (including the bureaucrat who issued the charter) wouldn't realize its true purpose.

The SHR was a small organization—only four named members—but was able to publish a newsletter, *Friendship and Freedom*. The group met in the home of Gerber and his partner, Henry Teacutter, to discuss legislative action, plan lectures, and build a community. About a year after it was founded, the wife of SHR's vice president tipped off a social worker, who got the police to raid Gerber's home. He and two others were arrested. After failing to find anything incriminating in Gerber's journals or newsletter, a detective introduced a powder puff as evidence that Gerber had been engaging in sodomy. The case was ultimately thrown out because authorities had failed to obtain a warrant.

Gerber was fired from his post office job after his superiors learned of his arrest. The SHR folded and he reenlisted in the army; Gerber retired with full honors at the end of World War II. In the 1950s he wrote under the pseudonym "parisex" for several gay rights publications, and in the 1960s under his own byline. He died in 1972. Chicago's LGBT archive, the Gerber/Hart Library, is named (in part) to honor his groundbreaking work.

LEARN MORE
www.gerberhart.org, (773) 381-8030

Jane Addams and Hull House
Jane Addams Hull House Museum, 800 S. Halsted Street, Chicago, IL 60607 · (312) 413-5353

The settlement house—the forerunner of today's social service agency—was a progressive idea that originated in Europe. In 1887 Jane Addams was traveling abroad and visited Toynbee Hall, a settlement house in London's East End. Two years later she brought the idea to Chicago, opening Hull House with her partner Ellen Gates Starr. Hull House addressed the social and cultural needs of the city's near west side, and would grow to include kindergarten and adult education classes, a swimming pool and gymnasium, a library and community kitchen, and dozens of clubs for children and adults. Addams formed the Juvenile Protective Association, which led to the nation's first juvenile courts and compulsory education laws, and an Immigrants' Protective League that advocated for workplace reform and consumer protection.

Addams was born into a wealthy family in Cedarville, Illinois (425 N. Mill Street), on September 6, 1860, but that didn't hamper her from understanding the needs of

Jane Addams, 1912

the poor. She was also a founding member of the NAACP (see page 102) and the ACLU, and the first president of the Women's International League for Peace and Freedom. For that she received the 1931 Nobel Peace Prize. Addams died at Hull House on May 21, 1935, and was buried in her family's plot at the Cedarville Cemetery.

> Progress is not automatic; the world grows better because people wish that it should, and take the right steps to make it better.
>
> —*Jane Addams*

LEARN MORE
www.uic.edu/jaddams/hull
Citizen by Louise W. Knight (University of Chicago, 2006)
Twenty Years at Hull House by Jane Addams (Dodo, 2006)

Lorraine Hansberry and *A Raisin in the Sun*
Hansberry House, 6140 S. Rhodes Avenue, Chicago, IL 60637

When *A Raisin in the Sun* debuted in 1959, it garnered critical acclaim for its 29-year-old playwright, Lorraine Hansberry. The play was based on a true Chicago story—Lorraine Hansberry's story. When she was just eight her father, real estate broker Carl Hansberry, bought a home in west Hyde Park. The family moved in on May 26, 1937, and the neighborhood reacted violently. Neighbors harassed the children as they played, and someone threw a brick through the Hansberry's front window.

And then Anna M. Lee, on behalf of the Woodlawn Property Association, filed suit against the Hansberrys claiming they were in violation of a local covenant. The Circuit Court of Cook County and the Illinois Supreme Court sided with Lee, but the U.S. Supreme Court overturned the lower courts' rulings in 1940. While *Hansberry v. Lee* did not universally abolish real estate restrictions based upon race, it dealt a major blow to the practice.

A Raisin in the Sun earned Hansberry the New York Drama Critics' Circle award for Best Play. Sadly, she was not able to enjoy her success for long; she died of pancreatic cancer on January 12, 1965, at the age of 34. The Hansberrys' former home still stands.

LEARN MORE

Readings on A Raisin in the Sun by Lawrence Kappel, ed. (Greenhaven, 2001)

To Be Young, Gifted and Black by Lorraine Hansberry (Vintage, 1996)

A Raisin in the Sun by Lorraine Hansberry (Random House, 2002)

Upton Sinclair and *The Jungle*
850 W. Exchange Street, Chicago, IL 60609

"I aimed at the public's heart," author Upton Sinclair reflected, "and by accident I hit it in the stomach." First published in serial form in *Appeal to Reason*, a socialist newspaper, *The Jungle* was a muckraking exposé of the working conditions in Chicago's stockyards and packinghouses. Sinclair dedicated the 1906 book version "To the Workingmen of America," but it was his grotesque descriptions of animal slaughter and meat production that moved readers. In its wake, overseas sales of American meat dropped by half, so to avert an industry-wide collapse, meatpacking executives *joined* the call for increased federal oversight. Congress passed the Meat Inspection Act and the Pure Food and Drug Act later that year.

Labor reform was not as forthcoming. The novel's protagonist, Jurgis Rudkus, is exploited by bosses, landlords, bankers, and politicians; his wife dies in childbirth and his son drowns in a slum mud puddle; and yet an unnamed worker who slips into a vat and is ground into sausage received more sympathy from the reading public. Actually, sausage eaters got the most sympathy.

Despite the bad press, the Chicago Union Stockyards continued to expand until 1920, when production peaked. Meaningful livestock-treatment reform didn't come until the late 1950s, pushed by the Humane Society of the United States and the Amalgamated Meat Cutters and Butcher Workmen of North America. On August 20, 1958, the Federal Humane Slaughter Act

> There were cattle which had been fed on "whiskey malt," the refuse of the breweries, and had become what the men called "steerly"—which means covered with boils. It was a nasty job killing these, for when you plunged your knife into them they would burst and splash foul-smelling stuff into your face.
>
> —*Upton Sinclair, in*
> *The Jungle, 1906*

was signed into law, which outlawed many of the industry's most barbaric practices.

The Union Stockyards eventually closed in 1971, and all that is left is the main entry's arch on Exchange Street.

LEARN MORE

The Jungle: The Uncensored Original Edition by Upton Sinclair (See Sharp, 2003)

Radical Innocent by Anthony Arthur (Random House, 2006)

Upton Sinclair and the Other American Century by Kevin Mattson (Wiley, 2006)

East Moline

Chad Pregracke and Living Lands & Waters

17625 Route 24N, East Moline, IL 61244 · (309) 496-9848

Growing up, Chad Pregracke lived 67 feet from the banks of the Mississippi River. By the time he reached high school he had worked as a shell diver and commercial fisherman, and understood the environmental problems of the river all too well. Most visibly, its banks and islands were strewn with garbage, from litter to abandoned cars, tires, and refrigerators. At the age of 16, he jumped in his skiff with a new mission: he was going to clean up the river. The *whole* river, from Minnesota to New Orleans.

And he just might. In the beginning, Pregracke worked summers through college, but in 1997 he approached the president of Alcoa—the first big company he found in the phone book—to sponsor a six-person operation to clean 435 miles. He needed $77,000, and got $8,400. With that, by himself, he launched the Mississippi River Beautification and Restoration Project. By the end of summer he'd collected 45,000 pounds of debris from 100 miles around the Quad Cities area.

> As I motored upstream with a heavy load of clams, a huge pile of more than 50 steel barrels that stood exposed in the mud on shore caught my eye. The ragged mess had probably been there for 30 years or more. . . . But this time a 60-foot yacht was anchored just offshore from the ugly tangle of barrels. . . . That was the moment I knew what I had to do.
>
> —*Chad Pregracke*

A year later Pregracke formed the nonprofit organization Living Lands & Waters (LL&W). He and a small crew of volunteers gathered 400,000 pounds of trash from St. Louis to Guttenberg, Iowa. The group then expanded into the Illinois and Ohio Rivers, and in 2002 adopted a donated rusty barge as a floating base of operations. They converted it into living quarters and an educational center to teach environmental workshops in riverfront communities. In 2003 LL&W launched the Riverbottom Forest Restoration Project to plant fruit and nut trees on the islands of the Mississippi. And following Hurricane Katrina in 2005, LL&W suspended its season and raced to New Orleans to assist in the cleanup, and repaired 70 homes.

Each summer LL&W takes on more volunteers and waterways, and considering that Pregracke is still in his early 30s, they'll probably complete the job before he retires. But don't count on him ever retiring.

LEARN MORE

www.livinglandsandwaters.org

From the Bottom Up by Chad Pregracke and Jeff Barrow (National Geographic, 2007)

Evanston

Frances Willard and the Women's Christian Temperance Union

Rest Cottage, 1730 Chicago Avenue, Evanston, IL 60201 · (847) 328-7500

Frances Willard was never one to retreat from a challenge, even during childhood. When told she couldn't ride a horse on her family's farm, young Frances—she preferred "Frank"—taught a cow to take a bridle, then saddled it up. After the cow tossed her off, Willard's father relented. As an adult, she refused to accept the Victorian convention that a woman was obligated to marriage and motherhood, and instead devoted herself to progressive causes: the eight-hour workday, women's suffrage, pure food and drug reform, uniform laws regarding women and men, and passive resistance as a method of bringing about social change.

Willard is best remembered, however, as the second (and most influential) president of the Women's Christian Temperance Union (WCTU), serving from 1879 to her death in 1898. She wrote and promoted the Polyglot Petition in 1885, which demanded that Congress outlaw alcohol, opium, and tobacco.

Though 7.5 million people signed the petition worldwide, it didn't have any immediate effect except to demonstrate the political muscle of active women, more than three decades before they gained the right to vote.

For years the WCTU was based out of her Evanston home, Rest Cottage. Today, as a museum, it appears much as it did when Willard lived there, preserved by her companion and secretary, Anna Gordon. Here you'll see rolls of the Polyglot Petition, WCTU and Willard family mementos, a huge bell cast from 1,000 confiscated opium and tobacco pipes, and Gladys . . . Willard's bike. At the age of 53, when presented with a bicycle by Lady Somerset, Willard taught herself to ride, peddling around Evanston to the shock of the local bluebloods.

LEARN MORE
www.franceswillardhouse.org
Frances Willard by Ruth Bordin (University of North Carolina, 2001)
How I Learned to Ride the Bicycle by Frances E. Willard (Fair Oaks, 1991)

Forest Park

Dissenters' Row
Haymarket Martyrs Monument, Forest Home (Waldheim) Cemetery, 863 S. Des Plaines Avenue, Forest Park, IL 60130 · (708) 366-1900

Chicago business and government leaders were correctly concerned that the graves of the men executed for the Haymarket Riot (see page 234) would become a shrine for anarchists and labor organizers, so they forbid the bodies from being buried within the city limits. Yet the five martyrs didn't go far; they were laid to rest just outside Chicago in Forest Park. Their three pardoned codefendants were also buried here as they died. A monument was erected and dedicated in 1893, and has been the location of many labor rallies since. Every year on the Sunday closest to May 4, feel free to join the Black Sunday memorial gathering.

The Haymarket martyrs aren't the only labor leaders buried in Forest Home. So were anarchist Emma Goldman, organizer Elizabeth Gurley Flynn, Lucy Parsons, and part of Joe Hill's and Bill Haywood's ashes. The graves are today known as "Dissenters' Row," sometimes jokingly referred to as "The Communist Plot."

Jacksonville

Packard v. Packard: **Women Are Not Their Husband's Property**
Jacksonville State Hospital (now the Jacksonville Developmental Center), 1201 S. Main Street, Jacksonville, IL 62650

One of the milestones in the long struggle for women's rights was achieved by a former inmate of Illinois's Jacksonville State Hospital for the Insane, Elizabeth Packard. Packard was *not* insane, nor had she ever been, but had been locked away for three years by her husband, Reverend Theophilus Packard Jr.

Why? Reverend Packard had grown tired of her constant questioning of his Calvinist beliefs, going so far as to withdraw from his church altogether. She had also asked that her husband weed the flower bed in front of their house, and when he refused she did it herself. *Crazy* behavior.

After three years in Jacksonville, Elizabeth Packard was returned to her husband, who then locked her in their home's nursery with the windows nailed shut. She managed to slip a note out to her friend, Sarah Haslett, who brought her in-home imprisonment to the attention of a local magistrate. Judge Charles Starr ordered Reverend Packard to bring his wife in to court. On January 18, 1864, after a ridiculous trial that focused more on theology than mental competence, a jury took a mere seven minutes to deliver a verdict: Elizabeth Packard was sane.

Though the court did not rule directly on the constitutionality of the law allowing husbands to institutionalize their wives, Elizabeth Packard made it her mission to overturn the law herself. Estranged (but not divorced) from her husband, Packard lectured on behalf of women's rights and was successful in changing four states' statutes, as well as Illinois's law denying married women the right to own property.

LEARN MORE
The Private War of Mrs. Packard by Barbara Sapinsley (Paragon House, 1991)

Mt. Olive

Mother Jones, "The Most Dangerous Woman in America"
Union Miners Cemetery, North Lake Avenue, Mt. Olive, IL 62069

Mary Harris Jones, better known as Mother Jones, did not become an activist until she was in her 40s, but she sure made up for lost time. Born in Cork

County, Ireland, in 1830 (some say 1837), she immigrated to the United States in 1859 by way of Canada. After her husband, George Jones, and four children died in Tennessee's 1867 yellow fever outbreak, she moved to Illinois. Four years later she lost everything else in the Great Chicago Fire.

Destitute, she joined the Knights of Labor and began organizing workers. A fiery orator with a salty tongue, she also worked with the United Mine Workers and the Socialist Party, and in 1905 helped found the Industrial Workers of the World (IWW). Jones was involved in most of the nation's labor battles between the 1880s and 1920s, and was so successful a West Virginia DA dubbed her "The Most Dangerous Woman in America." She was jailed dozens of times.

Mother Jones, 1902

> Pray for the dead, and fight like hell for the living.
>
> —*Mother Jones*

Jones had a knack for publicity, as in 1905 when she led mill waifs on a 125-mile march from Kensington, Pennsylvania, to Teddy Roosevelt's home in Oyster Bay, Long Island. "We want to go to school!" the children cried, but the president refused to meet with them. Jones denounced Roosevelt as a coward and a "monkey chaser," a slam at his passion for hunting. It was great newspaper copy, and raised child labor reform to a national issue.

Mother Jones died on November 30, 1930, and per her wishes was buried in the Union Miners Cemetery in Mt. Olive. Thirty-two years earlier, 10 men had been killed during a coal strike in nearby Virden, and four of the victims were laid to rest here. A large monument with a bronze portrait of Mother Jones now adorns her grave.

LEARN MORE
www.iww.org
Mother Jones by Elliott J. Gorn (Hill and Wang, 2001)
The Autobiography of Mother Jones by Mother Jones (Charles H. Kerr, 1996)

Princeton

Owen Lovejoy and the Emancipation Proclamation
Lovejoy Homestead, S. Sixth and E. Peru Streets, Princeton, IL 61356 · (815) 875-2616

Owen Lovejoy, the younger brother of Elijah Lovejoy (see page 231), made a vow to continue his brother's work after he was murdered in 1837. As minister of Princeton's Congregational Church, Lovejoy publicly spoke out against slavery, published a biography of his brother that inspired others to action, and used his home as a station on the Underground Railroad. Lovejoy was even put on trial for harboring runaway slaves in 1843, but was found not guilty by a sympathetic jury.

In 1856 Lovejoy was elected to the U.S. House of Representatives, and would become one of Abraham Lincoln's staunchest allies. On December 14, 1863, he introduced a "universal emancipation" bill that both supported Lincoln's signing of the Emancipation Proclamation and became the framework of the Thirteenth Amendment. Sadly, he did not live to see the end of the Civil War, dying in 1864. He is buried in Princeton's Oakland Cemetery.

LEARN MORE
www.lovejoyhomestead.com
His Brother's Blood by Owen Lovejoy (University of Illinois, 2004)

INDIANA

While it is true that Indiana gave the world Dan Quayle and Wonder bread, it has also given us Kurt Vonnegut Jr., and didn't he more than make up for the other two? Vonnegut was born in Indianapolis on November 11, 1922. While attending Shortridge High School (3401 N. Meridian Street) he began writing for the school's *Daily Echo*; at Cornell he was associate editor of the *Daily Sun* until World War II took him on another path. Vonnegut became a scout for the 106th Infantry Division and was captured on December 14, 1944, during the Battle of the Bulge. Imprisoned in Dresden, he was one of only seven American soldiers to survive the firebombing of the city on February 14–15, 1945, holed up in a meat locker named Schlachthof Fünf—Slaughterhouse Five.

The experience of seeing human depravity on such a grand scale led to his signature black humor. Yet his satiric novels never failed to offer islands of hope amid seas of pessimism, and throughout his 50-year career he returned often to antiwar and humanist themes. He retired from fiction in 1997, but continued writing essays and nonfiction, and was senior editor at *In These Times* magazine. His final book, *Man Without a Country*, offered his parting thoughts on the new century, and American imperialism run amok: "The highest treason in the USA is to say Americans are not loved, no matter where they are, no matter what they are doing there."

Vonnegut fell in his New York townhouse in the spring of 2007 and suffered an irreparable brain injury. He died on April 11.

And so it goes.

> I am a humanist, which means, in part, that I have tried to behave decently without expectations of rewards or punishment after I am dead.
>
> —*Kurt Vonnegut*

LEARN MORE
www.vonnegut.com
Man Without a Country by Kurt Vonnegut (Seven Stories Press, 2007)
Kurt Vonnegut's Crusade by Todd F. Davis (SUNY Albany, 2006)

Fountain City

Coffin House, Grand Central Station on the Underground Railroad

Levi Coffin House State Historic Park, 113 N. Main Street, Fountain City, IN 47341 · (765) 847-2432

Between 1839 and 1847 (and since 1827, before they lived in Indiana), Levi and Catharine Coffin helped more than 2,000 slaves escape to freedom in the North via their home in Fountain City (then called Newark). Because of this, it later earned the designation of "Grand Central Station of the Underground Railroad." Not one slave who passed through this station during those 20 years was ever captured. It certainly helped that Coffin was protected by a large network of sympathetic local politicians, lawyers, magistrates, and merchants who were willing to defend him from slave catchers.

The Coffins moved to Cincinnati, Ohio, in 1847, where they set up a new underground station, saved another thousand runaways, and met Harriet Beecher Stowe. She used them as the inspiration for Simeon and Rachel Halliday in *Uncle Tom's Cabin*. Catharine advocated on behalf of "free labor goods," clothing and other products that had not been manufactured with slave labor. In Cincinnati the couple opened the Free Produce Store, an idea that spread to other Northern states and markets.

The Coffins' Indiana home has been refurbished to its antebellum appearance with period furnishings. On the tour, you will see a hiding place in the attic located behind the headboard, and another between the mattresses on the bed. Levi and Catharine Coffin are buried at Spring Grove Cemetery (4521 Spring Grove Avenue) in Cincinnati.

> The Bible, in bidding us to feed the hungry and clothe the naked, said nothing about color.
> —*Levi Coffin*

LEARN MORE
www.waynet.org/nonprofit/coffin.htm
Levi Coffin, Quaker by Mary Ann Yannessa (Friends United Press, 2001)
Reminiscences of Levi Coffin by Levi Coffin and Ben Richmond, ed. (Friends
   United Press, 2006)

Indianapolis

Robert Kennedy on the Assassination of Martin Luther King Jr.
17th Street and Broadway, Indianapolis, IN 46202

Robert Kennedy learned about the assassination of Martin Luther King Jr. during a short flight from Muncie to Indianapolis on April 4, 1968. He was campaigning for the May 7 Indiana primary, the first state primary he'd entered as a presidential candidate.

Kennedy was scheduled to speak at a rally in an African American neighborhood, but his advisors warned him against appearing. He dismissed their advice and, to avoid confrontation, asked that police *not* escort him to the event. When he arrived outside the Broadway Christian Center he realized from the faces in the crowd that they had not yet learned of King's murder.

Standing on the back of a flatbed truck, he started, "I have bad news for you, for all of our fellow citizens, and for people who love peace all over the world, and that is that Martin Luther King himself was shot and killed tonight." He went on to give a short, heartfelt plea that Americans dedicate themselves to a new path, away from violence and toward justice and peace. Many cite it as the best speech he ever gave. Riots erupted in many U.S. cities that night, but not in Indianapolis.

> What we need in the United States is not division; what we need in the United States is not hatred; what we need in the United States is not violence or lawlessness; but love and wisdom, and compassion toward one another, and a feeling of justice toward those who still suffer within our country, whether they be white or they be black.
> —*Robert Kennedy*

Kokomo, Russiaville, and Cicero

Ryan White, an Early Face of AIDS

Western Middle School, 2600 S. County Road 600W, Russiaville, IN 46979

Ryan White was born in Kokomo on December 6, 1971, where doctors soon learned he suffered from hemophilia. With blood-derived Clotting Factor, most hemophiliacs can lead relatively typical lives, but in the early 1980s the nation's blood supply was compromised by the HIV virus, which in turn infected most hemophiliacs using Clotting Factor. Doctors believe White contracted HIV from a transfusion in 1984.

As if his medical challenges weren't enough, the pain he suffered at the hands of the local community was far worse. Restaurants would throw out his plates and silverware after he'd eaten at their establishments, or customers would march out at the sight of him. Garbage was dumped on the family's lawn. The pastor at St. Luke's United Methodist Church asked that Ryan sit only in the first or last pews. Other ministers claimed Ryan was infected because his family weren't "good" Christians. Kids flattened themselves against the lockers when he walked by and adults accused him of biting other children and spitting on vegetables at the grocery.

Through it all, Ryan White maintained a remarkably positive attitude. But when the local school district tried to get him banned from the classroom, the Whites fought back. At first Ryan was made to stay at home and attend classes through a telephone hookup. But in an agreement between both sides, White was allowed to return if he agreed to skip gym, eat from paper plates and plastic utensils, drink from a separate water fountain, and use a reserved bathroom. Yet by the time he returned to Western Middle School on February 21, 1986, half the school's students had been withdrawn by their parents. Before the end of the day, White was yanked back out by a court order secured by a group called Concerned Citizens and Parents of Children Attending Western School Corporation. They sued the Whites, their doctor, and the school for "endangering" three students. They even tried to get Jeanne White declared an unfit mother and have Ryan removed from her home.

But when their case was finally heard, it took the judge less than a minute to throw it out. Ryan returned to the school the same day. Shortly after Valentine's Day, 1987, his locker was vandalized with "Queer" and "Faggot" written on his school books. But after somebody fired a bullet through the front window of their home (3506 S. Webster Street) the family decided they'd had enough of Kokomo. With a loan from Elton John, the Whites moved to Cicero.

Unlike what the Whites had experienced in Kokomo, they were welcomed in Cicero. Jill Stewart, student body president of Hamilton Heights High

School (25802 Route 19, Arcadia), immediately befriended Ryan, as did other neighbors. Hamilton Heights had already launched an AIDS education program at the school in anticipation of White's arrival.

During the summer months, White performed as an extra in a movie about his life, and got a job at a local mall. Eventually, the virus caught up with him, and on April 8, 1990, Palm Sunday, White died at Riley Children's Hospital (702 Barnhill Drive) in Indianapolis. White's pall bearers included Howie Long, Phil Donahue, and Elton John, when he was laid to rest in the Cicero Cemetery (236th Street and Tollgate Road) beneath a large granite memorial.

LEARN MORE
www.ryanwhite.com
My Own Story by Ryan White and Ann Marie Cunningham (Dial, 1991)

Terre Haute

Eugene Debs, American Radical
Debs House, 451 N. Eighth Street, Terre Haute, IN 47807 · (812) 232-2163

In the pantheon of American political leaders, and certainly among those who have run for president, few have put themselves on the line as often, at great personal cost, as Eugene Victor Debs. He was born in Terre Haute (457 N. Fourth Street, torn down) on November 5, 1855. At 14 he began working on the railroads, and in 1875 became a founding member of the Brotherhood of Locomotive Firemen. He rose through the ranks of the labor movement and Indiana politics, and in 1884 was elected to the Indiana legislature as a Democrat.

Debs soon became convinced that labor needed to take an aggressive, national approach to address the needs of the working class, and in 1893 he founded the American Railway Union (ARU), the nation's first industrial union. The following year the ARU was involved in a bitter dispute with the Pullman Palace Car Company. Though the ARU did not represent the Pullman workers who had suffered pay cuts of 30 percent, they refused to work rail lines that carried Pullman cars. "Pullman, both the man and the town, is an ulcer on the body politic," Debs said. "And thus the merry war [on workers]—the dance of skeletons bathed in human tears—goes on, and it will go on, brothers, forever, unless you, the American Railway Union, stop it; end it; crush it out." Grover Cleveland sent the U.S. Army to Chicago to break the strike, and by the end of

July riots had left 13 dead. Debs was charged with "interfering with the mail": Cleveland had ordered mail cars to be attached to trains pulling Pullman coaches to entrap Debs. The labor leader eventually served six months for a contempt citation.

Released from prison in 1895, Debs helped found the Socialist Democratic Party in 1898 (renamed the Socialist Party of America in 1901), and in 1900 ran as its presidential nominee. His platform included a halt to child labor, suffrage for women, civil rights for African Americans, and the right for workers to unionize. Though he lost, he would repeat his campaign in 1904, 1908, and 1912, when he got 6 percent of the national vote. In 1918 he denounced America's participation in World War I, and was jailed for sedition (see page 273). In defiance, he ran for president that fall from his Atlanta jail cell, and received almost a million votes.

Eugene Debs, c. 1912

> I'd rather vote for something I want, and not get it, than vote for something I don't want, and get it.
>
> —*Eugene Debs*

Debs never quite recovered from his prison experience. He was nominated for the Nobel Peace Prize in 1924. He died at the Lindlahr Sanitarium in Elmhurst, Illinois, on November 20, 1926, and his ashes were buried in the family plot in Terre Haute's Highland Lawn Cemetery (4520 Wabash Avenue). Debs's longtime home is today a museum.

LEARN MORE

www.eugenevdebs.com

Eugene V. Debs by Nick Salvatore (University of Illinois, 2007)

Harp Song for a Radical by Marguerite Young (Knopf, 1999)

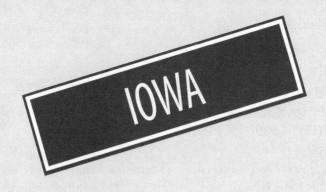

IOWA

Every four years the nation's political eyes turn toward Iowa and its unique candidate selection process: the Iowa caucuses. Though it is sometimes dismissed (usually by those who lose the contest) as unrepresentative of the national electorate's concerns—farm issues, for example, get considerable attention, while urban issues get less—the caucuses themselves are the epitome of participatory democracy. Neighbors gather in 1,800 schools, libraries, and churches around the state to debate their candidates' relative merits and suggest planks for their parties' platforms. Midway through the evening the participants divide into groups based on who they support, and a headcount is taken. Those groups not achieving a "viability threshold" (from 15 to 20 percent) are noted, and then participants are given 30 minutes to "realign." During that half hour, participants can lobby others into switching groups. One realigned, a new poll is taken. If a candidate's group is still not viable, they are not included when the delegates to the county conventions are nominated, in proportion to their support.

The Iowa caucuses have drawn significant national attention only since 1972, when George McGovern (see page 308) secured a strong second-place finish. Because they take place in January, prior to the New Hampshire primary, the caucuses can make or break a campaign. The Republican caucuses are also preceded by a "straw poll." The nonbinding contest is held five months earlier, in August, and the candidate who gets enough registered Republicans to participate, either by bussing them to the event or coaxing them through other . . . um . . . *incentives*, usually wins. Because the process can (and is) subverted, the results of the straw poll are usually dismissed as a mere "beauty contest."

Clarinda

Jesse Field and 4-H

Goldenrod School, Nodaway Valley Museum, 1600 S. 16th Street, Clarinda, IA
51632 · (712) 542-3073

Educator Jesse Field believed the Three Rs weren't nearly enough, so she
added Three Hs: Head, Heart, and Hands. Though her students at the Goldenrod School lived in the heart of farm country, they didn't seem to know
too much about the basics of rural life. So in 1901 she formed the Boys' Corn
Club to teach them about seed selection, livestock judging, and other farming
skills. A Girls' Home Club was also organized, but with domestic concerns in
mind: sewing, baking, and tending to a garden. Both clubs were a hit.

By 1906, Field was married—now she was Jesse Field Shambaugh—and
superintendent of the Page County school district. In 1907, O. H. Benson of
Clarion designed the now familiar 4-H emblem, though it only had three Hs
at the time. Shambaugh later added a fourth H leaf, for Home, which was later
changed to Health. You can still see Field's former one-room schoolhouse
where this innovative teacher first launched her big idea.

 **LEARN MORE**
www.clarinda.org/4-H.htm
www.4husa.org, (301) 961-2800

Des Moines

Tinker v. Des Moines: **Student Free Speech**

Warren Harding Junior High School, 203 E. Euclid Avenue, Des Moines, IA 50313

In December 1965, 13-year-old Mary Beth Tinker and a few friends decided
they would wear black armbands to school in protest of the Vietnam War.
Tinker's principal, Chester Pratt, suspended her for violating the district's
policy against such displays. Four students at Roosevelt High School (4419
Center Street)—Christopher Eckhardt, Ross Peterson, Bruce Clark, and Mary
Beth's brother John—were also suspended. Later, during a public meeting on
December 21, the school board upheld its policy that banned peaceful dissent.
And the controversy even followed the Tinkers home; on Christmas Eve they
received a threat to blow up their home, and later a right-wing radio talk show

host offered to pay the court costs of anyone willing to use a shotgun on their father.

Undaunted, the Tinkers and Eckhardt, with the help of the Iowa Civil Liberties Union, challenged the policy in district court. The ban was upheld, but the U.S. Court of Appeals reached a split decision. Finally, the U.S. Supreme Court rendered a verdict on February 24, 1969. In a 7–2 ruling, the justices declared the armband ban unconstitutional, ruling "[s]tudents do not shed their Constitutional rights to freedom of expression at the schoolhouse gate." The justices also pointed out that the Tinkers' protest did not disrupt classes. In fact, there had been no problems until the principals got involved.

> School officials do not possess absolute authority over their students. Students in school as well as out of school are "persons" under our constitution.
> —Justice Abe Fortas, in Tinker v. Des Moines, 1969

LEARN MORE
The Struggle for Student Rights by John W. Johnson (University Press of Kansas, 1997)

Orient

Henry A. Wallace and the Progressives
Henry A. Wallace Country Life Center (Catalpa), 2773 290th Street, Orient, IA 50858 · (641) 337-5019

Henry A. Wallace came from a breed of politicians in short supply today: a compassionate, creative intellectual who wasn't afraid to buck authority. He was born on his family's Iowa homestead, Catalpa, on October 7, 1888. His father, Henry Cantwell Wallace, published *Wallace's Farmer*, for which the younger Henry wrote and edited from 1910 to 1924. During that time he developed corn-hog ratio charts and high-yield corn varieties, and founded the Pioneer Hi-Bred corporation. Small wonder that in 1933 he was tapped by FDR to be Secretary of Agriculture.

Wallace would stay in the post until 1940, when he resigned to accept the Democratic Party's vice-presidential nomination. As veep, Wallace stumped on behalf of FDR's postwar vision, a contrast to the fascist regimes of Europe. His "Century of the Common Man" speech earned the wrath of corporate leaders, Republicans, conservative Democrats, and even Winston Churchill. In 1944 they were able to convince the president to drop Wallace in favor of Harry Truman (see page 265).

When Truman assumed the presidency, he nominated Wallace to be his Secretary of Commerce. Wallace held the post for a year and a half before being fired for criticizing Truman's Cold War rhetoric. From there he became editor of *The New Republic*, which he used to critique the administration, and in 1948 ratcheted up the pressure by running as the Progressive Party's presidential nominee. The party broke new ground by including African American candidates on its campaign stops in the South, though it failed to garner any electoral college votes.

> The American fascist would prefer not to use violence. His method is to poison the channels of public information. . . . They claim to be super-patriots, but they would destroy every liberty guaranteed by the Constitution. They demand free enterprise, but are the spokesmen for monopoly and vested interest. Their final objective toward which all their deceit is directed is to capture political power so that, using the power of the state and the power of the market simultaneously, they may keep the Common Man in eternal subjection.
> —Henry Wallace, 1944

Wallace was marginalized during the 1950s' Red Scare, and died in Connecticut on November 18, 1965. His ashes were returned to Glendale Cemetery (4909 University Avenue) in Des Moines. His birthplace is now a museum.

LEARN MORE
www.henryawallacecenter.com
American Dreamer by John C. Culver and John Hyde (Norton, 2001)

MICHIGAN

When Michael Moore's *Bowling for Columbine* won the Academy Award for Best Documentary in 2003, he invited his fellow nominees to the podium. "They're here in solidarity with me because we like nonfiction," he explained, training his sights on the Bush administration's war rhetoric. "We like nonfiction and we live in fictitious times. . . . We live in a time where we have a man sending us to war for fictitious reasons. . . ." And before he could finish his speech, before he was drowned out by the orchestra, the audience erupted in boos. Host Steve Martin tried to diffuse the wrath, telling viewers Moore was being hustled into his limo trunk by the Teamsters, and the "liberal" Hollywood audience snickered its approval. Funny stuff.

Well, who's laughing now? As has happened so many times before and since, Moore was denounced as a loudmouthed propagandist and dismissed . . . yet turned out to be entirely correct. If, for a change, the media were to take a fraction of the time it wastes on trying to debunk Moore's movies and use it instead to challenge corporate and government malfeasance, perhaps Moore wouldn't have to do their job for them.

Moore burst onto the national scene in 1989 with *Roger & Me*, an angry, heartbreaking, hilarious documentary about the destruction of the auto industry and the work-

Michael Moore, from *Roger & Me*, 1989

ing class in his hometown of Flint, Michigan. Moore has always returned to Michigan in his films, to investigate a local school shooting in *Bowling for Columbine*, to ride with army recruiters in *Fahrenheit 9/11*, and to take a Michigan Militia member to the county fair in *The Awful Truth*. Some have charged him with exploiting human misery, usually those most responsible for causing that misery.

LEARN MORE

www.michaelmoore.com

Dude, Where's My Country? by Michael Moore (Warner, 2003)

Michael Moore by Emily Schultz (ECW, 2005)

American Dissident by François Primeau (Lulu, 2007)

Roger and Me (1989)

Fahrenheit 9/11 (2004)

Ann Arbor

Judy and Alan Guskin and the Birth of the Peace Corps

Michigan Union, State Street and University Avenue, Ann Arbor, MI 48104

The initial concept of what became the Peace Corps was batted around by Hubert Humphrey in early 1960, but not until presidential candidate John F. Kennedy posed a series of rhetorical questions to students at the University of Michigan did the program begin to take shape. On a campaign trip through the state on October 14, 1960, he stopped in Ann Arbor to spend the night. Though it was 2:00 A.M., about 10,000 students turned out to greet him, and he was coaxed into an impromptu speech. "How many of you are willing to spend ten years in Africa or Latin America or Asia working for the U.S. and working for freedom?" he asked. "How many of you who are going to be doctors are willing to spend your days in Ghana?"

Two attendees, the newly married Judy and Alan Guskin, were in the crowd. They took Kennedy's words to heart and formed a committee of graduate students, Americans Committed to World Responsibility. On October 21, they published an article in the *Michigan Daily* asking how many readers would volunteer to serve the poor around the world. Petitions flooded in, and the Guskins delivered them to the Kennedy campaign. On November 2, less than

Peace Corps volunteer in Benin, West Africa, 1988

a week before the election, Kennedy announced in a speech at San Francisco's Cow Palace (2600 Geneva Avenue) that he would support this effort. The agency was created by executive order on March 1, 1961, and signed into law on September 22 the same year.

In the near-half century since its founding, 190,000 Peace Corps volunteers have served two-year commitments in 140 countries around the world. Though its mission is to aid underdeveloped communities, it has benefited the United States more than any other country. By offering development rather than military assistance, the Peace Corps has won millions of individual allies across the globe. And by learning about the world's hopes and needs firsthand, returning volunteers have brought deeper understanding back to their hometowns.

LEARN MORE

www.peacecorps.gov, (800) 424-8580

All You Need Is Love by Elizabeth Cobbs Hoffman (Harvard, 1998)

From the Center of the Earth by Geraldine Kennedy (Clover Park, 1991)

Battle Creek

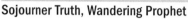

Sojourner Truth, Wandering Prophet

Kimball House Museum, 196 Capitol Avenue NE, Battle Creek, MI 49017 · (269) 966-2496

Isabella Baumfree was born a slave in New York in 1797, and was sold several times before being freed by the New York State Emancipation Act of 1827. At the time she had been hired out to another family, but once emancipated she returned to her owner to retrieve her five-year-old son Peter, only to learn that he had sold him to an Alabama plantation . . . *after* the boy was technically free. Baumfree registered a complaint with local authorities and was able to get her former owner thrown into jail. Charges were dropped when, remarkably, her son was returned.

Baumfree ended up in New York City where, at an 1843 service at the Mother A.M.E. Zion Church (140–146 W. 137th Street), she stood up and announced she would be changing her name to Sojourner Truth. "Sojourner, because I am a wanderer; Truth, because God is truth," she explained. When she wasn't touring the country lecturing against slavery and for women's rights, Truth made a home in Battle Creek, starting in 1857. Many in the town were abolitionists. Following the war, she lobbied to establish western land grants for

former slaves. She also spoke out against child labor and capital punishment, and for temperance and equal pay for men and women.

Truth died in Battle Creek on November 26, 1883, and was buried in Oak Hill Cemetery (255 South Avenue); a stone cairn was erected over her plot in 1929. Her home (38 College Street) burned down in 1898. Battle Creek's Kimball House Museum is the final repository of many of Truth's personal belongings, including a painting of her meeting with Abraham Lincoln, a silk dress given to her by Queen Victoria, and her only known signature.

Sojourner Truth, 1864

LEARN MORE

www.kimballhouse.org

Sojourner Truth by Nell Irvin Painter (Norton, 1996)

Narrative of Sojourner Truth by Sojourner Truth (Vintage, 1993)

Detroit

The Sweets and the McGhees Move In

Sweet Home, 2905 Garland Street, Detroit, MI 48214

McGhee Home, 4626 Seebaldt Avenue, Detroit, MI 48204

The desegregation of American society was achieved not through government action but through the determination of progressives willing to put their lives at risk by challenging restrictive covenants in court. In Detroit, Ossian and Gladys Sweet, and Orsel and Minnie McGhee paid the price, and won the victories, that eventually broke the stranglehold of institutionalized racism in housing.

Ossian Sweet was a prominent Detroit doctor who, with his wife, Gladys, purchased a home on the city's east side in 1925. On learning that their new neighbors were black, white residents met at the Howe School on July 14 where they formed the Waterworks Park Improvement Association. Its stated goal was to keep the neighborhood segregated, and members threatened to dynamite the Sweets' home if they dared move in. But the Sweets did just that on September 8, assisted by nine armed friends and the police. The next day a mob attacked the house, hurtling rocks and bottles through the Sweets' windows. When they rushed the front porch, shots from inside the house killed one attacker and injured another.

Ossian Sweet and 10 others were charged with first-degree murder, but only Sweet and his brother Henry went to trial. They were defended in court by Clarence Darrow, who had been hired by the local NAACP chapter. The doctor's trial ended in a hung jury, and his brother was found innocent by a second jury, which ruled that he had the right to defend his brother and sister-in-law against violence. Reunited, Ossian and Gladys Sweet lived in their Garland Avenue home until 1944.

The Sweets' victory, however, did not trigger a wave of desegregation in local housing. In fact, not until the McGhee family moved into an all-white community in 1944 did Detroit see another challenge to its racially divided neighborhoods. Orsel and Minnie McGhee were sued by their next-door neighbors, Benjamin and Anna Sipes, shortly after they moved in. The Sipes got a judge to order the McGhees and their two children to move out. The McGhees refused. Thurgood Marshall argued the McGhees' case all the way to the U.S. Supreme Court where, in its 1948 *Sipes v. McGhee* decision, the court ruled that restrictive covenants violated the Constitution's Fourteenth Amendment.

LEARN MORE

Arc of Justice by Kevin Boyles
(Henry Holt, 2004)

> I have to die like a man or live
> like a coward.
>
> —*Ossian Sweet*

Flint

The Flint Sit-Down Strike and the United Auto Workers
Fisher Body Plant #1 (torn down), 4300 S. Saginaw Street, Flint, MI 48507

Contrary to some histories, the first sit-down strike did *not* take place in Flint, Michigan, but in Akron, Ohio. In 1936, strikers at the Firestone rubber plant held out for a month until the company met their demands. But later that year, the new tactic—refusing to leave a factory, thereby preventing scabs from taking their places on assembly lines—was put to use against General Motors.

On December 26, workers in Cleveland went on strike against GM's Fisher body plant. Word leaked out that GM was planning on moving stamping dies out of its Flint facility in response, and the fledgling United Auto Workers (UAW) moved to stop it. On the afternoon of December 29, workers at the Fisher #1 Plant shut down the assembly line and refused to leave.

Over the next 40 days, the 2,000 strikers maintained discipline and morale by equally dividing chores and electing a mayor. Students from the University of Michigan came and taught classes. And though GM turned off the heat and electricity, the UAW was able to get food and water into the building.

GM secured two injunctions against the strikers, but wasn't able to enforce either one. On January 11, 1937, Flint police tried to raid the factory but were repelled by 5,000 autoworkers ringing the plant. Finally, the governor mediated a settlement between the two parties, and on February 11 an agreement was signed. The successful strike put the UAW on the map, and its membership exploded by 100,000 at GM facilities alone.

LEARN MORE

www.uaw.org, (313) 926-5000

Sit-Down by Sidney Fine (University of Michigan, 1969)

MINNESOTA

Minnesota has a long history of progressive politics and activism, and has been the birthplace and home of many liberal voices: Wisconsin's Senator Eugene McCarthy (Watkins, 1916), radical priest Daniel Berrigan (Virginia, 1921), songwriter Bob Dylan (Duluth, 1941), and comedian-activist Al Franken (1951), who grew up in St. Louis Park. Yet Minnesota's best-known progressive—Paul Wellstone—didn't arrive in the Land of 10,000 Lakes until he was an adult. He was born in Washington, D.C., on July 21, 1944, grew up in Arlington, Virginia, and attended the University of North Carolina. In 1963 he married Sheila Ison, and the couple had three children together.

Although Wellstone participated in the tail end of the civil rights movement, it wasn't until he accepted a position at Carlton College in Northfield, Minnesota, in 1969 that he began to flourish. One of the most popular professors in the political science department, his courses focused on people-powered movements and often included hands-on community service or political organizing elements as part of the off-campus curriculum. When the college announced in 1973 that it would not renew his contract, students rebelled with petitions and class boycotts. The college backed down, and a year later Wellstone was awarded tenure.

In 1982 Wellstone ran for state auditor and was trounced. That same year he was arrested in a Paynesville bank for leading a protest against farm foreclosures. Wellstone would return to the campaign trail in 1990 to unseat GOP senator Rudy Boschwitz. Barnstorming the backroads in a green, secondhand school bus, he attacked the incumbent's corporate connections: "Rudy Boschwitz is the senator from Exxon. I'll be the senator from now on!" Wellstone's campaign relied on humor and hard work, and it paid off; he was the only challenger to beat an incumbent senator that year.

Wellstone arrived in Washington on the eve of the Gulf War, and his brash and confrontational style earned him enemies. He later learned the art of consensus building, and one of his first bills to pass forced members of Congress to disclose lobbying gifts of more than $50. When Newt Gingrich's Contract with America arrived in 1994, Wellstone was instrumental in blocking and delaying several elements through skillful parliamentary maneuvers.

Boschwitz tried to unseat Wellstone in 1996, criticizing him for being liberal, something the voters were already aware of; Wellstone won reelection by 9 points. He went on to build coalitions around veterans issues, mental health, and passage of the Violence Against Women Act.

In 2002, during the buildup to the Iraq War (which he opposed), Wellstone faced a tough reelection. George W. Bush campaigned hard on behalf of challenger Norm Coleman. Then, on October 25, Wellstone's campaign plane crashed near Eveleth, killing Paul and Sheila, their daughter Marcia, three campaign aides, and the pilot.

Wellstone's legacy lives on through Wellstone Action, an institute that trains candidates and organizers interested in advancing progressive issues and economic justice.

> **Never separate the lives you live from the words you mean.**
> —Paul Wellstone

LEARN MORE
www.wellstone.org, (651) 645-3939
Paul Wellstone by Bill Lofy (University of Michigan, 2005)
The Conscience of a Liberal by Paul Wellstone (University of Minnesota, 2001)
Politics the Wellstone Way by Bill Lofy, ed. (University of Minnesota, 2005)
Wellstone! (2004)

Minneapolis

Birthplace of the American Indian Movement
Elaine M. Stately Peacemaker Center, 2300 Cedar Avenue S, Minneapolis, MN
55404 · (612) 724-3129

In the summer of 1968, Native Americans in the Minneapolis/St. Paul area saw an upsurge in police harassment. A group of 250 activists, mostly Chippewa, met in July at the Citizens Community Center and formed a new self-defense organization: Concerned Indians of America. Later, when they realized they'd named themselves the CIA, they changed to the American

Indian Movement—AIM. Modeled on the Black Panthers, teams formed AIM Patrols to monitor police activity; they'd listen to radio dispatches, then show up with cameras and tape recorders to make sure the officers were following proper procedure. For those who were arrested, legal assistance was given.

Originally led by Clyde Bellecourt, Dennis Banks, and George Mitchell, AIM quickly expanded to other cities—it was mostly an urban organization— including a Cleveland chapter led by Russell Means. His American Indian Center established a credit union, offered food and housing assistance, and protested Chief Wahoo, the Cleveland Indians' mascot. Means's creative, confrontational style helped him rise to a national leadership role, and he would later lead Thanksgiving protests at Plymouth Rock, as well as the occupation at Wounded Knee (see page 310).

Today Clyde Bellecourt carries on AIM's mission as the executive director of the Elaine M. Stately Peacemaker Center in Minneapolis.

> It is hereby suggested that we create a Department of White Affairs. . . . White people will be looked on as white savages unless they adopt the Indian religion and Indian way of life. White religious holidays such as Easter and Christmas will be outlawed. . . . It will be unlawful to wear a shamrock, eat haggis, fish and chips, pea soup, or wieners and sauerkraut.
> —*from an AIM "White Policy Proposal" pamphlet, 1970*

LEARN MORE
www.aimovement.org
Loud Hawk by Kenneth Stern (University of Oklahoma, 1994)

Sauk Centre

Sinclair Lewis, Main Street Rebel
Boyhood Home, 810 Sinclair Lewis Avenue, PO Box 222, Sauk Centre, MN 56378 · (320) 352-5201

Often the best way to force progress is to take a good, long look in the mirror. For middle America in the early 20th century, that mirror was author Sinclair Lewis. His popular novels explored and exposed a wide range of issues: *Main Street* (1920) looked critically at small-town life, *Babbitt* (1922) skewered businessmen and corporate culture, *Elmer Gantry* (1927) delved into the hypocrisy of a fictional Christian evangelist, *Ann Vickers* (1933) demanded equal rights for women, and *Kingsblood Royal* (1947) criticized American racism. But *It Can't Happen Here* (1935) is probably his most chilling work. Written during the rise of European fascism, Lewis imagined the same happening in the United States, with unsettling parallels to post-9/11 America. It can't happen here? Let's hope not.

Promotional poster for W.P.A. production of *It Can't Happen Here*, 1936

Lewis was born in Sauk Centre on February 7, 1885, in a building across the street from his eventual boyhood home. He left Sauk Centre for Yale in 1903, but returned via *Main Street* years later. The town, thinly disguised as the community of Gopher Prairie, did not appreciate the attention; the book wasn't taught in local schools until the mid-1960s. Lewis won the Pulitzer Prize twice, and refused it both times, and won the Nobel Prize for Literature in 1930, the first American author to do so. After Lewis died

> When fascism comes to America, it will be wrapped in the flag and carrying a cross.
>
> —*Sinclair Lewis*

in Rome in 1951, his ashes were returned to Minnesota and interred in the family plot at Greenwood Cemetery (Route 17).

Sauk Centre has since forgiven its native son. His boyhood home is open for tours and still has some of the family's heirlooms. The town has also opened a Sinclair Lewis Interpretive Center (Route 71 and I-94) and celebrates Sinclair Lewis Days each year in mid-July.

LEARN MORE

www.saukherald.com/ftp/lewis/default.html

Sinclair Lewis by Richard Lingeman (Random House, 2002)

MISSOURI

Only one U.S. president ever hailed from Missouri, but he was one of the nation's greatest. Harry S Truman was born in Lamar, Missouri (1009 Truman Avenue), on May 8, 1884. His family moved to a farm in Belton a year later, and to Independence in 1890, where he grew up and spent most of his adult life. As a young man he worked as an usher, a bank clerk, and a farmer, and led an artillery unit during World War I. He returned from France to marry his high school sweetheart, Bess Wallace, on June 28, 1919. After failing as a haberdasher, he began to work his way up through Kansas City politics, and in 1934 was elected to his first of two terms in the U.S. Senate.

Truman earned national praise when he established the Senate Committee to Investigate the National Defense Program, a.k.a. the Truman Committee, to investigate waste in military spending during World War II, saving taxpayers almost $3 billion from the era's Halliburtons. He did this on a $15,000 budget. FDR tapped him for vice president in the 1944 election, and four weeks after the inauguration Truman found himself in the Oval Office; Roosevelt died on February 12, 1945.

The list of Truman's progressive accomplishments is a long one. He oversaw the founding of the United Nations (see page 215), implemented the Marshall Plan to rebuild war-torn Europe, ordered the desegregation of the armed services (see page 71), launched the push to create Medicare, signed the Fair Employment Practices Act, organized and executed the Berlin Airlift, canned General Douglas MacArthur for threatening to expand the Korean conflict into China, limited presidential terms through the 22nd Amendment, and vetoed the infamous Taft-Hartley Act (which was overridden by the labor-hostile GOP). When the worst Southern elements of the Democratic Party threatened to bolt from its 1948 national convention over civil rights, Truman showed them the door (see page 139), then went on to win the election.

PROGRESSIVE THOUGHTS
OF HARRY S TRUMAN

- I have been fiercely partisan in politics and always militantly liberal. I will be that way as long as I live.

- When folks are given the choice between voting for a Republican or a Democrat who acts like a Republican, they'll vote for the Republican every time.

- I never did give anybody hell. I just told the truth and they thought it was hell.

- Those who want the government to regulate matters of the mind and spirit are like men who are so afraid of being murdered that they commit suicide.

- If there is one basic element in our constitution, it is civilian control of the military. Politics are to be made by the elected political officials, not by generals or admirals.

- I have never seen pessimists make anything work, or contribute anything of lasting value.

- I am sorry to see the growth of snobbery in the United States in recent years. I especially deplore the tendency to look down on people who work with their hands.

- I've got other things to do beside watch television.

 LEARN MORE
The Wit & Wisdom of Harry Truman by Ralph Keyes (Gramercy, 1995)

Truman was not without his faults; he ordered the bombing of Hiroshima and Nagasaki, and got the United States into the Korean War. He left office as one of the most unpopular presidents in the modern era, though historians give him high marks today. Back in Independence, Truman established

Harry S Truman, 1948. Tales of his electoral demise were greatly exaggerated.

his presidential library (Route 24 and Delaware Street) in 1957. The United Nations Charter was signed on the table that now resides in the front lobby. He died on December 26, 1972, and was buried at the library.

LEARN MORE
www.trumanlibrary.org, (816) 268-8200
Truman by David McCullough (Simon & Schuster, 1992)

Kansas City

Weeks v. United States: **No Illegal Search and Seizure**
1834 Penn Street, Kansas City, MO 64108

Little did the police know that when they entered the Kansas City home of Fremont Weeks on December 21, 1911, they would change law enforcement procedure forever. Acting on a tip that Weeks was involved in an illegal lottery, an investigator asked one of Weeks's neighbors where he might find a spare key to his home, and the neighbor obliged. Police discovered enough evidence to arrest Weeks. They also brought the evidence to the attention of the FBI, which made another, more thorough, raid on Weeks's place.

But the officers had failed to secure any sort of search warrant to conduct the original raids. The Fourth Amendment to the Constitution reads, "The right of the people to be secure in their persons, houses, papers, and effects, against unreasonable searches and seizures, shall not be violated, and no Warrants shall issue, but upon probable cause, supported by Oath or affirmation, and particularly describing the place to be searched, and the persons or things to be seized." Oops.

Weeks was indicted on nine counts of using the U.S. mail to conduct an illegal lottery. Before the trial began, his lawyer, Martin O'Donnell, asked the judge to order the prosecution to return all illegally seized items. They surrendered some, but kept enough evidence to pursue three of the original charges.

On November 9, 1912, Weeks was found guilty on one count—selling $1.50 worth of tickets to a single individual—and drew a six-month sentence and a $100 fine.

O'Donnell appealed the conviction to the U.S. Supreme Court, which, in a unanimous ruling, threw out Weeks's conviction. The decision was the basis for what is called the "exclusionary rule," which says prosecutors may not use evidence seized in an illegal manner, such as failing to obtain a search warrant. When it was issued, this ruling applied only to federal cases, but it was later extended to state and local courts in *Mapp v. Ohio* (see page 275).

> The tendency of those who execute the criminal laws of the country to obtain conviction by means of unlawful seizures and enforced confessions . . . should find no sanctions in the judgments of the courts, which are charged at all times with the support of the Constitution and to which people of all conditions have a right to appeal for the maintenance of such fundamental rights.
> —Justice William Rufus Day, in Weeks v. United States, *1914*

St. Louis

The Dred Scott Decision
Old Courthouse, 11 N. Fourth Street, St. Louis, MO 63102 · (314) 655-1600

Dred Scott was born into slavery in Virginia around 1800, and was owned jointly by Captain Peter Blow and John Moore. In 1830 Blow moved (with Scott) to St. Louis. When Blow died two years later, Scott was sold to John Emerson, an army surgeon. Emerson traveled with Scott to various forts in free states and territories, which later formed the basis of Scott's lawsuit. Emerson and Scott returned to St. Louis in 1839 where the doctor died in 1843. His widow, Eliza Emerson, hired Scott out to a military officer who released him in Texas in 1846. When he returned to St. Louis with $300 to purchase his freedom, as well as that of his wife and two daughters, Emerson refused, setting the lawsuit in motion.

Scott's original lawsuit alleged false imprisonment, battery, and assault. Under the 1820 Missouri Compromise, if a slave traveled to a free state or territory he or she was no longer a slave. Nevertheless, Scott lost at his first trial, though he won in county court in 1850. Meanwhile, Emerson turned over her legal affairs to John Sanford, her brother, whose name eventually appeared on the case. Scott lost in front of the Missouri Supreme Court in 1852.

Scott sued Sanford again in 1853 and lost in federal circuit court at St. Louis's Old Courthouse a year later. On appeal the case went before the U.S. Supreme Court as *Scott v. Sandford* (Sanford's name was improperly recorded); Scott lost 7–2 on March 6, 1857. The high court ruled that slaves were property, not people. Writing for the majority, Chief Justice Roger Taney claimed Scott had "no rights which the white man was bound to respect." The disastrous ruling effectively invalidated the Missouri Compromise, and started the countdown to the Civil War.

That year Emerson remarried and her new husband immediately transferred Scott's ownership back to Peter Blow's heirs, whose brother Taylor

Dred Scott, 1887

freed him. Scott would be free for only a year; he died on September 17, 1858, of tuberculosis.

LEARN MORE

Dred Scott and the Politics of Slavery by Earl M. Maltz (University Press of Kansas, 2007)

Dred Scott and the Problem of Constitutional Evil by Mark A. Graber (Cambridge, 2006)

Shelley v. Kraemer: No Private Racial Covenants
4600 Labadie Avenue, St. Louis, MO 63115

Shortly after the Shelley family moved to St. Louis's Grand Prairie neighborhood on September 11, 1946, a couple living 10 blocks away, whom they had never met, filed suit to have them evicted. The Shelleys, who were African American, had purchased their home in an area covered by a restrictive covenant. Though government-initiated restrictions had been outlawed since 1917, white homeowners were able to achieve the same goal by invoking the "freedom of contract" provision of the ruling. In this case, the private Marcus Avenue Improvement Association had established an all-white district, and the owner who had sold the home to the Shelleys had violated that contract.

The Shelleys chose to fight the lawsuit. The first time the case was heard the judge ruled that the family could stay, but only based on a technicality, not on constitutional grounds. The Missouri Supreme Court overturned the decision. When the case reached the U.S. Supreme Court only six justices heard the arguments; three had to recuse themselves because they owned restricted property. On May 3, 1948, the court ruled 6–0 that private racial covenants were illegal. While they did not constitute direct government discrimination, they were unconstitutional because their provisions were enforced by government bodies—courts and law enforcement agencies.

To demonstrate how strongly he endorsed the ruling, Harry Truman invited the Shelleys' lawyer, George Vaughan, to redeliver his closing arguments to the 1948 Democratic National Convention, the same convention from which the Dixiecrats bolted (see page 139).

LEARN MORE

Caucasians Only by Clement Vose (University of California, 1973)

OHIO

The 2004 presidential election was stolen in Ohio. The evidence has been available for some time, not that it has been given much attention in the corporate media. When it has, it's typically been preceded with a caveat that the claims are nothing more than wild conspiracy talk.

That's not altogether inaccurate—it *was* a conspiracy, carried out by state officials under the direction of the national Republican Party. Ohio's Secretary of State, J. Kenneth Blackwell, the man responsible for seeing that the election was handled smoothly, was at the same time cochair of the state's Bush-Cheney campaign. Virtually every time irregularities were discovered—and there have been hundreds of cases large and small—they worked in the favor of the Bush campaign. Remember Florida?

Here are just a few examples. Voting machines were distributed in greater numbers in Republican districts than in Democratic districts, sometimes resulting in 12-hour-long lines to vote, often in the rain. The state GOP deliberately disenfranchised more than 35,000 voters through "caging" voters in poor and minority communities, in direct violation of consent decrees from 1982 and 1987—the GOP had been busted twice before for this illegal tactic. Blackwell severely restricted the use of provisional ballots, contradicting the federal Election Assistance Commission's guidelines. Reporters were barred from observing the initial count in Warren County because of an unspecified "terrorist threat," and though the ban was lifted after the count, the officials went back into lockdown for a recount . . . and Bush emerged with an even larger margin than before. In Franklin County, 4,000 more votes were recorded for Bush than Kerry, in a precinct of only 800 voters. Miami County recorded an astonishing 98.55 percent turnout, unheard of in modern elections, and went for Bush by a 66–34 margin; the initial count was much lower, but 19,000 votes appeared during the recount, and almost all were added to the Bush column. And though exit polls showed Kerry winning the state by a 52–48 margin, the count recorded Bush winning by 2.5 percent. No other state showed a similar discrepancy.

The final disturbing element of the fraud was John Kerry's tacit complicity in the theft. Remembering the 2000 Florida debacle (see page 171), Kerry amassed a $7 million legal war chest *specifically* to support voters who had been disenfranchised and intimidated and to take the perpetrators to court. But when the Ohio election devolved into chaos, he sat on his hands, and his money. It was left to the Green and Libertarian parties to spend the $100,000+ needed to start an initial recount. The election irregularities listed above were only uncovered through the determination of active local progressives, investigative reporters, and commissions funded by the NAACP and Congressman John Conyers.

Election officials from Cuyahoga County have since gone to prison for rigging the initial electronic recount so that a full recount was averted. By 2007, more than two-thirds of the records pertaining to the election have been destroyed or "lost" in violation of election law. Wonder why?

LEARN MORE

www.bradblog.com

What Went Wrong in Ohio? by Congressman John Conyers (Academy Chicago, 2005)

Was the 2004 Presidential Election Stolen? by Steve Freeman and Joel Beilfuss (Seven Stories, 2006)

Armed Madhouse by Greg Palast (Dutton, 2006)

American Blackout (2007)

Akron

Bill Wilson, Robert Smith, and Alcoholics Anonymous

Dr. Bob's Home, 855 Ardmore Avenue, Akron, OH 44302 · (330) 864-1935

In the spring of 1935, Vermont stockbroker William G. Wilson came to Akron in an effort to take control of the National Rubber Machinery Corporation. The proxy fight failed, and Wilson found himself seeking consolation in the Mayflower Hotel bar (263 S. Main Street). Then, on May 11, he stood in the hotel lobby and faced his future: he could spend his final $10 on another round of cocktails or he could sober up. Wilson chose the latter. He phoned

Henrietta Seiberling of the Oxford Group, a self-help movement, who got him in touch with doctor Robert Smith. Wilson and Smith met the next day at the Gate Lodge (714 N. Portage Path) and talked for hours. Wilson swore off alcohol that day, and Smith pledged to help him by offering him a place to stay.

Anne Smith, Robert's wife, agreed to the visitor but had an ulterior motive. Her husband was also an alcoholic, and she thought Wilson could help *him* sober up. Sure enough, on June 10, Robert Smith followed Wilson's lead, and Alcoholics Anonymous (AA) was born.

In the months that followed, "Dr. Bob" and "Bill W." wrote up the basic framework for AA at the Smiths' dining room table. The home later served as the halfway house for new members following detox. The stories of these recovering alcoholics formed the backbone of *The Big Book*, which was written to inspire those in recovery.

Volunteers have restored Dr. Bob's home to its 1935 appearance, complete with Smith family furniture, a few of Dr. Bob's empty bottles found in hiding places, and first editions of *The Big Book* and other AA publications.

LEARN MORE
www.drbobs.com
www.alcoholics-anonymous.org, (212) 870-3400
Not God by Ernest Kurtz (Hazelden Information Education, 1998)
My Name Is Bill by Susan Cheever (Washington Square, 2005)

Canton

Eugene Debs Violates the 1917 Espionage Act
Nimisilla Park, 1075 Mahoning Road NE, Canton, OH 44075

In the nationalistic fervor surrounding the buildup to World War I, the federal government enacted a prototype of the USA PATRIOT Act: the 1917 Espionage Act. It made it a crime to interfere with military operations, including any action that might hamper troop recruitment. Authorities applied it broadly, arresting anyone who criticized the draft, including a four-time presidential candidate.

On June 16, 1918, Eugene Debs addressed a convention of the Socialist Party in Canton, Ohio. During his speech at Nimisilla Park he said, "They have always taught and trained you to believe it to be your patriotic duty to go to war and have yourselves slaughtered at their command. But in all the history of the world you, the people, have never had a voice in declaring war, and strange as it certainly appears, no war by any nation in any age has ever been declared by the people."

That was all the authorities needed, and two weeks after the speech Debs was arrested and charged with espionage. A jury found him guilty of obstructing army recruitment, and he was sentenced to 10 years in prison and stripped of his right to vote. The U.S. Supreme Court upheld the verdict.

Debs ultimately served 32 months in an Atlanta penitentiary. While there he ran for president a fifth time; Prisoner #9653 received 915,302 votes. Warren G. Harding, who won the 1920 election, pardoned Debs on Christmas Day 1921.

> I believe in the Constitution. Isn't it strange that we Socialists stand almost alone today in upholding and defending the Constitution of the United States? . . . I believe in the right of free speech, in war as well as peace. I would not, under any circumstances suppress free speech. It is far more dangerous to attempt to gag the people than to allow them to speak freely what is in their hearts. . . . There is an infinitely greater issue that is being tried today in this court, though you may not be conscious of it. American institutions are on trial here before a court of American citizens. The future will render the final verdict.
>
> —Eugene Debs, in his address to the jury, 1918

LEARN MORE
Walls and Bars by Eugene V. Debs (Charles H. Kerr, 2000)

Cleveland

LaFleur v. Cleveland Board of Education: An End to Pregnancy Discrimination

Patrick Henry Junior High School, 11901 Durant Avenue, Cleveland, OH 44108

On March 12, 1971, principal Henry Wilkins asked Jo Carol LaFleur to sign paperwork that forced her to take unpaid maternity leave from her teaching position, and she refused. Citing school board policy that any employee more than four months pregnant was not allowed to be in the school, Wilkins suspended her. But LaFleur demonstrated that pregnancy in no way impeded her ability to function by slapping Wilkins and the board with a discrimination lawsuit.

LaFleur, joined by another pregnant teacher, lost her first trial a month later. The judge bizarrely cited concerns of "children pointing, giggling, laughing, and making snide remarks" as one of his reasons for keeping her out of the classroom. A federal appeals court overturned the verdict as "arbitrary and unreasonable," and the U.S. Supreme Court agreed. The justices ruled 7–2 on January 21, 1974, that LaFleur had been unfairly suspended. Congress extended the same protection to women in the private sector by passing the 1978 Pregnancy Discrimination Act.

> This Court has long recognized that freedom of personal choice in matters of marriage and family life is one of the liberties protected by the Due Process Clause of the Fourteenth Amendment.
> —*Justice Potter Stewart,*
> *in* LaFleur v. Cleveland
> Board of Education, *1974*

Mapp v. Ohio: No Illegal Searches and Seizures
Mapp Home, 14705 Milverton Street, Cleveland, OH 44120

At 1:30 A.M. on May 23, 1957, Cleveland police came to Dollree "Dolly" Mapp's home in search of a bombing suspect. Mapp refused them entry without a warrant, but three hours later they forced themselves into her home, waving what they claimed was a judge's order. It wasn't.

Inside Mapp's home police found the suspect they were seeking (he was questioned and released), but they also found several books that were considered obscene under state law. Mapp was arrested. And even though the police's misconduct was introduced at trial, she was found guilty and sentenced to one to seven years in prison. Most states at the time had an exclusionary rule, preventing the introduction of improperly seized evidence, but not Ohio. Both the Eighth District Court of Appeals and the Ohio Supreme Court ruled

> Our decision . . . gives to the individual no more than that which the constitution guarantees him, to the police officer no less than that to which honest law enforcement is entitled, and, to the courts, that judicial integrity so necessary in the true administration of justice.
> —*Justice Tom Clark, in*
> Mapp v. Ohio, *1961*

that Mapp's Fourth Amendment rights hadn't been violated, but in 1961 the U.S. Supreme Court disagreed.

Writing for the 5–4 majority, Justice Tom Clark chided the authorities: "The State, by admitting evidence unlawfully seized, serves to encourage disobedience to the Federal Constitution which it is bound to uphold." *Mapp v. Ohio* went on to extend the exclusionary rule, which federal courts had operated under since 1914's *Weeks v. United States* decision (see page 267), to state criminal courts.

Dayton

Phil Donahue's Broadcast Democracy
WDTN-TV (formerly WLWD-TV), 4595 S. Dixie Drive, Dayton, OH 45439 · (937) 293-2101

Phil Donahue revolutionized television on November 6, 1967. That Monday on WLWD-TV, he launched the first TV talk show that included audience participation. His first guest was outspoken atheist Madalyn Murray O'Hair (see page 125). On Tuesday he explored "what single men want in a woman." On Wednesday, a Dayton obstetrician brought a graphic film of a baby's birth; on Thursday, Donahue visited with a local undertaker and reclined in a coffin; and on Friday, the discussion focused on a new, anatomically correct Little Brother doll.

Though the topics were tame by today's "standards," 1960s Dayton was aghast. And enthralled—Donahue quickly developed a loyal following. Writer Erma Bombeck later explained his appeal: he was "every wife's replacement for the husband that doesn't talk to her." Soon the show was being syndicated to stations nationwide, and in 1973 he moved the show to Chicago. Only Oprah could stop him . . . and ultimately did.

Phil Donahue, 2007

Years later, Donahue landed a new gig on MSNBC. In the months leading up to the Iraq War, he was the only mainstream broadcaster who routinely challenged the Bush administration's claims about WMDs and the need to go to war. Though he had the strongest ratings of anyone on the cable outlet, he was canned by programmers who worried he was "outside the mainstream."

LEARN MORE
Donahue by Phil Donahue (Simon & Schuster, 1979)

Macedonia

Bryan Drapp McUnionizes McDonald's
McDonald's, 6400 Macedonia Commons Boulevard, Macedonia, OH 44056 · (330) 467-9191

Just because you work at an entry-level, fast-food job doesn't mean you should have to put up with abuse. In April 1998, McDonald's manager Jerry Guffey blew up at a 66-year-old employee, Margaretha DeLollis, for leaving a box of clean garbage bags next to the garbage cans. She burst into tears and ran out. Guffey then ordered a 19-year-old burger-wrapper, Bryan Drapp, to take her place. Drapp refused, and left as well.

The following day, Drapp handed Guffey a list of employee grievances, and Guffey ignored him. So Drapp headed over to Wal-Mart, not to apply for another crummy job, but to pick up the supplies he needed to picket McDonald's. Soon, half of the restaurant's 40 workers were non–dues-paying members of Teamsters Local 416. The strike got Drapp on CNN, the *Tonight Show*, and Howard Stern, and management quickly caved. Employees were given a higher base pay, four days' notice on schedule changes, and one week's paid vacation after a year's worth of service. The agreement only applied to the three franchises owned by Drapp's employer, Jed Greene, but still, it was the first time a McDonald's was McUnionized.

For Drapp, the victory was short-lived. Several months after returning to work he was fired for showing up for his shift with "Go Union" defiantly painted on his face.

Ripley

John and Jean Rankin, John and Miranda Parker, and the "Hell Hole
of Abolition"

Rankin House, "Liberty Hill," 6152 Rankin Hill Road, Ripley, OH 45167 · (937)
392-1627

Parker House, 300 Front Street, Ripley, OH 45167 · (937) 392-4188

The home of Rev. John and Jean Rankin sits on a bluff overlooking the Ohio
River. Most nights, from 1825 to the Civil War, the Rankins lit a beacon in the
window facing Kentucky, in part to provide guidance to escaping slaves, and
in part to thumb their noses at slave owners across the river. By most estimates
the Rankins, with the help of their 13 children, were able to assist 2,000 runaways on the Underground Railroad, none of whom was ever captured. For his
efforts, a $2,500 reward was offered in Kentucky for Rev. Rankin's capture or
murder. It never happened.

NATIONAL UNDERGROUND RAILROAD FREEDOM CENTER

Downriver from Ripley, in Cincinnati, you'll find the National Underground
Railroad Freedom Center (50 E. Freedom Way). Cincinnati was the perfect
location for the first major U.S. museum of its kind in the United States, for
it was here that Harriet Beecher Stowe, while living at the home of her father
Lyman Beecher (2950 Gilbert Avenue), gathered most of the stories that
became *Uncle Tom's Cabin*. It was also here that Levi and Catharine Coffin
(see page 246) lived out their final years. The stories of passengers, stations,
and conductors are told through movies, multimedia, time lines, and artifacts,
including a restored slave pen from Mason County, Kentucky.

 LEARN MORE

www.undergroundrailroad.org, (513) 333-7500

Bound for Canaan by Fergus M. Bordewich (Amistad, 2005)

Traveling the Underground Railroad by Bruce Chadwick (Citadel, 1999)

But the Rankins weren't the only conductors in Ripley. Down by the river John Parker, a former slave who in 1845 had purchased his freedom for $1,800, ran a foundry . . . and a station. Between 1849 and the war, he and his wife Miranda helped 440 runaways head north. For the most part, the Rankins and Parkers operated independently; should one couple be stopped, the other could continue. John Parker was fearless, and often ventured into Kentucky to retrieve passengers—a dangerous tactic for anyone, but particularly for a free black.

Is it any wonder that Southerners called Ripley the "hell hole of abolition"?

LEARN MORE
www.ripleyohio.net
Beyond the River by Ann Hagedorn (Simon & Schuster, 2002)
His Promised Land by Stuart Seely Sprague, ed. (Norton, 1996)

Toledo

Baldemar Velásquez and the Farm Labor Organizing Committee
1221 Broadway Street, Toledo, OH 43609 · (419) 243-3456

What the United Farm Workers (see page 383) is to migrant farm workers in the West, the Farm Labor Organizing Committee (FLOC) is in the Midwest. Founded in 1969 by Baldemar Velásquez, the union did not have much of an impact until its first strike in 1978. That year, FLOC launched a boycott against the Campbell Soup Company, which was refusing to pay higher prices for its tomatoes. Despite a 560-mile march from Toledo to the company's headquarters in Camden, New Jersey, the strike dragged on for six years.

But in 1984, FLOC brought pressure to Campbell's financial doorstep. It got nuns and community leaders to purchase single shares of the company, then had them show up at the annual shareholders' meeting to denounce the management's intransigence. The tactic worked. In 1985 Campbell's sat down with FLOC, and a year later signed a collective bargaining agreement with the union. They not only got higher wages, but addressed issues from pesticide safety to housing to day care. Soon Heinz, Vlasic, and Dean Foods came to the table as well.

In 1998, FLOC announced a second boycott, this time against Ohio's largest pickle processor, the Mt. Olive Pickle Company. That campaign lasted five years and was settled in 2004. It marked the first time in U.S. labor history that a union was allowed to represent guest workers.

LEARN MORE
www.floc.com
The Farm Labor Movement in the Midwest by W. K. Barger and Ernesto M. Reza (University of Texas, 1994)

Wellington

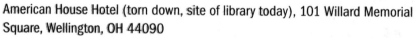

The Oberlin Rescuers
American House Hotel (torn down, site of library today), 101 Willard Memorial Square, Wellington, OH 44090

John Price was walking between Oberlin and Wellington on September 18, 1858, when he was approached by four men who told him about day labor available at a local farm. Price agreed to go with them, but was tied up and thrown in the back of a wagon. His abductors turned out to be slave catchers; Price was a runaway who had been living for the previous two years in Oberlin using counterfeit documents.

Price was taken to Wellington where the kidnappers looked for a judge to approve his return to the South. Meanwhile, abolitionists in Oberlin had been alerted to the situation. More than 200 men and women raced to the American Hotel in Wellington where Price was being held. The crowd charged the building, nabbed Price, and spirited him away in a waiting wagon. Wellington police arrested 39 men—later dubbed the Oberlin Rescuers—and shipped them off to the Cuyahoga County jail, charged with violating the 1850 Fugitive Slave Act.

Rather than post bail the Rescuers used their incarceration to their advantage. Protests erupted across the North, and more than 2,000 marched in Cleveland demanding their immediate release. The men gave speeches from their cells to crowds outside, and even began publishing a newspaper, *The Rescuer.* Two men were put on trial, found guilty, and sentenced to prison. The backlash grew, and after three months the federal government dropped all charges and released the Rescuers. They returned triumphant to Oberlin, where they were hailed by a throng of 3,000 singing *La Marseillaise,* and given a thanksgiving service at the First Church (Main and Lorain Streets).

WISCONSIN

Wisconsin senator Robert "Fighting Bob" La Follette certainly earned his pugilistic nickname—if there was a moneyed interest or a corrupt politician, he took them on, often to the consternation of his Republican Party.

La Follette was born three miles north of Stoughton on June 14, 1885. He was elected to three terms in the U.S. House, starting in 1884, served as Wisconsin governor from 1901 to 1906, and then as senator from 1905 to 1925 (serving simultaneously as senator and governor in 1905). La Follette was part of the "Insurgent" wing of the GOP, foes of railroads and other trusts that backed the party's powerful machine. He even exposed the state's sitting Republican senator, Philetus Sawyer, for trying to bribe him to fix a legal case. As governor he launched the "Wisconsin Idea" where University of Wisconsin faculty developed progressive reforms that the state legislature implemented. These included open primaries, workmen's compensation, transparent government, the minimum wage, women's suffrage, and more.

While senator, Fighting Bob began publishing *La Follette's Weekly* (today known as *The Progressive*), a forum for progressives and home to muckraking journalists. He opposed the United States' entry into World War I, the draft, and the 1917 Espionage Act, and after the war was over, the League of Nations. He helped launch the Teapot Dome investigation, and in 1924 formed the Progressive Party to challenge Calvin Coolidge and the Republicans in

> Every nation has its war party. It is not the party of democracy. It seeks to dominate absolutely. It is commercial, imperialistic, ruthless. It tolerates no opposition. It is just as arrogant, just as despotic, in London, or in Washington, as in Berlin.
> —Robert La Follette

Robert La Follette, c. 1911

the general election. The Progressives' platform included union protection, an end to child labor, government control of utilities and railroads, and cheap farm credit. La Follette also called for a restoration of civil liberties lost in the war, the end of American military intervention in Central and South America, and a national plebiscite any time the United States wanted to declare war. He won 17 percent of the popular vote, and carried Wisconsin.

La Follette died on June 18, 1925, and was succeeded by his son, Robert M. La Follette Jr., who would represent the state until being defeated in the 1946 Republican primary by Joseph McCarthy. Fighting Bob's Maple Bluff home (733 Lakewood Boulevard) is today a National Historic Landmark. Each year FightingBob.com hosts a Fighting Bob festival for progressives across the nation.

LEARN MORE
www.fightingbob.com
Fighting Bob La Follette by Nancy C. Unger (University of North Carolina, 2000)

Portage

Aldo Leopold and *A Sand County Almanac*

Aldo Leopold Legacy Center, Leopold Memorial Reserve, E13701 Levee Road, Portage, WI 53901 · (608) 355-0279

The concept of a "land ethic"—that humans have a responsibility to the natural environment—is a relatively new development in environmentalism. Conservationism, as envisioned by Teddy Roosevelt (see page 304), was humancentric—nature was to be preserved for people to enjoy, not for its own sake. But the 1949 publication of Aldo Leopold's *A Sand County Almanac* moved interconnectedness to center stage.

"The land ethic simply enlarges the boundaries of the community to include soils, waters, plants, and animals, or collectively: the land," Leopold wrote. It was an ethic he lived every day, beginning in 1905 and his first job with the U.S. Forest Service. Then, in 1935, the same year he helped found the Wilderness Society, Leopold purchased 80 acres along the Wisconsin River where he converted a chicken coop to a writing sanctuary he dubbed "The Shack." Over the next 14 years he worked to restore the property to its original habitat. While there he penned *A Sand County Almanac*, a collection of essays and observations that was published posthumously in 1949; Leopold died of a heart attack a year before while helping a neighbor fight a grass fire.

The book inspired a new breed of environmentalists determined to take an active role in preserving the land and finding a suitable balance between humans and the rest of the world. Today his retreat is part of the 1,300-acre Leopold Memorial Preserve, and his work is carried on by the Aldo Leopold Foundation of nearby Baraboo.

> We abuse land because we regard it as a commodity belonging to us. When we see land as a community to which we belong, we may begin to use it with love and respect.
> —*Aldo Leopold, in* A Sand County Almanac, *1949*

LEARN MORE

www.aldoleopold.org

www.wilderness.org, (920) THE-WILD

A Sand County Almanac by Aldo Leopold (Ballantine, 1986)

Aldo Leopold's Odyssey by Julianne Lutz Newton (Island Press, 2007)

Aldo Leopold by Curt Meine (University of Wisconsin Press, 1988)

Watertown

Margarethe Schurz and America's First Kindergarten

Octagon House Museum, 919 Charles Street, Watertown, WI 53094 · (920) 261-2796

Educators today credit Friedrich Frobel with the revolutionary concept that young children should be prepared for entry into a school routine. In 1837 he founded Europe's first kindergarten—"a garden for children"—in Hamburg, Germany. Frobel's experiment made an impact on one of his students, Margarethe Meyer Schurz, who later founded America's first kindergarten in her front parlor in Watertown.

There were only six students in the first class on August 26, 1856. Two were hers. The other four children were their cousins. Schurz's lessons were conducted in German. Her students made such advancements that neighbors noticed and encouraged Schurz to expand her enrollment to include their children. So Schurz set up a formal kindergarten in a storefront (N. Second and Fourth Streets) in downtown Watertown.

Though the kindergarten lasted only two years, Schurz's effort had a tremendous impact. A friend, Elizabeth Peabody, copied Schurz's model and opened the first English-speaking kindergarten in Boston in 1860. But Peabody did more than open a single school; she advocated that they be part of every child's education through the *Kindergarten Messenger*, which she edited from 1873 to 1877.

Schurz's home was restored in 1956 and the building was moved from downtown to its present site next to the Octagon House. The storefront school is long gone.

LEARN MORE
www.watertownhistory.org

5
The Great Plains

★ Kansas ★ Nebraska ★

★ North Dakota ★

★ South Dakota ★

KANSAS

While most of the nation was focused on the 2004 presidential race, Kansas politicians were debating an even larger issue: the origins of life on this planet. Backed by the Seattle-based Discovery Institute and the Kansas Intelligent Design Network, religious conservatives were able to secure a 6–4 majority on the Kansas State Board of Education, and they didn't waste any time going after Charles Darwin. In early 2005 board member Connie Morris sent a taxpayer-funded flyer to constituents denouncing evolution as "an age-old fairy tale." As a fundamentalist Christian, she believed the Book of Genesis—no fairy tale, that. The board suggested 20 pages of revisions to the state's science standards, even though those changes had been rejected earlier by the Kansas Science Standards Committee, which comprised local educators and scientists.

In an effort to cloak their decision in legitimacy, the board scheduled a week's worth of hearings in early May 2005. Kansas Citizens for Science, a pro-evolution group, organized a boycott of what it felt would be a kangaroo court, and its concerns were confirmed. Republican board member Kathy Martin opened the hearings by saying, "Evolution has been proven false. [Intelligent Design] is science-based and strong in facts." Several scientists spoke about evolution, but most of the testimony was given by ID proponents, many of whom had no science credentials whatsoever. And though it had received letters from 70+ science societies and a petition signed by 38 Nobel Prize laureates, all supporting the teaching of evo-

> I think the people of Kansas are tired of being a laughingstock not only of the nation but the world.
>
> —Janet Waugh, pro-evolution board member, on the 2006 primary election

lution, the board had heard all it needed; it approved the new standards by a 6–4 vote in November.

Kansas was nationally lambasted, and apparently the majority of its citizens didn't appreciate being characterized as backward thinking and anti-science. Less than a year later, in August 2006, two of the six pro-ID board members were defeated by moderates in the *Republican* primary, including Connie Morris. "I feel bad for them when they face God on Judgment Day," said Morris, of her GOP opponents. On February 13, 2007, the new Kansas State Board of Education voted 6–4 to throw out the revised science standards.

LEARN MORE
www.kcfs.org
Unintelligent Design by Robyn Williams (Allen & Unwin, 2006)

Abilene

Dwight D. Eisenhower and the Military-Industrial Complex
Dwight D. Eisenhower Library and Museum, 200 SE Fourth Street, Abilene, KS 67410 · (877) RING-IKE

Since George Washington, every president who hasn't died in office has delivered a farewell address, and it has been a tradition for the president to include in the text a warning or a sobering truth. (Why these warnings and truths aren't delivered in *inaugural* addresses, when the presidents can still do something about them, is a mystery.)

When it was Dwight Eisenhower's turn on January 17, 1961, he cautioned against the rising influence of the "military-industrial complex," the unholy alliance between defense contractors, the Pentagon, and the federal government. The defense industry buys influence in Congress and receives lucrative contracts in return, and all of it is blessed by military brass, many of whom later end up working in the private sector . . . on weapons programs. If you doubt it, ask yourself how the nation moved from having enough nuclear weapons to wipe out every human on the planet 20 times to 40 times, and 60 times.

Coming from a former four-star general, the speech should have been taken more seriously, particularly in light of the 1960 election. But John F. Kennedy had been able to paint Richard Nixon, Eisenhower's vice-president, as part of an administration that allowed a "missile gap" to develop between the United States and the Soviet Union. Eisenhower's original draft referred to the military-industrial-*congressional* complex, but he deleted reference to the third leg of the monster so as not to offend legislators—congressmen, senators, folks like Senator Kennedy.

> In the councils of government, we must guard against the acquisition of unwarranted influence, whether sought or unsought, by the military-industrial complex. The potential for the disastrous rise of misplaced power exists and will persist.
> —*Dwight D. Eisenhower, in his Farewell Address, 1961*

So in the end the burden falls on the public, the ones who finance this cascading insanity. Ike knew that, too, and said so later in his address: "Only an alert and knowledgeable citizenry can compel the proper meshing of the huge industrial and military machinery of defense with our peaceful methods and goals so that security and liberty may prosper together."

Don't say you weren't warned.

LEARN MORE
www.eisenhower.archives.gov/farewell.htm
www.MilitaryIndustrialComplex.com
The Sorrows of Empire by Chalmers Johnson (Metropolitan, 2004)
War Is a Racket by Smedley Butler (Feral House, 2003)
Addicted to War by Joel Andreas (AK Press, 2004)
Why We Fight (2005)

Argonia

Susanna Salter, America's First Female Mayor
Salter House National Historic Site, 220 W. Garfield Street, Argonia, KS 67004

Women achieved the right to vote and hold local office in Kansas in 1887, and they took their civic responsibility seriously, certainly more than some men did. A couple of drunkards in Argonia, in an effort to razz the head of the local WCTU, placed 27-year-old Susanna Medora Salter's name on the ballot for mayor. Salter was as surprised as anyone to learn she was a candidate when she showed up to vote on April 4, 1887. The pranksters were even more surprised when Salter won by a two-to-one margin.

Salter accepted the office she hadn't sought or expected, and the one-dollar-a-year salary. She served one term and would likely have been reelected—the townfolk agreed she was a fine and capable leader—but Salter decided against it after her first child died shortly after being born.

Today, Salter's red brick home is a museum, open by appointment.

Lawrence

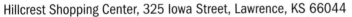

The Day After
Hillcrest Shopping Center, 325 Iowa Street, Lawrence, KS 66044

On Sunday, November 20, 1983, more than 100 million viewers tuned in see the end of the world—and they were not disappointed. That night ABC broadcast *The Day After*, a made-for-TV movie dealing with the effects of a nuclear war between the Soviet Union and the United States. Unlike other no-nuke films, such as *On the Beach* or *Testament*, it showed in graphic detail the immediate impact on an American community, in this case Lawrence, Kansas. Well, *almost*—ABC's censors demanded that for every three humans shown being vaporized it had to show seven inanimate objects melting, burning, or being blown to bits. The film was shot on location in Lawrence and Kansas City—the film's memorable supermarket riot sequence was filmed at the Hillcrest Shopping Center.

The movie was aired at a time when Ronald Reagan was saber-rattling mid-range nuclear missiles in Europe, and the USSR was returning the gesture. Though the movie left unresolved the question of who started the imaginary conflict, its victorless moral was hard to avoid. Still, blowhards like Jerry Falwell, Phyllis Schlafly, and William F. Buckley Jr. complained that the film evoked "unnecessary fear" in viewers.

The Day After encouraged mainstream dialogue on the issue among citizens, and for that reason should be recognized as an important milestone in the antinuclear movement. Viewed today, the images of the collapse of government and social order after the catastrophe look eerily Katrina-esque.

> The catastrophic events you have just witnessed are in all likelihood less severe than what would actually occur in the event of a full nuclear strike against the United States.
> —*Coda appearing at the end of* **The Day After**

Leavenworth

The Fort Leavenworth General Strike

Leavenworth Federal Penitentiary, 1300 Metropolitan Avenue, Leavenworth, KS 66048

During World War I, a conscientious objector had to be willing to go to prison for his principles. The U.S. government locked up hundreds of pacifists in 1918, but as guards quickly learned, pacifism isn't the same thing as passivity. In an effort to gather intelligence on "socialistic and anarchistic activities," 300 COs were sent to the Leavenworth Federal Penitentiary. That November, the prison saw its first strike. Twenty-four men refused to work because fellow COs, Russian Molokan immigrants who spoke no English, were being abused by guards. The strikers were tossed into solitary confinement and fed rations of bread and water. Word got out, and complaints flooded into Washington. The men were soon returned to the general population, which was generally impressed.

Then in January 1919, two Huttrian COs who had recently been trans-ferred from Alcatraz died while in solitary. On January 29, 150 members of the "first work gang," few of whom were COs, spontaneously quit working. The next morning, Warden Rice threatened to *kill* any prisoner who refused work, on a charge of mutiny. That afternoon, 2,300 men were lined up to report for work detail. When called to step forward, all stood with their arms crossed. The Fort Leavenworth General Strike was on.

One man eventually did step forward, a CO named W. Oral James. "I make myself a marked man among your officers," he admitted. "I am willing to do this, sir, if it can enlighten this protest." He then gave a general summary of their complaints.

The warden requested 1,000 troops for the 49th Infantry Regiment to "main-tain discipline," but that only attracted outside attention. The COs helped the inmates elect a strike committee and make a formal list of demands: forma-tion of a grievance board, letter writing privileges, better food, elimination of bed bugs, amnesty for strike leaders, and the right to present evidence when accused of a rule infraction. The warden finally agreed, and added one more: reduction in the COs' sentences. By July, all COs were released or transferred to other prisons. The warden then reneged on all the demands.

LEARN MORE
Jailed for Peace by Stephen M. Kohn (Praeger, 1986)

Medicine Lodge

Carry A. Nation, Hatchet-Swinging Radical

Carry A. Nation Home and Museum, 211 W. Fowler Avenue, Medicine Lodge, KS
67104 · (620) 886-3553

Carry A. Nation is often dismissed as a violent, puritanical kook, yet she also possessed a strong progressive streak. Born Carry Moore in Lancaster, Kentucky, on November 25, 1846, her family moved to Missouri in 1856. In November 1867 she married Dr. Charles Gloyd and moved into a home near Holden. But in May 1868 she returned to her parents, pregnant, to escape her husband's spiraling alcohol abuse. She gave birth to a daughter, Charlien, that fall, and in March 1869 learned that her husband had drunk himself to death.

Five years later Carry married David Nation; the couple lived in Richmond, Texas, until 1889 when they moved to Medicine Lodge. David Nation served as an elder of the Campbellite Christian Church, and Carry began to throw herself into the local temperance movement. A fiery orator, Carry Nation lectured on topics such as "How, When, and Where I Saw 800 Drunkards," often at African American churches. She always donated the entrance fees, usually 25¢ a head, to her hosts to support and build their congregations.

But Nation's outspokenness, not to mention her "unladylike" assertive behavior, got her expelled from the Campbellite church. (Members were also not happy that she insisted on inviting some of the community's working poor to their services.) From that point on she forged her own spiritual and activist path. In the beginning, Nation focused on securing food and clothing for the area poor. She would pressure merchants for donations, and if they turned her away she would stand in front of their establishments and shout to anyone within earshot that the business was run by "thieving gougers of widows and orphans." That often worked.

Then, on June 5, 1900, Nation claimed to receive a heavenly message during an electrical storm: "Go to Kiowa," a voice commanded, and she did, the following day. Armed with "smashers" (rocks), she entered Dobson's Saloon and announced, "Men, I have come to save you from a drunkard's fate," and broke every liquor bottle in the place. She then repeated the process at Kiowa's other two saloons.

And she didn't stop there. Nation's campaign spread, as did her fame. On December 28, 1900, she demolished Wichita's Carey Hotel Bar (523 E. Douglas Avenue), including a nude painting titled *Cleopatra at the Bath*, while delivering a Christmas message: "Glory to God and peace on earth, good will to men!" After the Wichita campaign, her husband joked that she could have been more efficient with a hatchet. "That's the most sensible thing you have said since I married you," she responded.

Nation was arrested more than 30 times for her "hatchetations." She paid her fines and legal fees through donations from WCTU members and fees from speaking engagements. In her lectures, she not only opposed alcohol, but tobacco, gambling, immodesty, and women's corsets, and spoke in behalf of equal rights for women.

The Nations divorced in 1901, and Carry eventually retired to Eureka Springs, Arkansas, where she ran Hatchet Hall (35 Steele Street), a boarding house for abandoned families of alcoholics. She died on June 9, 1911, and was buried beside her mother in the Belton (Missouri) Cemetery. The Kansas State Historical Society in Topeka (6425 SW Sixth Avenue) has several of the smashed remnants of Nation's handiwork.

Carry A. Nation, c. 1905

"She hath done what she could."

—*Epitaph on Carry Nation's grave*

LEARN MORE
www.kshs.org, (785) 272-8681
Carry A. Nation by Fran Grace (Indiana University, 2001)

Topeka

Brown v. Board of Education: "Separate but Equal" Is Inherently Unequal
Brown v. Board of Education National Historic Site, Monroe Elementary, 1515 SE Monroe Street, Topeka, KS 66612 · (785) 354-7213

Oliver Brown saw no need for his eight-year-old daughter Linda to attend Topeka's Monroe Elementary when Sumner Elementary (330 SW Western Avenue) was so much closer to their home on First Street. So in the fall of 1950 he brought Linda to Sumner to register for third grade. The principal turned them away; Sumner was for white children only. Of course, Oliver Brown already knew that Topeka's schools were segregated. He was taking the first step toward abolishing the practice.

Brown had been recruited, along with 19 other African American parents, by the president of the local NAACP chapter, McKinley Burnett. Thurgood Marshall filed the landmark lawsuit. A three-judge panel from the U.S. District Court in Topeka heard the case in the spring of 1951 and ruled that the school board was within its power to segregate the district. The justices did, however, acknowledge that segregated facilities harmed black students. "Segregation of white and colored children in public schools has a detrimental effect on colored children," they wrote. That legal finding was the key Marshall used to unlock the doors of Sumner Elementary for Linda Brown.

When it was argued before the U.S. Supreme Court on December 9, 1952, *Brown v. Board of Education* was a combination of five cases (see pages 52, 60, 212, and 225). Together they formed a scathing indictment of the damage caused by institutionalized racism in American society. Marshall's team was assisted as well by an amicus brief from the Truman administration, which included an observation by Secretary of State Dean Acheson: "The continuation of racial discrimination in the United States remains a source of constant embarrassment to this Government in the day-to-day conduct of its for-

Thurgood Marshall, 1957

eign relations, and it jeopardizes the effective maintenance of our moral leadership of the free and democratic nations of the world."

The *Brown* decision was pushed to the court's next term after several justices asked lawyers to address five legal issues that had come up in conference. Before the next session convened, Chief Justice Fred Vinson died and was replaced by California's governor, Earl War-

> We conclude that in the field of public education the doctrine of "separate but equal" has no place. Separate educational facilities are inherently unequal.
>
> —*Chief Justice Earl Warren,* in Brown v. Board of Education, *1954*

ren. Because he was a politician, Warren understood the need for a single voice from the bench on such a monumental decision. He was able to cobble together a unanimous vote to overturn *Plessy v. Ferguson* (see page 196) on May 17, 1954. The ruling declared that all public schools should begin desegregation "with all deliberate speed." That phrase would be abused by Southern bigots to drag their feet for years to come.

LEARN MORE

www.nps.gov/brvb

http://brownvboard.org

Jim Crow's Children by Peter Irons (Penguin, 2002)

All Deliberate Speed by Charles J. Ogletree Jr. (Norton, 2005)

Simple Justice by Richard Kluger (Vintage, 1977)

NEBRASKA

While there are plenty of good reasons for the U.S. Congress to be organized into two bodies, based on the size and diversity of American states, it is not at all clear why states, with much smaller populations, should be similarly organized. Still, every legislature in the nation functions under a two-body arrangement . . . except Nebraska.

It wasn't always that way. When it became a state in 1867, Nebraska had both a House and a Senate. But citizens looked at the endless back-and-forth between the bodies and decided there had to be a better, less expensive way to run their government. Why not a unicameral legislature? The idea gained supporters, chief among them Senator George Norris (see page 297) who traveled the state stumping for an amendment to the state constitution. In 1935 the electors approved the new plan and the first unicameral legislature was seated in 1937. The first unicameral session passed 214 bills in 98 days, at a cost to taxpayers of $103,445. In contrast, the 1935 bicameral session passed 192 bills in 110 days, and cost $202,593. You do the math.

Originally organized with 43 senators, the legislature has since grown to 49. Senators are elected to four-year terms on a nonpartisan basis. (The state's executive offices are still filled through a multiparty process.) Fourteen states have looked into making their legislatures unicameral, yet none have done so.

LEARN MORE
www.unicam.state.ne.us

Blair and Bancroft

Black Elk Speaks

Tower of the Four Winds, Black Elk/Neihardt Park, W. College Drive, Blair, NE 68008 · (800) 444-DANA

John G. Neihardt State Historic Site, Elm and Washington Streets, PO Box 344, Bancroft, NE 68004 · (402) 648-3388

When it was first published in 1932, *Black Elk Speaks* was a revolutionary work, if for no other reason than it treated the Native American experience with the respect to which it was entitled. Some believe it to be the only religious classic written in the 20th century. It is the autobiography of an Oglala Sioux holy man, as told through his son Ben Black Elk to poet John G. Neihardt.

> When I look back now from the high hill of my old age, I can still see the butchered women and children lying heaped and scattered all along the crooked gulch as plain as when I saw them with eyes still young. And I can see that something else died there in the bloody mud, and was buried in the blizzard. A people's dream died there. It was a beautiful dream.
>
> —*Black Elk, in* Black Elk Speaks

Black Elk was a second cousin of Crazy Horse, and from an early age had had visions. He was present at the Battle of Little Bighorn (see page 360), and would eventually participate in the Ghost Dance Movement that ended with the massacre at Wounded Knee (see page 310). His life story was collected through a series of interviews on the Pine Ridge Indian Reservation in South Dakota, where Black Elk lived two miles west of the Manderson post office.

Today, the 45-foot Tower of the Four Winds, on a hill overlooking Blair's Dana College, captures Black Elk's vision of peace and brotherhood in a 50,000-piece mosaic. Even more information on Black Elk can be found at Neihardt's former home in Bancroft.

LEARN MORE
www.nebraskahistory.org/sites/neihardt/index.htm
Black Elk Speaks by John G. Neihardt (Bison Books, 2000)
Black Elk by Michael F. Steltenkamp (University of Oklahoma, 1993)

McCook

George Norris, "Gentle Knight of Progressive Ideals"

Senator George Norris State Historic Park, 706 Norris Avenue, McCook, NE 69001 ·
(308) 345-8484

Long before there were "Reagan Democrats" there were "New Deal Republicans," and Nebraska's longtime senator George Norris was their champion. Born near Clyde, Ohio (2148 County Road 270), on July 11, 1861, he did not make it to Nebraska until 1883, after graduating from law school. He set up a practice in Beaver City but moved to McCook in 1900 and lived there the rest of his life.

In 1902 Norris was elected to the U.S. House as a Republican. He supported most of Theodore Roosevelt's progressive reforms and in 1911 helped found the National Progressive Republican League, serving as its first vice president. When Roosevelt broke with the GOP to run on the Progressive Party ticket in 1912, Norris ran as a Republican for the U.S. Senate, and won. In 1917 he was one of only six senators to vote against declaring war on Germany.

Norris continued to be an independent voice for progressive causes. He endorsed Democrat Al Smith for president in 1928, and FDR in 1932, and tried and failed to abolish the antiquated Electoral College. He wrote the Twentieth Amendment, which limited the lame-duck session of Congress, as well as moved forward the date of the presidential inauguration to January. His support of the New Deal, including the creation of the Tennessee Valley Authority and the Rural Electric Administration, was too much for the Republican Party to stand; it voted Norris out of its ranks in 1936. That same year he ran as an Independent, and won. However, he was defeated for re-election in 1942.

Norris died on September 2, 1944, and was buried in McCook's Memorial Park Cemetery (L and 14th Streets). His nearby home is today a museum. John F. Kennedy selected Norris for one of his chapters in *Profiles in Courage*.

LEARN MORE

www.nebraskahistory.org/sites/norris/index.htm

Fighting Liberal by George W. Norris (University of Nebraska, 1992)

Nebraska City

J. Sterling Morton and the Birth of Arbor Day

Arbor Lodge State Historical Park and Arboretum, 2300 W. Second Avenue,
Nebraska City, NE 68410 · (402) 873-7222

Nebraska City calls itself "The Town That Gave the World a Great Idea," the
great idea being Arbor Day. Truth be told, it wasn't the town that came up with
it; J. Sterling Morton did. As founding editor of Nebraska's first newspaper,
Morton promoted tree planting as a means of improving the environment and
the quality of life on the prairie. In 1872 he was able to convince the State
Board of Agriculture to sponsor a holiday—a competition actually—where
counties and individuals could win prizes for planting trees. This first Arbor
Day took place on April 10, when more than a million trees were planted.

Three years later the governor signed a bill making April 22, Morton's birthday, a legal holiday in Nebraska. The idea eventually spread to other states,
due in large part to the work of Dr. Birdsey Northrup, a New England educator who also saw the value in tree planting. It did not become an official
national holiday until 1970. Today, Arbor Day is typically celebrated each year
on the last Friday in April.

Morton's final home, which was completed the year he died, is open to the
public as a museum. It sits adjacent to a 72-acre arboretum with more than
270 species of trees and shrubs. When Morton passed away he was buried in
Nebraska City's Wyuka Cemetery (S. 19th and 6th Corso Streets) beneath a
tree sculpted from granite, with a stone tree fence winding around his family
plot.

LEARN MORE

www.ngpc.state.ne.us/parks/guides/parksearch/showpark.asp?Area_No=4
www.arborday.org, (888) 448-7337
Arbor Day by Robert Haven Schauffler (Omnigraphics, 1990)
Arbor Day by Harry Banker (Self-published, 1989)

Omaha

Standing Bear v. Crook: Native Americans Are "Persons" Under Law

General Crook House, 30th and Fort Streets, Omaha, NE 68111 · (402) 455-9990

Among the U.S. Army's "Indian fighters," Brigadier General George Crook, commander of the Department of the Platte, stood out as one whose sympathies frequently rested with the people he battled. He often worked around orders from Washington he felt were unjust, and earned the respect of many native leaders, if not his military superiors.

In 1879 chief Standing Bear of the Ponca tribe, which two years earlier had been marched from its land in northeast Nebraska to Oklahoma, led a group of 29 Ponca back to their ancestral land to bury his son. Crook was ordered to arrest the Ponca and return them to Oklahoma. He did arrest them, but before they could leave Crook collaborated with Thomas Tibbles, a progressive editor at the Omaha *Herald*, to have Standing Bear sue the U.S. government to block their removal. Crook was named as the defendant in the case; only Tibbles knew Crook was in on the plan.

Standing Bear petitioned for a writ of habeas corpus, saying the army should either charge him with a crime or release him. But his lawyer, A. J. Poppleton, had to first convince the judge that Standing Bear was even eligible to make such a motion. Armed with the just-ratified Fourteenth Amendment, Poppleton claimed that if Standing Bear wanted to waive his "right" to live on the Oklahoma reservation, he should be able to live and farm back in Nebraska. In an emotional speech before the bench, Standing Bear asserted, "I want to be buried in the land of my fathers."

Judge Elmer Dundy's ruling was a bombshell: "An Indian is a person within the meaning of the habeas corpus act." It was the first time

General George Crook, c. 1875

> General Crook came. He, at least, had never lied to us. His words gave people hope.
> —*Oglala chief Red Cloud*

a Native American had been so designated in a U.S. court, and Standing Bear and the Ponca were released. The government did not appeal the case to the Supreme Court, fearing that if they lost it would set an even stronger precedent.

Crook lived in Omaha until 1882, when he was assigned to track down and capture Geronimo. Years after his death Tibbles revealed the true role Crook had played in Standing Bear's case. Crook's Victorian home is open today as a museum.

LEARN MORE

www.omahahistory.org/museum.htm

Standing Bear Is a Person by Stephen Dando-Collins (Da Capo, 2004)

The Standing Bear Controversy by Valarie Sherer Mathes and Richard Lowitt (University of Illinois, 2003)

General Crook and the Western Frontier by Charles M. Robinson III (University of Oklahoma, 2001)

When Bright Eyes Talks to George W. Bush

Saddle Creek Records, PO Box 8554, Omaha, NE 68108

If you've never seen or heard the performance of Conor Oberst, frontman for the band Bright Eyes, on *The Tonight Show with Jay Leno*, do yourself a favor: go to his Web site and download the free version of "When the President Talks to God," or check out the video on YouTube.

On May 2, 2005, in the wake of Bush's "reelection," this Nebraska-based musician appeared on the late-night talk show and raised a few unanswered questions about Bush's claim that he converses with the Almighty. To Leno's credit, he allowed the performance to be broadcast with only one bleep.

Oberst has remained faithful to his indie rock and Nebraska roots, keeping Bright Eyes based in Omaha, where he started the band in the eighth grade and the Saddle Creek record label in 1993. He is a

> When the president talks to God, does he fake that drawl or merely nod?
>
> —*Bright Eyes, in "When the President Talks to God"*

tireless critic of media consolidation, particularly regarding Clear Channel's stranglehold on radio stations, venues, and events, and has boycotted all Clear Channel–sponsored concerts and award shows.

LEARN MORE
www.saddle-creek.com
www.ThisIsBrightEyes.com

North Dakota does not have a Democratic Party, it has a Democratic-NPL Party. And what is the NPL? The Non-Partisan League, founded in 1915 by A. C. Townley, a longtime organizer with the Socialist Party. The NPL's members' individual political philosophies covered the spectrum from isolationist libertarians to fire-breathing socialists, but they banded together in a pro-farmer platform that was extremely popular with the Scandinavians of the upper Great Plains. The NPL advocated state-owned mills, banks, and grain elevators to combat the Eastern trusts.

The NPL started as a nonparty party, and in its first electoral outing offered up a slate of *Republicans* in the 1916 race. The NPL's gubernatorial candidate, Lynn Frazier, won with 79 percent of the vote, and its House candidates took control of the chamber. In 1918 the NPL won a majority of the seats in the Senate, and began putting its platform into action. It established the Bank of North Dakota and the North Dakota Mill and Elevator, created hail insurance and workmen's compensation funds, and reorganized the state income tax to account for earned versus unearned income. And to prevent its new power from going to its members' heads, lawmakers established a means for popular recall of any elected official.

Unfortunately, commodity prices fell after the end of World War I, and the NPL's ventures struggled to survive. They were also undermined by private banks, railroads, and business interests who wanted to see them fail. The citizens even recalled the governor (using the law he signed) in 1921 when an auditor declared the Bank of North Dakota insolvent. Were it not for a resurgent interest in the NPL during the Depression, it might have vanished as quickly as it appeared.

Most of the right wing of the NPL drifted back to the GOP, and the remaining NPL merged with the state Democratic Party in 1956. A fictionalized version of the league's early history was captured in the film *Northern Lights*.

LEARN MORE
www.demnpl.com, (701) 255-0460
The Story of the Nonpartisan League by Charles Edward Russell (University Press
  of the Pacific, 2002)
Northern Lights (1979)

Dunseith

International Peace Garden
RR 1, PO Box 116, Dunseith, ND 58329 · (888) 432-6733

With so many conflicts between nations, it is heartening to recognize that the United States and Canada have maintained friendly relations since the War of 1812. In 1932 folks from both sides dedicated 2,339 acres of land straddling the border for the International Peace Garden, and pledged "that as long as man shall live we will not take up arms against one another." Though not legally binding, it certainly was an admirable declaration.

In addition to the formal gardens, the park contains a wildlife refuge, camp-grounds, picnic areas, and a nondenominational Peace Chapel with pews in both countries. Kids are invited to attend the International Music Camp or the Royal Canadian Legion Athletic Camp held at the gardens each summer.

LEARN MORE
www.peacegarden.com

Fargo

Big Ed Schultz and Progressive Talk Radio
The Ed Schultz Show, 1020 25th Street South, Fargo, ND 58103 · (877) WE-GOT-ED

Who says a person can't change his or her opinions when presented with the facts? That's what happened to "Big Ed" Schultz. In 1992 the former college football star and sports color commentator launched "News and Views," a conservative regional talk show on KFGO-AM in Fargo. Schultz became the station's star talent, a prairie Limbaugh (without the drugs), and was the winner of several broadcasting awards.

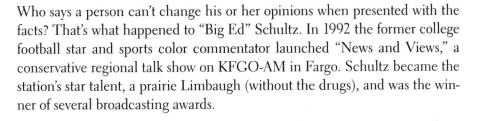

But then he met Wendy, a psychiatric nurse who thought Schultz could use an introduction to the real world. She invited him to lunch at the local Salvation Army shelter where she worked, to meet some of the "bums" he railed against on the air. He got to meet struggling farmers and laborers, and to his credit, admitted that he may have been mistaken in his beliefs. He also fell in love, and the couple later married. Wendy Schultz would eventually become Ed's producer, and the pair hit the road in the Big Eddie Cruiser to tell the stories of his listeners in the northern plains.

Schultz's transformation into a progressive populist apparently worried the suits at KFGO—they didn't think his new format would last. So in a leap of faith, Schultz left KFGO and launched a new, independent show on January 5, 2004, and offered it for national syndication. Unlike conservative talk radio, Schultz made a point of not screening his calls to fit his world view, and the format worked. Within three years he could be heard on more than 100 affiliates and had more than three million regular listeners.

LEARN MORE
www.wegoted.com
Straight Talk from the Heartland by Ed Schultz (Regan Books, 2004)

Medora

Theodore Roosevelt, Conservationist
Theodore Roosevelt National Park, South Unit, PO Box 7, Medora, ND 58645 · (701) 623-4466

In 1883, shortly after graduating from Harvard, Theodore Roosevelt headed west to hunt buffalo. He enjoyed himself so much that he bought a spread near Medora, North Dakota, and renamed it the Maltese Cross Ranch. It was only supposed to be a getaway spot, but a year later his wife Alice and mother died . . . on the very same day. Grief stricken, Roosevelt returned to his cabin to sort out his thoughts, and stayed two years. He ended up developing a new love: nature.

Years later, as president, Roosevelt made conservation a top priority. In 1903 he set aside the nation's first bird

> I have always said I never would have been president if it had not been for my experience in North Dakota.
>
> *—Theodore Roosevelt*

Theodore Roosevelt, 1910

reservation (see page 176), the forerunner of the National Wildlife Refuge. His friend Gifford Pinchot urged him to transfer the nation's forest reserves to the Department of Agriculture, and on February 1, 1905, Roosevelt signed them over. On July 1 a new agency was formed to manage them: the U.S. Forest Service. Within a year, 107 million acres were under its protection.

And Roosevelt went even further, signing the Antiquities Act on June 8, 1906. While its stated goal was to protect archeological sites, it could also be used to set aside any land that had significant historic, scientific, or natural merit, for the public benefit. Before he left office, he used it to create 18 new National Monuments.

Today you can visit Roosevelt's Maltese Cross Cabin, itself part of a National Park, where you'll see his cowboy gear, trunk, and writing desk.

LEARN MORE

www.nps.gov/thro

www.theodoreroosevelt.org, (516) 921-6319

Hunting Trips of a Ranchman & The Wilderness Hunter by Theodore Roosevelt
    (Modern Library, 1998)

SOUTH DAKOTA

In 2004 the legislators of South Dakota passed a sweeping law to outlaw abortion, but the Republican governor, who was sympathetic to the cause, vetoed it based on a technicality . . . and conveniently pushed the controversy off the political radar screen until after the presidential election. But in 2005, feeling its oats after Bush's reelection, the GOP-dominated legislature passed five bills restricting abortion, followed in 2006 by the Women's Health and Human Life Protection Act (WHHLPA). Its authors made no effort to deny that it was intended to directly challenge *Roe v. Wade* (see page 337). It contained no exceptions for rape or incest, and its only exception was if the procedure would prevent the death of the pregnant woman, and if performed, doctors would have to spend as much effort to save the fetus as the woman.

And the WHHLPA went even further than that: it defined life as beginning at conception, which would have made IUDs, emergency contraception, and even the Pill illegal. Yet before a legal challenge could be mounted, the residents of South Dakota launched their own revolt. In just three months an upstart organization named the South Dakota Campaign for Healthy Families collected 38,000 signatures—twice the 17,000 required—to place a repeal referendum on the 2006 ballot. The measure passed by a 56–44 margin, and the WHHLPA was removed from the books.

LEARN MORE
www.sdhealthyfamilies.org, (605) 221-4363
Abortion Under Attack by Krista Jacob, ed. (Seal, 2006)

Keystone

The Six Grandfathers, not Mount Rushmore

U.S. Highway 16A, Keystone, SD 57751 · (605) 574-2523

It probably comes as no surprise that the Black Hills, known to the Lakota as Paha Sapa, were stolen from Native Americans by the U.S. government. Paha Sapa, as well as most of South Dakota, North Dakota, Nebraska, Montana, and Wyoming, were covered under the Treaty of 1868; no white settlers were allowed to set foot on the land without permission. Nevertheless, George Armstrong Custer rode into Paha Sapa in 1874, looking to build a fort. He brought gold miners with him, and when they discovered nuggets on July 27, the treaty was unofficially tossed out. Ulysses S. Grant secretly told the army in 1875 to stop preventing prospectors from entering the hills.

In 1877 the Black Hills were taken back in the wake of the Battle of Little Bighorn (see page 360), and in 1889 the Dawes Act broke the remaining territory into six divided reservations. The best-known "hill" in the stolen land, the mountain on which the "Shrine of Democracy" was carved, was named Mount Rushmore in 1885 by lawyer Charles Rushmore, in honor of himself. The Sioux had always called it the Six Grandfathers.

With the rise of Native American activism in the late 1960s, Mount Rushmore posed an ideal target for civil disobedience. In the summer of 1970 several groups, including AIM and Indians of All Tribes (see pages 262 and 395), descended on Mount Rushmore to protest the Department of the Interior's plans to expand Badlands National Park to include the decommissioned Sheep Mountain Gunnery Range. Finding grisly photos of the frozen corpses of the Wounded Knee victims for sale in the gift shop, AIM demanded Native Americans be given control of the park's concessions. Yet that was secondary to the protesters' primary demand: for the U.S. government to resolve a land reparations lawsuit filed in 1923. They refused to leave until they had a face-to-face meeting with the Secretary of the Interior, and several climbed up to make a camp on Roosevelt's head, and wait. Later they unfurled a banner over Lincoln's forehead reading "Crazy

> No white person or persons shall be permitted to settle upon or occupy any portion without the consent of the Indians.
> —*Treaty of 1868*

Horse Monument Indian Power." However, most left by September, and the rest before winter set in.

The attention did elicit one response: in 1980 the U.S. Supreme Court awarded the Sioux $17 million for the stolen land, with interest accrued from 1877, roughly $300 million. The Sioux have never cashed the check. Since the Black Hills were never sold, they reasoned, taking a payoff would be like having a thief send you a money order—it didn't address the underlying crime. Not only that, by accepting it they'd be nullifying all future claims. The legal battle continues to this day.

LEARN MORE

www.nps.gov/moru

Mount Rushmore by Jesse Larner (Thunder's Mouth Press/Nation Books, 2002)

Great White Fathers by John Taliaferro (PublicAffairs, 2002)

Mount Rushmore by Gilbert Fite (University of Oklahoma, 1952)

Mitchell

George McGovern, American Hero

McGovern Library, Dakota Wesleyan University, 1201 McGovern Avenue, Mitchell, SD 57301 · (605) 995-2618

Though the citizens of South Dakota, along with 48 other states, made the mistake of casting their electoral college votes for Richard Nixon in 1972, at least they had the good sense to elect George McGovern their senator . . . three times. McGovern started in the U.S. House, serving two terms, the first in 1956. He campaigned for the senate in 1960 and lost, but won in 1962, 1968, and 1974.

McGovern was born in Avon on July 19, 1922; his family later moved to Mitchell, where he grew up, when he was six years old. Here he met his future wife, Eleanor Stegeberg, when she trounced him in a high school debate tournament. The couple wed on October 31, 1943.

During World War II, McGovern piloted a B-24, the *Dakota Queen*, on 35 missions over North Africa and Italy and was awarded the Distinguished Flying Cross for his service. "Most of my close friends were killed in the war," he later reflected, "I vowed from the depth of my heart that if I survived, I would devote the rest of my life to the cause of peace."

And he has. After his 1960 senatorial defeat, McGovern was appointed the first director of JFK's Food for Peace program, and served until 1962. Back in the senate, he became one of the Johnson and Nixon administrations' harshest war critics. In 1970 he cosponsored a bill with Oregon's Mark Hatfield calling for the immediate withdrawal of U.S. troops from Vietnam. "Every senator in this chamber is partly responsible for sending 50,000 young Americans to an early grave," he spoke from the floor. "[I]t does not take any courage at all for a congressman or a senator or a president to wrap himself in the flag and say we are staying in Vietnam, because it is not our blood that is being shed!"

In 1972, with the traditional Democratic machine in disarray and the Nixon administration engaging in clandestine dirty tricks, McGovern secured his party's presidential nomination with a truly progressive agenda: withdrawal from Vietnam, support of the Equal Rights Amendment (see page 57), an increase in the minimum wage, environmental safeguards, and more. But he stumbled out of the convention with the vice-presidential nomination of Thomas Eagleton, who was later replaced with Sargent Shriver, and lost to Richard Nixon by a 61–38 popular margin.

> The highest patriotism is not a blind acceptance of official policy, but a love of one's country deep enough to call her to a higher standard.
> —George McGovern

After losing his fourth bid for the senate in 1980, McGovern returned to private life to write and teach. He also served in various capacities with the United Nations on hunger eradication programs.

LEARN MORE

www.mcgovern72.org

www.mcgovernlibrary.com

Vote Your Conscience by Richard Michael Marano (Praeger, 2003)

George McGovern by Robert P. Watson, ed. (South Dakota State Historical Society, 2004)

One Bright Shining Moment (2006)

Wounded Knee

Bury Your Heart at Wounded Knee, Twice
Big Foot Trail, Wounded Knee, SD 57794

The final bloody campaign against the Native American people during the 19th century took place on December 29, 1890. Chief Big Foot and 350 of his followers were camped out along the shores of Wounded Knee Creek. Colonel James W. Forsyth had been instructed to bring all of the men to the military prison in Omaha, and leave the women and children to continue on to Pine Ridge alone. Ordered to give up their weapons, one refused and discharged his gun. The cavalry opened fire, and before it was over, 300 of the original group were dead, including Big Foot. They were not buried for three days, and some were carried off by animals, making an exact body count uncertain. Seventeen soldiers who participated in the slaughter were given the Congressional Medal of Honor.

It seems only obvious that the Wounded Knee massacre site would forever generate intense emotions among those on the Pine Ridge Reservation, on which it sits. However, a "trading post" was built there by non-Natives to exploit the tragedy, advertised with "VISIT THE MASS GRAVE!" billboards. On February 27, 1973, about 200 AIM activists (see page 262) arrived to declare the village liberated territory, the Independent Oglala Sioux Nation. They demanded the Senate begin investigating the BIA, the Department of Interior, and every treaty ever ratified by the U.S. Congress. FBI and BIA officers quickly surrounded the town. Supporters smuggled food, medical supplies, water, and ammunition into the encampment throughout the 71-day standoff. Gunfire often erupted between the sides, and one AIM follower, Frank Clearwater, was shot while sleeping. He later died. Some time later another occupier, Buddy Lamont, a Vietnam veteran, was killed too. AIM and the FBI finally negotiated a stand-down, which took place on May 8. The U.S. government promised to review the Treaty of 1868, and found the natives' claims valid . . . yet said the law of eminent domain overrode the treaty.

LEARN MORE

www.woundedkneemuseum.org

Bury My Heart at Wounded Knee by Dee Brown (Holt, Reinhart & Winston, 1970)

The Politics of Hallowed Ground by Mario Gonzalez and Elizabeth Cook-Lynn
    (University of Illinois, 1999)

Wounded Knee 1973 by Stanley Lyman (University of Nebraska, 1991)

6
The Southwest

★ Arizona ★ New Mexico ★
★ Oklahoma ★ Texas ★

ARIZONA

When it comes to progressive politics in Arizona, few stories are as encouraging as the short, unhappy administration of Republican Governor Evan Mecham. The conservative Pontiac salesman from Glendale was elected to the state's highest office in 1986. One of his first official acts was to cancel Arizona's new Martin Luther King holiday. In response, progressives called for a boycott of the tourist industry. Before it was over 166 national conventions rescheduled to other states, costing Arizona an estimated $200 million.

As buyer's remorse washed over Arizona voters, Mecham opponents were able to collect twice the number of petition signatures required for a recall election. But the names weren't even needed. On February 9, 1988, before the secretary of state could schedule a special election, the legislature impeached Mecham for high crimes and misdemeanors. Mecham had been found guilty of laundering $350,000 in campaign contributions, misusing an $80,000 state loan to his car dealership, and obstruction of justice. With Mecham out, the legislature reestablished the MLK holiday, though it cancelled the state's Columbus Day under the same bill.

Mecham did not go quietly; he ran for governor in the 1989 special election to replace himself, but failed to get the GOP nomination. And in 1990 he endorsed a referendum to recancel the MLK holiday and reestablish Columbus Day. Crazy as it sounds, voters *approved* the measure. A second boycott was organized and Arizona paid dearly: the NFL cancelled its contract for the 1993 Super Bowl in Phoenix, to the tune of $300 million. Finally, spearheaded by suffering businesses in Phoenix, the voters were given another chance in 1992 to make things right; the MLK holiday was approved in a statewide vote, and remains in place to this day. The 1996 Super Bowl was played in Phoenix.

LEARN MORE
High Crimes and Misdemeanors by Ronald J. Watkins (William Morrow, 1990)

Benson

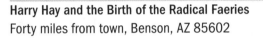

Harry Hay and the Birth of the Radical Faeries
Forty miles from town, Benson, AZ 85602

The gay and lesbian liberation movement made tremendous headway in the 10 years following the 1969 Stonewall Riot (see page 111). But Harry Hay, one of the cofounders of the Mattachine Society (see page 377) worried that with success came a new danger: assimilation. He believed gay men—Hay chose not to speak on behalf of lesbians—were losing sight of their unique sexual identities in an attempt to mimic heterosexual roles. And at the very least, gay men were becoming boring.

So in 1979, along with activists Don Kilhefner and Mitch Walker, Hay announced the first-ever Faerie Gathering, to be held over Labor Day weekend at the Sri Ram Ashram in Arizona's Sonora Desert. This new development (Hay disliked the term "movement") was intended to establish a "flamboyant anti-assimilationist fringe of gay liberation."

Between August 31 and September 2 more than 200 men joined Hay to chant, form healing circles, bang drums, and openly explore a new pagan spirituality. One of the weekend's highlights, according to participants, was a "spontaneous mud ritual" along an old creek bed. Sometime after dusk a horned black bull came upon the naked, mud-covered throng and stayed nearby until frightened off by a fireworks display. The faeries took the bull's spontaneous appearance as a positive omen; the Radical Faeries had been born. Today, Radical Faerie chapters can be found across the nation.

> The call goes out to all who know there is more to us than hetero-imitation. To all who are ready to move on. To all who have broken through and are ready to share those breakthroughs with your faerie brothers.
> —*Don Kilhefner, Harry Hay, and Mitch Walker, in their invitational flyer, Spring 1979*

LEARN MORE
www.radfae.org
Radically Gay by Will Roscoe, ed. (Beacon, 1996)
Faeries by Keri Pickett (Aperture, 2000)

Phoenix

Miranda v. Arizona: The Right to Remain Silent
Old City Hall, 17 S. Second Avenue, Phoenix, AZ 85003

Though today his name is synonymous with a basic civil liberty, Ernesto Miranda was hardly a champion of the U.S. Constitution. He was a hotheaded career criminal who, by chance, became the focal point in a legal battle over police procedure.

On November 27, 1962, a Phoenix woman was kidnapped as she entered her car downtown and was driven to a nearby alley. The assailant robbed the victim of eight dollars and fled. Then, on February 22, 1963, an 18-year-old woman was abducted after getting off a bus, taken to a remote area, and raped.

Two days later the second victim's cousin spotted a 1953 Packard fitting the description of the perpetrator's car and wrote down its license number. The vehicle belonged to Twila Hoffman, Ernesto Miranda's girlfriend. The victim viewed Miranda in a lineup with two other men, but could not identify him with absolute certainty. The police, however, told Miranda he'd been positively identified, and he started to confess. There, in Interrogation Room Two, police asked Miranda to put it in writing. The top of the printed form read, in part, that he did so "of my own free will . . . with full knowledge of my legal rights, understanding any statement may be used against me."

But did he really understand? Miranda did not have a lawyer when he wrote out his confession, and for his two trials was assigned a barely competent public defender who the state paid $50. During Miranda's robbery trial the police investigator admitted that he had not informed him that his statements would be used against him, nor that he had the right to an attorney (see page 175). The judge did not see a problem with either admission, nor did the jury, which found Miranda guilty. Miranda's kidnapping and rape trial the next day went just as quickly: guilty on both counts. He was sentenced to a total of 20 to 30 years in prison.

The Arizona Supreme Court upheld Miranda's convictions. But the Phoenix chapter of the ACLU appealed to the U.S. Supreme Court, which agreed to review it alongside three similar cases. In 1966, in a 5–4 ruling, the justices established a set of guidelines for police to follow to protect suspects' rights under the Fifth Amendment. Miranda's convictions were overturned and new trials were ordered.

Miranda's 1967 retrial for kidnapping and rape was almost as quick as the original. Even without a confession and the evidence gathered from that admission, prosecutors had a strong case. The jury found him guilty. A 1971 retrial on the robbery also ended in a guilty verdict.

Has *Miranda* tied the hands of law enforcement? Chief Justice Warren Burger, who dissented on the original ruling, admitted in 1988 that it had led to increased professionalism on the part of police, citing statistics that less than one percent of dismissed criminal cases were done so because of unwarned confessions.

LEARN MORE
Miranda by Gary L. Stuart (University of Arizona, 2004)
Miranda by Liva Baker (Atheneum, 1983)

MIRANDA RIGHTS

1. A suspect must be informed of his/her right to remain silent *before* questioning.

2. A suspect must be informed that anything he/she says can be used against him/her in a court of law.

3. A suspect has a right to have an attorney present at all times.

4. If a suspect cannot afford an attorney, one will be provided *before* questioning.

Tucson

Elfbrandt v. Russell: An End to Loyalty Oaths

Amphitheater Junior High, 4350 N. Fourth Avenue, Tucson, AZ 85705

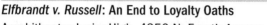

As much as the sins of the Red Scare are heaped on Joseph McCarthy, plenty of other politicians and citizens contributed to the climate of fear. In Arizona the red-baiting continued into the 1960s, long after McCarthy's 1954 censure by the senate. The 1961 Arizona Communist Control Act established, among other provisions, a loyalty oath for all public employees, including teachers. By signing the oath an employee asserted that he or she was not a member of the Communist Party, nor "any other organization having for one of its purposes the overthrow of the Arizona government." Right-wing backers of the bill suggested the ACLU, the NAACP, CORE, and SNCC were just such subversive organizations, but probably weren't thinking about folks like Barbara and Vern Elfbrandt of Tucson.

The Elfbrandts were devout Quakers and social activists; Barbara worked as an English and social studies teacher at Amphitheater Junior High and Vern (on leave from teaching) was an organizer for the State, County and Municipal Workers Union. When Barbara was asked to sign the oath she refused. Not only that, she filed suit against the school board, chaired by Imogene Russell, the state attorney general, and the governor. Oddly enough, the legislation was written so that employees already working for the state could not be fired for refusing to sign the oath, but could be denied their salaries. The couple's friends and landlord chipped in with rent and meals as the case made its five-year journey through state and district courts. (During this time Vern returned to teaching, unpaid because he did not sign the loyalty oath.)

The Elfbrandts lost every ruling prior to the U.S. Supreme Court, but on April 18, 1966, the high court ruled 5–4 that Arizona's loyalty oath was unconstitutional based upon Barbara Elfbrandt's First Amendment right of association. Writing for the majority, Justice William O. Douglas also asserted the obvious: "People often label as 'communist' ideas which they oppose." The Elfbrandts' salaries were immediately reinstated, as were the civil liberties of state employees, but it took several years before the Tucson school board coughed up the couple's back pay.

LEARN MORE

"Barbara Elfbrandt v. Imogene Russell" in *The Courage of Their Convictions* by Peter Irons (Penguin, 1990)

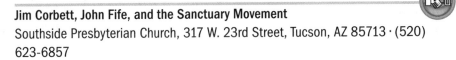

Jim Corbett, John Fife, and the Sanctuary Movement
Southside Presbyterian Church, 317 W. 23rd Street, Tucson, AZ 85713 · (520) 623-6857

In the late 1970s and early '80s thousands of Salvadoran refugees fled death squads in their home country for the United States. Because the American government supported the ruling junta in El Salvador, these refugees' applications for political asylum were rejected 97 percent of the time. Worse still, they were routinely deported to their home country where they were clear targets for state-sponsored torture and murder.

As the Reagan administration turned a blind eye to Central American atrocities, progressive citizens filled the moral void. In the early 1980s Arizonans John Fife and Jim Corbett launched the Sanctuary Movement, offering legal assistance, shelter, and food to refugees. Fife was the pastor of Tucson's Southside Presbyterian Church, and Jim Corbett was a retired rancher.

Though originally a clandestine operation, they went public on March 24, 1982, on the two-year anniversary of the assassination of Archbishop Oscar Romero. Five churches announced that their members were offering sanctuary to refugees. That number soon swelled to 300 churches and synagogues, 20 universities, 19 cities, and the state of New Mexico. More than 70,000 volunteers risked legal repercussions for their work on this modern underground railroad.

Corbett and 15 others were indicted on alien-smuggling charges in early 1985, and eight (though not Corbett) were convicted of felonies. All were given probation.

> **One day we will be as ashamed of borders as we are of slavery.**
> **—Jim Corbett**

LEARN MORE
Convictions of the Heart by Miriam Davidson (University of Arizona, 1988)
The American Sanctuary Movement by Robert Tomsho (Texas Monthly, 1987)
Sanctuary by Renny Golden and Michael McConnell (Orbis, 1986)

No More Deaths
Arivaca Road, Tucson, AZ 85736

Too often lost in the debate over immigration in this country is the human toll along the U.S.–Mexico border. To hear the Minutemen rant about the thousands who perish from heat stroke and dehydration in the desert southwest each year, you'd think the punishment for crossing the border illegally—a *misdemeanor*—is death. To understand the magnitude of the disaster, between October 30, 2004, and November 1, 2005—one year—282 immigrants were found dead in the Arizona desert, to say nothing of Texas, New Mexico, or California. Or Mexico.

But there are organizations, such as No More Deaths, Samaritan Patrol, and Christian Peacemaker Teams, who provide water and emergency medical assistance for humans in desperate need. In July 2005 two 23-year-old volunteers with No More Deaths, Daniel Strauss and Shanti Sellz, found three immigrants in the desert who were vomiting after drinking water from a contaminated cow tank. Straus and Sellz called a doctor using a cell phone, and were told to rush the trio to a hospital south of town. Along the way, on Arivaca Road, they were stopped by the U.S. Border Patrol and arrested and charged with transporting illegal aliens. If found guilty, they could have faced 15 years in prison. Months later, under intense public pressure, the federal government eventually dropped the charges.

LEARN MORE
www.nomoredeaths.org, (520) 495-5583
www.samaritanpatrol.org, (520) 620-0725
www.cpt.org, (773) 277-0253
The Devil's Highway by Luis Alberto Urrea (Little, Brown and Company, 2004)
Dead in Their Tracks by John Annerino (Four Walls Eight Windows, 2003)

NEW MEXICO

At 5:29:45 A.M. on July 16, 1945, the world's first nuclear device was detonated about 55 miles NNW of Alamogordo, New Mexico. Local residents were not forewarned, and when they asked what happened they were told a remote munitions dump had exploded. Three weeks later, on August 6, the United States dropped the first atomic bomb used in warfare on Hiroshima, killing 140,000 people. Three days later a second bomb was dropped on Nagasaki, killing 74,000 more.

Did any of the Nobel Prize–winning physicists or government officials ever slow down to consider the long-term consequences of their decision to develop the Bomb? In fact, Albert Einstein, who in 1939 urged FDR to launch the Manhattan Project, later regretted his role. "The unleashed power of the atom has changed everything save our modes of thinking, and we thus drift toward unparalleled catastrophes," he said.

Those wanting to reflect on the nuclear genie uncorked in the New Mexico desert have two opportunities a year to visit the Trinity site, on the first Saturdays in April and October. Visitors are permitted onto the White Sands Missile Range, and can drive the bumpy dirt road out to the site. A simple stone cairn marks the point where the device detonated, and changed the world forever.

LEARN MORE
www.atomictourist.com/trinity.htm
The Making of the Atomic Bomb by Richard Rhodes (Simon & Schuster, 1986)
Hiroshima by John Hersey (Knopf, 1946)
The Fate of the Earth by Jonathan Schell (Knopf, 1982)

Bayard

Salt of the Earth
All Over Town, Bayard, NM 88023

The late 1940s and early '50s were frightening years in Hollywood, when even the whisper of involvement with socialist politics could get an artist or technician blacklisted. Unable to find work in the studios, one group of blacklistees, including Will "Grandpa Walton" Geer, banded together to film *Salt of the Earth*.

Though the movie is fictional, it was based upon a real 15-month strike in Bayard, New Mexico. After several avoidable accidents, the consequence of understaffed crews, the International Union of Mine, Mill and Smelter Workers Local 890 called a strike against the Empire Zinc Corporation. The Grant County sheriff sought and received a Taft-Hartley injunction preventing the strikers from blocking the road to the mine. But the injunction did not apply to the miners' wives, mothers, and daughters, who formed a Ladies Auxiliary. These women maintained the picket lines for 15 months, driving away some strikebreakers and being assaulted by others, but ultimately winning a compromise with Empire.

The film, set in the town of San Marcos, is told from the perspective of Esperanza Quintero, played by Mexican actress Rosaura Revueltas. Her husband, Ramón, was played by Juan Chacón, the real-life president of Local 890. It explored issues seldom seen at the time in American films, such as sexism and anti–Mexican American racism. The actors understood these issues well; many had participated in the original strike.

Salt of the Earth was directed by Herbert Biberman, one of the Hollywood Ten (see page 386). The U.S. government, the studios, and some New Mexico residents did all they could to stop its production. Crew members were beaten and fired upon, and the union local's office was set afire. Labs refused to develop the film, and editing had to be done in secret locations. And two weeks before filming wrapped, Revueltas was deported on an immigration technicality—border officials hadn't stamped her passport when she entered the United States.

Only 13 American theaters would screen the film, but it played well overseas. Today it is seen as both a document of 1950s labor issues and a testament to the creative spirit in the face of government-sanctioned tyranny. It was eventually selected by the Library of Congress as one of 100 films to be preserved for posterity.

LEARN MORE
Salt of the Earth (1954)

Capitan

Smokey Bear Prevents Forest Fires
Smokey Bear Museum, 102 Smokey Bear Boulevard, PO Box 246, Capitan, NM
88316 · (505) 354-2247

Before there was Smokey Bear the bear, there was Smokey Bear the cartoon character, and before there was Smokey Bear the cartoon character there was an ill-conceived media campaign to save our nation's forests from wildfires. In 1937 the U.S. Forest Service launched a fire safety campaign with an Uncle Sam in a ranger outfit, nagging: "Your Forests—Your Fault—Your Loss."

But seeing the popularity of *Bambi*, released in 1944, the department decided to introduce a cartoon character, and named him Smokey Bear. (No, not Smokey *the* Bear.) He was so popular with children that he was given his own zip code for fan mail.

Then, on May 9, 1950, firefighters battling a blaze in the Lincoln National Forest found a five-pound black bear cub trapped in a tree. His paws and hindquarters were burned, so they nicknamed him Hotfoot Teddy. Game warden Ray Bell took him to Santa Fe for treatment, where Bell's daughter Judy helped nurse him back to health. The cub was renamed Smokey Bear when he was turned over to the chief of the Forest Service, and shipped to the National Zoo in Washington, D.C.

When Smokey died in 1976, his body was returned to New Mexico and buried not far from where he was born. Today a mini-chapel/museum stands near his grave with a stained glass window of the firefighting icon. A sculpture of young Smokey, up a tree, stands out front.

> Only *you* can prevent forest fires.
>
> —*Smokey Bear*

LEARN MORE
www.zianet.com/village/museum/museum.html
www.smokeybear.com
Guardian of the Forest by Ellen Earnhardt Morrison (Morielle Press, 1989)

OKLAHOMA

Your right to procreate is a fundamental human right. Yet the U.S. Supreme Court had little opportunity to weigh in on whether it was a *constitutional* right until the case of an Oklahoma inmate came before it in 1942.

Jack Skinner was caught stealing chickens in 1926 and was sent to state prison. After his release he ran afoul of the law in 1929, this time for armed robbery. And when, in 1934, Skinner was convicted a third time, again for armed robbery, the judge imposed a harsh sentence under the state's 1935 Habitual Criminal Sterilization Act: he ordered Skinner to undergo a vasectomy.

Skinner challenged the constitutionality of the eugenic statute; his case eventually reached the U.S. Supreme Court as *Skinner v. Oklahoma*. In a unanimous ruling the court held that the law violated the Equal Protection Clause because it exempted white-collar crimes, such as embezzlement and "political offenses." Furthermore, the justices warned, "In evil or reckless hands [punitive sterilization] can cause races or types which are inimical to the dominant group to wither and disappear," and that "Marriage and procreation are fundamental to the very existence and survival of the race." *Skinner* set a precedent that would later be used to argue *Roe v. Wade* (see page 337) and other cases regarding reproductive freedom.

Crescent

Karen Silkwood, Nuclear Whistleblower
7.3 miles south of the Hub Cafe on Route 74, south of Route 33, Crescent, OK 73028

On November 13, 1974, labor activist Karen Silkwood was scheduled to meet with *New York Times* reporter David Burnham at the Northwest Holiday Inn in Oklahoma City. She claimed she had damning evidence regarding safety violations, quality control, and missing plutonium at Kerr-McGee's Cimarron River processing facility, where she worked in the metallography laboratory. Silkwood never made it; one mile south of the plant her car crossed the northbound lane, ran off the road, and struck a concrete culvert. Silkwood was killed.

Or was she *murdered?* Many believe so. In the preceding months Silkwood, a member of the Oil, Chemical, and Atomic Workers Union, had collected evidence of faked safety reports, doctored photos of fuel rods, and 40 pounds of unaccounted-for plutonium, enough to build three nuclear bombs. Plant managers were suspicious of her activities and had gotten local law enforcement to tap her phone, break into her car, and bug her apartment—all in violation of the law—by suggesting she was a plutonium smuggler. Worse still, someone "seeded" Silkwood's apartment with plutonium. (Kerr-McGee would later claim Silkwood deliberately poisoned herself to embarrass them.)

After the crash, Silkwood's 1973 Honda Civic was taken to a local garage where a mechanic claimed two teams in hazmat suits, saying they were from the Atomic Energy Commission, picked over the wreckage. They seemed particularly interested in a brown file folder . . . a folder that vanished before the Oklahoma State Highway Patrol's investigation. The crash report claimed Silkwood had fallen asleep at the wheel, and made no attempt to explain the mysterious scratch found along the side of vehicle, nor the dents in its rear fenders.

Silkwood's family sued Kerr-McGee in 1979 and won a $505,000 damage settlement, along with a $10 million punitive award. Kerr-McGee motioned for a mistrial because the Three Mile Island accident occurred three weeks after the trial had commenced. The judgment was overturned in 1981. The U.S. Supreme Court sided with the family in 1984, ordering Tenth Circuit to retry the case; in 1985 the family settled for $1.38 million.

If there is an "up" side to Silkwood's death, it's that the Cimarron River facility closed in 1975, and Kerr-McGee got out of the nuclear business altogether in 1987.

LEARN MORE

The Killing of Karen Silkwood by Richard Rashke (Houghton Mifflin, 1981)

Who Killed Karen Silkwood? by Howard Kohn (Summit, 1981)

Okemah

Woody Guthrie, Folk Song Hero
Birthplace (burned down), Second and Birch Streets, Okemah, OK 74859

The hand-printed sticker on Woody Guthrie's guitar said it all: "This Machine Kills Fascists." His ammunition? More than 3,000 songs written during his lifetime.

Guthrie was born to a poor family in Okemah, Oklahoma, on July 14, 1912. As a young man he was attracted to a 1929 oil boom in Pampa, Texas, where he married his first wife and started his musical career. To find work, Guthrie hitchhiked and hopped trains between gigs at low-wattage radio sta-

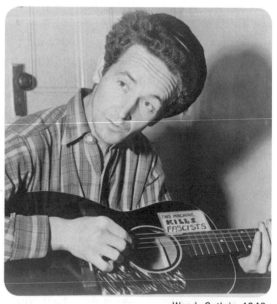

Woody Guthrie, 1943

tions and honky-tonks. Then in 1937 he landed a job singing traditional folk ballads on KFVD radio in Los Angeles. As his popularity grew he felt more comfortable weaving social and political themes into his lyrics and on-air commentary. Guthrie's original folk songs chronicled the struggles of bankrupt farmers, hoboes, and working-class Americans, from "Talking Dust Bowl Blues" to "Union Maid" to "I Ain't Got No Home."

In early 1940 Guthrie brought his common man message to New York. It was here, on February 23, in a cheap hotel off Times Square, Guthrie penned his best-known ballad: "This Land Is Your Land." It was originally titled "God Blessed America," a parody of Irving Berlin's "God Bless America." The song's original refrain was "God blessed America for me," a sarcastic turn on Berlin's lyrics, particularly in light of Guthrie's final stanza:

> One bright sunny morning in the shadow of the steeple
> By the relief office I saw my people—
> As they stood there hungry,
> I stood there wondering if
> God blessed America for me.

Guthrie didn't record it until April 1944, when he changed the refrain to "This land was made for you and me." When the ballad was published in songbooks, however, the biting final verse was almost always absent.

In the early 1940s the Guthries' marriage fell apart. Woody soon remarried and had four children by his second wife, including Arlo (see page 24). During World War II Guthrie joined the Merchant Marine where he wrote songs about fighting the Axis and, for the soldiers, advice on avoiding VD. After the war he began to show symptoms of Huntington's disease. His behavior became increasingly erratic, and he left his family and headed for California with another woman.

During the McCarthy era Guthrie was blacklisted for his involvement in left-of-center causes, which further fueled his downward personal spiral. In 1954 he was institutionalized at the Greystone Park Psychiatric Hospital in Morris Plains, New Jersey. While there his work was rediscovered by a new generation of folk singers. Many made the pilgrimage to his bedside, including Joan Baez, Bob Dylan, and Phil Ochs. Guthrie died on October 3, 1967.

> Any song that points out something that is wrong, needs fixing, and shows you how to fix it—is the undying song of the working people. If it is made a little jazzy or sexy that ain't wrong—what book could you read to a crowd that would make them dance?
> —*Woody Guthrie*

LEARN MORE

www.woodyguthrie.org, (212) 541-6320

Prophet Singer by Mark Allan Jackson (University Press of Mississippi, 2007)

Ramblin' Man by Ed Cray (Norton, 2006)

Woody Guthrie by Joe Klein (Delta, 1999)

Oklahoma City

"Oklahoma Kate" Barnard, Social Reform Pioneer
Fairlawn Cemetery, 2700 N. Shartel Avenue, Oklahoma City, OK 73103

When Oklahoma became a state in 1907 it ratified a constitution that included restrictions on child labor, opting instead for compulsory childhood education. This radical idea was inserted into the document by "Oklahoma Kate"

Barnard who, in 1907, was elected Commissioner of the Department of Charities and Corrections. She was one of the first American women to hold elected office, and her first order of business was to reduce her own salary from $2,500 to $1,500 a year.

Barnard served for almost two terms. Near the end of her second term she was openly critical of a state program that was created to manage the land of Native American wards of the state. Businessman (and later governor) William Murray was up to his elbows in graft, and saw to it that Barnard's department was defunded to zero.

Though she was driven from politics, she remained active in social causes, and when Barnard died in 1930 several Oklahoma governors acted as pallbearers. Her grave remained unmarked, however, for many years, until the Oklahoma County Historical Society recognized the reformer's contributions in 1992. A statue of Barnard stands on the first floor of the Oklahoma State Capitol building.

> How can a woman wear diamonds in a country where little children starve?
>
> —*Kate Barnard*

LEARN MORE

One Woman's Political Journey by Lynn Musslewhite and Suzanne J. Crawford (University of Oklahoma, 2003)

Oologah and Claremore

Will Rogers, Cowboy Philosopher
Birthplace, Will Rogers Birth Place Road (Route 38), Oologah, OK 74053 · (918) 341-0719

Will Rogers Shrine and Grave, 1720 W. Will Rogers Boulevard, PO Box 157, Claremore, OK 74108 · (918) 341-0719

"My ancestors didn't come over on the *Mayflower*, but they met 'em at the boat," claimed Will Rogers, who was 9/32 Cherokee. But journalist Damon Runyon calculated Rogers's constitution differently: "[Rogers is] America's most accomplished human document. One-third humor. One-third humanitarian. One-third heart." Indeed, during the Depression Rogers became the common-sense voice of working-class Americans in a world that seemed disinterested in their plight.

Despite his humble personality, Rogers did not come from a humble background. His parents owned a 60,000-acre spread in northeast Oklahoma—Dog Iron Ranch—and on it built one of the largest homes in the territory. Rogers was born there on November 4, 1879.

When Rogers was 10 his mother died. To help him get over his grief, his father bought him a horse. Rogers learned to ride and rope, and his skill with a lasso landed him a job with Texas Jack's Wild West Show, and eventually the Ziegfeld Follies. Ad-libbing when he botched tricks,

Will Rogers, c. 1930

Rogers found that audiences responded to his folksy wit, and he launched his career as a humorist. The vaudeville stage led to radio and a syndicated newspaper column, "Will Rogers Says."

In 1928 Rogers ran for president on the "Anti-Bunk" ticket—a publicity stunt dreamed up by *Life* magazine. But in 1932, several years into the Depression, there was serious talk of him running on a populist platform. Few Americans garnered such universal affection, though his political skills were untested. In the end he endorsed Roosevelt, who won in a landslide. Rogers became a roving humanitarian ambassador, raising money for disaster relief on behalf of the Red Cross and the Salvation Army, and any cause he thought worthy.

Rogers's life was cut short on August 15, 1935. An enthusiastic booster of the nascent aviation industry, he was killed in a plane crash near Point Barrow, Alaska, along with aviator Wiley Post. His body was placed in a holding vault in Los Angeles before being moved to Claremore on May 22, 1944. In addition to his grave, the Will Roger Shrine today includes a museum where you can see his saddles, lariats, and other personal effects. You can also visit his nearby birthplace, which is still a working ranch.

LEARN MORE
www.willrogers.org
Will Rogers by Ben Yagoda (Knopf, 1993)

PROGRESSIVE THOUGHTS
OF WILL ROGERS

- This country is bigger than Wall Street. If they don't believe it, I show 'em the map.
- Our distribution of wealth is getting more uneven all the time. . . . You can't get money without taking it from somebody.
- This country has come to feel the same when Congress is in session as when the baby gets hold of a hammer.
- [To the board of directors of Standard Oil:] Your motto is "Service." Back on the farm, when I heard that the bull was "servicing" the cows, I looked behind the barn. And gentlemen, what the bull was doing to the cow is exactly what you people have been doing to the public all these years.
- When you get into trouble five thousand miles from home you have got to have been looking for it.
- I am not a member of any organized political party. I am a Democrat.
- They may call me a rube and a hick, but I'd rather be the man who bought the Brooklyn Bridge than the man who sold it.

LEARN MORE
The Quotable Will Rogers by Joseph Carter (Gibbs Smith, 2005)

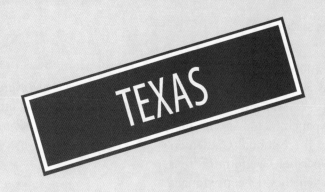

TEXAS

What's a progressive to say about Texas? Sure, George W. Bush has no doubt soured many on the Lone Star State, but that one person should not be allowed to eclipse the Texans who have contributed so much to the nation's advancement. Congresswoman Barbara Jordan? Texan. Journalist Bill Moyers? Born and raised in Marshall. Populist Jim Hightower, and columnist Molly Ivins, and Governor Ann Richards. Texan, Texan, and Texan. Willie . . . Freakin' . . . Nelson? You get the point.

Not only that, several important (and progressive) legal decisions made by the U.S. Supreme Court originated in Texas: *Roe v. Wade, Texas v. Johnson, Lawrence v. Texas,* and Thurgood Marshall's first case before the high court, *Smith v. Allwright.* So before you paint the nation's second largest state with a red Bush brush, perhaps you should brush up on your Texas progressive history.

And just for the record, George W. Bush was born in New Haven. *Connecticut.* As the great braided Buddha Willie Nelson once observed, "He's not from Texas, and he ain't a cowboy, so let's stop trashin' Texans and cowboys." Amen to that.

Amarillo

Howard Lyman and Oprah Beat the Meat Industry
Federal Courthouse, 205 SE Fifth Avenue, Amarillo, TX 79101

Think you can't slander a hamburger? Think again! During an April 1996 broadcast of *The Oprah Winfrey Show* Howard Lyman, a fourth-generation dairy farmer and president of Earth Save International, informed viewers of the dangers posed by BSE—bovine spongiform encephalopathy—better known as

Mad Cow Disease. Lyman's descriptions moved Winfrey to swear off hamburger forever. And though her onstage panel included Dr. Gary Weber of the National Cattlemen's Beef Association, a group of Texas ranchers felt they'd been wronged.

> Cows are herbivores. They shouldn't be eating other cows.
> —Oprah Winfrey, during her broadcast

Pointing to a dip in the futures market, they sued Lyman, Winfrey, and Harpo Productions under the Texas Food Disparagement Act, claiming they'd suffered "shame, embarrassment, and mental pain and anguish."

In January 1998 the case went to trial in Amarillo. During the proceedings jurors heard more than a few of the dirty little secrets of the meat industry, including the practice of feeding the discarded and rendered remains of slaughtered cattle back to other cattle, which many scientists believe is responsible for the transmission of BSE. In fact, the FDA banned the practice in the wake of the broadcast . . . five months before the trial began.

On February 26, 1998, the jury delivered its verdict after deliberating less than six hours: not guilty. On the steps of the courthouse Winfrey told reporters, "The First Amendment rocks!!"

She's right, you know.

LEARN MORE
www.madcowboy.com
Mad Cowboy by Howard F. Lyman with Glen Merzer (Touchstone, 1998)
No More Bull! by Howard F. Lyman, Glen Merzer, and Joanna Samorow-Merzer
    (Scribner, 2005)

Austin

Barbara Jordan, Champion of the Constitution
Jordan Grave, Texas State Cemetery, 909 Navasota Street, Austin, TX 78702 · (512) 463-0605

Many Americans were introduced to Barbara Jordan during the 1974 House Judiciary Committee hearings on the impeachment of Richard Nixon. She had only been on the committee for two years, but became a key figure in Congress's final action to hold the president accountable for his criminal behavior.

Jordan was born on February 21, 1936, in Houston's Fifth Ward. After attending Texas Southern University and Boston University Law School, she returned to Houston and volunteered on the Kennedy campaign. She ran for state office in 1962 and 1964, and lost both times. But in 1966, after the 1964 Civil Rights Act forced Texas to fairly redraw its voting districts, Jordan was elected the first African American to serve in the Texas Senate since Reconstruction. There she introduced the state's first minimum wage bill, established the Texas Fair Employment Practices Commission, worked on environmental issues, and earned the admiration of fellow legislators.

In 1972 Jordan was elected the first African American woman from the South to serve in the U.S. House of Representatives. After the national spotlight of the impeachment hearings, she was asked to give the keynote address to the 1976 Democratic National Convention. And though many hoped she would run for higher office, diagnosed with

Barbara Jordan, at the 1976 Democratic National Convention

My faith in the Constitution is whole. I am not going to sit here and be an idle spectator to the diminution, the subversion, the destruction of the Constitution.
—*Barbara Jordan, in her opening statement on impeachment hearings for Richard Nixon, July 25, 1974*

multiple sclerosis, she retired from Congress in 1979. That she was also a lesbian with a partner in a very conservative state might have had something to do with her decision.

Jordan accepted a position at the University of Texas Lyndon B. Johnson School of Public Affairs, where she taught public policy. Jordan testified against the nomination of Robert Bork to the U.S. Supreme Court, was awarded the Presidential Medal of Freedom in 1994, and died on January 17, 1996.

LEARN MORE
www.utexas.edu/lbj/barbarajordanforum/home.htm, (512) 471-8288
www.cemetery.state.tx.us
Barbara Jordan by Mary Beth Rogers (Bantam, 1998)
Barbara Jordan by Max Sherman, ed. (University of Texas, 2007)
Barbara Jordan by Barbara Jordan and Shelby Hearon (Doubleday, 1979)

John Henry Faulk Kills the Broadcast Blacklist
Faulk Grave, Oakwood Cemetery, 1601 Navasota Street, Austin, TX 78702 · (512) 478-7152

In 1956 John Henry Faulk had the second-highest-rated show on CBS radio. A year later the folksy Texas storyteller was fired, his canning explained away as "format changes" by the network brass. But Faulk knew better—he had been blacklisted.

The extent of Faulk's "subversive" activities during the 1950s Red Scare was to challenge the blacklist itself. As a member of the American Federation of Television and Radio Artists (AFTRA) he advocated that the union condemn the activities of AWARE, a right-wing organization that compiled lists of "Communist sympathizers," lists that included anyone in radio or TV they found objectionable or a threat to their racket of fear. AWARE was allied with Laurence Johnson, the owner of a large chain of grocery stores based in Syracuse, New York. Johnson would threaten to boycott products from any advertiser who sponsored programs on which blacklistees appeared. Networks crawled to AWARE for the lists . . . and had to pay five dollars a head to "clear" every actor, musician, announcer, writer, or director involved in a project. AWARE was running a Mafia-style protection racket—"Nice little radio show you've got there. It would be a shame if anything happened to it."

Unemployed and unemployable, Faulk made fighting AWARE his full time job. In 1957, with the help of lawyer Louis Nizer and funded by Edward R. Murrow, he filed a libel suit against AWARE and Johnson. It was five years before the case ever came to trial, due mostly to legal blocks put up by AWARE's counsel, Roy Cohn. Shortly before the verdict was read, Johnson committed suicide in a Bronx motel room; few knew it at the time, but his grocery empire was teetering on bankruptcy. On July 19, 1962, a jury awarded Faulk a combined $3.5 million judgment for compensatory and punitive damages, even *more* than he asked for. It was reduced to $550,000 on appeal, but the money was never the goal—killing the blacklist was. AWARE closed its doors for good after the U.S. Supreme Court refused to hear its final appeal.

LEARN MORE
Fear on Trial by John Henry Faulk (University of Texas, 1983)
A Shadow of Red by David Everitt (Ivan R. Dee, 2007)

Crawford

Cindy Sheehan and Camp Casey
Camp Casey, Prairie Chapel and Morgan Roads, Crawford, TX 76638
Camp Casey II, Prairie Chapel and Carmen Church Roads, Crawford, TX 76638

Cindy Sheehan had heard enough. George W. Bush was speaking about the Iraq War and described it as a "noble cause." Sheehan, whose son Casey had been killed in Sadr City on April 4, 2004, asked herself, "What *noble cause?*" She knew Bush couldn't answer the question, but she decided to go to Crawford and ask him anyway.

Sheehan showed up at the gates of Bush's ranch on August 6, 2005, at the beginning of his scheduled month-long Texas vacation. She boldly declared, "This is the beginning of the end of the occupation in Iraq." And history will probably prove her correct.

Camp Casey started as a grieving mother in a pup tent beside a two-lane road, but it quickly grew to a movement. White House staff tried to diffuse the situation, but Sheehan demanded to talk directly with the president. They said no, so she pledged to stay. Others joined her. Authorities threatened to arrest the group if they did not disperse by August 11, but the vigil was getting too much attention and the police and Secret Service backed down.

On day six Veterans for Peace erected 200 crosses along Prairie Chapel Road, including one for Sheehan's son Casey. A day later Bush and his motorcade passed by the camp and the crosses on the way to a fundraiser, but did not stop. A small group of Bush supporters were bussed in by right-wing talk radio host Mike Gallagher; they protested across the road from Camp Casey, then later moved to the parking lot of Crawford's Pirate Field.

On day nine Larry Mattlage, who owned the property adjacent to Camp Casey, drove out near the fence line, shouted at the protesters, then fired a shotgun five times into the sky, away from the group. He later told police he was practicing "hunting doves." Another Bush supporter, Larry Northern, plowed down dozens of soldiers' crosses in his speeding pickup a day later. One of the crosses became lodged in his tire and he could drive no farther; police arrested him at the scene.

Disgusted by his neighbors' behavior Fred Mattlage, third cousin of Larry Mattlage, opened 180 acres of his land to establish Camp Casey II . . . even closer to the Bush Ranch. Sheehan had to fly to California on August 18 after her mother suffered a stroke, but the vigil continued, coordinated through the Crawford Peace House (9142 E. Fifth Street), and included a concert with Joan Baez. Sheehan returned August 24.

Cindy Sheehan, 2005

Events culminated on Saturday, August 27, and the following day. Sheehan's supporters held a rally at Camp Casey II, with several thousand in attendance. A "You Don't Speak for Me, Cindy!" rally was held at Pirate Field. An interfaith service was held on Sunday at Camp Casey.

> We want to show him there are people who oppose him. This is real democracy. There are real people that really oppose him.
> —*Cindy Sheehan, at Camp Casey*

The next morning, with Bush still at his ranch, Hurricane Katrina struck the Gulf Coast and the nation began focusing on a new failure of his administration. Sheehan left Crawford on August 31; Camp Casey's tents and supplies were transported to the hurricane disaster area by veteran volunteers, and arrived before many of the FEMA crews did.

LEARN MORE
www.crawfordpeacehouse.org, (254) 486-0099
The Vigil by W. Leon Smith and the Staff of the *Lone Star Iconoclast* (Disinformation, 2005)
Peace Mom by Cindy Sheehan (Atria, 2006)
Not One More Mother's Child by Cindy Sheehan (Koa Books, 2005)

Crystal City

Los Cinco, José Angel Gutiérrez, Severity Lara, and La Raza Unida Party
Crystal City Town Hall, 101 E. Dimmit Street, Crystal City, TX 78839

In 1963, the population of Crystal City, Texas, was 85 percent Mexican American, yet it had never had a representative from the community on the city council. But that year a slate of five candidates—Los Cinco—shocked the political establishment by sweeping the old guard out of office. They were assisted by the Political Association of Spanish-Speaking Organizations (PASSO) and local unions. But the victory didn't last long; the deposed politicians fought back and were able to capitalize on the inexperienced missteps of Los Cinco to defeat them in the next election.

Then, in 1969, a new political organization rose from the ashes: La Raza Unida Party (LRUP), led by José Angel Gutiérrez. It recaptured city hall and the school board in 1970, with Gutiérrez as the new school board president. It was a sweet victory, as Gutiérrez had earlier assisted Severity Lara when she led a walkout at Crystal City High School to protest unfair treatment of Mexican Americans in the school's curriculum and activities. LRUP was able to address many of the needs of the underserved population, including bilingual education and fair housing practices.

The success of the LRUP led to new chapters across the nation, and while they did not elect a tremendous number of candidates, they were able to force the political establishment to be more inclusive. Severity Lara went on to serve on the city council, and later became mayor of Crystal City. Gutiérrez was elected a county judge.

> We believe that by virtue of birth we're entitled to dignity, to respect, to a free, clean environment, and the opportunity to make oneself worth something.
> —José Angel Gutiérrez

LEARN MORE
The Making of a Chicano Militant by José Angel Gutiérrez (University of Wisconsin, 1999)

Dallas

The Dixie Chicks Stand Up and Sing
American Airlines Center, 2500 Victory Avenue, Dallas, TX 75219

"Just so you know, we're on the good side with y'all. We do not want this war, this violence. And we're ashamed that the president of the United States is from Texas." Little did Natalie Maines know when she uttered those words from the stage of London's Shepherds Bush Empire theater on the eve of the Iraq War that she'd be punished for speaking her mind. But she found out fast.

At the time the Dixie Chicks had a #1 hit, "Travelin' Soldier," about a young woman waiting stateside for her boyfriend fighting in Vietnam. Almost overnight the song disappeared from country music radio, driven by a campaign organized by the ironically named Free Republic. Radio stations held rallies where listeners burned their Dixie Chicks CDs, or crushed them with steamrollers. By the time the group returned from their European tour they were country music pariahs. Both the Cox and Cumulus radio networks had banned them from their stations' playlists.

To their ultimate credit, Maines, Martie Maguire, and Emily Robison stuck together and called the overreaction what it was: bullshit. Were American citizens no longer able to speak their minds? They defiantly appeared on the cover of *Entertainment Weekly* and gave a candid interview to Diane Sawyer. And on the same day George W. Bush landed on the USS *Lincoln* to announce "Mission Accomplished," the Dixie Chicks opened their U.S. tour in Greenville, South Carolina, while protesters picketed outside. Their true fans stood by them, but album and ticket sales fell off. And at the end of the tour Maines received a letter threatening that she would be shot while performing in Dallas on July 6, 2003. They went ahead with the concert at the American Airlines Center anyway.

Following the tour the Dixie Chicks took time off to write and record a new album and to grow their families. They returned to the music scene in 2006 with *Taking the Long Way*. Its single, "Not Ready to Make Nice," explained what they'd gone through, and why they weren't apologizing. And though it got almost no attention from country stations, it won Grammys for Record of the Year and Album of the Year, and two country awards.

LEARN MORE
www.dixiechicks.com
Shut Up & Sing (2006)

Roe v. Wade: Abortion Rights
Fifth Circuit Federal Court, 600 Commerce Street, Dallas, TX 75202

Norma Nelson had a rough early life. In and out of reform institutions, she dropped out of high school, got married at 16, and moved to California. Six weeks later she was pregnant. Her 24-year-old husband "Woody" McCorvey accused her of sleeping around, and beat her. She fled McCorvey, returned to Dallas, and surrendered custody of her newborn to her mother, who was angry that her daughter worked in a lesbian bar. Two years later McCorvey became pregnant again, and signed away custody to the child's father. And in October 1969, while working as a ticket-taker in a traveling carnival, she got pregnant a third time. Without family support or financial security, she looked to get an abortion.

Under Texas law the procedure was illegal unless her life was in jeopardy. Denied her request, McCorvey met with lawyers Linda Coffee and Sarah Weddington to file a lawsuit. The complaint was filed in federal court on March 3, 1970, alongside the case of married couple Marsha and David King. McCorvey was "Jane Roe," and the Kings were "John and Jane Doe." Henry Wade, the Dallas County district attorney, was named the defendant. Coffee and Weddington threw every constitutional argument they could at the Texas law, saying it violated the First, Fourth, Fifth, Eighth, Ninth, and Fourteenth Amendments. Because McCorvey's pregnancy would come to full term during the course of the trial, and any appeals, the case was filed as a class action suit.

On June 17 the three-judge panel on the Fifth Circuit Court in Dallas ruled in favor of Roe: "[T]he Texas abortion laws must be declared unconstitutional because they deprive single women and married couples of the right, secured by the Ninth Amendment, to choose whether to have children." But because the court issued "declarative relief," rather than "injunctive relief" (which would have invalidated the Texas law), the case was appealed to the U.S. Supreme Court.

Roe v. Wade was heard alongside a case from Georgia, *Doe v. Bolton*, in December 1971. Associate Justices Lewis Powell and William

> I think one of the purposes of the Constitution was to guarantee to individuals the right to determine the course of their own lives.
>
> —Sarah Weddington, in oral arguments before the U.S. Supreme Court in Roe v. Wade, 1971

Rehnquist joined the bench while the case was being decided, so to allow them to participate in the ruling, Chief Justice Warren Burger moved to have the case reargued in October 1972. Many believe he did so also to delay the undoubtedly contentious decision beyond the 1972 presidential election.

In a 7–2 ruling handed down on January 22, 1973, the justices ruled that, under the Fourteenth Amendment, abortion on demand was legal during the first three months, or trimester, of a pregnancy, during the second trimester for the health of the woman, and during the third trimester if the woman's life was at risk.

LEARN MORE

www.naral.org, (202) 973-3000

Roe v. Wade by Marian Faux (Cooper Square, 2001)

A Question of Choice by Sarah Weddington (Penguin, 1993)

How the Pro-Choice Movement Saved America by Cristina Page (Basic Books, 2006)

Texas v. Johnson: Freedom of Dissent
Dallas City Hall, 1500 Marilla Street, Dallas, TX 75201

August 22, 1984, was a hot day in Dallas—about 110 degrees—but it got even hotter when the Revolutionary Communist Youth Brigade showed up. About 100 demonstrators, not all of them members of the group, marched around downtown to protest the renomination of Ronald Reagan as the GOP's candidate for the upcoming presidential election. They ended up at Dallas City Hall, about two blocks from the Republicans' gathering. There they set fire to an American flag pulled from the front of the nearby Mercantile National Bank. Had the protesters immediately dispersed they may have escaped arrest, but they jumped into the fountain in front of City Hall to cool off, and were arrested a half hour later. Daniel Walker, a Korean War veteran who witnessed the events, collected what remained of the charred flag, brought it home, and buried it in his backyard.

Four protesters were eventually charged under a Texas statute prohibiting "desecration of a venerated object." Two of the four jumped bail before answering the charges, and a third pled guilty and received a 10-day jail sentence. But Gregory Lee "Joey" Johnson decided to go to court . . . and took his case all the way to the U.S. Supreme Court.

Johnson was originally found guilty, sentenced to a year in prison, and fined $2,000. The sentence was upheld in District Court, but reversed by the Texas Court of Criminal Appeals. Then, on June 21, 1989, the U.S. Supreme Court ruled 5–4 in Johnson's favor, deciding that his actions, offensive as many found them, were symbolic speech protected by the First Amendment. William Rehnquist sang the first verse of "The Star-Spangled Banner" from the bench as part of his dissent. Joey Johnson celebrated the decision by posing with several charred flags outside the court.

> If there is a bedrock principle underlying the First Amendment, it is that the government may not prohibit the expression of an idea simply because society finds the idea itself offensive or disagreeable. . . . We have not recognized an exception to this principle even when our flag has been involved.
> —Justice William Brennan, in Texas v. Johnson, 1989

Public reaction was mostly negative, and provoked a lot of grandstanding. George H. W. Bush, then president, proposed a constitutional amendment against flag burning; the U.S. House passed 39 different resolutions condemning the ruling; and Congress quickly drafted and passed the Flag Protection Act of 1989. The new law provoked even *more* flag burning. Two cases challenging the statute made it to the U.S. Supreme Court, consolidated as *United States v. Eichman*. In a quick 5–4 ruling in 1990, the justices confirmed that they meant what they said the first time, and the federal law was declared unconstitutional.

LEARN MORE

Flag Burning and Free Speech by Robert Justin Goldstein (University Press of Kansas, 2000)

Burning the Flag by Robert Justin Goldstein (Kent State, 1996)

Galveston

Juneteenth

Ashton Villa, 2328 Broadway, Galveston, TX 77550 · (409) 762-3933

Although Abraham Lincoln issued the Emancipation Proclamation on September 22, 1862, and it went into effect on January 1, 1863, it wasn't until June 19, 1865, more than two months after the end of the Civil War, that slaves around Galveston were informed about it. The news was delivered by the Union's Major-General Gordon Granger from the balcony of Ashton Villa. He also read aloud Lincoln's General Order #3, announcing that all slaves were henceforth free.

A year later, on June 19, African Americans in Texas commemorated the day the news of their freedom arrived. Though the holiday was originally called Freedom Day, or Emancipation Day, somehow "June 19th" was shortened to "Juneteenth," and the name stuck. As Texas blacks migrated to new states, they took with them what was once a local celebration, and Juneteenth became a nationwide event. Though Juneteenth ceremonies vary to include services, picnics, and parades, they always include a rereading of the Emancipation Proclamation and/or General Order #3.

> The people are informed that in accordance with a proclamation from the Executive of the United States, all slaves are free. This involves an absolute equality of personal rights and rights of property, between former masters and slaves . . .
>
> —*Abraham Lincoln,*
> *in General Order #3*

LEARN MORE

www.juneteenth.com

Oh, Freedom! by William H. Wiggins Jr. (University of Tennessee, 1987)

Hillsboro

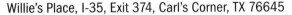

BioWillie Biodiesel
Willie's Place, I-35, Exit 374, Carl's Corner, TX 76645

In 2004 Annie Nelson bought a new Volkswagen Jetta that ran on biodiesel—a fuel made from plants and animal fats. Historians may one day point to her decision as the moment the United States charted a new course toward energy independence. It wasn't that she started a trend or invented a new type of engine—diesel technology has been around for over a century—she just had the good fortune of being married to Willie Nelson. For all his work with Farm Aid (see page 232), the country music legend had never given biodiesel much thought until he drove his wife's car.

Now he gives it a lot of thought. As it turns out, biodiesel is an answer to several modern dilemmas. Biodiesel emits 78 percent less carbon dioxide (the earth's primary greenhouse pollutant) than fossil fuels. It emits no sulfur dioxide (the main cause of acid rain) when burned, and only half the smoke particulates of standard engines. And because it opens a huge new market for American agriculture, biodiesel could become a lifeline for struggling farmers, not to mention break the country's dependence on foreign imports.

Today Willie Nelson is biodiesel's biggest booster. He started by converting all of his tour buses to run on it. When he was having difficulty finding the fuel on tour, he committed himself to making it available nationwide. He started by renovating the legendary Carl's Corner Truckstop near his hometown of Abbott into a biofuel Mecca called Willie's Place. It now sells Nelson's signature brand, BioWillie Biodiesel, brewed right on site. That's another advantage to biodiesel—there's no need for a stinky, cancer-causing refinery to produce it. BioWillie is now available at dozens of gas stations from California to South Carolina, and its network is growing fast.

> I'd like to see biodiesel and ethanol processed within a few feet of the fields the products were grown in. The key to efficiency is going to have to be localized production.
>
> —*Willie Nelson*

LEARN MORE
www.biowillieusa.com, (866) 765-4940
On the Clean Road Again by Willie Nelson (Fulcrum, 2007)
The Tao of Willie by Willie Nelson with Turk Pipkin (Gotham, 2006)

Houston

The Battle of the Sexes

Reliant Astrodome (former Harris County Domed Stadium), 8400 Kirby Drive, Houston, TX 77001

It was billed as the "Battle of the Sexes," a best-of-five tennis match between Billie Jean King and Bobby Riggs. It was the early 1970s and chauvinists like Bobby Riggs were on the ropes. Though 55 at the time, Riggs was no slouch; he'd been a pro since 16 and had just beaten Margaret Court, the top female player at the time, in a match on Mother's Day 1973. "I want Billie Jean King," he announced after his victory. "I want the women's lib leader!"

And he got her. Well, she got *him*. On September 20, 1973, 40 million television viewers from 36 countries tuned in to watch the match. King entered the stadium a modern Cleopatra, carried on a litter by toga-clad football players. Riggs arrived via rickshaw, pulled by four female models. But once the match began, it was serious. King promptly handed Riggs his ass in three straight sets. In defeat, Riggs reneged on his pledge to jump off a California bridge if he lost.

Following the Battle of the Sexes, women's tennis saw a marked increase in fans, purses, and endorsements. For King, who had founded the Women's Tennis Association, it made the victory even sweeter. Riggs and King remained close friends until his death in 1995.

LEARN MORE

A Necessary Spectacle by Selena Roberts (Crown, 2005)

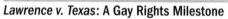

Lawrence v. Texas: A Gay Rights Milestone

Colorado Club Apartments, 794 Normandy Street, Houston, TX 77015

The U.S. Supreme Court's 1986 *Bowers v. Hardwick* decision (see page 182) offered law enforcement a convenient pass on the constitutionality of Georgia's anti-sodomy statute; because it applied to all citizens, gay or straight, nobody (technically) was being singled out for persecution, even though police selectively enforced the law. But Texas had no such fig leaf of impartiality—only members of the same sex could be charged under the state's anti-sodomy statute.

John Lawrence and Tyrone Garner found that out on September 17, 1998. Police were called to the Colorado Club Apartments by a citizen claiming a man was "going crazy" with a gun. Harris County sheriff's deputy Joseph Quinn responded, entered Lawrence's apartment, and found him having sex with Garner. Rather than charge the individual who had made the false 911 report (a person who had been harassing Lawrence), the officer arrested and charged Lawrence and Garner for engaging in intercourse.

The case made its way to the nation's high court, which handed down its decision on June 26, 2003. Writing for the 6–3 majority, Justice Kennedy made a not-so-common admission: "*Bowers* was not correct when it was decided, and it is not correct today. . . . *Bowers v. Hardwick* should be and now is overruled."

Not surprisingly, Justice Scalia blew a gasket. His dissent left little doubt of his own bigotry: "Many Americans do not want persons who openly engage in homosexual conduct as partners in their business, as scoutmasters for their children, as teachers in their children's schools, or as boarders in their home." Just be happy he wasn't on the bench when *Brown v. Board of Education* was unanimously decided.

> The petitioners are entitled to respect for their private lives. The state cannot demean their existence or control their destiny by making their private sexual conduct a crime.
> —*Justice Anthony Kennedy, in Lawrence v. Texas, 2003*

Muhammad Ali Resists the Draft
U.S. Customs House, 701 San Jacinto Street, Houston, TX 77022

As beloved as Muhammad Ali is today, it's easy to forget that he was a lightning rod for criticism in the late 1960s for his opposition to the Vietnam War. On April 28, 1967, Ali appeared before Houston's Local Draft Board 61 on the third floor of the U.S. Customs House (having been transferred from his home board in Louisville, Kentucky) and stated his intention to apply for conscientious objector (CO) status. This was no surprise to the board; Ali had been seeking the classification since converting to Islam several years earlier.

What made Ali's case unique was that he sought his CO status based upon his opposition to the Vietnam War. The military routinely granted CO status to members of certain religious groups, but refused to grant it for those opposing a specific conflict, even though his objections were based on religious reasoning. On June 19, 1967, an all-white Houston jury convicted Ali of refusing to submit to the draft. He was given a five-year sentence and a $10,000 fine, and was ordered to surrender his passport. Ali had already been stripped of his heavyweight title—the New York State Athletic Commission suspended his boxing license an hour after he made his original declaration.

> Why should they ask me to put on a uniform and go 10,000 miles from home and drop bombs and bullets on brown people in Vietnam while so-called Negro people in Louisville are treated like dogs and denied simple human rights? . . . This is the day when such evils must come to an end. . . . If I thought the war was going to bring freedom and equality to 22 million of my people they wouldn't have to draft me, I'd join tomorrow.
>
> —*Muhammad Ali*

Because of the nature of his petition, Ali's case was appealed through higher courts before being taken up by the U.S. Supreme Court in 1971. On June 28 the court ruled 8–0 (with one abstention) that Ali's CO request should be honored on religious grounds, establishing a new precedent for CO status. Two years later he regained his title as Heavyweight Champion of the World.

LEARN MORE

Muhammad Ali Handbook by Dave Zirin (M. Q. Publications, 2007)

Muhammad Ali, the People's Champ by Elliott J. Gorn (University of Illinois, 1998)

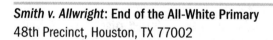

Smith v. Allwright: End of the All-White Primary
48th Precinct, Houston, TX 77002

Following the ratification of the Fifteenth Amendment, which established voting rights for African American men, state legislatures—mostly in the South—came up with new methods to thwart black voter participation. In Texas the primary system was used. Starting in 1903, African American voters were barred from voting in the Democratic primary. How was this possible?

The state had turned the primary elections over to the parties themselves, and the Democratic Party in Texas did not allow blacks to join. Nonparty members could not receive a ballot. And since Texas was essentially a one-party state, whoever won the Democratic primary went on to win the general election.

But on July 27, 1940, Dr. Lonnie Smith walked into Houston's 48th Precinct and requested to vote in the Democratic primary. Election judges S. E. Allwright and James Liuzza turned him away. Their refusal was exactly what Smith, a respected local dentist and officer of the Houston NAACP, was seeking. His would become the test case to challenge the all-white primary.

> The United States is a constitutional democracy. Its organic law grants to all citizens a right to participate in the choice of elected officials without restriction by any State because of race.
>
> *—Justice Stanley Reed, in the majority opinion of Smith v. Allwright, 1944*

The case was handled by the NAACP's Legal Defense and Education Fund's new lead counsel, 33-year-old Thurgood Marshall. As Marshall eventually argued before the U.S. Supreme Court, voting consisted of three stages: qualifying to vote, picking candidates, and voting in the election. Anything that interfered with citizens' participation in all three stages violated the Fifteenth Amendment. The primary was unconstitutional because it was not open to African Americans.

The state argued that the Democratic Party was a private organization, and that it was free to run its primaries according to its own rules. It made no difference that more people (knowing how the system worked) voted in the state's primaries than general elections, or that the Republican candidates never won. The justices did not buy the state's reasoning, and the Texas primary system was struck down 8–1 on April 3, 1944.

LEARN MORE

The Battle for the Black Ballot by Charles L. Zelden (University Press of Kansas, 2004)

San Antonio

Rodriguez v. San Antonio: Challenging School Funding
Edgewood Independent School District, 5358 W. Commerce Street, San Antonio, TX 78237

The main legal hurdle for equal education in the United States—equal access—was cleared with *Brown v. Board of Education* (see page 293) in 1954. However, what good was access if state and local boards routinely underfunded predominantly poor (and predominantly minority) districts?

Demetrio Rodriguez and six other parents from San Antonio's Edgewood Independent School District filed suit in 1968, charging that Texas officials were unfairly funding their district in violation of the constitution's Equal Protection Clause. Indeed, though the residents of the Edgewood district voted to tax themselves at a higher rate than the residents of Alamo Heights, another San Antonio community, Edgewood students were funded at $356 per student, as opposed $594 for Alamo Heights. Why? Property values in Alamo Heights far exceeded those of Edgewood, and the taxpayer-to-student ratio was higher as well. According to the formula, state contributions mirrored local contributions, which by design funneled more money to rich districts than poor ones.

The U.S. Supreme Court did not hear the case of *Rodriguez v. San Antonio* until 1973, when it turned a blind eye to the obvious disparity of the system, stating that the right to an education was not a fundamental right under the constitution. Rodriguez summed up the decision: "The poor people have lost again."

Yet the poor people came back for another round. Rodriguez joined another suit in 1985, this time challenging the funding formula under the *state* constitution. This time it worked. In 1987 the Texas district court threw out the property-tax-based plan and ordered Texas lawmakers to devise a more equitable formula. It still has a long way to go, but it was a step in the right direction.

Santa Fe

Santa Fe Independent School District v. Doe: No Prayer at Games
Santa Fe High School, 16000 Highway 6, Santa Fe, TX 77510

The oft-made assertion that only nonbelievers, or non-Christians, are pushing to keep prayer out of public schools is simply false. There are places like Santa Fe, Texas, where followers of nondominant religions would prefer that the schools leave their children's religious instruction up to them. In 1995 the parents of two Santa Fe High School students, one Catholic and the other Mormon, challenged the school's overwhelming (and often inappropriate) Baptist influence. Santa Fe teachers routinely led prayers in classes and the lunchroom, invited students to revivals, and had a Baptist minister give an invocation over the PA system before Friday night football games.

The ACLU, on behalf of the parents, challenged the invocations. The school district tried to diffuse the issue by holding a student election to determine whether the pregame prayers should continue, and if so, which *student* should give them. It passed and (big surprise!) a Baptist student was chosen to lead them. The district then tried to have the lawsuit dismissed, claiming the prayer was now "student initiated" and "voluntary," even though players, marching band members, and cheerleaders were all required to attend the games.

The U.S. Supreme Court wasn't convinced; in a 6–3 decision, the justices struck down the student-led prayers. Of course, nothing in the ruling prevented any student, parent, or teacher who wanted to pray at the game to do so . . . they just couldn't ask anyone else to.

> We are not persuaded that the pregame invocations should be regarded as "private" speech. These invocations are authorized by a government policy and take place on government property at government-sponsored school-related events.
> —Justice John Paul Stevens, in Santa Fe Independent School District v. Doe, 2000

Seadrift

Diane Wilson, Environmental Activist
San Antonio and Lavaca Bays, Seadrift, TX 77983

Diane Wilson's love of the Texas gulf coast ran deep. She came from four generations of shrimpers, and when she got her own vessel she was the first female shrimp boat captain in the area. Then, in 1989, Wilson learned that the EPA had placed her county first on a national list for toxic waste discharge sites, citing chemicals dumped into the bays in which she fished. She hadn't read about the report in local papers—they hadn't covered the story—but in an article passed along from a cancer-ridden employee.

Wilson called a community meeting to let her neighbors know, and earned the wrath of political and business leaders. When she couldn't get authorities to stop the nearby Formosa Plastics plant from illegally dumping chemicals into Lavaca Bay, she tried to sink her shrimp boat over the discharge site. The Coast Guard stopped her and confiscated her boat. And though Formosa was later fined $150,000 and cited for workplace safety violations by OSHA, the plant remained open, and even expanded.

As her activism grew, Wilson trained her sights on obtaining justice for the victims of the 1984 disaster in Bhopal, India, where a poison cloud from a Union Carbide plant killed 28,000. The Indian government later charged Union Carbide executives with various crimes but, failing to get any cooperation from U.S. authorities, was going to let them off the hook. So Wilson went to India and launched a hunger strike outside the plant. Soon 1,000 people in eight countries joined her, and forced the Indian government to file an extradition request with the U.S. Justice Department for CEO Warren Andersen.

The FBI claimed it couldn't find Andersen, but Wilson did, while standing outside his home in South Hampton, New York, with a sign reading, "Warren, shouldn't you be in India?" In 2002 she climbed a 70-foot chemical tower at the Dow Chemical plant in her hometown of Seadrift to unfurl a 20-foot banner that read, "Dow—Responsible for Bhopal." (Dow Chemical had purchased Union Carbide and assumed all of its domestic assets and liabilities, yet ignored its foreign liabilities, including Bhopal.) Convicted of a misdemeanor, Wilson left Texas saying she would return to serve her time only if Andersen was extradited to India to face justice. But when she was picked up in 2005 for protesting Dick Cheney at a Houston fundraiser for Tom DeLay, she was transferred to Victoria County to serve out her three-month sentence.

Wilson continues her activism through CODEPINK (see page 60) and the Bioneers, whose mission is to promote "practical environmental solutions and innovative social strategies for restoring the Earth and communities."

LEARN MORE
www.anunreasonablewoman.com
www.bioneers.org, (505) 986-0366
An Unreasonable Woman by Diane Wilson (Chelsea Green, 2005)

7

The Mountain West

★ Colorado ★ Idaho ★

★ Montana ★ Nevada ★

★ Utah ★ Wyoming ★

COLORADO

In 1992 the voters of Colorado made a *big* mistake. That November they voted on Amendment 2, which stated that no town, nor the state legislature, could enact a law establishing minority status or legal protection from discrimination for gays, lesbians, or bisexuals. Pushed by the religious right, the initiative carried by a 53–47 margin.

The backlash was immediate as civil rights groups called for a boycott of Colorado tourism. Celebrities bashed voters for approving the law, and the voters got indignant. "How *dare* Barbra Streisand stick her nose into our business?" the complaint went. Yet the same could be said for the folks who backed the measure: "How dare Colorado Springs stick its nose into Denver's business?" At the time, only Denver, Boulder, and Aspen had laws on the books that could be nullified by Amendment 2, and those communities rejected the amendment.

Conventions were cancelled. State products were boycotted. Businesses rethought plans to relocate to the Centennial State. Still, the economic impact was far less damaging than the black eye Colorado received from being labeled the "Hate State." The conflict was ultimately resolved by a gay man, Richard Evans, who sued the state to have the law overturned. Ironically Governor Roy Romer, who had opposed the amendment all along, was named the defendant in the lawsuit. The case of *Romer v. Evans* made it to the U.S. Supreme Court in 1996, which ruled 6–3 that the voters of Colorado had violated the Constitution by putting the civil rights of a class of citizens up to a

> [Amendment 2] seems inexplicable by anything but animus toward the class that it affects; it lacks a rational relationship to legitimate state interests.
> —Justice Anthony Kennedy, in Romer v. Evans, *1996*

popular vote. By the time the decision was handed down, many Coloradoans were thrilled to see the whole embarrassing episode just go away.

LEARN MORE
Strangers to the Law by Lisa Keen and Suzanne Goldberg (University of Michigan, 1998)

Denver

Corky Gonzalez and the Crusade for Justice
Crusade for Justice Headquarters (closed), 1500 Downing Street, Denver, CO 80128

Rodolfo "Corky" Gonzales was born in Denver on June 18, 1929, and while he achieved success as a featherweight boxer and businessman, by the early 1960s he had also worked his way up through the Democratic Party, organizing the Colorado branch of "Viva Kennedy." In 1965 he was picked to lead the city's War on Poverty programs, but resigned within a year when he discovered the party wasn't interested in promoting Latino candidates—it just wanted their votes.

As an alternative, Gonzales founded the Crusade for Justice (CFJ), a community service organization for Mexican Americans. The CFJ offered legal assistance on civil rights issues, organized high school walk-outs, documented police misconduct, and led opposition to the Vietnam War. And when the city neglected swimming pools in its poorer neighborhoods, the CFJ organized a "splash-in" in an affluent, predominantly white neighborhood in southeast Denver.

Meanwhile, Gonzales and Reies López Tijerina drew national attention when they led the Mexican American contingent to the 1968 Poor People's March. On returning, Gonzales proposed "El Plan del Barrio," a manifesto for Chicano empowerment, and organized an annual National Chicano Youth Liberation conference to help implement its goals.

The CFJ eventually collapsed after confrontations with police in 1973. On March 17 a man was arrested for jaywalking in front of the CFJ headquarters. A crowd gathered and guns were fired, and suddenly the upper floor of a nearby apartment house exploded. One person was killed and 17 were injured.

Police blamed militant members of the CFJ; the CFJ claimed the police were involved. The organization never recovered from the incident. Gonzales died in Denver on April 12, 2005.

LEARN MORE
Message to Aztlán by Rodolfo "Corky" Gonzales (Arte Público, 2001)
Crusade for Justice by Ernesto B. Vigil (University of Wisconsin, 1999)

The Denver Three
Wings Over the Rockies Air and Space Museum, 7711 E. Academy Boulevard, Denver, CO 80230

Following the 2004 election George W. Bush announced plans to "privatize" (read "gut") Social Security and immediately faced opposition. Bush said he would take his case directly to the people, and by "people" he meant "hand-picked audiences that supported his agenda." Critics dubbed the nationwide town hall–style PR events the Bamboozapalooza Tour.

One such "public" forum took place in a hangar at the Wings Over the Rockies Air and Space Museum on March 21, 2005. Alex Young, Leslie Weise, and Karen Bauer requested and received tickets to the event. As they approached security they were singled out by a volunteer. He brought them to a man with an earpiece who identified himself as a member of the Secret Service. After a brief discussion the three were allowed to go to their seats. But then, before the president arrived, seven men (including the original two questioners) demanded they leave and escorted them out.

Why were the three citizens ejected? Had they done something wrong? At the gate the trio demanded answers. A *real* Secret Service member later told them they had been ejected because they had shown up driving a car with a "No More Blood for Oil" bumper sticker.

Wrong answer. This was not a private campaign rally, but a taxpayer-funded event, and as such was open to the general public. The volunteer who flagged them turned out to be Jay Bob Klinkerman, leader of the Colorado Federation of Young Republicans. The guy with the earpiece was Michael Casper, a building manager in the federal General Services Administration, not a Secret Service agent. (Casper was never disciplined for impersonating a federal officer, though it is a felony.) Weise and Young filed suit against Casper and Klinkerman for violating their First Amendment rights to free speech and association. The case is currently pending.

LEARN MORE
www.denverthree.org

Frank Rice and the Liberal Church
Liberal Church Site, Labor Hall/Loop Building, 1450 Lawrence Street, Denver, CO 80202

"You want the kids to come to church?" Frank Rice asked his fellow parishioners at the Grant Avenue Methodist Episcopal Church. "Then throw a few dances." He even cited scripture that *supported* the sinful pastime. But the very suggestion, in 1918 Denver, got the popular magazine editor excommunicated from the congregation.

Not that Rice cared much. Undaunted, he decided to take his crusade against Puritanism directly to the people. In May 1922 Rice filed legal paperwork to create the Big Church. The Secretary of State was not amused, and rejected the application. After reorganizing the structure of the as-yet-unformed assembly (to include a university), and renaming it the Liberal Church, Rice reapplied for incorporation in February 1923. This time his request was approved. Rice promptly ordained himself the church's first bishop.

The Liberal Church ministered to Denver's working class and poor, and never passed a collection plate. Rather than ply them with dogma, Rice encouraged them to think for themselves. Congregants were told "to do good" and given a communion of candy, cigars, and cigarettes. The church's annual Prohibition-era allotment of sacramental wine—a mere 12 gallons—was consumed in a single blowout party . . . er . . . *service*. Rice denounced vagrancy and panhandling laws aimed at harassing the poor and presided over burials at the city's potters' fields. He advocated sex education for teens and condemned the KKK, which had a stranglehold on local politicians. Rice expelled the governor (who had an honorary membership) when he failed to commute the sentence of a prisoner on death row, led demonstrations against unemployment and hunger during the Depression, opened soup kitchens, and baptized his congregation's pets.

Rice eventually ordained more than 4,300 clerics and bishops, including the Bishop of Atheism, the Bishop of Righteous Hell, and the Bishop of Say It with Flowers. Sister churches popped up in 11 other states. The Liberal Church even had saints—Robert Ingersoll, P. T. Barnum, and Thomas Paine—and well-known supporters, such as Will Rogers, Clarence Darrow, Babe Ruth, and Robert Ripley, whom he awarded an honorary degree.

> We believe in the United States . . . Our religion is to do good.
> —*Official doctrine of the Liberal Church*

Bishop Rice ran for mayor of Denver as an Independent, as governor of Colorado on the Andy Gump ticket, and for the U.S. Senate on the Liberal ticket. He failed at all three campaigns. He died penniless on February 26, 1945, and was buried in a simple ceremony attended by hundreds, from Larimer Street vagrants to justices on the Colorado Supreme Court.

LEARN MORE

Horsefeathers and Applesauce by Inez Hunt and Wanetta W. Draper (Sage Books, 1959)

The Seamy Side of Denver by Phil Goodstein (New Social Publications, 1993)

Pagosa Springs

Peace Prevails

Bell Tower, Pagosa Springs, CO 81147

"Take it down," commanded Bob Kearns, president of the Loma Linda Homeowners Association of Pagosa Springs, "or you'll be fined $25 for each day it's up." But Lisa Jensen and Bill Trimarco refused, even if it ended up costing them $1,000. What had they done to so offend Kearns? They'd hung a four-foot Christmas wreath on their home shortly after Thanksgiving 2006, and had modified it to look like a peace symbol.

The subdivision's rules stated that homeowners couldn't erect signs, billboards, or advertisements without first getting the approval of the architectural control committee. Kearns claimed to have gotten "three or four complaints" that the peace sign offended supporters of the Iraq War, or was a "symbol of Satan." Jensen and Trimarco countered that for them, peace was "a spiritual thing" in keeping with the season. It wasn't a sign. It wasn't a billboard. It wasn't an advertisement. Still, Kearns demanded that the committee fine the couple, and when it refused, he fired all five members.

> Now that it has come to this, I feel I can't get bullied. What if they don't like my Santa Claus?
> —Lisa Jensen

As news spread, Pagosa Springs residents rallied behind the couple. Two dozen residents marched through the business district, caroling and carrying peace flags, then stomped out a 300-foot-wide peace symbol in a snow-covered soccer field. Kearns and two other board officials resigned, and the issue was dropped.

Almost. Town manager Mark Garcia ordered a large peace wreath . . . and hung it from the town's bell tower. Peace on earth. Pagosa Springs, too.

Sedalia

Billy Kreutzer, America's First Forest Ranger
Plum Creek Timber Preserve (now part of Pike National Forest), Sedalia, CO 80135

William "Billy" Kreutzer was born on a ranch west of Sedalia on October 3, 1877, the son of German immigrants. His father was a trained forester and passed along his love of the outdoors to his son, and his son put it to good use.

The U.S. Congress set aside the first "timber land reserves" in 1891, but due to opposition from Western business interests, funding to enforce the statute was not approved until 1897. Two years later Kreutzer rode his horse into Denver and applied to be the federal government's first forest ranger. His job was to manage the land on the Plum Creek Timber Reserve, federal property that was adjacent to his family's ranch. Working alone, Kreutzer put out fires, educated other ranchers on the best way to graze their livestock, and confronted those who were cutting timber illegally. His work as a forest ranger actually preceded the U.S. Forest Service by six years; that agency was not established until 1905.

Kreutzer apparently did his job too well, and was shot at on several occasions. Mining and lumber trusts worked to have him transferred to more remote locations, out of their way, first to Battlement Mesa Reserve (near Collbran) and then to Grand Mesa National Forest (near Cedaredge). But Kreutzer gained the respect of locals wherever he worked, and was eventually named supervisor of the Gunnison National Forest (near Gunnison). He accepted his final position as supervisor of the Colorado National Forest (surrounding Rocky Mountain National Park) in 1921, where he worked until he retired in 1939. Kreutzer died in Fort Collins on January 2, 1956.

LEARN MORE

www.firstforestranger.com

Saga of a Forest Ranger by Len Shoemaker (University of Colorado)

The Forest Service and the Greatest Good by James G. Lewis (Forest History Society, 2005)

IDAHO

In 1967 the laws regarding estates and inheritances in Idaho were still quite Victorian, as they were in most of the country. So when the teenage son of Sally and Cecil Reed died intestate, control over his estate was given to Cecil. The couple was separated at the time, and Idaho law stated "males must be preferred to females" when two parties of the same class (in this case, parents) had competing claims.

Sally Reed challenged the law, and the Idaho Supreme Court rejected her claim. But on appeal in 1971, the U.S. Supreme Court ruled unanimously that the law was unconstitutional under the Fourteenth Amendment's Equal Protection Clause. It was the first time the century-old amendment had been applied in the case of discrimination against a woman. One of Sally Reed's lawyers before the high court was Ruth Bader Ginsburg, a volunteer attorney with the ACLU who would later go on to become an associate justice on the high court.

> To give a mandatory preference to members of either sex over members of the other, merely to accomplish the elimination of hearings on the merits, is to make the very kind of arbitrary legislative choice forbidden by the Equal Protection Clause of the Fourteenth Amendment.
> —Chief Justice Warren Burger, in Reed v. Reed, 1971

Hayden Lake

Goodbye Aryan Nations
Hayden Lake, ID 83835

Nobody paid much attention when Richard Butler, a white supremacist from California, purchased 20 acres near Hayden Lake in 1973. But in 1980, when anti-Semitic graffiti was found on a local Jewish-owned restaurant, many in the surrounding community decided to take action: they formed the Kootenai County Task Force on Human Relations. Every time the bigots marched the Task Force was there to protest, and even though the Task Force had more active members than the Aryan Nations, Idaho gained an undeserved reputation as a haven for hate mongers.

For almost 20 years neo-Nazis and the KKK would come to the compound for training, and some would go on to attack and murder innocent Americans, yet Butler and the Aryan Nations somehow escaped prosecution . . . until 1998. That September Victoria and Jason Keenan, a mother and son, were driving past the compound when their car backfired. Two guards hopped in a car and chased the Keenans, shot out their tires, and assaulted them after they drove into a ditch. With the help of Morris Dees of the Southern Poverty Law Center (see page 160) and Norm Gissel, a lawyer from the Task Force, the Keenans sued Butler, the guards, and Aryan Nations chief-of-staff Michael Teague.

In September 2000 a Coeur d'Alene jury awarded a total of $6.3 million in compensatory and punitive damages to the Keenans. As Butler left the courtroom in Coeur d'Alene he shrugged it off. "This is nothing," he said, which was a lie. In order to file an appeal he would have had to put up a $9 million bond, money he didn't have. Instead, the Keenans took possession of Butler's Hayden Lake property, his printing press, his Web server, and even the copyright to the Aryan Nations name (now *permanently* retired).

That fall the new owners bulldozed the compound's guard shack, watchtower, and swastika-adorned commissary. The remaining buildings were offered to local fire departments for practice, and were burned to the ground. The Keenans sold the land to a philanthropist, who then donated it to a local college.

MONTANA

With all due respect to the citizens of New Hampshire, Montana residents are a decidedly "live free or die" bunch, too. Increasingly, the state's libertarian element has been channeling its energy through progressive networks and lawmakers. In 2007 Montana became the first state in the union to pass a law stating it would not comply with the Real ID Act. Under the new federal law, states will soon be required to standardize their driver's licenses, as well as link their information through a national database. In the future, U.S. residents will be required to produce the Real ID when taking a flight or entering a government building.

"No, nope, no way, hell no," said populist Democratic governor Brian Schweitzer as he signed the state bill on April 17, 2007, effectively telling the Bush administration to take a hike. The bill had reached Schweitzer's desk with the unanimous approval of both houses of the Montana legislature, and was enthusiastically endorsed by the Montana ACLU—and how often do you think that happens?

Other states are now considering similar bills. Montana's freshman senator, Democrat Jon Tester, might beat them to the punch; he's pushing to have the draconian statute repealed altogether.

> This is still a free country, and there are no freer people than the people we have in Montana.
> —*Brian Schweitzer, rejecting the Real ID Act, 2007*

LEARN MORE
Real ID, www.realnightmare.org

Crow Agency

The Battle of Little Bighorn

Little Bighorn Battlefield National Monument, I-90 (Exit 510), PO Box 39, Crow Agency, MT 59022 · (406) 638-3204

File this one under He Had It Coming. On June 25, 1876, George Armstrong Custer marched 262 soldiers from the Seventh Cavalry into the heart of a 10–12,000-person encampment of mainly Sioux and Cheyenne, 4,000 of whom were warriors. In less than an hour the troops were all dead.

Custer's blunder befit his graduating rank from West Point—65th out of 65. His commander during the Yellowstone Expedition, General Alfred Terry, had wanted Custer's regiment to reach the encampment on June 26, but the lieutenant colonel wanted to seize the glory, and possibly the White House, as a war hero. When he came upon the gathering along the Greasy Grass River a day early, he divided his troops into three battalions, one of which he commanded himself . . . the one that got slaughtered.

The Native American warriors were led by Sitting Bull, Crazy Horse, and Gall. Sitting Bull later summed it up: "We did not go out of our country to kill them. They came to us and got killed themselves." News of the battle reached the East Coast just in time for the nation's Centennial celebrations. Custer was hailed as a martyr, and his "Last Stand"—which nobody has ever documented—entered into the American psyche.

Only in the last few years has the national monument made any effort to offer a balanced interpretation of the battle waged here. In 1972 one arm of the Trail of Broken Treaties (see page 74) passed through Montana on its way to Washington and demanded that a plaque honoring the Indian warriors be installed; the park superintendent promised it would. Russell Means of the American Indian Movement

Sitting Bull, c. 1885

(AIM) returned in 1976 for the battle's centennial, and still no plaque. Means mounted the stage at the ceremony and again requested a monument to the Native warriors. Again the park promised . . . and like so many treaties, violated the pact. So in 1988 Means erected a concrete memorial on the site, U.S. Park Service be damned. It was removed two months later and placed in the park's museum.

Finally, in 1991, the U.S. Congress changed the name from the Custer Battlefield National Monument to the Little Bighorn Battlefield National Monument, and authorized a monument to Native Americans be erected. A winning design was finally chosen in 1997.

> In honor of our Indian Patriots who fought and defeated the U.S. cavalry. In order to save our women and children from mass-murder. In doing so, preserving our rights to Homelands, Treaties and Sovereignty.
> —*Inscription on the 1988 AIM monument*

LEARN MORE
www.nps.gov/libi
Lakota Noon by Gregory F. Michno (Mountain Press, 1997)
Custer Died for Your Sins by Vine Deloria Jr. (University of Oklahoma, 1988)

Missoula

Jeannette Rankin, America's First Congresswoman
Jeannette Rankin Peace Center, 519 S. Higgins Avenue, Missoula, MT 59801 · (406) 541-3997

When the U.S. Congress first voted on the Nineteenth Amendment, giving women the right to vote, one of the "Yeas" was cast by Congresswoman Jeannette Rankin. How was that possible? Look no further than Rankin herself. In 1910 she wrote a letter to the Montana legislature, asking for the opportunity to speak to it on the topic of women's suffrage. They agreed, and on February 1, 1911, the 30-year-old Rankin addressed a packed chamber. Her passionate speech inspired lawmakers to take the issue seriously (they had been dithering around it for eight years), and though it took a few more years, on November 3, 1914, Montana women were extended the franchise. Two years later Rankin ran for Congress and won, making her the first woman elected to the U.S. House of Representatives.

During her 1916 campaign Rankin had promised that, if elected, she would do everything to keep the United States from entering the war in Europe. Her position was not based on isolationism, but pacifism. "You can no more win a war than you can win an earthquake," she said. Six days after she was sworn in, the House scheduled a vote on whether to enter the conflict. Rankin was urged by her suffragist allies to vote for the declaration of war, if for no other reason than to demonstrate that women could be as "tough" and "patriotic" as men. But Rankin's vote against the declaration took more guts and principle than going along with the crowd; she was one of only 50 "nays" recorded that day. Over the next 18 months 116,000 American GIs perished in the conflict.

Jeannette Rankin, 1916

Congress eventually turned its attention to women's suffrage, and on January 18, 1918, Rankin opened the floor debate on the Nineteenth Amendment. The House later voted to send the bill to the states for ratification, but the Senate balked. The amendment was reintroduced a year later and passed, but Rankin was not able to vote for it a second time; she had been defeated for reelection, primarily because of her vote against the war.

But Rankin wasn't through yet. She helped establish the Women's International League for Peace and Freedom, moved south and founded the Georgia Peace Society, and lobbied both political parties to

> I felt at the time the first woman [in Congress] should take the first stand, that the first time the first woman had a chance to say no to war she should say it.
>
> —*Jeannette Rankin*

add peace planks to their national platforms. They refused, and as Europe descended into chaos once again, Rankin's path became clear: she would run for Congress again, from Montana, pledging to vote "No" on entering the war. And she won!

The day after Japan attacked Pearl Harbor, Franklin Delano Roosevelt asked for a declaration of war. Rankin cast the only "No" vote from either chamber, adding "As a woman I can't go to war, and I refuse to send anyone else." Reporters chased her into a Capitol Hill phone booth where she calmly called police for an escort back to her office.

Rankin did not run for reelection in 1942. After the war she traveled to India to study Gandhi, and became an unofficial ambassador for pacifism. And in January 1968, at the age of 88, she led a march on Washington against the Vietnam War called the Jeanette Rankin Peace Brigade.

Rankin died on May 18, 1973, and was cremated. Her work for peace is carried on by the Jeannette Rankin Peace Center, founded in 1986. The organization promotes peace and social justice through education, media activism, art, and a Free Trade Store.

LEARN MORE
www.jrpc.org
Jeannette Rankin by Norma Smith (Montana Historical Society, 2002)

NEVADA

Though the first atomic bomb was detonated in New Mexico (see page 319), since 1951 most of the nation's nuclear testing has taken place at the Nevada Test Site in Nye County, Nevada, northwest of Las Vegas. Between 1951 and 1962, the Department of Defense conducted 126 aboveground tests in the open desert. Following the ratification of the Nuclear Test Ban Treaty, it has performed 828 belowground tests.

The first protests at the Nevada Test Site took place in 1957, and have continued to this day. In 1979 residents of Nevada and Utah filed suit in federal court to put a halt to the government's ongoing radioactive contamination. The U.S. District Court ruled on behalf of the residents in *Allen v. U.S.*, but the verdict was overturned on appeal. In 1988 and 1989, more than 1,000 people were arrested for trying to block access to the site.

Since 1994 much of the opposition has been coordinated through the Shundahai Network. Founded by Newe (Western Shoshone) spiritual leader Corbin Harney, it is a collective of indigenous, environmental, peace, labor, and human rights groups working to abolish all nuclear weapons. Harney points out that the Nevada Test Site is located on his tribe's ancestral land, Newe Sogobia, and is a violation of the 1863 Treaty of Ruby Valley.

The Shundahai Network has worked to block the Yucca Mountain nuclear dump, sponsored national and international lecture tours, established a Las Vegas chapter of Food Not Bombs (see page 19), and organized nonviolent direct action at the entrance to the site through an annual Peace Camp.

 LEARN MORE

www.shundahai.org

The Way It Is by Corbin Harney (Blue Dolphin, 1995)

Uncertainty Underground by Allison M. Macfarlane and Rodney C. Ewing, eds.
(MIT, 2006)

UTAH

Utah is one of the most conservative, Republican states in the union, hardly the place you'd expect to find an outspoken mayor who supports gay rights, a woman's right to choose, immigration reform, living wage ordinances, gun control, and affirmative action, and is a card-carrying member of the ACLU . . . right?

Wrong! Meet Ross C. "Rocky" Anderson, the popular two-term mayor of Salt Lake City. First elected in 1999, Anderson launched an ambitious environmental agenda: the Salt Lake City Green Program. The city built cogeneration plants at its waste disposal and water treatment plants, improved the energy efficiency of its buildings and fleet (trading in SUVs for hybrids), made the city more vehicle- and pedestrian-friendly, and doubled the input to its recycling program. The mayor even signed on to the Kyoto Protocol in 2002, and by 2006 had achieved its benchmarks seven years ahead of schedule, earning Salt Lake City the World Leadership Award for the Environment.

Reelected in 2003, Anderson continued his progressive agenda and drew criticism for his outspokenness. On August 30, 2006, George W. Bush spoke to the American Legion's national convention in Salt Lake City, while the mayor led a simultaneous anti-Bush rally at nearby Pioneer Park. "Blind faith in bad leaders is not patri-

> A patriot does not tell people who are intensely concerned about their country to just sit down and be quiet; to refrain from speaking out in the name of politeness or for the sake of being a good host; to show slavish, blind obedience and deference to a dishonest, war-mongering, human-rights-violating president.
>
> —*Rocky Anderson*

otism," he told the cheering crowd of 4,000. He soon lent his voice to the growing calls for the president's impeachment. And though he chose not to seek reelection on 2007, expect to see him play an expanded role in progressive and Democratic politics in the future, in Utah or the national scene.

Kanab

America's First All-Female Government
City Hall, 76 N. Main Street, Kanab, UT 94741

In January 1912 the voters of Kanab did something no town had ever done before: they elected an all-female government. Mary W. Howard (in reality, Mary Woolley Chamberlain, who used the pseudonym to mask her polygamous marriage) was chosen as mayor, and Blanche Hamblin, Tamar Hamblin, Vinnie Jepson, and Luella McAllister were elected to the town board. Though it was a major step forward for women, their administration was hardly a feminist cabal. They enacted laws banning alcohol, slingshots, and livestock on the streets, as well as foot races, ball games, horse races, and "noisy sports" on the Sabbath.

At the end of their two-year terms, many hoped that the women would run again, but they declined. "We are not at all selfish, and are perfectly willing to share the honors with others," said Mayor Howard. "We are in hopes [voters] will elect ladies to fill the vacancies."

They didn't; the next mayor and town board were all men. And don't expect to find any trace of Kanab's forward-thinking history today. In 2006 the city council passed Resolution 1-1-06R—the so-called "Natural Family Resolution"—which stated, in part, "We envision a local culture that upholds the marriage of a woman to a man, and a man to a woman, as ordained of God. . . . We envision young women growing into wives, homemakers, and mothers; and we see young men growing into husbands, home-builders, and fathers."

Talk about a giant step backward . . .

Moab

Edward Abbey's *Desert Solitaire*
Arches National Park, PO Box 907, Moab, UT 94532 · (435) 719-2299

When it was first published in 1968, *Desert Solitaire* was hailed as a modern-day *Walden*. Author Edward Abbey had written three novels, but this was his first work of nonfiction. The book is a collection of essays and reflections on his two seasons as a park ranger at Arches National Monument (today Arches National Park), from river running to helping a search-and-rescue team recover the body of a dead hiker. But it was his condemnation of the growth of "industrial tourism" in our national parks that appealed to most readers. "We have agreed not to drive our automobiles into cathedrals, concert halls, art museums, legislative assemblies, private bedrooms, and other sanctums of our culture," he wrote "We should treat our national parks with the same deference, for they, too, are holy places."

Abbey's writing would grow more militant over time, and would include the *The Monkey Wrench Gang* (1975), a tale of four environmental activists fighting corporate exploitation of the wilderness though unconventional, destructive tactics. They burn billboards, vandalize construction equipment, and crush a pickup with a boulder. The book became the inspiration for more radical environmental organizations such as Earth First! and the Earth Liberation Front.

When he died on March 14, 1989, Abbey's family and friends placed his unembalmed body in a sleeping bag and buried it in Arizona's Cabeza Prieta Desert. Only they know where.

> Growth for the sake of growth is the ideology of the cancer cell.
> —*Edward Abbey*

LEARN MORE

www.abbeyweb.net

www.nps.gov/arch

Desert Solitaire by Edward Abbey (McGraw-Hill, 1968)

Edward Abbey by James M. Calahan (University of Arizona, 2001)

Epitaph for a Desert Anarchist by James Bishop Jr. (Scribner, 1994)

The Best of Edward Abbey by Edward Abbey (Sierra Club, 1984)

Wyoming calls itself "The Equality State," and rightfully so, for it was here on December 10, 1869, that American women first achieved the right to vote and hold public office. (It was a territory at the time.) The first election under the new statute took place on September 6, 1870 (see below). And when Wyoming joined the union on July 23, 1890, women's suffrage was included in its new constitution.

The state's women took up the mantle of public service with enthusiasm. Esther Morris of South Pass City became the nation's first female office holder, appointed justice of the peace on February 12, 1870. She served for eight months. On March 7 of the same year, five women were empanelled on a Laramie grand jury. However, because of a legal loophole in the suffrage bill, Wyoming women did not sit on juries again until 1950; on the first panel after their return the Green River jury voted for the nation's first female foreman, Louise Spinner Graf.

In 1894 Estelle Reel was elected Wyoming's superintendent of public instruction, the first time a woman had been elected to a statewide office in the United States. Mary Godat Bellamy was elected the state's first female legislator in 1910, and in 1911 Susan Wissler of Dayton became Wyoming's first female mayor. Reelected, she became the first woman in America to serve consecutive terms in office . . . but soon had company. The town of Jackson elected, by a two-to-one margin, an all-female slate to the town council in 1920; Grace Miller served as mayor. They were all reelected by an even larger margin a year later.

Finally, Wyoming was the first state to have a woman governor: Nellie Tayloe Ross, who served from 1924 to 1927. Her husband, William Ross, who was governor, died in office on October 2, 1924, and she was asked to run on the ticket in the special election to succeed him. Ross served until the end of

the original term. In 1933 she was appointed director of the U.S. Mint—yet
another first for women.

Cheyenne

Birthplace of Women's Suffrage
Suffrage Memorial, 17th Street and Carey Avenue, Cheyenne, WY 82001

On November 27, 1869, the Wyoming senate approved "An Act to Grant to
the Women of Wyoming the Right to Suffrage, and to Hold Office." The bill
had been authored by Senator William Bright of South Pass City. He had
been urged on by Esther Morris, the state's "Mother of Suffrage," who would
soon be elected the first woman to hold public office in the United States (see
above).

The bill went to the house, which met in a small building on 17th Street.
After some debate the bill passed on December 10 and was sent to the governor
for his signature. A group of women kept a silent vigil outside John Campbell's
office until he signed the bill into law. The first general election ballot was cast
by Elizabeth "Grandma" Swain of Laramie on September 6, 1870. Reporters
flocked to Laramie to watch her do it.

Morris later moved to Cheyenne where, in 1895, she welcomed Susan B.
Anthony on a western lecture tour. Her home (2114 Warren Avenue) is designated by a historic marker today. Morris died there on April 2, 1902, and was
buried in Lakeview Cemetery (25th Street and Seymour Avenue).

Laramie

The Murder of Matthew Shepard
Fireside Bar (closed), 201 Custer Street, Laramie, WY 82001

If the gay and lesbian community was beginning to feel comfortable in American society during the later half of the 20th century, those feelings were challenged with the murder of Matthew Shepard. In the early morning hours of
October 7, 1998, Shepard left the Fireside Bar with Aaron McKinney and Russell Henderson, two men who had told Shepard they were gay and had offered

him a ride. Driving east out of town the pair pistol-whipped the 21-year-old as he sat between them, yelling, "We're not gay, and you just got jacked!"

McKinney and Henderson parked along Snowy Mountain View Road near the Sherman Hills subdivision, tied Shepard to a fence, and began beating their 102-pound, five-foot-two victim to death. The coroner later estimated that Shepard had been struck in the head by a blunt object—the butt of a .357 Magnum—about 20 times. They then stole Shepard's wallet, keys, and shoes and left him to die.

Later that morning, drunk and high, Henderson and McKinney ended up in a fight with two Laramie men near the corner of Seventh and Harney Streets. Police arrived and found the bloody gun and Shepard's shoes and credit card in the cab of the truck, and the two were placed under arrest. They were released on bail later that day, before Shepard had been found.

About 18 hours after the original assault, a bicyclist discovered Shepard's unconscious body still lashed to the fence. He was rushed to Ivinson Memorial Hospital (255 N. 30th Street) and then to the Poudre Valley Hospital (1024 S. Lemay Avenue) in Fort Collins, Colorado. Shepard died there on October 12.

His body was returned to Casper, his hometown. A memorial service was held at St. Mark's Episcopal Church (1908 Central Avenue). Rev. Fred Phelps picketed the services, but was drowned out by mourners singing "Amazing Grace."

Henderson pleaded guilty to kidnapping, robbery, and felony murder, and drew two life sentences without parole. McKinney tried to invoke the "gay panic" defense, but the jury didn't buy any of it. Found guilty, McKinney was spared the death sentence after the moving testimony of Shepard's father.

If there was anything positive to come out of the tragedy, it was *The Laramie Project*. Four weeks after Matthew Shepard's murder, Moisés Kaufman and nine members of the Tectonic Theater Project traveled to Laramie to interview those closest to the case. Over the next year and a half they captured more than 200 interviews, which were later compiled into a powerful play, an unflinching *Our Town* for the new century.

> I would like nothing better than to see you die, Mr. McKinney. However, this is the time to begin the healing process. To show mercy to someone who refused to show any mercy.
>
> —Dennis Shepard,
> at the sentencing hearing
> for Aaron McKinney

LEARN MORE
www.matthewshepard.org, (307) 237-6167
Losing Matt Shepard by Beth Loffreda (Columbia, 2000)
The Laramie Project by Moisés Kaufman (Vintage, 2001)

Yellowstone

Yellowstone, the First National Park
Yellowstone National Park, PO Box 168, Yellowstone, WY 82190 · (307) 344-7381

Yellowstone National Park was created by an act of Congress and signed into law by Ulysses S. Grant on March 1, 1872. The idea of setting aside a large parcel of government land for the benefit of the public was not entirely new; six years earlier the U.S. Congress deeded the Yosemite Valley to the state of California with the purpose of it being used as a state park. But not until Yellowstone was a park created under federal control.

Unfortunately, Yellowstone was under federal control in name only—the National Park Service was not created until 1916. Early visitors, mostly wealthy tourists from the East Coast, damaged the land by carving their names into rock formations, bathing in the hot springs, and walking off with mineral formations and petrified wood as souvenirs. To protect the park, it was placed under the control of the U.S. Army in 1896, and much of the vandalism and poaching ceased. Today Yellowstone is one of the largest wildlife sanctuaries in the United States.

In recent years the park has been the focus of two heated debates pitting environmentalists against commercial interests. The U.S. Forest Service's policy of allowing naturally ignited wildfires to burn them-

Old Faithful, 1917

selves out was widely criticized after fires in the summer of 1988 torched 800,000 acres, about one-third of the park. Tourism boosters forced Yellowstone to suspend "Let It Burn" and actively combat the blazes. Yet the forest ecosystem, even in the most damaged areas of the back-

> **For the Benefit and Enjoyment of the People**
>
> *—Inscription on the arch over the north entrance to Yellowstone*

country, quickly rebounded . . . just as the biologists predicted it would.

Similar howls of protest greeted the park's plan to reintroduce the gray wolf in 1995. Once native to the region, gray wolves had not been spotted in Yellowstone since the 1930s, having been killed off by ranchers and poachers. In an effort to restore the balance between natural predators and prey, three packs (15 wolves in all) were captured in Alberta, Canada, and released into the park. Several have since been shot, but on the whole the gray wolf has thrived, and concerns about attacks on cattle and sheep turned out to be largely unfounded.

LEARN MORE

www.nps.gov/yell

The Yellowstone Story by Aubrey L. Haynes (University Press of Colorado, 1996)

Scorched Earth by Rocky Barker (Island Pres, 2005)

The Yellowstone Wolves by Gary Ferguson (Falcon, 1996)

8
The Pacific Rim

★ Alaska ★ California ★

★ Hawaii ★ Oregon ★

★ Washington ★

ALASKA

In the early morning hours of March 24, 1989, the *Exxon Valdez* ran aground on Bligh Reef in Alaska's Prince William Sound. Though he was not on the bridge at the time (as he should have been), captain Joseph Hazelwood came up and, against protocol, tried to free the tanker from the rocks. His efforts made the hole in the ship's hull even larger, and 11 million gallons of crude spilled into the ocean.

Public outrage forced Congress to write and pass the 1990 Oil Pollution Act. It mandated double-hulled tankers in U.S. waters and established guidelines for avoiding future spills and coordinating cleanups. The nonprofit Coalition for Environmentally Responsible Economies wrote up the Valdez Principles, today known as the CERES Principles, by which industry signatories pledge to conduct business in an environmentally responsible manner: reducing pollutants, conserving energy, informing the public when problems occur, and remedying damage.

If only Exxon were that responsible. The company spent $3.5 billion to clean up the sound (it recovered only 14 percent of the spilled oil), but has vigorously battled any attempts to pay punitive damages for the disaster. Though levied a $5 billion fine in 1994, the judgment was halved on appeal. The case is now before the U.S. Supreme Court.

 LEARN MORE
www.ceres.org, (617) 247-0700
Not One Drop by Riki Ott (Chelsea Green, 2008)
Out of the Channel by John Keeble (Eastern Washington University, 1999)
Living with the Spill (1990)

Amchitka

Don't Make a Wave Committee and the Birth of Greenpeace
Amchitka Island, AK

The organization known today as Greenpeace originated with a singular mission. Since 1965 the U.S. government had used one of the westernmost Aleutian Islands, Amchitka, as a belowground nuclear testing site. When the Atomic Energy Commission announced in 1970 that it would be detonating a five-megaton device—Cannikin, about 400 times the strength of the Hiroshima bomb—Jim and Marie Bohlen called a meeting of environmentalists in Vancouver, British Columbia. They decided to do everything in their power to stop the test, even if it meant putting their lives in danger. Several geologists had expressed concern that such a large explosion along the Pacific Rim might trigger earthquakes or a tsunami, so the group called itself the Don't Make a Wave Committee (DMWC).

After all legal maneuvers failed, DWMC launched the *Phyllis Cormack* toward Amchitka Island, hoping to prevent Cannikin by sailing into the restricted area. The fishing boat was hampered by bad weather, and on November 6, 1971, the test took place. The explosion registered 7.0 on the Richter scale—strong, but no tsunami. All did not go well, however; since that time, scientists have documented radioactive plutonium and americium seeping into the open sea.

DMWC vowed to fight on, and in 1972 changed its name to Greenpeace. It has gone on to battle international whaling, harp seal hunting, deep sea dumping, and more through regional offices in 42 countries.

> Greenpeace's goal is to ensure the ability of the earth to nurture life in all its diversity.
> —*from Greenpeace's Mission Statement*

LEARN MORE
www.greenpeace.org, (202) 462-1177
Greenpeace by Rex Weyler (Rodale, 2004)
Making Waves by Jim Bohlen (Black Rose, 2000)

Juneau

Elizabeth Peratrovich, Champion of Native American Rights
Alaska State Capitol, Main and Fourth Streets, Juneau, AK 99801

Each year on February 16 Alaska celebrates Elizabeth Peratrovich Day. Who was she? More than anyone else, Peratrovich was responsible for ending official discrimination against the state's native population. From its early days as a territory, Alaska allowed businesses to openly refuse service to non-Europeans; neighborhoods were redlined and theaters had segregated seating.

Elizabeth and Roy Peratrovich experienced this firsthand when they moved to Juneau in 1941. They found a home they wanted to rent, but were later refused when the owner learned they were Native American. But the bigots had met their match. Elizabeth was grand president of the Alaska Native Sisterhood, and Roy was former grand president of the Alaska Native Brotherhood. Together they campaigned and lobbied for a bill outlawing racial discrimination that came before the state legislature in 1943. It failed to pass.

But the bill came up again in 1945. In the Alaska legislature at the time, citizens present at debates were allowed to make speeches for or against bills. On February 8 Elizabeth Peratrovich rose and delivered an impassioned speech on the senate floor. Dismissing earlier speeches that stereotyped natives, the 34-year-old began, "I would not have expected that I, who am barely out of savagery, would have to remind gentlemen with five thousand years of recorded civilization behind them of our Bill of Rights." She went on to relay her own life experiences and the injustices her community suffered due to institutionalized racism. When she finished, Peratrovich received a standing ovation and the senate approved the bill by a two-to-one margin.

Elizabeth Peratrovich died on December 1, 1958, and was buried in Juneau's Evergreen Cemetery (601 Seater Street). The state first recognized her with an official holiday in 1989. February 16 marks the day that Alaska's Anti-Discrimination Act was signed into law.

CALIFORNIA

It's hard for a progressive not to feel some antipathy toward California—after all, both Richard Nixon and Ronald Reagan began their political careers in the Golden State. Yet it is also where César Chávez gave voice to thousands of migrant farmworkers, where Harvey Milk was elected the first openly gay public official in America, and where Mario Savio led the Free Speech Movement. What's more, it's the birthplace of three of the earliest LGBT organizations in the United States: the Mattachine Society, ONE, and the Daughters of Bilitis.

The Mattachine Society was formed in 1950 by a group of five men who met at the home of Harry Hay (2328 Cove Avenue) to discuss issues related to homosexuality. As the organization grew, it held its first public meeting at the First Universalist Church (755 Crenshaw Boulevard) in April 1953. About 50 people attended what was the first *open* gathering of gay men in America.

Still, Jim Kepner and several other activists found Mattachine too tame, so in 1952 they launched ONE at a meeting in Los Angeles (232 S. Hill Street). The group began publishing ONE magazine in January 1953, the first "homophile" journal since Henry Gerber's *Friendship and Freedom* newsletter (see page 235). But unlike *FaF*, which ran for only two issues, *ONE* was printed for about a decade, despite the U.S. Post Office's numerous attempts to shut it down. The organization also launched the ONE Institute for Homophile Studies in 1956.

> It should barely be necessary to state that I am interested in defending my right to be as different as I damn please. And somewhere, I've picked up the notion that I can't protect my own rights in that quarter without fighting for everyone else's.
> —Jim Kepner, as Lyn Pederson
> in ONE, 1954

Farther north, in San Francisco, Del Martin and Phyllis Lyon founded the Daughters of Bilitis (DoB) in October 1955. They started with eight members. DoB was the first civil rights organization for lesbians in the United States, which a year later published the first lesbian journal in history: *The Ladder*. It ran for 16 years, ceasing publication around the time that the DoB dissolved.

LEARN MORE

Gay L.A. by Lillian Faderman and Stuart Kimmons (Basic, 2006)

Wide Open Town by Nan Alamilla Boyd (University of California, 2003)

Behind the Mask of the Mattachine by James T. Sears (Harrington Park, 2003)

Different Daughters by Marcia M. Gallo (Carroll & Graf, 2006)

Lesbian/Woman by Del Martin and Phyllis Lyon (Bantam, 1983)

Berkeley

Jake Weinberg, Mario Savio, and the Free Speech Movement
Sproul Hall, University of California at Berkeley, Bancroft Way and Barrow Lane, Berkeley, CA 94720

Students who enjoy political freedom on their college campuses today have Jake Weinberg, Mario Savio, and a few thousand former UC Berkeley students to thank. Until the fall of 1964, political expression (other than joining Democratic and Republican clubs) was forbidden at many schools. Then, on October 1, Weinberg was passing out CORE literature at UC Berkeley in support of civil rights workers in the South. Police arrested him when he refused to provide identification. After they loaded him into their squad car, angry students surrounded the vehicle at the corner of Bancroft and Telegraph Avenues and refused to let it leave . . . *for 32 hours.* They used its hood as a podium, and when it became clear that the

> There's a time when the operation of the machine becomes so odious, makes you sick at heart, that you can't take part, you can't even passively take part, and you've got to put your bodies on the gears and upon the wheels, upon the levers, upon the apparatus, and you've got to make it stop!
>
> *—Mario Savio*

3,000+ students had no intention of backing down, the police dropped all charges.

The outburst of free speech boiled over and became a movement all its own. Students took 24-hour control of nearby Sproul Hall, the university's administration building. Though many participated, Mario Savio emerged as the Free Speech Movement's most eloquent spokesperson. The sit-in/teach-in continued until December 3, when 800 students were arrested. The charges against the demonstrators inflamed the campus, and in early January the acting chancellor issued new rules regarding "open discussion areas" and tables used for leafleting.

A statewide backlash against the protests swept Ronald Reagan into the governorship in 1966, who then attacked the UC Board of Regents for "coddling" students.

LEARN MORE

www.fsm-a.org

The Free Speech Movement by Robert Cohen and Reginald E. Zelnik, eds. (University of California, 2002)

Berkeley at War by W. J. Rorabaugh (Oxford, 1989)

People's Park
2556 Haste Street, Berkeley, CA 94704 · (510) 390-0830

It's the kind of thing that, had it happened in Topeka, would have been praised as "citizenship in action:" hundreds of folks descended on an empty city block with shovels and plants and playground equipment to build a public park they all could share. But this was Berkeley in the late 1960s, and if there was anything Governor Ronald Reagan couldn't abide it was a bunch of lazy, dirty hippies efficiently cleaning up a state government eyesore. The land had been stolen from local taxpayers by the university in 1967 using eminent domain. The school wanted to construct a parking lot and practice field—not too complex, architecturally speaking—yet the plot sat idle, covered in trash and abandoned cars, for more than a year. Local merchants wanted the muddy mess fixed and students stepped in to help. The first flowers and trees were planted on April 20, 1969. People's Park was born.

But less than a month after it was created, Reagan (who sat out World War II in Hollywood) declared war against the people and petunias: "If there has to be a bloodbath, then let's get it over with." On May 15, more than 250 California Highway Patrol officers and Berkeley police "swept" the park, then sealed it off with an eight-foot chain-link fence, but not before they bulldozed the landscaping to show who was boss.

Students rallied at Sproul Plaza that afternoon and were soon chanting "Take the park!" But by then, Reagan had called in 800 more officers from various local jurisdictions. They opened fire with tear gas and shotguns, killing one bystander and blinding another, and shooting 128 unarmed protesters, mostly in the back as they fled.

Reagan then called in the National Guard. On May 20, people gathered in Sproul Plaza to remember James Rector, the murdered bystander. Gas-masked police surrounded the event with bayonets drawn. Helicopters then dropped so much CS gas that the drifting fumes poisoned patients at a nearby hospital and children at two local elementaries.

The university never did build the parking lot. Some today complain about the park's large homeless population, as if the park was responsible. No, if you want a culprit, look to those who call Reagan their political hero.

LEARN MORE
www.peoplespark.org
People's Park by Alan Copeland, ed. (Ballantine, 1969)

Fair Oaks

Cari Lightner, Laura Lamb, and Mothers Against Drunk Driving (MADD)
Sunset Avenue at New York Avenue, Fair Oaks, CA 95628

On May 3, 1980, Cari Lightner was hit by a car in broad daylight while she walked to a church carnival with a friend. The car's 47-year-old driver had been drinking for three days, ever since his release from jail . . . for driving drunk. Candace Lightner didn't learn any of this until the day after her 13-year-old daughter's funeral. Driving past the crime scene while the police were measuring the skid marks, she stopped and asked the officer if he thought the perpetrator would go to prison. He responded, "Lady, you'll be lucky [if he sees] jail time, much less prison. That's the way the system works."

Well, not any more. That day Lightner vowed to change American's attitudes toward drunk driving, and get laws passed to back her up. She soon met Cindi Lamb, a mother from Maryland whose infant daughter Laura had been left paralyzed from the neck down after a head-on collision a year earlier. That accident was caused by a man with five drunk driving convictions.

On October 1, 1980, Lightner and Lamb held a press conference on Capitol Hill, and Mothers Against Drunk Drivers—MADD—catapulted onto the national stage. States began passing tougher DUI and DWI penalties, and lowering the blood alcohol levels needed for conviction. The number of alcohol-related accidents and deaths soon began to drop, and continue to do so. MADD won't be happy (nor should they be) until that number is reduced to zero.

LEARN MORE
www.madd.org, (800) GET-MADD
America Gets MADD! by Micky Sadoff (Mother Against Drunk Driving, 1990)

Independence

Challenging Executive Order 9066
Manzanar National Historic Site, PO Box 426, Independence, CA 93526 · (760) 878-2194

If there is a lesson behind the signing of Executive Order 9066, it is how quickly and callously the government can dispose of our civil liberties. On February 19, 1942, just two months after the Japanese attack at Pearl Harbor, Franklin Roosevelt established "zones from which any or all persons may be excluded." With the stroke of a pen, he uprooted 110,000 people of Japanese ancestry on the West Coast and threw them into 10 "detention centers" across the nation. Of these, 75,000 detainees were American citizens, Nisei who were born in the states; the remainder were Issei, foreign-born immigrants who had been prevented from becoming Americans due to racist citizenship policies.

Several individuals challenged the constitutionality of Executive Order 9066 in court. Minoru Yasui, an Oregon native, was a reserve officer in the

U.S. Army living in Chicago. Following Pearl Harbor he returned to his home base in Oregon to report for active duty, but the army turned him away. Yasui came back *eight times*, and each time was rebuffed. After a nighttime curfew was imposed, Yasui presented himself to a Portland policeman on March 28, 1942, and demanded to be arrested. He was tossed in solitary confinement for nine months, awaiting trial.

In Seattle Gordon Hirabayashi, a student at the University of Washington, was told to report for "evacuation" on May 16, 1942. Instead, Hirabayashi presented himself at the local FBI office to announce he was a conscientious objector who refused to obey the order. The former Eagle Scout was thrown into the King County jail.

A third individual, Fred Korematsu, was picked up in San Leandro, California, on May 30, 1942, while walking with his girlfriend. He had been trying to avoid detection, and had gone so far as to have plastic surgery and alter the name on his draft card to Clyde Sarah.

Yasui, Hirabayashi, and Korematsu were all convicted in lower courts on charges related to the curfew and evacuation orders, and all appealed. The U.S. Supreme Court unanimously upheld Hirabayashi's and Yasui's convictions on June 21, 1943.

Meanwhile, a young Sacramento clerk named Mitsuye Endo, who had been taken to the Tule Lake War Relocation Center (near Newell, California) challenged her imprisonment by filing a petition for a writ of *habeus corpus*. She lost in district court, but appealed. The U.S. Circuit Court of Appeals requested clarification on several legal matters from the U.S. Supreme Court, which demanded that the case be sent to them for consideration with Korematsu's.

Shockingly, Roosevelt's lawyers tried to argue that 9066 had been issued to *protect* Japanese Americans from racial violence. The court decided 6–3 on December 18, 1944, to uphold Korematsu's conviction for failing to comply with the order, but on the same day ruled in *Ex parte Endo* that Endo, who had not violated the curfew, was improperly detained. "Loyalty is a matter of the heart and mind, not of race, creed, or color," Justice William O. Douglas wrote. The decisions were released one day after the War Department rescinded 9066 and "permitted the same movement throughout the United States [for Japanese descendents] as other loyal citizens and law-abiding aliens." What a coincidence.

Order 9066 was not officially rescinded until February 1976, by Gerald Ford. Then in 1983, after three years of testimony, the Commission on Wartime

Relocation and Internment of Citizens issued a unanimous report blasting the government for its unconstitutional actions. In 1987 the wartime convictions of Yasui, Hirabayashi, and Korematsu were vacated, and in 1988 the federal government paid $20,000 to each living survivor of the internment camps. (By then 60,000 survivors had already died, and thus received nothing.)

All that remains of the most infamous detention center, Manzanar, where 10,000 people were held against their will without charges, are two sentry posts, an auditorium, and the cemetery.

LEARN MORE
www.nps.gov/manz
Justice at War by Peter Irons (Oxford, 1983)
Only What We Could Carry by Lawson Fusao Inada (Heyday, 2000)

Keene
César Chávez, Dolores Huerta, and the United Farm Workers
National Chávez Center, 29700 Woodford-Tehachapi Road, Keene, CA 93531 ·
(661) 823-6134

César Chávez was born on a small farm near Yuma, Arizona, on March 31, 1927. During the Great Depression his family was swindled out of their homestead and forced into migrant labor. They eventually settled in San Jose's Sal Si Puedes (Get Out if You Can) barrio, though they traveled to follow the harvests. When his father was injured in an accident, Chávez left school after the eighth grade and began working full time in the fields.

During World War II Chávez served a two-year stint in the navy, then returned and married Helen Fabela. The couple moved to Delano in 1948 where César became an organizer for the Community Services Organization (CSO), a grassroots self-help and civil rights group. Using methods he learned at CSO, Chávez founded the National Farm Workers Association (NFWA) in 1962. He was soon joined by Dolores Huerta, another CSO alum.

The NFWA had more than 1,000 members by November 1965 when it called for a grape boycott alongside the Agricultural Worker Organizing Committee, a union of Filipino farmworkers. The NFWA garnered national attention in April 1966 when members marched 340 miles from Delano to

Sacramento. When they arrived on Easter Sunday, Governor Ronald Reagan fled town rather than meet with them.

In 1966 the NWFA became the United Farm Workers (UFW) when it formally affiliated with the AFL-CIO. The move brought them added strength, but not all elements of labor were in the UFW's camp—growers later tried to bust the UFW by turning the Teamsters against them. When it looked as if the sides would erupt in violence, Chávez launched a hunger strike on February 15, 1968, to force his followers to remain peaceful. He broke the fast after 25 days when the NWFA recommitted itself to a pacifist strategy.

> Once social change begins, it cannot be reversed. You cannot uneducate the person who has learned to read. You cannot humiliate the person who feels pride. You cannot oppress the people who are not afraid anymore.
>
> —*César Chávez*

Grape growers did not sign a contract with the UFW until 1970, and the union called off the boycott. There would be more boycotts and more fasts throughout the 1970s as the UFW's rolls grew to 50,000 members. The UFW's final grape boycott was launched in 1984 over pesticide exposure.

Chávez died of a heart attack in Arizona on April 23, 1993. His body was returned to Delano for a funeral at the UFW's Forty Acres compound (30168 Garces Highway), then was buried in nearby Keene. A year after Chávez's death, his wife accepted the Presidential Medal of Freedom from Bill Clinton on her husband's behalf.

LEARN MORE

www.ufw.org, (661) 823-6250

www.chavezfoundation.org, (213) 362-0260

www.nationalchavezcenter.org

César Chávez by Jacques E. Levy (University of Minnesota, 2007)

The Fight in the Fields by Susan Ferriss and Ricardo Sandoval (Harcourt Brace, 1997)

The Moral Vision of César Chávez by Frederick John Dalton (Orbis, 2003)

Los Angeles

The Assassination of Robert Kennedy

Ambassador Hotel (torn down), 3400 Wilshire Boulevard, Los Angeles, CA 90005

The political life of Robert Kennedy demonstrates that not all politicians become more insensitive and entrenched over time—sometimes a person can be shaped by circumstances for the better. In his early years, Kennedy was an opportunistic Hill staffer who desperately wanted to work as Joe McCarthy's right-hand man, only to lose out to Roy Cohn. As his brother's attorney general, he was far less aggressive on civil rights than he could have been, and typically calculated the political implications of the department's policies before making a move.

But John F. Kennedy's assassination affected him in profound ways, and by 1968, as senator from New York, he had become a critic of the Vietnam War. Four days after Senator Eugene McCarthy nearly defeated Lyndon Johnson in the New Hampshire primary, Kennedy announced that he would be getting into the 1968 race. Two weeks after that, Johnson announced that he would not seek the party's nomination.

Kennedy appealed to the same youthful optimism his brother had, yet spoke more vigorously on issues of economic justice. He toured Appalachia and America's inner cities, and during the California primary met with César Chávez. On June 4, 1968, Kennedy won the California primary and spoke in Los Angeles at an early-morning victory rally at the Ambassador Hotel. Leaving the stage via a kitchen service entrance, he was shot three times by Sirhan Sirhan, as were five other people. He died at Good Samaritan Hospital (1225 Wilshire Boulevard) the next day.

Robert Kennedy's funeral was held at New York's St. Patrick's Cathedral, where his brother Edward eulogized, "My brother need not be idealized or enlarged in death beyond what he was in life, to be remembered simply as a good and decent man, who saw wrong and tried to right it, saw suf-

> I do not run for the presidency merely to oppose any man, but to propose new policies. I run because I am convinced that this country is on a perilous course and because I have such strong feelings about what must be done, and I feel that I'm obliged to do all I can.
>
> —*Robert Kennedy,*
> *announcing his candidacy*

Robert Kennedy, campaigning in California, 1968

fering and tried to heal it, saw war and tried to stop it." His body was laid to rest in Arlington National Cemetery, steps from his brother's eternal flame.

LEARN MORE

Make Gentle the Life of This World by Maxwell Taylor Kennedy (Broadway, 1999)
Robert Kennedy by Evan Thomas (Simon & Shuster, 2000)

The Hollywood Ten
Blacklist Sculpture Garden, 823 Exposition Boulevard, Los Angeles, CA 90034 ·
(213) 740-7676

The 1950s Red Scare hit Hollywood long before Joseph McCarthy became a national figure. In fact, the movie industry launched its own witch hunt in the late '40s when the Motion Picture Alliance for the Preservation of American Ideals (whose members included Ronald Reagan, Ayn Rand, Gary Cooper, and Walt Disney) testified before the House Committee for the Investigation of Un-American Activities (better known as HUAC) that Tinseltown was more like Trotskytown.

In October 1947, HUAC subpoenaed 11 individuals it suspected of Communist sympathies. Most were writers or directors. Screenwriter John Howard Lawson was called first, but was denied the right to read aloud his opening statement. He would have begun, "For a week this Committee has conducted an illegal and indecent trial of American citizens, whom the Committee has selected to be publicly pilloried and smeared." Instead, he was asked if he was, or ever had been, a member of the Communist Party. He refused to answer, and was cited with contempt of Congress.

Lawson was followed by Dalton Trumbo, Albert Maltz, Alvah Bessie, Samuel Ornitz, Herbert Biberman, Adrian Scott, Edward Dmytryk, Lester Cole, and Ring Lardner Jr., all of whom refused to respond to HUAC's unconstitutional bullying. Together they became known as the Hollywood Ten. (Bertolt Brecht, the eleventh witness, denied any Communist sympathies . . . then fled to East Germany after being released by the Committee.)

Meanwhile, studio heads got together and issued a statement—they'd cooperate with HUAC to blacklist anyone the Committee accused of un-American sympathies. The chair of HUAC brought the Ten's contempt citations before the full House in November 1947, and they were approved 346 to 17. Lawson and Trumbo were then put on trial and found guilty. The other eight joined them on appeal before the U.S. Supreme Court, which refused to overturn the convictions. All served time behind bars for exercising their constitutional freedoms.

The blacklist got much longer over time, and few of the original Ten ever fully recovered from the taint (except Dmytryk—he eventually "named names"). Some wrote under pseudonyms, and several Academy Awards have since been reissued to their rightful recipients, reclaiming the artists from anonymity and finally recognizing their contributions to film.

> You violate the most elementary principles of constitutional guarantees when you require anyone to parade for your approval his opinions upon race, religion, politics, or any other matter.
> —Dalton Trumbo, 1947

LEARN MORE
www.fishergallery.org
Blacklisted by Dave Wagner and Paul Buhle (Palgrave Macmillan, 2003)
Naming Names by Victor S. Navsky (Hill and Wang, 2003)
The Hollywood Ten (1950)

Martinez

John Muir, Pioneer Preservationist

John Muir National Historic Site, 4202 Alhambra Avenue, Martinez, CA 94553 ·
(925) 228-8860

John Muir's life changed forever in 1863 while standing under a black locust tree outside North Hall at the University of Wisconsin. He was taking his first botany class, and learned that the black locust was a member of the pea family. "This fine lesson charmed me and sent me flying to the woods and meadows in wild enthusiasm," he later wrote.

Muir was born in Scotland on April 21, 1838. Eleven years later his family came to the States and settled near Portage, Wisconsin. After his college-age epiphany, he dropped out of school and enrolled in the "university of the wilderness," rambling around the United States, Mexico, and Canada taking odd jobs and enjoying the great outdoors. In 1868 he arrived in California, and that spring saw Yosemite for the first time. He fell in love. Muir spent that summer herding sheep in the Sierra Nevada and began to develop his environmental theories, the most radical of which being that Yosemite was formed by glaciers, not earthquakes. Originally dismissed as a kook, he was later proven correct.

In 1880 Muir married Louie Strentzel and took over management of her family's orchard and ranch in Martinez. The work took its toll on his health, so in 1887 he returned to the wild to recuperate.

> Most people are on the world, not in it; have no conscious sympathy or relationship to anything about them, undiffused, separate, and rigidly alone like marbles of polished stone, touching but separate.
>
> *—John Muir*

John Muir, c. 1902

Two years later he convinced Congress to preserve Yosemite, though the park was placed under state control. In 1892 Muir helped found the Sierra Club and was elected its first president. From there he led the preservationist wing of the nascent environmental movement. (Preservationists wanted land set aside for its own sake, but conservationists wanted land set aside for hunting, grazing, and other human enterprises.)

When Teddy Roosevelt (see page 304) came to California in 1903, Muir convinced him to take a hike into the backcountry to see how the state had mismanaged the park through overgrazing and logging. By the time the president came back down from the mountains he was a preservationist. In 1905 the park was put under federal control, as was Muir's original wish.

Muir died in Los Angeles on December 24, 1914. The National Park Service was created as its own agency two years after his death, taking Yosemite and other parks out from under the umbrella of the U.S. Forest Service.

LEARN MORE

www.nps.gov/jomu

www.nps.gov/yose, (209) 372-0200

www.sierraclub.org, (415) 977-5500

www.johnmuir.org

John Muir: Nature Writing by John Muir and William Cronon, ed. (Library of America, 1997)

John Muir and His Legacy by Stephen R. Fox (University of Wisconsin, 1985)

The History of the Sierra Club, 1892–1970 by Michael P. Cohen (Sierra Club, 1988)

Pacific Palisades

Gandhi's Ashes

Self-Realization Fellowship Temple and Ashram Center, Lake Shrine, 17190 Sunset Boulevard, CA 90272 · (310) 454-4114

OK, so he's not exactly an *American* progressive, but Mahatma Gandhi was inspired by, and has inspired, many in this country. He developed his own method of nonviolent resistance by studying Henry David Thoreau (see page 20), and his work influenced Bayard Rustin, James Lawson, Martin Luther King Jr., and César Chávez in their civil rights struggles.

After Gandhi was cremated in 1948, some of his ashes were given to Paramahansa Yoganada, an Indian spiritual leader who had taught Gandhi. In 1950 Yogananda brought his ashes to the States, where they were kept by his followers at the Self-Realization Fellowship. In 1996 they built the Gandhi World Peace Memorial and his cremains were placed inside.

LEARN MORE

www.yogananda-srf.org/temples/lakeshrine

Non-Violent Resistance by M. K. Gandhi (Dover, 2001)

The Essential Gandhi by Mahatma Gandhi and Louis Fisher, ed. (Vintage, 2002)

Rancho Mirage

Betty Ford Center
3900 Bob Hope Drive, Rancho Mirage, CA 92270 · (800) 434-7365

Though Eleanor Roosevelt was the greatest progressive First Lady of the 20th century, Betty Ford ran a close second. Her independence and candor in the wake of the Watergate era won the hearts of most Americans, with the exception of GOP conservatives who disapproved of her support of the Equal Rights Amendment (see page 57) and legalized abortion. In September 1974, shortly after her husband took office, she underwent a mastectomy for breast cancer. By publicly discussing her diagnosis and treatment, she saved the lives of thousands of women who might otherwise have put off visits to their doctors.

Two years after Gerald Ford's presidential defeat in 1976, Betty faced another battle, this time against alcoholism and addiction to prescription painkillers. After her recovery, she went on to found the Betty Ford Center in 1982. Since opening, it has treated more than 56,000 patients and continues on under the chairmanship of her daughter Susan.

Betty Ford, 1976

LEARN MORE
www.bettyfordcenter.org
Healing and Hope by Betty Ford (Putnam, 2003)
Betty Ford by John Robert Greene (University Press of Kansas, 2004)

San Francisco

Harvey Milk, "The Mayor of Castro Street"
Camera Shop (gone), 575 Castro Street, San Francisco, CA 94114

In 1977 Harvey Milk became the first openly gay person elected to a major public office in the United States. A year later, he became the first openly gay public official assassinated. And though he held office for a little more than a year, his impact on the LGBT community, not just in San Francisco, cannot be underestimated.

Milk was born in New York on May 22, 1930. He served in the navy and had successful careers as a Wall Street broker and assistant director on Broadway. And like many gay men in the late 1960s, he packed up and headed to San Francisco. In 1972 he opened a camera shop on Castro Street in the heart of the city's "gay ghetto." It soon became the neighborhood's unofficial gay community center.

After organizing the first Castro Street Fair, Milk was nicknamed "The Mayor of Castro Street." It was only a matter of time before he tried his hand at electoral politics. In 1973 he ran for the city's board of supervisors and lost. He ran for office twice more, and lost both times. But then in 1975 George Moscone was elected mayor. Moscone backed an initiative called Proposition C by which city supervisors would be elected from districts, rather than at large. By running from neighborhoods, it would allow candidates from minority communities to have a greater say in the governance of their city. Prop C passed, and in 1977, the first election after it became law, San Francisco saw its first African American woman, its first Chinese American man, and its first openly gay man—Harvey Milk—take seats on the board of supervisors.

Milk won not only due to the strong support from the LGBT community, but also because he ran a populist campaign that included everyone within the district, from union rank and file to senior citizens to fellow small business owners. Once in office, he tackled issues such as voting machines, rent control, an antidiscrimination ordinance, and a pooper scooper law.

In 1978 Milk found himself thrust into a statewide leadership role to defeat Proposition 6, the so-called Briggs Initiative. Buoyed by Anita Bryant's hate campaign in Florida, state senator John Briggs got a referendum placed on the California ballot that would prevent gays and lesbians from teaching in the public schools. Though the campaign against Proposition 6 started in the hole, polling at a 61–31 deficit (with 8 percent undecided), the measure was defeated by a 41–59 margin.

Harvey Milk, 1977

Three weeks after the victory, on November 27, 1978, city supervisor Dan White walked into the mayor's city hall office and shot Moscone four times, reloaded, then walked to Milk's office and shot him five. Both men died at the scene. White was a frustrated, self-marginalized board member who had resigned his seat in protest earlier that month, but was trying to be reinstated. When the mayor refused, White unleashed his rage on the two people he blamed for his own personal and political

> My name is Harvey Milk, and I want to recruit you. I want to recruit you for the fight to preserve your democracy from the John Briggs and the Anita Bryants who are trying to constitutionalize bigotry.
> —Harvey Milk, at the Gay Freedom Day Parade, 1978

failings. Milk long suspected he would be a target of a crazed homophobe; he had left a cassette with his will, and on it he stated, "If a bullet should enter my brain, let that bullet destroy every closet door."

San Franciscans responded to the murders with a huge, spontaneous, peaceful candlelight vigil that evening. The following spring White, who had preplanned the killings (he had crawled through a window to avoid the building's metal detectors), was found guilty of only voluntary manslaughter. His lawyers argued that he had overdosed on junk food—the infamous Twinkie Defense—

and snapped. The city erupted on May 21, as protesters smashed windows at city hall and burned squad cars. White was sentenced to seven years in prison, served five, and a year after he was released committed suicide.

Milk's story was made into an Academy Award–winning documentary in 1984. There is currently a drive to erect a statue of Milk at city hall.

LEARN MORE
www.milkmemorial.org
The Mayor of Castro Street by Randy Shilts (St. Martins, 1982)
The Times of Harvey Milk (1984)

GAVIN NEWSOM AND THE GAY MARRIAGE STAMPEDE

The murder of Harvey Milk in his city hall office cast a pall over the building (at 1 Dr. C. B. Goodlett Place) for a quarter century. But in February 2004, Mayor Gavin Newsom purged its bad karma when he ordered the county clerk to begin issuing marriage licenses to same-sex couples. Just after midnight on February 12, Phyllis Lyon and Del Martin (see page 378), partners of 51 years, walked into city hall and received the first same-sex marriage license in California history. They were followed by 89 other couples who had waited for hours in the rain. Over the next 29 days, 4,037 couples pledged their commitment to one another in the offices, hallways, and rotunda of the building. Newsom's bold move was copied by mayors and clerks in New York, New Mexico, Oregon, and New Jersey, and would have continued had the California Supreme Court not issued an injunction. (On August 12, 2004, the court invalidated all the marriages.)

LEARN MORE
We Do by Amy Rennert, ed. (Chronicle Books, 2005)

The Indians of All Tribes Take Alcatraz

Alcatraz Island, Golden Gate National Recreation Center, Fort Mason, B201, San Francisco, CA 94123 · (415) 561-4900

Early in the morning on November 20, 1969, 12 men left Sausalito in several boats headed for Alcatraz. Led by activist Ed Castillo, they weren't headed to prison—the facility had been closed since 1963—they were going to claim the Rock on behalf of the Native American people. By sunup, others had landed on the island, a total of 78 occupiers known as the Indians of All Tribes (IAT). Under the Fort Laramie Treaty of 1868, Sioux tribal members were entitled to claim any federal land that had been abandoned by the U.S. government, which is exactly what they did. The Coast Guard quickly blockaded the island, with some success, and attempted to land at the dock, but a group of Indian vets just back from Vietnam fought them off.

In the days to come, Richard Oakes, a Mohawk, emerged as the group's spokesman. Public sentiment was overwhelmingly with IAT, at least in the beginning. The Coast Guard was told to stand down, and food and supplies arrived by the boatload, including dozens of turkeys on Thanksgiving Day. Creedence Clearwater Revival held a concert in a boat off shore, then donated the boat to the protesters. The IAT launched Radio Free Alcatraz, hosted by John Trudell, and broadcast its message to the Bay area. And in a gesture of good faith, the group offered to compensate the government for the land—a few glass beads, a swatch of red cloth, and some trinkets.

A long-range plan for the island soon emerged: it would be home to a new museum, university, spiritual institute, and ecology center. None of it came to pass, however, after the liberated island became a refuge for mostly non-Native miscreants fleeing police and social workers in the city. As chaos grew, so did resentment of Oakes, who in January was ousted from the occupiers' leadership. By February the remaining protesters had finalized a plan for the Rock's development, but the early good will was long gone.

On June 1, mysterious fires engulfed four buildings. IAT managed to occupy the island for another year, though they were largely ignored by the press and the government. The protest ended on June 11, 1971, when the Coast Guard arrested 15 remaining holdouts.

LEARN MORE

www.nps.gov/alcatraz

Like a Hurricane by Paul Chaat Smith and Robert Allen Warrior (New Press, 1996)
American Indian Activism by Troy Johnson, Joan Nagel, and Duane Champagne,
   eds. (University of Illinois, 1997)

Yick Wo v. Hopkins: No Discrimination in the Administration of Laws
Yick Wo Elementary School, 2245 Jones Street, San Francisco, CA 94133

Yick Wo is not a household name today, but this Chinese immigrant was the plaintiff in one of the U.S. Supreme Court's first decisions against racial discrimination. Though he had been running a laundry in San Francisco for 22 years at the same location, in 1885 Yick Wo was denied a new laundry permit by fire marshal Peter Hopkins. The city of San Francisco had recently passed an ordinance stating that anyone wanting to operate a laundry out of a wooden building had to have a permit. Hopkins used his power to deny 200 Chinese applicants, yet barely gave a second thought to white-owned establishments. Yick Wo defied the ordinance and kept his laundry open anyway. Taken to court, he was fined $10 and ordered to spend 10 days in jail.

Yick Wo appealed the ruling to the California Supreme Court and lost. But in front of the U.S. Supreme Court, he fared much better; the justices unanimously agreed that Hopkins had discriminated against Yick Wo. The decision was important, for it said that even though a law could be impartially written, if it was applied unfairly, the government could be found to be acting in an unconstitutional manner. Unfortunately, the ruling was not widely applied to subsequent cases, as the burden of proof was often difficult to achieve, particularly in front of unsympathetic judges and juries.

> Though the law itself be fair on its face and impartial in appearance, if it is applied and administered by public authority with an evil eye and an unequal hand, . . . the denial of equal justice is still within the prohibition of the Constitution.
>
> —*Justice Stanley Matthews, in*
>   *Yick Wo v. Hopkins, 1886*

Santa Barbara

Gaylord Nelson and Earth Day
Santa Barbara Harbor, Cabrillo Boulevard, Santa Barbara, CA 93101

Senator Gaylord Nelson came to Santa Barbara to see the disaster for himself. On January 29, 1969, an offshore oil platform suffered a blowout, and 200,000 gallons of crude spewed from the ruptured pipeline before it was capped a week and a half later. The slick covered 800 square miles of open water and 35 miles of California coastline from Goleta to Rincon Point.

Nelson, a lifelong environmentalist from Wisconsin, called for a national teach-in and service day in response. The effort was organized by Denis Hayes. The first Earth Day was held on April 22, 1970, the birthday of J. Sterling Morton (see page 298). About 20 million people celebrated by cleaning up their communities and learning what they could do to protect the planet. Under pressure, Congress soon passed the Clean Air Act Extension and created the EPA.

Today Earth Day is observed by a half-billion people in 175 countries worldwide. In many areas, Earth Day has expanded to Earth Week. The Earth Day Network coordinates events internationally; Keep America Beautiful sponsors community cleanups across the United States.

LEARN MORE
www.earthday.net, (202) 518-0044
www.kab.org, (203) 323-8987
Beyond Earth Day by Gaylord Nelson, Susan M. Campbell, and Paul A. Wozniak
(University of Wisconsin, 2002)

Santa Monica

The Pentagon Papers
Chez Jay, 1657 Ocean Avenue, Santa Monica, CA 90401

In 1967, Daniel Ellsberg was working for the RAND Corporation when he was given the task of compiling the Defense Department's assessment of the ongoing conflict in Vietnam. What he read shocked him. Lyndon Johnson had funneled money to secret military operations, had misled Congress about war activities and the justification for the conflict, and had, along with Nixon, abused presidential power on a regular basis. Sound familiar?

Ellsberg felt the public had a right to the truth. He and friend Anthony Russo photocopied a report titled "History of the U.S. Decision-Making Process on Vietnam Policy" and another titled "Command and Control Study of the Gulf of Tonkin Incident," and released them to the New York Times. The exchange took place at Chez Jay, a restaurant in Santa Monica, California.

The first installment of the so-called Pentagon Papers was published on June 13, 1971, under the byline of Neil Sheehan. Another article appeared the next day, and that evening the Nixon administration sent a telegram to the Times demanding that it cease publication. When the paper refused, the White House obtained an injunction against the paper. It was the first time the federal government had succeeded in obtaining prior restraint on the press. But it didn't stop anything; the Washington Post picked up the baton on June 18, followed by the Boston Globe.

The Times asked the U.S. Supreme Court to immediately lift the injunction. The justices ruled 6–3 that the federal government had to meet a high threshold to be granted prior restraint, and it had not met it in the case of the Pentagon Papers. Justice Black addressed the subject: "In revealing the workings of government that led to the Vietnam War, the newspaper nobly did precisely that which the Founders hoped and trusted they would do." Henry Kissinger had a different opinion; he called Ellsberg "the most dangerous man in America."

The Justice Department eventually charged Ellsberg and Russo with 15 counts of theft, espionage, and conspiracy. Meanwhile, on September 3, 1971, Nixon had G. Gordon Liddy and Howard Hunt break into Ellsberg's psychiatrist's Beverly Hills office to look for damaging personal information. Later, during Ellsberg and Russo's pretrial phase, the judge learned of the break-in and the illegal phone tapping and dismissed all charges against the pair.

> Both the history and the language of the First Amendment support the view that the press must be left free to publish news, whatever the source, without censorship, injunctions, or prior restraints.
>
> —Justice Hugo Black, in New York Times Company v. United States, 1971

LEARN MORE
www.chezjays.com
Secrets by Daniel Ellsberg (Viking, 2002)
The Pentagon Papers by George C. Herring (McGraw Hill, 1993)
The Papers & the Papers by Sanford J. Ungar (Columbia, 1989)

Stafford

Butterfly and Luna
Highway 101, Stafford, CA 95562

In late 1997 Julia Hill headed west to recover from an automobile accident and found herself in northern California. There she came upon the violent disbanding of a protest at the Headwaters Forest near Stafford. Environmentalists, including Earth First!, had been blocking Maxxam/Pacific Lumber's access to a stand of old-growth forest and were being run out by authorities armed with a court order and pepper spray. As the group scattered, they needed somebody to continue a "tree sit" for a few days until they regrouped. And though she had no experience in rope climbing, much less tree sitting, Hill volunteered. She was given a two-minute crash course in climbing knots, hiked up the hill to a 1,000-year-old redwood named Luna, and pulled herself 180 feet up to the sitters' six-by-eight-foot platform. Butterfly, as she became known, stayed in the canopy for six days and then was relieved by another volunteer. But when Maxxam began clear-cutting the surrounding hillside, she returned to her perch on December 10, 1997, and stayed.

And stayed. And stayed. Maxxam continued to cut trees near Luna and sent helicopters to harass Hill in her treetop perch. They tried wearing her down with floodlights and air horns at all hours of the night. They tried starving her out by preventing supporters from getting food to her. (Several managed to get through.) She stayed through one winter, and then another, at times facing 90-mph winds. Throughout her sit, many people climbed the tree to visit with Hill and lend their support, or interviewed her via cell phone.

Hill did not descend from Luna until December 18, 1999, after the Sanctuary Forest organization negotiated a settlement between Hill and Maxxam to preserve Luna forever. The tree and a 2.9-acre buffer grove were placed in a conservation easement under Sanctuary Forest's control. Hill went on to establish the Circle of Life Foundation to bring together environmental, youth, social justice, indigenous, and religious organizations to continue preserving the delicate ecosystem called Planet Earth.

> I want the world to know that the destruction happening to our environment is a direct reflection on the destruction of our lives.
>
> —*Julia Butterfly Hill*

LEARN MORE
www.circleoflife.org, (510) 601-9790
www.sanctuaryforest.org, (707) 986-1087
The Legacy of Luna by Julia Butterfly Hill (HarperSanFrancisco, 2000)

Westminster

Méndez v. Westminster: Educational Opportunity for Latino Children
17th Street Elementary (replaced by Smith Elementary), 770 17th Street, Westminster, CA 92646

Méndez v. Westminster is sometimes called the *Brown v. Board of Education* for Latinos. In 1945 a group of Mexican American parents sued four Orange County school districts for discriminating against their children. Unlike in *Brown*, where racial separation was officially mandated on a statewide level, *Méndez* addressed more subtle, but no less destructive, forms of segregation on the district level. School boards would routinely gerrymander boundaries to isolate Latino neighborhoods and "track" Latino children into remedial classes using bogus educational criteria.

Gonzalo and Felicitas Méndez wanted their three children to attend Westminster's 17th Street Elementary, a clean, modern, brick-and-mortar school attended by the city's white children, rather than Hoover Elementary, a ramshackle wooden structure in the city's Mexican barrio. They joined with parents from three other communities—El Modina, Garden Grove, and Santa Ana—and sued on behalf of 5,000 segregated students. They won in district court, but the decision was appealed. On April 14, 1947, the 9th Circuit Court of Appeals ruled that under state law the districts could not discriminate against Latino children.

Sadly, however, *Méndez v. Westminster* preserved districts' right to segregate Asian students. Spurred by the ruling, Governor Earl Warren erased that final racial distinction two months later when he pushed through a repeal of all segregation language in the California Education Code. (Warren was later appointed Chief Justice of the U.S. Supreme Court, and ushered through the unanimous *Brown v. Board of Education* decision in 1954.) A middle school in Santa Ana—Gonzalo and Felicitas Méndez Intermediate (2000 N. Bristol Street)—has since been named in the couples' honor.

LEARN MORE
The Other Struggle for Equal Schools by Rubén Donato (SUNY, 1997)

LAU V. NICHOLS: BILINGUAL EDUCATION IS A RIGHT

In the 1970s the parents of Kinney Lau sued the San Francisco Unified School District for failing to provide a meaningful education for their child. Under the 1964 Civil Rights Act he was entitled to an education regardless of his national origin, which was directly tied to his language of origin. The high court ruled that the district was hiding behind the issue of access to its *buildings* while ignoring the issue of access to its *curriculum*. "Imposition of a requirement that, before a child can effectively participate in the educational program, he must already have acquired those basic [English] skills is to make a mockery of public education," the justices wrote. "We know that those who do not understand English are certain to find their classroom experiences wholly incomprehensible and in no way meaningful." *Lau v. Nichols* is considered the legal foundation for modern bilingual education.

HAWAII

When Hawaii became a state in 1959, it specifically wrote its constitution to outlaw discrimination based upon sex. That progressive clause was later used to challenge the state's ban on gay marriage; *Bachr v. Lewin* was filed in state court on behalf of three couples in March 1991. It argued that the same-sex marriage ban violated the state constitution because it denied a person the right to marry a partner of his or her choice based solely on the other partner's sex. On May 5, 1993, the Hawaii Supreme Court agreed, and ruled that gay marriage was legal. However, the justices allowed for some wiggle room by giving the voters the opportunity to amend the constitution, should they so choose.

Well, they did just that. In November 1998, after a bitter and emotional debate, Hawaii voters enshrined discrimination into their constitution. "Aloha," at least for the time being, now means hello to special rights for heterosexuality, and goodbye to equal rights for all citizens.

> People talk about their marriages being threatened. I find it implausible that two men deciding to commit themselves to each other threatens the marriage of people a couple blocks away.
>
> —*Barney Frank, on the Hawaii Supreme Court ruling*

LEARN MORE
http://hawaiigaymarriage.com

OREGON

In 1998 the voters of Oregon approved Ballot Measure 67—the medical marijuana law—by a 55–45 margin. It legalized the cultivation, possession, and use of marijuana for those who'd secured a prescription from a doctor and a license from the state. Physicians could prescribe medical marijuana to anyone with a debilitating medical condition that could reasonably be expected to benefit from its use, including those with cancer, HIV, seizures, multiple sclerosis, glaucoma, muscle wasting, nausea, chronic pain, epilepsy, or any disease or treatment that decreased appetite.

There were, of course, limits built into the law. A patient could not have more than seven plants at a time, only three of which could be fully grown, and he or she could not amass more than three ounces of cultivated pot. Oregon kept a confidential register of licensees, and each patient had to designate a single growing location, should police have a question. The first license was issued to Jeannelle Bluhm in early 1999.

The federal government has refused to recognize the Oregon law, and opponents of the measure, some from organizations funded by pharmaceutical companies, predicted dire consequences. But when the sky didn't come crashing down, the Oregon legislature took another look at the provisions in 2005, and *expanded* the program to further assist those who had benefited from its implementation. Currently there are more than 14,000 Oregon residents on the state registry.

LEARN MORE
www.oregon.gov/DHS/ph/omp/index.sthml
www.norml.org, (202) 483-5500
Reefer Madness by Eric Schlosser (Mariner, 2003)

Marylhurst

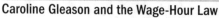

Caroline Gleason and the Wage-Hour Law
Sister Miriam Theresa Lounge, Shoen Library, Marylhurst University, 17600 Pacific
Highway, Marylhurst, OR 97036 · (503) 699-6261

Caroline Gleason was working for the Oregon Consumers League in 1912
when she conducted a survey of labor conditions around the state. What she
reported shocked (or at least embarrassed) the political establishment in Salem.
Unsafe and unsanitary working conditions, long hours and low pay, corrupt
management, and it was all virtually unregulated. The 26-year-old even went
undercover, accepting a job in a shoe factory gluing labels on boxes. For a 10-
hour day she earned 52¢. Total.

Gleason's report got the attention of lawmakers, who passed the Wage-Hour
Law in 1913. It was the first state law in the nation to protect women and
children in the workplace. The legislation was so successful it was later used
as the model for the federal Fair Labor Standards Act of 1938. The FLSA not
only established a minimum wage but also outlawed all nonfarm child labor
and guaranteed time-and-a-half overtime for many occupations. It has been
expanded and amended many times since its enactment.

In 1916 Gleason joined the Sisters of the Holy Names of Jesus and Mary
religious order and became Sister Miriam Theresa. She headed up the Social
Science Department at Marylhurst College (now University) for 30 years.
Under her leadership, the department's coursework emphasized an activist,
social justice approach to the field.

Portland

Muller v. Oregon: A Small Victory for Working Women
Lace House Laundry (gone), Portland, OR 97086

In the early 1900s, Oregon law stated that women could not be asked to work
more than 10 hours per day. That apparently wasn't enough for Curt Muller,
proprietor of Portland's Lace House Laundry. In 1905 he was charged with
abusing his employees by forcing them to work longer hours or be fired. He
challenged the statute in court . . . but probably wished he'd kept his mouth
shut.

At the request of the Oregon Consumers League (see page 404), lawyer (and later Justice) Louis Brandeis joined the case when it finally reached the U.S. Supreme Court. There he presented what became known as the Brandeis Brief, a summary not of case law but of medical and sociological data pertaining to the detrimental effects of overwork on women. It was a new legal strategy, and would later be used successfully in other cases, most famously in *Brown v. Board of Education*.

Given the impact of the data, the justices voted unanimously to support the maximum hours law. Their 1907 decision, while good for blue-collar Americans, included antiquated observations regarding women in the workplace. Under the guise of chivalry, Justice David Brewer stated, "[W]oman has always been dependant on man," and that legislation was justified "to protect her from the greed as well as the passion of man."

Not every victory is pretty.

WASHINGTON

Elsie Parrish had worked as a maid at the Cascadian Hotel in Wenatchee, Washington, for almost two years—1933 to 1935—when she was let go. Parrish later learned that her employer had underpaid her, that she had been entitled to $14.50 per week under the state's minimum wage law. So she demanded $216.19 in back pay from the hotel's owners, the West Coast Hotel Company. They offered her $17. She took them to court instead.

In a 5–4 decision in 1937, the U.S. Supreme Court ruled in *West Coast Hotel Co. v. Parrish* that the state of Washington was within its right to establish a minimum wage, and that Parrish should be given her missing salary. A year later the federal government instituted the first minimum wage under the 1938 Fair Labor Standards Act: 25¢ an hour.

Home

There's No Place Like Home Any More
All Over Town, Home, WA 98349

They fled to Joe's Bay in 1896 to get away from their closed-minded neighbors, but the prudes eventually caught up with them. The Mutual Home Association started as a 26-acre anarchist colony with only three families, but within 10 years had 120 residents and 217 acres. The land was owned by the association, but members could have up to two acres each on which to build their homes. Nobody was expected to join a church, think a certain way, or do anything except live peacefully with those around them.

And it worked. The colony attracted all stripes of freethinkers, radicals, independent women, and naturalists who spent much of their time reading, talking, and enjoying the great outdoors. One resident, Professor Thompson, wore a skirt as a way of advancing progress between the sexes; he found the attire to be "aesthetic and comfortable." Occasionally they would gather at the association's Liberty Hall to hear lectures or debate. The town even had two newspapers, *Discontent* and the *Agitator*.

But William McKinley's 1901 assassination by an anarchist brought undue attention to Home. Postal authorities closed down its post office in 1902, fearful that *Discontent*'s advocacy of "free love" might influence the outside world. Yet it was the "Great Nude Sunbathing Case" that ultimately killed the colony. In 1911 four women and two men were charged with skinnydipping in the bay. Jay Fox, editor of the *Agitator*, defended the naturalists and was arrested for encouraging disrespect of the law. He served six weeks in jail before the governor pardoned him.

Things in Home were never the same after that, with residents breaking into three warring factions: nudes, prudes, and skunks. Their association was dissolved in 1919.

Seattle

The Battle in Seattle
Convergence Center (closed), 420 E. Denny Way, Seattle, WA 98122

The World Trade Organization delegates who arrived in Seattle in late November 1999 were expecting protests. They probably weren't anticipating they'd need to slink out of town a week later. For that, they should thank the Seattle police.

Throughout the 1990s, progressives' warnings of the downside of unfettered world trade had largely fallen on deaf ears. The North American Free Trade Agreement (NAFTA) was negotiated, ratified, and signed with broad public support, people who were no doubt influenced by the corporate-friendly media. Not until 40,000 protesters converged on Seattle to shut down the WTO conference did globalization's critics get a foothold in the American press.

Working out of a rented former warehouse on Capital Hill called the Convergence Center, organizers devised a plan to occupy 13 downtown intersections surrounding the Washington State Convention and Trade Center (800 Convention Place) where the WTO was meeting. Labor groups, peace and justice organizations, and students from all over the world joined forces, and on November 30 clogged the streets. Police overreacted, firing tear gas and rubber bullets into the crowd.

> **The people owned the streets that day and it was as much a lesson for us as it was for corporate America.**
>
> *—Mike Brannan, participant in the WTO protests*

While the overwhelming majority of the protesters were nonviolent, several small groups of anarchists smashed windows at Nike Town, Starbucks, and other stores . . . and grabbed all the early attention. Yet as the days wore on, it was clear to even the dullest television viewer that the police were *causing* the riot, wading into crowds of innocent bystanders and residents, beating unarmed marchers, and indiscriminately arresting citizens who were exercising their free speech rights.

Because of the protests, Bill Clinton was never able to address the organization, and the WTO failed to come to an agreement before adjourning early. Citizens who had not yet begun to consider the downside of globalization were now intrigued, and minds changed. The Battle in Seattle was a public relations disaster for not only the WTO but the International Monetary Fund and any multinational corporations.

LEARN MORE

The Battle in Seattle by Janet Thomas (Fulfrum, 2000)

5 Days That Shook the World by Jeffrey St. Clair and Alexander Cockburn (Verso, 2001)

Fences and Windows by Naomi Klein (Picador, 2002)

Index